CW00541916

EDGEHILL
AND BEYOND

CHARLES I. Drawn by the King's children's drawing master, Wenceslaus Hollar, in 1639, probably on the march to Scotland when the King camped outside Berwick-on-Tweed. The heroic equestrian portrait, complete with a sterotyped battle scene in the background, became a standard icon, and Hollar himself produced almost identical ones of the parliamentary generals Essex and Waller. This portrait was re-issued in 1644, perhaps after the battle of Cropredy.

EDGEHILL

AND BEYOND

The People's War in the South Midlands
1642 - 1645

PHILIP TENNANT

ALAN SUTTON

THE BANBURY HISTORICAL SOCIETY
VOLUME 23

First published in the United Kingdom in 1992 by
Alan Sutton Publishing Ltd · Phoenix Mill · Far Thrupp · Stroud · Gloucestershire
in association with
The Banbury Historical Society

First published in the United States of America in 1992
Alan Sutton Publishing Inc · Wolfeboro Falls · NH 03896–0848

British Library Cataloguing in Publication Data

Tennant, P. E.
  Edgehill and Beyond: People's War in the
  South Midlands, 1642–45
  I. Title
  942.4062

  ISBN 0-7509-0049-0

Library of Congress Cataloging in Publication Data applied for

Typeset in 11/12 pt Garamond.
Typesetting and origination by
Alan Sutton Publishing Limited.
Printed in Great Britain by
The Bath Press, Avon.

My dear Country-men: to you I direct this Story, for it is yours. In your Land were these Battels fought, these Actions done, for your sakes and by your hands . . . Tell me, Did you ever read such a Story as this? of so many Actions, so considerable, done in so short a time?

Joshua Sprigge, *Anglia Rediviva, England's Recovery*, 1647, Preface

CONTENTS

List of Illustrations

MAPS

ACKNOWLEDGEMENTS

No man is an island, and no work of this kind is produced without the author accumulating a huge and multifarious debt; in the first instance to the vast resources of the Public Record Office and the British Library and to their staff, and secondly to all the company of previous historians, from the often unreliable contemporary commentator to this more circumspect descendent, the modern scholar. The Notes and Bibliography will suggest the nature and the extent of that debt, and of my corresponding gratitude for such stimulating company over the past two years. I am also especially grateful for the generous facilities provided by the libraries and staff of the Senate House and the Institute of Historical Research of the University of London. More specifically, I wish to thank Jeremy Gibson and the Banbury Historical Society ·for providing the initial impetus and, following the publication of my article in *Warwickshire History* in the winter of 1989/90, encouraging me to attempt something more ambitious; and Alan Sutton, for his immediate and generous support. I am also very grateful to Stephen Beck, for responding so promptly and delightfully to my request for new line illustrations; to both Gordon Norwood, former director of the Roundwood Press at Kineton, and Barracuda Books of Buckingham, for allowing reproduction of Stephen Beck's earlier drawings originally published in Peter Young's *Marston Moor* and *Cropredy Bridge* and Wilfrid Emberton's *Skippon's Brave Boys* respectively; to Julia Nicholson and her staff at Banbury Museum and the Oxfordshire Centre for Local Studies, for many of the photographs; to Gladys Mary Coles, for permission to reprint 'After Edgehill, 1642', from *Leafburners: New and Selected Poems*, Duckworth, 1987; and to Thelma, for the heady cocktail of photocopying and somewhat desperate sandwich-making which neither of us will be sorry to see much diluted now. Knowingly or not, all these helped smoothe the way into previously unfamiliar territory. The path from nineteenth-century French poetry to the English Civil War was not an obvious one, and only the reader can judge whether I was wise to take it.

PREFACE

In recent years academic interest in the English Civil War has often turned to focus on its regional and social context, and one result has been increasingly to undermine some long-cherished traditional notions. One of those is of a power struggle, confined essentially to politicians, priests and military commanders, which culminated in the outbreak of a war in which a few set-piece battles did admittedly take place, but in areas so conveniently remote as to leave the bulk of the population relatively unscathed; parish life, consequently, was largely unaffected. No doubt the serious historian never subscribed to such a view; yet the deafening silence of most of the earlier *Victoria County History* volumes on the impact of the war at parish level – in articles contributed by professional historians – inevitably tended to reinforce such an impression. Typical were the volumes devoted to south Warwickshire, where virtually no mention of the war is made over the entire succession of individual parish histories filling literally hundreds of pages. Either the Civil War took place elsewhere, or some historians can evidently be as economical with the truth as politicians. Even much more recently, at least one eminent scholar has seemed to share the old view in suggesting that 'we may have exaggerated the impact of the war itself upon daily life in the provinces'.

Curiously, such a myth tended also to perpetuate itself in a very different kind of history, that of those picturesque, faintly condescending folk legends illustrating the ignorance of quaint villagers of momentous events unfolding on their very doorstep. The story of the Marston Moor ploughboy astonished at being interrupted at his work by the arrival of two mighty armies may appear inherently implausible, but has often been repeated; while nearer home, Dugdale's tale of Richard Shuckburgh blithely intent on a morning's hunting near Edgehill, oblivious to his king's preparations for a supposedly decisive battle, or the anecdote of the Tysoe youth surprised by the arrival of soldiers and quite unable to identify them – these surely have the ring of authenticity? Moreover, the general recognition of how few real partisans there were during the war in any given locality, and the reluctance of the majority to take sides at all, might also suggest that most people succeeded in avoiding involvement.[1]

How questionable these notions are is nevertheless apparent to anyone who simply examines a representative selection of contemporary archives. Among these are two collections in particular of supreme importance, on which much of the following enquiry is based: the vast hotchpotch of pamphlets, news-sheets and reports collected by the London bookseller George Thomason, housed in the British Library; and the almost equally voluminous collection of accounts scattered among the so-called Commonwealth Exchequer Papers in the Public Record Office, compiled by each parish in response to local parliamentary committees' instructions in the hope of receiving compensation for war damage. The former, despite being often blatantly partisan and certainly unreliable in points of detail, is one of the most basic of all the now commonly-used Civil War sources; the latter, frequently offering a graphic insight into the impact of the war at parish level and with a surprisingly good survival rate for Warwickshire at least, complements and sometimes corrects the former, yet has been curiously ignored by many historians, even those concentrating on military campaigns which the accounts in fact often illuminate. Only by a detailed examination of both of these vital sources, placed in the national context by use of more orthodox sources like the State Papers, can the effects of the war on the local community begin to be assessed; and when that is done one conclusion appears inescapable: that in spite of the permanent popularity of the Civil War as a subject of research and general interest alike, justice has still not been done to the fate of ordinary people in the war. For if the extent to which the war fundamentally and permanently changed English society is still cause of legitimate debate, the more one examines a specific area the more it becomes clear that, for a few short years at least, the lives of ordinary villagers, with their age-old preoccupations of field and market, weather and harvest, labour and rest, were profoundly disrupted. The purpose of this book is to substantiate this claim by exploring the impact of the war on a limited area of midland England for the short period 1642–5, in an attempt, partly, to discover whether it is true that, as has been said, 'the Civil War from below remains hidden'. What follows devotes less space, consequently, to ideology, polemics and the battle-field than to what actually took place in lanes and villages across the rolling English shires from the Vale of Evesham to the Northamptonshire Heights, and in the process Marlowe's stately tents of war are much less in evidence than Shakespeare's grim-visaged one, particularly in its more mundane and sordid aspects. For if part of England's history may well be encapsulated in T.S. Eliot's broken king in the falling light of a winter's afternoon in a secluded chapel, part also is in the lice-infested soldiers trudging through the dripping lanes towards Aston Cantlow, in the captain caught with his mistress in an Alcester bedroom and forced to flee in his shirt-tails, in the deputation of Kilsby wives demanding the release of their imprisoned husbands at Banbury, in Sir William Waller's fall through rotten floorboards into the cellar at Great Bourton, and in the theft of Shakespeare's granddaughter's red petticoat by the soldiers from New Place, Stratford-upon-Avon. To learn this may not, perhaps, advance one's knowledge of historical processes, but it is living history, and, as such, is valuable. In the study of history above all others, generalization must make way for the particular, and, as the doyen of local historians, W.G. Hoskins, has written well on the English landscape, 'the interest of an enquiry such as this, and one cannot say it too often, lies in the detail of the subject'.

Although a straightforward chronological approach has been adopted, it is, of course, impossible, after three-and-a-half centuries, to reconstruct a continuous narrative, since although thousands of individuals were caught up in events, few thought to speak or write directly of them, and there is much on which the records remain silent. The extracts from official reports, private correspondence, the odd diary, the semi-official tabloid-type journalism, the reports of the parish constable, the verbal testimony of parson and squire, and the patchy communiqués of military commanders are valuable exceptions, but for all of these survival is random and fragmentary. Nevertheless, one should beware of parish histories which tend to assume that because a village's name is absent from a particular archive the war must have passed it by untouched, for it is unlikely to have been so. There can be little doubt that the contemporary sources quoted here, although in themselves substantial in quantity, represent the mere tip of a once-considerable iceberg, and that for every single event recorded countless others were not. The testimony of that scholarly eye-witness Richard Baxter is both significant and authoritative: 'I think there were very few Parishes where at one time or another Blood had not been shed'. Extensive use of contemporary quotation has therefore been made to illustrate this, and not only to inform but to convey something of the feeling of the period by allowing actors and commentators alike to speak directly of their own times and experiences in their own way.

The major battles, on the other hand, already well documented in many standard works, are only cursorily described, in order to allow greater focus on the build-up and the usually scandalously-neglected aftermath of the respective campaigns, since these affected the local community in ways the actual brief fighting itself could not. In that sense many actions insignificant nationally, but traumatic for the neighbourhood, assume almost equal – it may be thought undue – prominence. But it must be remembered that for the local people, deprived of wider perceptions by defective communications and the habit of local rather than national thinking, there was little 'before' and 'after'; for them, Edgehill or Cropredy presented no greater significance necessarily than having to live with a garrison in the next town or endure a siege at the nearby manor-house. Both could bring equal devastation and ruin. Finally, in these days of an ever-growing interest in genealogy, a glance at the indexes will reveal the attention paid to ordinary people in unimportant villages on the road to nowhere in particular, rescued momentarily, as it were, from their customary anonymity. Their very obscurity testifies to the all-embracing nature of the conflict in which they were unavoidably caught up. 'History' is about them, too.[2]

September 1992

P.T.
London

AUTHOR'S NOTE

In all contemporary quotations the original spelling and standard abbreviations have been retained except very occasionally, where to do so might have resulted in unnecessary confusion for the general reader. For convenience, however, these have been punctuated according to modern usage. Similarly, in transcribing money values the modern £ has been substituted for the usual abbreviated latin, though pre-decimal currency (£ s. d.) has been kept. All maps are intended merely as graphic simplifications; on each, space has allowed only a selection from events to be recorded. Dates are given Old Style, except that the year has been taken to begin on 1 January.

CHAPTER ONE

INTRODUCTION:
THE BACKGROUND TO WAR

THE WARWICKSHIRE CROSSROADS

Although at the outbreak of the English Civil War the geography of allegiance to the two sides was complex and fluid at local level, the old, long-established basic picture still remains broadly valid: a relatively economically-advanced south and east predominantly parliamentarian in sympathies, and an economically-backward west and north mainly royalist. This divide was exemplified at the outset by the King's removal first to York, later to Shropshire, leaving Parliament to consolidate its authority in London and East Anglia. Within this broad pattern the Midlands constituted a wide frontier zone, albeit ill-defined and constantly shifting, in which loyalties were fairly evenly divided and local divisions peculiarly intense. It was a region in which underlying tensions might surface at any time if committed minorities attempted to organize support, sway the uncommitted, contact outspoken allies or secure a base. By the time that it had become increasingly clear, in June 1642, that political reconciliation between King and Parliament was unlikely, that is precisely what took place. The King himself began to prepare for war by issuing Commissions of Array for each county, in effect calls to arms, and Warwickshire was the first to receive such instructions, on 6 June; it was an act which polarized issues and galvanized some of the leading gentry into action. A petition to Parliament from Warwickshire could later claim, with some justice therefore, that the county had been the first to mobilize. As the country stumbled towards war rival musters began to be organized as loyalists and, soon, actual armed men made preparations by recruiting, drilling, collecting arms, fortifying town walls and manor houses and establishing garrisons.

The Midlands were therefore implicated in events from the very outset, and nowhere was this more so than in the south, where a combination of strategic factors, apparently random events, deep and long-standing religious divisions and, not least, the presence

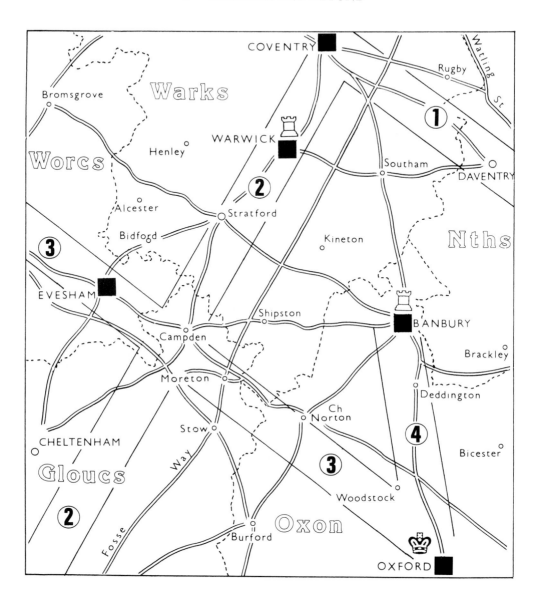

CIVIL WAR ROUTES   ■ Military HQ   ♛ Court at Oxford

1   London–Coventry via Northampton, the main parliamentarian route
2   Coventry–Gloucester via Warwick, heavily used by Parliamentarians
3   Worcester–Oxford via Evesham, the major royalist supply route
4   Oxford–Banbury and beyond, heavily used by Royalists

PT

of influential and energetic local leaders made the whole area, from Worcester and the Vale of Evesham in the west to Oxford and the Northampton uplands in the east, the scene of intense social conflict, as well as an actual military arena. It was in Warwickshire that the first, key, critical decisions were taken to determine the onset of war. It was from near Warwick that the King issued his ultimatum to the rebels, planned to set up his standard on Dunsmore Heath before marching, supposedly triumphantly, to seize Warwick Castle and so end the war before it could begin, and near here, at Meriden, that he first reviewed his full army, symbolically at the very heart of his kingdom. It was here that were staged not only the 'dress rehearsal of the entire English civil war' at Edgehill but an almost continuous chronicle of violence from month to month and year to year throughout the entire duration of the war and after, and not just briefly, during the Edgehill campaign, as is sometimes imagined. Successive armies, including Essex's, Waller's and the King's own marched and counter-marched across these counties. Equally, it was through this district that Cromwell marched to the rendezvous with Fairfax that was to preface the ultimate parliamentary triumph at Naseby, and through it again that Cromwell and Fairfax marched to the south-west after annihilating the King there, to be followed exactly a year later by the enactment of the three-part *dénouement* of the war in the successive capitulations at Banbury, Oxford and Worcester.[1]

The whole of the south Midlands was a constant military thoroughfare, and strategically there were at least two crucial factors determining Warwickshire's major role throughout the war. The first was its key position on the national road network, wedged between two busy north–south trunk roads radiating from London: the Roman Watling Street, whose great arc formed part of the county's eastern border, and the equally ancient route from Oxford entering Warwickshire at the Rollright Stones (see Map 1). The former of these had long ago become one of what the pioneer cartographer John Ogilby described as 'the six prime Post-ways . . . one of the most frequented Roads in the Kingdom', and gave direct access to Coventry, the hub of the Midlands, and the long-established staging posts of St Albans, Towcester and Daventry ensured a continuous flow of traffic along it in both directions. The latter, more westerly, route gave access through south Warwickshire to Worcester, Wales, the Cotswolds and the north. Both of these highways were heavily used in the war. Successive parliamentarian convoys and armies took the Watling Street route to Northampton and Daventry before veering west across Dunsmore Heath to Coventry and Warwick, and almost continuous military activity of one sort or another took place near it, while the other route carried constant royalist supplies from Wales and Worcester to Oxford. Between these two routes lay a third busy thoroughfare, the Oxford–Banbury–Coventry one, with Banbury and Southam placed on it as nodal points for traffic from the four points of the compass.

Outside this major national network of approach roads, however, caution is necessary in attempting to speculate on the use of more local routes, what little evidence there is being inconclusive. Surprisingly little evidence exists, for example, to suggest heavy use of the ancient Fosse Way, although Halford was the scene of isolated skirmishes, quartering was heavy in villages adjacent to it, and Fairfax and Cromwell evidently used it on their lightning march to the south-west after Naseby. One village situated on it, Stretton-on-Fosse, appended a weary note to its claims for compensation: 'as touching Free quarter, we saye that we have bene charged so often wth so many [soldiers] that we cannott make any certeyntie thereof'. But when Sir William Waller marched north from

Stow in June 1644, much of his army evidently took a route parallel to rather than via the seemingly obvious Fosse Way one, as has sometimes been assumed, even though the hot weather might be expected to have made the way more passable than usual. Troops marching south-west seem largely to have ignored it, in fact, preferring the Warwick–Stratford–Chipping Campden route. For the Roman Ryknield Street there is even less evidence of heavy military use. Although both of these ancient roads figure on the maps prepared for Dugdale's 1656 edition of his *Antiquities*, the assumption must be that by the mid-seventeenth century the Fosse Way and Ryknield Street had become marginalized by the economic domination of the south-east. Significantly, shortly after the war, Ogilby virtually ignored them when compiling his celebrated road-maps. Apart from the major routes indicated above, in fact, any attempt to match movements of troops and their quarters to known local roads is fraught with problems. It must never be forgotten that the precise destination of an army on the march (as opposed to local expeditions) was rarely known in advance, and that although local 'scouts' were used, signposts, maps and compasses were virtually non-existent. Although towns and villages providing quarter for soldiers are scrupulously named by parishes hopefully expecting later compensation, there is of course rarely any indication of why particular villages were chosen or which routes were taken to arrive there, and many soldiers lodged almost accidentally, it would seem, in isolated hamlets remote from any obvious route. Mystery often surrounds even the major commanders; it is unclear, for example, why Lord Willoughby of Parham should have quartered at Brailes when marching from Birmingham to Edgehill, why Cromwell should have chosen Tadmarton in May 1645 or Fairfax Clifford Chambers in June. Similarly for civilian traffic: more is known of the precise London destinations of weekly carriers from all parts of the Midlands than on the local routes they took on first setting out. The silence of contemporaries can only mean that they saw nothing to report on the subject; in other words, that travellers took whichever sections of local roads happened to be negotiable at the time, as conditions permitted, deviating across open country wherever preferable. Much of the eastern part of the district under consideration was unenclosed, corresponding to the undulating Warwickshire Feldon and north Oxfordshire 'champion' country, and this region felt the full impact of the war correspondingly more than the relatively thickly-wooded Forest of Arden district to the west. With river crossings rare, bridges often dilapidated and fords treacherous, both civilian and military traffic must often have meandered, improvising routes according to prevailing conditions rather than venturing into the dangerous quagmires of known local roads. Interestingly, local tradition in individual parishes often confirms this picture of even eminent travellers using quite minor trackways, like those associated with the King himself near Banbury and Dunchurch. Altogether, apart from the case of the major national highways, which were well frequented despite their universally bad condition, the subject of the use of local roads is one needing scrupulous study by historians with detailed local knowledge before further conclusions can be drawn.

The second major factor in determining the central role that the south Midlands were to play in the Civil War was the early establishment of the court at Oxford, exactly midway between parliamentary London and royalist Worcester, with Banbury assuming the role, according to one early historian of the war in this locality, of Oxford's 'most important outpost . . . and an integral part of the Royalist scheme of operations in the southern midlands'. The early royalist reoccupation of Herefordshire and Worcestershire provided a corridor between the King's base at Oxford and the loyal strongholds of Worcester and the south-west, a corridor soon broadened by Prince Rupert's conquest of Cirencester and Bristol. Equally important was the King's dependence on Wales, the west Midlands and the Marches as a treasury house and major recruiting base, as well as a vital manufactory containing iron-working districts, arms depots and workshops, factors painstakingly analysed by Ian Roy's valuable study of the royalist ordnance accounts. Throughout the war the King relied on these areas for men, money and materials, as well as on the prodigality of loyal individuals like the Earl of Worcester, the richest Catholic peer in the kingdom, who immediately donated £5,000 to raise a regiment and contributed the quite spectacular sum of almost £1 milion to the King's cause over the duration of the war. Among other important aids to the Royalists in the district was the Court of the Welsh Marches, which exercised jurisdiction over a wide area including Worcestershire, and gave the Crown large and arbitrary powers over individuals and property.

The King's base at Oxford itself was progressively and systematically surrounded by a circle of protective garrisons extending north into Warwickshire and south into Berkshire, while at the same time a string of east–west staging posts was established between Oxford and the west, ensuring a constant stream of convoys escorted by local commanders and guaranteeing recurrent skirmishes as they came under attack, while garrisons near the route were activated and periodically changed hands with the ebb and flow of the war, creating almost continuous disruption far and wide throughout Worcestershire, Warwickshire and Oxfordshire. When a post-war Warwickshire petition to Parliament pleaded the 'continual passage through the county from Oxford and Banbury to Worcester, Hereford, Dudley and Lichfield, with other of the King's garrisons', or a tenant, Henry Cowper, on the Earl of Middlesex's estate at Milcote, near Stratford-upon-Avon, claimed a reduction of rent because of 'the great dangers these parts are in by the passage of armies and soldiers', they were merely stating the simple truth.[2]

From the parliamentary viewpoint the region was equally important. Although after Turnham Green the King displayed little inclination to venture towards London, he could not be allowed to dominate the Midlands with impunity either, since he would thereby block the vital Severn Valley communications route to the ports of Gloucester and Bristol on the one hand, while containing and neutralizing powerful northern allies like Brereton and the Fairfaxes on the other, preventing them bringing their aid to Parliament's south-eastern base.

The whole of the region, with south Warwickshire at its heart, was therefore unavoidably implicated in the approaching conflict, with the result that not only the major market towns like Evesham, Stow, Warwick, Stratford and Banbury assumed strategic importance disproportionate to their modest size, but communities now little more than rural backwaters on the modern tourist circuit attracted major military operations as Sudeley, Bourton-on-the-Water, Chipping Campden, Woodstock and Burford were raised to garrison status and witnessed dramatic days. Even in lulls of activity, temporary 'courts of guard' were kept in countless hitherto sleepy villages throughout the Warwickshire Feldon and beyond, like Kineton, Ratley, Balscote, Burton Dassett, Adderbury, Combrook, Shottery, Bidford, Snitterfield, Napton-on-the-Hill, Exhall and many others – all necessitating local provisioning besides presenting a stressful reminder of the wider, more violent conflict in the rowdy presence of armed soldiers molesting villagers, manning a checkpoint at the lane's end or lording it in the squire's hastily-vacated manor-house. It is not suggested that such villages became centres of prolonged military activity; they were not garrisons as such. But not even the presence of troops there has usually been suspected by the local historian, and the parish archives tell us that that presence was rarely benign. Moreover, the historian's stress on 'localism' or 'county-mindedness' (whose validity is debatable, in any case, as far as Warwickshire is concerned) and on the notorious reluctance of unprofessional soldiers to serve outside their home district, should not obscure other facts: that recruitment was far from being exclusively local and regions were closely interdependent across largely irrelevant county borders. Such regional interdependence is often acknowledged by contemporaries: a royalist commander writes to Prince Rupert that 'the loss of Evesham . . . cut off all the intercourse between Worcester and Oxford'; John Corbet, the parliamentary chaplain at Gloucester, bewails the loss of Sudeley as 'a great stop to our entercourse with Warwick, which was the only way of commerce with London'; and the parliamentary Colonel Whetham, writing of Banbury, notes that 'the taking of this Den of Theeves would much conduce to the straitning of Oxon, and give liberty of Trade to London from many parts'.

One of the features of the war which particularly affected the Midlands is thus the regularity with which 'foreign' troops crossed regions far distant from their point of origin, and the sheer distances covered by footsore soldiers, flying cavalry and lumbering convoys remain impressive. The parliamentary relief of Gloucester in the summer of 1643, seen by some modern historians and at least one informed contemporary as the turning-point of the war, was largely achieved by an expeditionary force of Londoners trekking across the Midlands, but many other, less well-known assignments using forces recruited in distant shires affected the region under discussion. Similarly, when the conflict took the form of a major siege, as at Banbury twice, forces were called in from everywhere to supplement local contingents and billeted in the neighbourhood in often huge numbers for considerable periods of time. The Warwickshire parish archives refer with almost monotonous regularity to such events, and to forces from Newport Pagnell, Aylesbury, Tewkesbury, Evesham and Northampton criss-crossing their territory on some mission, besides the unwelcome later incursions of the standing armies like Fairfax's New Model and the dreaded Scots which, if the parish reports are to be believed, left a trail of desolation in their wake. Often the conscientious parish constables are explicit in their reports: 'Nuport men when they came from Worcester'; 'the carryage of Coll. Whalleys amunition to Evisham & other places'; 'when the seege was at Banbury'; 'Northampton men going to Worcester'; 'Coll. Crumwells when they went to Stow fight'; 'when Sir Thomas Fayrfaxe marcht by Stratford'; 'the Scots Army when they came throughe Warrwicke'. Sometimes, on the other hand, a minor reference remains obscure: why were parliamentary troops from the small garrison of Gaunt House, near Standlake, Oxon, stationed in Brailes, well over 20 miles to the north; and what mission were soldiers from 'a castle in Wales' undertaking in Tysoe? Virtually all the parishes record such mysteries: the tiny Ashow, near Kenilworth, for example, notes the passage not only of local volunteers but others from Evesham, Norfolk, Lincolnshire, 'Darby men as they went to Bristol' and 'Darby men as they came back', as well as the Scots on their return march from Hereford. Similarly, Sherbourne quartered 'dragoneers when they came from Yorke fighte'. Inevitably, such manoeuvrings seem particularly motiveless to the unfortunate villagers, like Richard Randall in Little Wolford who wearily reports: 'For 8 weekes last I have had foote Souldiers under [blank] and for this last Fortnight 3 Horsmen, & how long they will Continew I know not'.

It has perhaps not been sufficiently recognized, therefore (particularly by military historians understandably concentrating on the main battle routes converging on the climax of the battle itself), to what extent even minor military offensives well outside a given district had an unpredictable local impact, and only detailed examination of the surviving parish archives reveals the full extent of this random fall-out. Each of the military expeditions referred to above brought to the villagers the realities of war, in the shape of harassment and impoverishment through quarter and plunder, if no worse.[3]

RIVAL LOYALTIES

If the whole region was therefore, as it were, geographically predestined to become a major military thoroughfare, it was the presence in south Warwickshire of two powerful rivals, Lord Brooke and the Earl of Northampton, which precipitated matters and ensured that actual conflict would break out in the region sooner rather than later. Public inertia, fear or incompetence might easily have delayed the onset of war indefinitely in Warwickshire as it did, for example, in neighbouring Staffordshire which remained at first stoutly uncommitted. But neither Lord Brooke nor the Earl of Northampton, nor their influential allies, were prepared simply to sit back and wait or be conciliatory. On the contrary, both peers seemed to relish the approach of what none could have suspected to be their finest hour, the tragic climax to their respective careers. So although until this date Warwickshire had in effect no single dominant peer, the Civil War here almost instantly crystallized into a series of confrontations between these two, almost as though the baronial conflicts of the past were about to be revived. Nor is this personalization of the conflict simply a modern, retrospective view, contemporary commentators themselves stressing the 'many troubles . . . occasioned by those broyles between the Lord Brooks and the Earle of Northampton'. In this context therefore, the pointed replacement of the one by the other as Lord Lieutenant of the county by Parliament on 5 March 1642 was a significant and, seen in retrospect, prophetic step.

The pre-war careers of these two formidable opponents, both experienced campaigners on a national rather than a purely local level, need not delay us here. It is almost too easy to see in them polar opposites. Robert Greville, Lord Brooke, was a long-standing puritan intellectual of uncompromisingly radical views, and with a network of influential contacts among puritan preachers as well as leading political subversives like John Pym and the more radical peerage like Lord Saye. He published philosophical and religious tracts and sermons and had already been busy campaigning in Warwickshire and inducting puritan protégés into local churches, and the display of his impressive organizational skills in 1642 presented a model of radical ideological leadership to an as yet uncommitted county. The royalist Dugdale pictures him as a fanatical zealot, albeit, trying to be fair, 'in his own nature a very civil and well humour'd man'. Spencer Compton, Earl of Northampton, by contrast, was a straight-forward unintellectual aristocrat, long a court favourite and personal friend of the King, whose courtship of Henrietta Maria he had promoted as Master of the Robes in happier times, and who had seen service on the continent in some of Charles's ill-fated military ventures. Apparently converted overnight from a life of courtly pleasure to firm political resolve, he was prominent among the group of peers declaring loyalty to the King at York on 5 June 1642; one assumes his loyalty to Charles to have been as unswervingly automatic as was Brooke's hostility. The two peers were even opposed physically and temperamentally: Brooke, athletic, austere and chess-playing, Northampton, preferring his hounds in spite of having become, according to one contemporary critic, 'grosse and corpulant'. By a curious irony, once they had set the wheels of war in motion the two rivals were shortly to be killed in action, almost at the same time and almost at the same place; Northampton was barely forty, Brooke in his mid-thirties. It is almost tempting to see the two opponents characterized in their respective seats of Warwick Castle and Compton Wynyates, the grim inviolability of the one challenging the gem-like flamboyance of the other. Roughly halfway between the two was the as yet undisturbed Edgehill where, undreamt of by either, the first full battle of war would shortly be enacted.

Of the many associated with the two rival peers in the early stages of the war little needs recording. There was never a cohesive war group on either side, each party discovering convenient local allies as the situation evolved. On the royalist side were several hitherto undistinguished conservative magnates with local landed interests, the most active being Francis Leigh, Lord Dunsmore, of Kings Newnham, one of the King's chosen Commissioners of Array for Warwickshire, a cousin of the wealthy Sir Thomas Leigh of Stoneleigh and a 'quarrelsome and unpopular man'; the young Robert Dormer, Earl of Carnarvon, of Grove Park, Warwick; and the prickly and ambitious Henry, later Lord, Wilmot, of Adderbury; while from just outside the county the energetic Sir John Byron and spirited young Henry Hastings, son of the Earl of Huntingdon, eagerly contributed to the Earl of Northampton's appeals. The precise contribution of such allies is difficult to evaluate, but they immediately raised valuable troops of horse and prepared to indulge in whatever opportunities for plundering, harassment and armed skirmishing presented themselves. Wilmot and Carnarvon in particular soon became highly experienced, competent cavalry commanders, at Edgehill and after. The ruthless Wilmot enjoyed a successful, if controversial, military career throughout the war, but Carnarvon, 'a high-tempered young man with a mop of yellow curls', was killed in action at Newbury in 1643. Apart from their military expertise, however, none of these allies brought political or moral distinction to the royalist cause, or even the organizational skills and sheer charisma which Prince Rupert was soon to display.

The parliamentary camp of Lord Brooke presented a somewhat different picture, however, including a number of more substantial, impressive local personalities, usually ideologically committed, of which two deserve special mention: William Fiennes, Lord Saye and Sele, of Broughton Castle, near Banbury, and William Purefoy, of Caldecote, from the north Warwickshire minor gentry. Both, already elderly, were experienced political campaigners and as such added an intellectual dimension to Lord Brooke's circle of a kind patently lacking in the Earl of Northampton's. Lord Saye, termed by Dugdale 'that great Rebel' and by another contemporary the 'Godfather to the Puritan faction', was alleged, in a tradition established at the time and often subsequently popularized, to have held secret meetings with leading subversives, including John Hampden, in:

> . . . Lord Saye's house, wherein was a roome and passage which his servants were prohibited to come neare, where great noises and talkings have been heard to the admiration of some who lived in the house, yet could never discerne their Lords Companions.

The hidden 'council chamber' under the roof at Broughton, with its thick stone walls, narrow stairway, subterranean escape passage under the fields and the tradition that discussions were sometimes continued on the adjacent leads of the roof, are as inviolably part of the local folklore as the ghosts of Edgehill.[4]

As an opposition leader Saye was as uncompromising as Brooke: both peers had objected to the imposition of Ship Money, both had been imprisoned for refusing the Oath of Allegiance, both implicated in puritan colonizing projects in America. In August 1642 he was appointed Lord Lieutenant for Oxfordshire by Parliament, as Brooke had already been for Warwickshire, and immediately set about raising forces and a loan of £1,000 for Parliament. Although he was very active in and about Oxford in August and September 1642, he soon withdrew from active combat, leaving his sons, John and Nathaniel Fiennes, to become leading parliamentary commanders. Like Brooke, too, he wrote tracts and made speeches in Parliament against episcopacy and royal despotism.

The extraordinary politician-turned-soldier William Purefoy, already a veteran sixty-year-old puritan campaigner having sworn the ruin of the monarchy as a young man, was perhaps the most implacable opposition figure of all, and even without the provocation of Prince Rupert's ill-advised assault on his home at Caldecote in August 1642 would have been an uncompromising opponent of all King-and-Church circles. Already charged by Parliament with putting the Militia Ordinance into effect in Warwickshire in May, he soon gravitated into Brooke's circle and was almost certainly the co-defender, with Edward Peto of Chesterton, of Warwick Castle during the royalist siege of August 1642. Along with his undoubted political skills and formidable energies, however, he also has a less enviable claim on the local historian's attention in that, as a dogmatic puritan, he is the only Warwickshire leader to have achieved notoriety in condoning, if not actually instigating, the wave of church vandalism beginning to sweep the countryside as war approached. Consistent to the last, he was later a member of the High Court which tried Charles and personally signed his death warrant. Either as committeeman or military commander, this imperious and tireless parliamentarian and his equally committed kinsmen are met at every corner of Warwickshire's fraught history throughout the 1640s and '50s.[5]

Such, then, were the main protagonists and their leading supporters in at least the initial stages of the conflict in the south Midlands; the energetic initiative-takers who by their example – mixed, it must be added, with a degree of coercion and crude propaganda – attempted to sway the uncommitted and secure the region for their cause. To what extent were they followed by the rest of the community? It has already been noted that pre-war Warwickshire was a profoundly divided county with deep underlying tensions. The drift to war was marked by unprecedented pressures on the leading families to declare themselves, and many, most perhaps, resisted these pressures for as long as they could. Which way, finally, did they vote? To this simple question there is, of course, no simple answer. Most historians are agreed that, whatever it was, the Civil War was not a class war, that loyalties in aristocracy and gentry alike were almost equally divided, and that the family unit itself was frequently split, with some tragic, well-publicized cases, like the Feildings, Earls of Denbigh, of Newnham Paddox. It is equally true that allegiance, once established, was not necessarily permanent or definitive. Participants could and did, for a variety of reasons not necessarily disreputable, change sides: their ardour might cool once the personal cost of loyalty became clear; some were so financially ruined that they were unable to continue their support; and there was in any case an in-built reluctance on the part of the majority to become involved at all. Certainly there was no doubt in the mind of that perceptive contemporary sociologist Thomas Hobbes that 'there were very few of the common people that cared much for either of the causes, but would have taken any side for pay or plunder'. The reluctance to take sides was in itself due not merely to inertia or indifference. Quite apart from the fact that the aristocracy, gentry, substantial yeomen and even smallholders all had much to lose if they chose the 'wrong side', there was genuine bewilderment at the complexities of the issues raised and how to reconcile conflicting duties, some involving matters of deep moral and spiritual conviction, as in the well-attested case of John Fetherston of Packwood. Fetherston confessed his dilemma in a touching letter to his 'good brother', explaining how the contradictory demands of the day left him quite unable to act with an easy conscience:

> I am in a great distraction concerninge my armor (beinge all-togeither unable to satisy my self in point of judgement and conscience what to doe) by reason of the severall commands of the Kinge and parliament. My protestation [Oath] putts me in mind that I am bound in conscience to serve both, and yet there seems now a very great difference betweene them, which I humbly desyer allmighty god, if it be his will, may be peaceably & timely composed and settled for the good of this churche and kingdome. I have not yet sent in my armes, eyther to my lord of Northampton or my lord Brooke, because you know I am joyned with Mr Bettom, who is a known profest papist [Walliston Betham of Rowington]; hee is to find the horse & man, and I the armor, pettronells and sadle. If I should deliver my armes to Mr Bettomes man, I should then have done an act contrary both to the Kinge & parliament, who have both declared that papists are to be disarmed. I have therefore left my armor at your house & my pettronells I have sent by my man now, & as for my sadle, I cannot have it from Mr Bettome. I understand that Mr Dugdale lyeth at your howse. I pray you present my respects to him, & tell him my armes are there ready, & I desyer they may be imployed for the safety of the church and kingdome . . .

Matters were indeed far from clear-cut, when troops were being raised 'for the defence of the King, Parliament and Kingdom', in the standard, often-repeated and all-embracing formula of the day, or when confusing distinctions between the King in person, his advisers and his constitutional (or, indeed, spiritual) role were constantly being invoked. Many were unable or unwilling to opt for one side or the other. As we have seen, John Fetherston was friendly with both the Royalist Dugdale and the recusant Betham, yet in the general uncertainty appeared shortly after at one of Lord Brooke's musters, in June or July, and was accordingly listed as a Parliamentarian by Dugdale (see Appendix A). But his allegiance was always suspect and he was later taken prisoner by the Roundheads, apparently on the Earl of Denbigh's orders, and escorted to London where he lodged at the Chequers tavern in the Strand, awaiting interrogation. A classic Warwickshire example of prevarication is provided by Richard Shuckburgh, who persisted in putting off an irrevocable decision as long as possible, blandly declaring that he had 'horses in readiness to defend the King, the Commonwealth, the Laws and Parliament'. The ploy seems not to have convinced Parliament, however, for although Dugdale, curiously, judged him a neutral, he was shortly after accused of 'entertaining cavaliers in his house, having suspicious Irish-men being brought to him, & making derogatory remarks about Parliament'. He did indeed opt for the King, apparently decisively, at Edgehill.[6]

Warwickshire was therefore as deeply divided and uncommitted a county as any, and any selection of names from the leading families could illustrate ambiguous loyalties even among the apparently staunch. Two random examples may suffice. Hastings Ingram, of Little Wolford, was at first neutral before opting belatedly for Parliament. As an apparently committed activist he then suffered imprisonment by the Royalists before escaping, commanding a cavalry unit and becoming briefly governor of the Kenilworth parliamentary garrison, only to suddenly lay down his arms (he alleged, somewhat unconvincingly, through local hostility to him) and be subsequently accused by the authorities of political unreliability. The wealthy William Combe, of the prominent Stratford-upon-Avon family with long-standing connections with the Shakespeares, is another curious case. Combe was captain of the town militia in 1632 and considered ten years later such a committed parliamentarian as to be bracketed with William Purefoy as a principal rebel to the King's cause in Warwickshire. Although then approaching sixty he immediately raised troops for Lord Brooke as war approached and, in consequence, was ruinously plundered by royalist soldiers, only to be accused by the parliamentary authorities of political treachery a few years later. Similar stories could be repeated from all parts of the county, each slightly different, and each, no doubt, would offer fascinating insights into local and family history which only painstaking research could uncover.

The task of identifying precisely how the leading families opted initially has been made immeasurably easier by the contemporary antiquary William Dugdale, who at the beginning of the war, compiled a detailed list of Royalists, Parliamentarians and neutrals for Warwickshire (see Appendix A). While Dugdale is not infallible and while the list, by its very nature, ignores the fluid and impermanent nature of loyalties which was to be a major feature of the war, he was fair-minded, scrupulous and involved, and this unique document must serve as the starting-point for any comprehensive discussion of allegiance in Warwickshire during the Civil War. The large number of neutrals in the list is particularly significant, and although many of those named there soon committed themselves, this particular section, when seen alongside those many who changed sides, withdrew or sat on the fence throughout, confirms that the subject of Warwickshire's loyalties is indeed a complex one. Comprehensive debate on the many issues raised by the Dugdale list is well outside the scope of the present work, but overriding all considerations must remain the point already made of an almost universal reluctance to opt for one side or the other, as illustrated in Clarendon's sardonic comment, that 'the number of those who desired to sit still was greater than of those who desired to engage in either party'.[7]

CHAPTER TWO

THE DRIFT TO WAR

POLITICAL AND RELIGIOUS TENSIONS

Once the King had left London, in January 1642, a feverish, excitable mood began slowly but remorselessly to build up throughout the country. In Warwickshire there was already heightened tension in the wake of scares over alleged Catholic conspiracies: violence had been forecast in the county in November 1641 and warrants issued to prevent unlawful assemblies, as the county was considered one 'most stored with Papists and in that respect most dangerous'. Plots, real or imagined, were in the air everywhere. As early as January, following the doubling of the watch throughout Warwickshire and with similar precautions taking place in Worcestershire, Leicestershire and elsewhere, warlike preparations were afoot in some towns, as at Stratford-upon-Avon where the corporation thought it advisable to replenish the town's armoury: 'itt is ordered thatt 1 c.waite of powder shall be forthwith bought'. At Warwick, it was learnt later, Lord Brooke was beginning a systematic strengthening of the castle's fortifications.

At the same time, in a developing war of words, January saw the resumption of the previous year's county lobbying of Parliament, and a bewildering flurry of petitions and counter-petitions was delivered to Westminster as each side, in a clear political act, attempted to pressurize opinion, rally support and gain at least moral ascendancy. In February, one Warwickshire text prayed for the 'thorough reformation of the church, punishment of delinquents and vindication of the privileges of Parliament'. So numerous had these petitions become by the summer of 1642, that one contemporary later referred to the period as 'those petitioning times'. Naturally, the petitions addressed to Parliament are the most well known: they are not only more numerous but, with the King self-exiled at York, Parliament could also operate untrammelled, printing and circulating thousands of copies of, for example, its declaration against the Commission of Array. In many counties, therefore, evidence exists of real awareness among the common people of what the issues were. As for the petitions to the King, these were couched in similar terms, one typical 'Humble Remonstrance, Protestacion and Peticion of the knights, gentlemen and others of the Countie of Warwick' expressing loyalty and readiness to 'adventure the utmost hazard of our lives and fortunes' in the Sovereign's defence, ending by begging for a visit from the King to counteract the 'allurements' and 'terrors' instigated by 'Lord Brooke and other disaffected persons'. One parliamentary diarist, reflecting the ambiguities of the times already referred to, sums up one Warwickshire petition: 'they wilbe ready to spend there bloode for the King and parlya; they desyre the malygnante spiritts may be removed from the king'.

It is debatable to what extent such petitions were, as Anthony Fletcher has claimed in his lucid analysis, 'an authentic expression of deeply-felt local opinion', or, rather, an efficient stage-managed exercise by skilful political operators like Lord Brooke. Certainly the displays of loyalty sound exaggerated and the fulsome rhetoric suspect, as do the obsequious thanks to the organizers and the neatness with which they easily become pleas for enhanced powers to be given to those already powerful enough. At one of Brooke's musters, for example, a petition was drawn up requesting that the county magazine 'be removed [from Coventry] and laid up in your Lordship's Castle at Warwick, as the safest place of the Countie, with a sufficient Guard provided by the Countie for the securing of it'. This was very promptly done. It is clear that the leading militants were heavily involved in the process, even if they did not engineer the whole operation. The orchestration of the final stages certainly could often become a family affair. Lord Brooke had no family, but Lord Saye's eldest son James Fiennes announced Oxfordshire's delegation to Parliament, while his brother John presented the actual petition.[1]

A substantial part of this almost continuous petitioning process concerned religious, as well as purely political, matters; indeed, it was almost impossible to separate the two in an area which reflected the entire religious spectrum, from the Catholic strongholds of south Worcestershire and Warwickshire, through districts of incipient quakerism, to the radical puritan heritage of 'cakes and zeal' Banbury, where the town cross had long since been pulled down and maypoles, May Day celebrations, Whitsun ales and Morris dancing suppressed. The long-standing religious dissensions of many years began to sharpen, and petitioning clashes over religious matters occurred in places, sometimes complicated by personal feuding. Both Warwickshire and Oxfordshire had deep fears over papism: Oxfordshire wanted wider powers given to JPs for the searching of Catholic properties and pressed the House of Lords to interrogate heads of colleges about whether Parliament's order to destroy images, altars and crucifixes had been fully implemented, even though it had been reported as early as January 1641 that 'all . . . the painted glasse windows in most of the Colledges [are] pulled downe voluntarily, and the Alters turned into Tables and stand East and West'. Sir William Walter challenged the Fiennes family over the county petitioning and had a rival conservative one printed, and was promptly accused by them of 'great labouring to raise a faction'. Everywhere religious tensions were evident: substantial numbers of recusants were repeatedly presented in many parishes; the Warwickshire anti-papist scares in November 1641 implicated several of the leading families of the region, like the Throckmortons, Morgans and Sheldons; there was an increase in religious cases in Warwick Quarter Sessions indictments; and some parishes witnessed ugly incidents as hints of what was to come during the actual war. The position of the royalist Bishop of Worcester, whose diocese included much of south Warwickshire, was becoming politically untenable under parliamentary attacks and '. . . menaced to be sent for in a disgracefull maner . . . as if indeed he were a notorious malefactor and delinquent', while the Bishop of Oxford had already thought himself obliged to suspend the veteran puritan divine, John Dod, rector of Hanwell, 'a centre of puritanism for a far wider area than north Oxfordshire'.[2]

Local clergy could not avoid being sucked into the controversy even if they would have preferred otherwise. Their response naturally varied from parish to parish. Some, like the 'sententious and pedantic' Thomas Pilkington, vicar of Claverdon, kept a low profile, hoping to sit it out for as long as possible, and survived the wars unscathed. Others faced these unprecedented pressures resolutely, often paying the price for their principles. The elderly conservative scholar Francis Holyoak, vicar of Southam, whose son Thomas became a captain of foot in the King's forces at Oxford, was later alleged to have pressurized parishioners in church to enlist for the King and offered arms in his house to those who volunteered; he was condemned by parliamentary soldiers as 'of very evil and dissolute conversation' and was one of the first parsons to be harassed. Among the conscientious, some were perhaps genuinely bewildered over the issues. Christopher Harvey, the poet-vicar of Clifton-on-Dunsmore, petitioned Parliament in March 1642 to resolve certain 'doubts and scruples' before his conscience would allow him to espouse its cause. As he later published a tract against rebellion he seems not to have been convinced by the advice he received. In the most clear-cut cases, as will be seen, the parson simply deserted his cure to enlist. Yet others preferred to contribute verbally, like the scholar and grammarian Thomas Merriott, vicar and schoolmaster of Swalcliffe, summoned to appear before the House of Commons in July 1642 for 'using some reproachful terms upon the Parliament, and publishing the last Declaration of his Majesty's'. Merriott had long had an uneasy relationship with his parishioners, and the war brought things to a climax: his living was sequestrated. Others went even farther and lost no opportunity for abusing the enemy, like the obstreperous Walwyn Clarke, parson of Oxhill, who, not content with sending men and material assistance to the Royalists and having relatives enlist, publicly:

> . . . called Parliament rogues, scorned that his man[servant] should be in their Roundhead service, threatened a constable for executing his office, said the Kings army would soon get the better, and the constable should be hanged for it.

Others, like Roger Jones, vicar of Long Compton, and John Williams, of Halford, both later ejected for habitual drunkenness, were presumably beyond decision-making.

The personal danger in being indiscreet or, perhaps merely foolish, is well illustrated in the case of John Howes, the vicar of Banbury. In December, 1640, in a strongly puritan parish, he inadvisably drew attention to his political views by refusing to read the annual commemorative thanksgiving for deliverance from the Gunpowder Plot or pray for divine retribution against all rebels against the state, making matters worse by abusing the dominant peer of the neighbourhood, the prickly Lord Saye, 'in foul and scandalous words'. His parishioners petitioned Parliament against their 'wicked vicar' and he was promptly hauled in front of judges who condemned him to the Fleet prison. After a few chastening days he apologized, was graciously pardoned by Saye and released. The episode illustrates clearly how inextricable Church and politics had become by this date, and how the war was to exacerbate and bring into the open such profound divisions.[3]

In some parishes therefore, as at Banbury, vicar and parishioners were clearly at loggerheads, causing intolerable tensions. Samuel Clarke at Alcester castigated the town's drunkenness and wickedness, a result, he claimed, of its being 'placed in the midst of many great papists, which made it their rendezvous', while at Warwick, Clarke was constantly under attack from a rival vicar, Thomas Hall, of St Mary's. Hall himself illustrates one other side to the story, that of the conscientious clergyman desperately trying to steer an honourable path through the irreconcilable conflicts of these times, when he later recalled his career:

> So soon as I began to exercise [my ministry] my refusing to read the Book of Sports on the Sabbath endangered me . . . [later] I was threatened by the episcopal party for non-conformity; since I am come to you I have suffered deeply by the cavaliering party, oftentimes plundered, five times their prisoner; oft cursed, accused, threatened etc. And now at last I have been set upon by the sectaries who sometimes have spoken to me in the middle of sermons, sometimes after, sometimes challenge me to dispute.

Many parishes were indeed deeply divided among themselves. In one of the most populous of all, Brailes, and in the face of budding quakerism soon to blossom, the influential Catholic William Bishop, closely associated with the great Sheldon family of Weston, Long Compton, kept a private priest and, after suffering the sequestration of his large estate, would soon go abroad to avoid further victimization by the authorities. Elsewhere, adjacent parishes might have ideologically-opposed incumbents: at Cropredy Edward Bathurst was 'a distinguished royalist academic', while at neighbouring Hanwell, patronized and even lodged by the leading puritan gentry of the district, the Copes, the elderly rector John Dod, scholarly, conscientious but hostile to the established Church, had had a long and distinguished lecturing and preaching career before finally being replaced by the equally radical Robert Harris. Nor, at parish level, could bitter controversies, once aroused, cool overnight. Later isolated references suggest that ordinary people could occasionally take the law into their own hands within their church, as at Adderbury in December 1643, when the village carpenter, John Harris, a veteran of Edgehill, committed a 'desperate outrage' against the royalist vicar, William Oldys:

> . . . when, after he had seasoned his wicked hands by tearing into peeces the Booke of Common prayer . . . this desperate wretch tooke the Holy Bible, looked into it, and rent it all to peeces, from the first page of the Creation to the last of the Revelation, and . . . trod it under his feet.

In some parishes, as is clear from later, incidental records, animosities aroused between vicar and parishioners in these troubled times could simmer for years, sometimes culminating, as at Sutton-under-Brailes, in lengthy court cases which must have totally disrupted parish life. Inside the church itself, too, there was change, and although there is disappointingly little hard evidence to illustrate this locally, at least one oft-quoted observation hints at this, and is well worth repeating. Anna Temple, Lord Saye's sister, writing from Broughton with, presumably, local information, to her sister in Sussex, piously enthuses over the puritans' removal of sacramental communion tables and altar rails, to allow the congregation to gather around in the body of the church:

Wee shall see idolatry and superstition rooted out and God's ordinances sett up in the puritie and power of them; altars begin to goe downe apace, and railes, in many places . . .[4]

Finally, one further significant aspect of the politicized religious debate of the day was the contribution of the more radical puritan clergy of the district under discussion. In particular, as Ann Hughes has well revealed, there existed a local network of puritan intellectuals, often associated with or actual protégés of Lord Brooke, some of whom had in the 1630s taken refuge in Warwick from Archbishop Laud's harassment: 'Through Warwick Castle young provincial ministers and schoolmasters forged personal contacts with men who in the 1640s became influential national figures'. A number had been carefully placed by Brooke in nearby parishes and had been busy disseminating radical views from local pulpits, rotating with colleagues in the district, giving lectures at Warwick, Coventry and elsewhere. Establishing close contacts with local parliamentary gentry like William Combe of Stratford and Anthony Stoughton of Warwick, who would travel to hear them preach, some promptly volunteered for active service as parliamentary chaplains as war became imminent while others took refuge in parliamentary strongholds like Coventry, acquiring official positions. Among the more prominent of these intellectuals were Simeon Ashe, already ejected from Staffordshire and a regular preacher in Warwick before enlisting and riding into battle at Edgehill; John Bryan, rector of Barford, treasurer and preacher to the Warwick garrison, close associate of Lord Brooke and later a leading Parliamentarian in Coventry; Samuel Clarke, vicar of Alcester, close associate of Lord Brooke and a frequent preacher at Warwick and consequently one of the first local ministers to be plundered by the Royalists; Thomas Dugard, vicar of Barford and schoolmaster at Warwick, connected also with Lord Brooke, Lord Saye and others, including Pym; John Trapp, vicar of Weston-on-Avon, then Welford, later minister to Warwick garrison and headmaster of Stratford grammar school; and the most celebrated of all, Richard Baxter, who gave a graphic account of the local bigotry in neighbouring Worcestershire which forced him to flee for his life and gravitate to Coventry, where he regularly preached to the soldiers before attending the siege of Banbury. Although there were doctrinal differences between them, all such were at the opposite end of the ideological spectrum to incumbents like the Laudian vicar of Southam, a strong advocate of episcopacy and author of a celebrated 'Sermon of Obedience, especially unto Authority Ecclesiastical'.

Clearly it would be impossible to evaluate in precise terms the exact contribution of such intellectuals to the religious debate of the neighbourhood. After all, morale-boosting 'heavenly sermons' to the troops by the chaplains among them, much appreciated by the more pious in the Earl of Essex's ranks, must have been rather different from the lengthy pulpit sermons to parishioners, guest lectures to the already converted at Warwick or Coventry, or the learned disquisitions which many of them later wrote. But common sense suggests that they must have contributed significantly to the heightening of tension and polarization of issues which were such a marked feature of the times. The Church was still 'the most efficient mass-media system of the age', and the parish pulpit a powerful instrument for the large and relatively unsophisticated congregations for whom regular church attendance was still obligatory. Church services and long sermons were infinitely susceptible to political slant, as Clarendon recognized when he complained of the perversion of scripture for political purposes, or indeed

Parliament itself when it later issued a request to the bailiff of Warwick 'to deliver these inclosed papers to both the ministers that preacheth this afternoone for them to publish in theire severall churches, thereby the better to sturr up the people to expresse their affections to the Parliamt'. Certainly Royalists like Dugdale had no doubt that the puritan zealots were pernicious opinion-formers: Lord Brooke himself had been 'strangely tainted with fanatic Principles by . . . some Schismatical Preachers', who had virtually corrupted the nation:

> Nor were the Lecturing-Preachers and others of that strain less active every where in this desperate, and afterwards bloudy, Scene; the cheif of which, throughout all England, were then got into London, Westminster and the Suburbs; it being very well known, both by their public Sermons and seditious Pamphlets, what endeavours they sedulously used to stir up all persons.

A diametrically-opposed view, on the other hand, is given by parliamentarian correspondents from adjacent Leicestershire and Northamptonshire in August, 1642, equally adamant that 'Altar-Priests have poysoned the best of the people'.

There is little doubt, therefore, that religious tensions which had been steadily rising throughout the 1630s were now sharper than ever: 'all the Pulpetts doe now ring of the disorders of the Clergy, both in doctrine and discipline', reported one newsletter at the end of 1640. The strains in some parishes were all too evident: Richard Baxter's experience in Worcestershire, where, although a moderate, he was jeered and taunted with cries of 'Down with the Roundheads!', prompted his oft-quoted observation: 'The war was begun in our streets before the King or Parliament had any armies'. A fascinating insight into this sharply divided community and the intensity of the passions aroused is given by a Parliamentarian's bitter portrait of the state of Worcester at the outbreak of the war. His city has become a 'distracted place' invaded by 'the birds of darknesse and prey', full of quarrelsome and opinionated turncoats seen in some sombre vision:

> In that new world I saw strange creatures: some Salamanders, which live in the fire of contention; and Proteuses, changing from the forme they were of but a few dayes before . . .

His city has been occupied by unruly, blaspheming Welsh cavalrymen on their way to royalist billets, stealing purses and taking all the cheese from the market stalls, while hordes of soldiers were destroying pastures in the common meadow 'as if they would root up our grasse with our Religion and Liberties', frightening citizens with their violence and attending evensong in the cathedral carrying muskets instead of bibles. Plundering and skirmishing are reported from nearby towns and hayricks are on fire. Although nearby churches are full of 'malignants', only one in ten has 'a constant preaching Minister', so that there is 'such a scarcity of the Word' throughout this benighted land. The cathedral itself is home to fearful refugees and the chancel is reflecting the recent anti-Laudian changes:

> The great Candlesticks are gone, and we hope better Lights will be set up; and the Marble Altar . . . is confined within a Vault under the Quire, there to remaine till a day which I hope they shall never see . . .

The cathedral staff are unworthy, and the bishop himself under threat of imprisonment, even though 'he is loath to change his pallace for a prison, though it were the Tower of

London'. Such a picture, luridly partisan though it is, offers a glimpse of what was to come. By the end of the war, as we shall see, the disintegration of the old Church had affected many a Midland parish almost as much as the arrival of the soldiers, as spiritual life was disrupted, congregations were divided, parochial relief suspended and parsons harassed or, in many cases, ejected and ruined. There is indeed 'a real sense in which the English Civil War was a war of religion'.[5]

THE CALL TO ARMS

By the time the King had arrived in York, in March 1642, the war of words had long since begun, but now leaders on both sides began, in effect, to prepare for the eventuality of war itself. The immediate problem was that England had no professional army at this date, and each side promptly attempted to rectify this by manoeuvring to secure control of the nearest equivalent, the county militia or 'trained bands' and their long unused armoury, and by organizing regional recruitment drives to raise more substantial numbers of men. In actual fact the first moves towards asserting parliamentary, rather than royal, control over the militia had taken place the previous year, but this constitutional struggle was now intensified and preoccupied polititicians for most of the year. In the spring of 1642 the passage of the Militia Bill through Parliament 'polarized the politically conscious nation as no other issue of these troubled times had done'. The King rejected this direct challenge to his supreme authority, whereupon on 15 March both Houses of Parliament passed it as the 'Militia Ordinance', without the King's consent, commanding all subjects to obey it notwithstanding. Charles's response was to withdraw to York and begin reviving the rival, archaic process of the royal 'Commission of Array' addressed to the county authorities with the identical purpose, essentially, of raising bodies of armed loyalists. It was in effect a call to arms on both sides, and it has been well remarked that if there was a single point at which civil war became inevitable, this was it.

Both Parliament's Militia Ordinance and the royal Commission of Array were of dubious legality, and Parliament, particularly sensitive to the charge of acting unconstitutionally, called in the leading lawyer of the day, John Selden, to give an authoritative judgement. He duly pronounced the Commission of Array unlawful, but then inconveniently spoilt the effect by judging the Militia Ordinance equally illegal, and promptly withdrew from the debate. Undeterred, both sides began making arrangements for open-air rallies to mobilize support, check what weapons were serviceable, enlist volunteers and raise money by collecting 'contributions', a word soon to be dreaded by every villager in the land. The first such rally was an impressive parliamentarian parade and gala in London's Finsbury Fields on 10 May, but the King soon followed suit by addressing a stream of Commissions of Array to each county, Warwickshire's being the first to be issued, on 6 June. Charles entrusted his Warwickshire directive to the group of notables duly recorded by Dugdale (see

Appendix A), and from the outset the Earl of Northampton, prominent among the group of peers publicly declaring loyalty to the King at York on 5 June, was his most trusty and energetic Midlands representative.

For both sides the procedure was broadly similar. Warrants were sent out to each hundred in the county and thence to individual constables, giving only about a week's notice, summoning males between the ages of sixteen and sixty to assemble at designated local rendezvous, 'with as many volunteers as each Constable could raise', as one local newsletter put it. Village constables, therefore, and without doubt estate stewards and bailiffs and the more politicized clergy, were being drawn into the preparations for war now percolating down to village and hamlet. No doubt typical of most, the constable and churchwardens of Offchurch were expected to provide volunteers for military training and carts for military transport, send their trained bands to musters at Warwick and Southam, and themselves attend the deputy lieutenant at Coventry to receive instructions. Warrants from both sides were couched in the same peremptory language as that addressed to the constable of Alveston and Tiddington, near Stratford-upon-Avon:

> Whereas we his Mats. Commissioners nominated in a Commission of Array under the great seale of England for the County [of Warwickshire] are authorised to traine and muster the Trained Band of this Countie for the Defense of the Kinge and Countrey; We therefore according to the authoritie thereby given us Doe require you in his Maties name to warne and bringe in all the Trained souldiers both of Horse and Foote wthin your said Constablerie of Alston and Teddington; And in any case any of ye trained soldiers be dead or unfitt for yt service that you doe likewise bringe sufficient supplies to come and appeare before us at Stratford upon Avon upon Friday next beinge the 29th Day of this Instant July, then & there to be exercised beinge compleatly armed; as you and they will answere the contempt hereof at your p[er]ill. You are likewise to give notice to all the Inhabitants of your sd Towne yt as many of them as will then voluntarily offer themselves wth such Armes & Weapons as they have to be trained & exercised for the Safetie of his Matie pson, the protestant Religion, the knowne Lawes of the Land, the just Kingdome in this time of soe publique distraction, will be taken to be a verie acceptable service to his Matie and the Kingdome. Hereof we desire you not to faile. Given under our hands ye 22th day of July 1642.

The signatories, headed by the Earl of Northampton, include all but one of those named by Dugdale: Sir Charles Adderley of Nether Whitacre, Robert Arden of Park Hall, near Coleshill, Sir William Boughton of Little Lawford, Richard Chamberlain of Temple House, near Nuneaton, Sir Simon Clarke of Bidford, Sir Roger Feilding of Newnham Paddox, Sir Robert Fisher of Great Packington, Robert Lee of Billesley, Francis Leigh, Lord Dunsmore, Sir Thomas Leigh of Stoneleigh and Spencer Lucy of Charlecote.[6]

The size of the eventual turnout would have depended to a large extent less on ideology than on the effectiveness of the attempts to coerce apathetic villagers, the availability of dedicated local activists and the sheer efficiency, not to say personal popularity, of the organizers. There is a suggestion of justifiable wariness on the part of the villagers to enlist. One Alcester correspondent reports that Lord Brooke's first summons to assemble at Stratford was largely ignored because the warrant was issued in Parliament's name, not the King's, and that he had to reword it before achieving a respectable response, at Coleshill a few days later. Actual numbers attending these rallies are uncertain, because surviving accounts are unreliably impressionistic and biased, but most reports agree that hundreds took part on each occasion, and one parliamentary report estimates a total of around three thousand at the early July meetings. At the best-organized meetings – likely in Warwickshire to have been the parliamentary rallies of the efficient Lord Brooke – the leader would make a speech stressing the justice of the cause, denouncing the illegality of the opposition's tactics, the reasons for the muster, and the case for ridding the King of evil counsellors, traitors or rebels, depending on the viewpoint (there was as yet no suggestion of removing the King himself). Handsome financial inducements would then follow to further attract volunteers, Brooke offering initially 4s. 8d. per week, or 5s. according to one report, a sum soon capped by the Earl of Northampton's astonishing 2s. per day, described by one contemporary as 'extraordinary wages'. Identifying 'colours' would be distributed to wear in hats. At some assemblies, 'entertainment' in the form of refreshments were supplied, like the 'wine and strong drinke' generously offered by Lord Brooke along with overnight accommodation, both extremely welcome in the summer weather to the many who, if the reports are to be believed, had travelled many weary miles from outlying parishes or even, apparently, from well outside the county: the royalist Commission of Array at Southam on 28 July was said to have attracted men from as far afield as Buckinghamshire and Gloucestershire as well as the adjacent counties. Lord Brooke's accounts include payments of over £85 for refreshments at the parliamentary musters at Coventry, Stratford and Coleshill. At such meetings there would have been much waiting about with nothing to do, as is clear from the reports of activities at Coleshill or at Southam, where participants recorded that 'they were there and in the Field for one day, & returned home . . . at night'. Although Lord Brooke's initiative seems in retrospect impressive, its success appeared much less a foregone conclusion to even sympathetic contemporaries: 'My Lord Brooke I hear is not like to do much in the militia in Warwickshire, but I know he hath a good zeal, he will do as much as he can'. Nor was his authority unchallenged, the royalist Robert Lee of Billesley presenting an indictment against him at Warwick assizes on 21 July for opposing the Commission of Array, causing a near-riot in the courtroom. Lee's temerity was promptly punished by his being summoned by Parliament as a delinquent and, shortly afterwards, comprehensively plundered by Colonel John Needham, on the orders of the governor of Warwick's parliamentary garrison:

> Collonell John Bridges . . . gave mee order to goe to the house of Sr Robert Lee (a man actually in Armes agt ye Parliamt) & from there to bringe awaye Moneyes, Plate, Corne & Cattell or any other goodes yt might serve for ye use of ye Garrison, upon wch Order I tooke from ye sd house betwixt threescore & fourscore poundes in silver, A teame of free horses & Mares wth a Carte loaden wth Corne, some plate (but of wt value I knowe not), one fatt brawne & two or three fatt swyne, all which was brought into Warwicke Castle & disposed of by Coll. Bridges.[7]

Nearly all of these gatherings took place at, or rather outside, the major market towns of the region, in effect the capitals of the ancient administrative districts or 'hundreds' traditionally associated with the musters of Tudor times, the timetable being as follows:

Lord Brooke's, for Parliament:	30 June	Stratford
	1 July	Warwick
	2 July	Warwick (replacing Southam?)
	4 July	Coleshill
	5 July	Coventry

Earl of Northampton's, for King: 28 July   Southam
                                                     29 July   Stratford
                                                     30 July   Coleshill (postponed?)
                                                     30 July   Warwick
                                                      1 Aug   Coleshill

The whole town would have been humming with activity, as is clear from the Coleshill muster, the only Warwickshire one for which a fairly detailed picture may be pieced together: streets and taverns bustling with soldiers, officers recruiting by drum beat at the last minute, notables like Dugdale prominent on horseback, brisk trading, colours being distributed prior to the actual exercises themselves 'upon the heath' or 'in the meadow' as the arrival of the lordly organizers was announced. Although some participants dressed for the occasion (hats were particularly prized), with muskets, pistols and swords much in evidence, clearly many recruited by such improvised means must have presented a bedraggled, distinctly unsavoury appearance, similar to those caricatured by Shakespeare in Falstaff's celebrated muster. One critical observer described, no doubt fairly accurately, such an assembly at Pitchcroft Meadow, outside Worcester, attended by 'a great number of men – of mean and base quality as they seemed to me – and having hedgebills, old calivers, shep pikes and clubs', while at Warwick on 2 July some 'came many miles, with good trunchions in their hands'. Equally clearly, the military potential of such volunteers was limited. Even after training, they 'were yet as a cake not turned; a kind of souldiers not wholly drawn off from the plow or domesticke employments, having neither resolution nor support . . . .'. Not surprisingly, many soon deserted, fleeing at the first sight of danger when confronted by a professional fighting force, as at the first engagement at Powick Bridge, near Worcester, or were expelled by the commander even before then as useless. Lord Saye, having struggled ineffectually to maintain a semblance of discipline among some of his local recruits, eventually told them 'he cared not for their helpe and bid them begone', he himself taking coach to return home to Broughton. The professionals were quick to draw their own lessons, and the disparaging but just comments of both Cromwell and Waller have often been quoted, Cromwell dismissing the 'old decayed servingmen and tapsters and such kind of fellows' among Hampden's Edgehill soldiers and Waller later reporting to his superiors that 'an army compounded of these men will never go through with their service'. Yet such assemblies nevertheless produced a nucleus of soldiers, however variable in professionalism, to supplement those among the local gentry who promptly joined on both sides often bringing with them their own equipment, horses and servants, together with the sons and close relatives of the various commanders: the sons of both Northampton and Saye were all to play distinguished roles in the unfolding drama. According to Bulstrode, who served under him, Northampton's troop at Edgehill was staffed by his two sons and an officer nucleus of about a hundred gentlemen, some very local, like Matthew Clarke and Daniel Blackford from Oxhill, Flammock Colbourne from Barcheston, Robert Arden, possibly a distant relative of Shakespeare and certainly 'a Gentleman of one of the most ancient Families in Warwickshire', and, from across the county border, James and George Chamberlaine, the brothers of the High Sheriff of Oxfordshire, Sir Thomas Chamberlaine. The Earl of Northampton is estimated to have had about three hundred foot already by the battle of

Southam on 23 August, possibly many more by Edgehill a few weeks later, and of these many, as will be seen, must have been recruited locally at his own personal Commission of Array at Winderton and Tysoe. Similarly, another of the Warwickshire Commissioners of Array, Sir William Boughton of Little Lawford, was later alleged to have attended the Southam meeting, taking with him several local recruits, all well armed: John Glass, Thomas Greene, Jonathan Mason and John Collins. Some energetic local activists evidently did their own private recruiting, actively encouraged, no doubt, by the local magnate, like Thomas Tibbot, the head of the Rowington family and an ally of Northampton's, who recruited some twenty Solihull men for the King's service 'with colours in their hats, and acted as their captain'. Such personal commissions to local loyalists to raise men were probably, at least initially, the most effective method of recruitment, with the result that something not unlike the small private armies of the medieval barons was becoming possible: 'last night, Lord Brooke asked me to provide ten horse and muskets to accompany him to Banbury', writes one proud Parliamentarian on one occasion.[8]

On the parliamentary side, once the series of rallies was completed early in July, Lord Brooke's organizational skill ensured that suspiciously fulsome petitions, confirming the success of the Militia Ordinance and expressing the iron resolve of all, were sent within days to Westminster, being promptly published and circulated for maximum propaganda value. Back in Warwickshire, training sessions continued during August at various venues, bands of men often travelling long distances to attend, like those from Nether Whitacre at Warwick on 13 August. It is quite likely, such was the confusion in these early days, that some 'exercised' with both sides.

The most important musters naturally took place, therefore, at the major towns of the region. But this did not necessarily preclude others; it has usually escaped notice that less 'official' ones could be improvised elsewhere if circumstances warranted. In the only recorded instance from the south Warwickshire countryside, for example, one such took place in the common meadow at Winderton, in the parish of Brailes, at the dependable heart of the extensive Northampton estates, where local allegiance could presumably be exploited to guarantee an impressive turnout. No description of the proceedings at this gathering survives, but it cannot have been very different from the hillside assembly picturesquely evoked by Richard Gough in his classic example from Shropshire, where the organizer stood on the hilltop, paper in hand, in a prominent position marked off by three or four soldiers' pikes stuck upright in the ground, before reciting a proclamation promising a generous 4s. per week for every volunteer. The Winderton mission was assigned to William Baldwin, whose loyalty to the King's cause would have been unquestioning, his family having provided several generations of stewards for the ancient royal manor of Brailes in the Middle Ages. He later suffered the sequestration of his estate for this day's work. The dependence initially of both sides on locally-recruited estate tenants at the expense of the landowning lord offering handsome wages has already been noted. This, surely, must be one example of the process at work. Here, under the lee of Winderton hill and overlooked by the ancient Compton Pike which itself, according to local tradition, had provided a beacon to alert of an earlier national emergency, the Spanish Armada, several hundred villagers met on that unrecorded day in August 1642, before the whole process was repeated soon afterwards in neighbouring Tysoe. Many must have pledged themselves there and then to the King's cause, and of those, equally certainly, some were to die nearby only weeks later, across those same harvest fields, at Southam and Edgehill.

It is, of course, impossible to assess accurately the effect of the whole cumulative process of petitioning and mustering on the local inhabitants, but it seems probable that in the summer of 1642 significant numbers of villagers enlisted for one side or the other: if Richard Gough's example from his tiny Shropshire village is generalized, the local contribution to early recruitment patterns was impressive. What is even more certain is that by the summer of 1642 few Warwickshire villagers could have been unaware of the dangerous trend of events and, apart from a few hotheads, not seriously alarmed at what they could gather from hearsay and first-hand accounts from their village constable, estate officials and parson, as well as travellers to nearby markets. The huge numbers reportedly attending the musters must have provided the most dramatic news that the countryfolk had heard for many a long day. Issues and personalities were now increasingly polarized:

> . . . so that now, every one as his fancy leads him takes upon him with open invectives to censure his Majestie or Parliament . . .; such things as these do raise disputes and set heart burnings one against another, and do present the Country [i.e. district] like a Cockpit, one spurring against another . . . as if open Wars were already proclaimed betwixt us; our Fears are renewed every night . . .

Apprehension and fear are the keynotes of newsletters and much of the private correspondence which has survived, one regular Warwickshire letter-writer prefacing his report of the latest events by doleful forebodings of impending tragedy:

> I will not omit this week's sending unto you, God knows whether wee shall ever send to you againe; for we have a mighty distracted Countrey. Here is mighty providing for warres . . .

Thomas Johnson, writing from Sambourne, near Alcester, at about the same time, is similarly fearful: '. . . here in Warwicke Shire wee are like to fall into great calamities and distresses', and continues, 'here is nothing but providing of armes', before concluding that if the King should come to Warwick in peace, he will be royally received, but 'if otherwayes, I am afraid wee shall have a wofull time of it'. Another correspondent refers to the 'many troubles and distractions' which Warwickshire has 'groned under these late dayes'. During August rioting was reported from several counties, including Warwick-shire. Like many others, no doubt, John Fetherston's hopes of remaining insulated from the preparations for war were abruptly dashed. He thought it prudent to attend the local muster, and then troops desperate for arms began scouring the countryside and arrived one day at remote Packwood: 'wee weare lately very much affrighted by reason of a troop of horsemen that cam to some of my neighbours howses and did disarme them, & took away what they pleased under coulor of takinge of their armes'.

Others tried to take comfort in pious pleas, one correspondent composing a thirty-page sermon, or 'most serious Exhortation, both to the King and subjects, to embrace and preserve peace and abandon Civill Warres', inspired by the biblical text 'Blessed are the peacemakers'. Even those fully committed to one side or the other and prepared to indulge in their own private scaremongering cannot hide their alarm at reporting the 'many and great troubles here, being never quiet night nor day, but full of fears and dangers', or:

the miseries and distractions that are now ready to be put into execution . . . and the plots and projects that are now hatched . . . ready to take place and possession, inasmuch that a Civill Warre is beginning to play its part in this Kingdome.

One nervous commentator considers Lord Brooke as primarily responsible for these dangerous tensions, for 'fuelling jealousies and fears in these days . . .', while others, as we have seen, speak of the 'great joy amongst the People, that the Parliament had put such a Noble Lord in trust with the safety of their County'. Seen clearly in retrospect, the darkening mood and apprehension of these months concealed a stark fact: that the drift to war had, in effect, already begun. All that was needed was a spark or two of actual violence to precipitate matters.[9]

THE BANBURY MAGAZINE

At no single, identifiable point did the villagers of Warwickshire wake one morning to find their county at war; the drift though in retrospect real enough, was imperceptible. Over many months the usual country concerns of cultivating strips of land, rotating beasts and crops, scouring ditches and travelling to market had been interspersed with news of more ominous happenings from over the horizon, news of petitions and confrontation, of fortifications being prepared, volunteer soldiers enlisting, papist plots discovered, and all this had, as we have seen, created a mood of expectancy and foreboding. But it was not until July 1642 that actual armed confrontation took place in the neighbourhood, and immediately escalated into violence. What provoked this was a series of interlocking events the previous month, beginning with an unsuccessful attempt by the Earl of Northampton, who was Recorder of Coventry, to secure that city for the King as a counterweight to Warwick, which Lord Brooke was continuing to fortify for Parliament.

Following the peers' declaration of loyalty to the King at York on 5 June, Charles had immediately made preparations for calling the country to arms by issuing Commissions of Array to all the counties, and by 17 June many were reported ready to 'go down to the several counties'. Emboldened by this and attempting to force the pace, the Earl of Northampton suddenly arrived in Coventry from York the following week, in mid-morning on Saturday 25 June, and in his official capacity attempted to coerce the divided corporation into joining with him in proclaiming the Commission of Array in the council house. As the county's principal city and commercial centre, the hub of communications in the Midlands, and housing the county magazine, Coventry would clearly represent a major prize for the royalist cause. In spite of its puritan tradition, the city was as yet uncommitted to either side, with a split corporation and a conciliatory mayor. However, the parliamentary sympathizers among the city aldermen, led by John Barker, blocked this move by invoking Parliament's earlier pronouncement that the Commission of Array was illegal. Northampton was, in any case, unable to produce the King's authorization which he claimed to have brought, admitting that 'he had nott yett hys commission, for twas nott fynyshed when he came from Yorke', and the strength of hostility to his mission was such, according to one report, as to force him to leave the city via the back door of the Black Bull. A parliamentary news-sheet gleefully summed up the incident:

> . . . the whole County refused to obey him, whereupon finding himself wholy neglected by the County, hee returned againe to Yorke, and told his Majesty that if hee had no other service to command him, he knew not how to doe his Majesty any at all.

The result of this fiasco was that Parliament immediately designated Northampton as a 'delinquent' and, more important, took immediate steps to forestall further royal initiatives in Warwickshire, ordering a general state of alert, the sending of a strong force headed by Lord Brooke to secure the county and the enforcement of the Militia Ordinance. To these decisions the King responded in kind; the pace was quickening.[10]

Lord Brooke was by now fully engaged in masterminding the series of Militia Ordinance rallies already described. But while completing these, on 5 July, he took further precautionary steps by transferring the county magazine, comprising by one account 'two great Cart loades and a Waggon loaded with Gun-powder, bullets and match', from Coventry to Warwick, having previously taken care to get official authorization from Parliament for this unusual step. Parliament shortly after ordered a further consignment of nine cannons to be sent from London with an armed escort, 'for the better fortification of his castle', to be paid for out of public subscription, together with permission to strengthen his garrison: 'my Lo: Brooke should take men ynto Warwycke Castle for the defence of the magasyn there'. By now Lord Brooke's high-handed activities were beginning to alarm moderate royalist opinion in the neighbourhood, as is evident from the report of Sir Thomas Leigh's servant writing from Stoneleigh to his master:

> My Lord Brooke hath made greate preperacon for his Castle. Hee hath great store of men in it, & they say hee gives to diverse men 4s. 8d. a weeke, but how this money is to be paid none doe know, but supposed by the Country, wch they can very ill spare when there is noe need of that unnecessarie charge; but jeolosies and feares in these daies arise, when there is none, or very little, reason for it. His Lordp. would have had the Armor wch the Country brought to one Tibbots shop in Warwick to be dressed; but the man told his Lordp. that if hee or any other of his company tooke any away hee would kill them, though hee were hanged wthn an houre after; and Sr [Edward] Peto would have had the fellow committed to prison, but his Lordp. let him alone; and he was sent for to the Castle, but hee went not.

The response of the loyal Tibbots to this affront was, rather, to offer more active support to the King's cause: he was later accused of having been at the Coleshill Commission of Array, '& tooke a longe with him out of Solihull neere upon xx men, & marched before them as their Captaine & gave them Colours in theire hatts'.

Fully satisfied with their recent tactical successes, however, Lord Brooke and Parliament exchanged self-congratulatory reports of the musters and the allegedly overwhelming enthusiasm of the common people for the parliamentary cause at the respective assemblies. Nevertheless, as Anthony Fletcher comments, violence was beginning to take precedence over normal civilized behaviour. In mid-July, Judge Reeve had to quell a near-riot in court when many members of the public were 'about the Hall with swords' as a court action against Lord Brooke was presented by a local Royalist.[11]

The King for his part countered the parliamentary activity by issuing his own order from York to put the Warwickshire Commission of Array into effect, following this a day or so later with further instructions from Beverley, addressed principally to the Earl of Northampton and Lord Dunsmore, demonstrating once again the inseparability of politics and religion at this stage of the conflict:

> . . . to make all enquiry after such seditious Preachers and other persons of what degree soever who endeavour by their Sermons, Councells, and other discourses to lessen and deprave our just legall Authority and to incense our good subjects against us, and that you proceede against them as stirrers of Sedition and Promoters of Rebellion against us, especially against those who shall presume to execute that pretended Ordinance which in this tyme wee can enterprett to be noe other then leavying Warr against us.

Empowered by the King at last to act decisively, aware of having been outmanoeuvred by his rival over both the Coventry magazine and the musters, and doubtless, with the personal humiliation of the Coventry rebuff rankling, Northampton determined at all costs to prevent the further strengthening of Warwick. Nothing had so far come of earlier royalist plans to hold their own musters, now rescheduled to begin at Southam on 28 July. Northampton urgently wrote from Compton Wynyates to allies for help, warning the bellicose young Henry Hastings, son of the Earl of Huntingdon, whose forces had recently attempted to seize the county magazine at Leicester and been noisily parading 'in a warlike manner . . . beating up their drummes and displaying their Colours', of 'forces . . . coming from the Parliament, together with a great quantity of ammunition sent to Lord Brooke'. At the same time he assured himself of the active cooperation of other staunch Royalists like the Nottinghamshire Byrons and his young ward, Lord William Petre at Burton Dassett, and increased his local recruitment campaign, enlisting 'many hundreds of men out of severall Shires and Counties . . . by faire and alluring speeches [and] extraordinary wages, not commonly exhibited unto souldiers, [of] two shillings a day'. An imminent assault on Warwick Castle was thought likely by parliamentary commentators.[12]

In spite of this activity Northampton, now fully absorbed in organizing the series of Commissions of Array, was unable to prevent the parliamentary convoy arriving at Banbury on Friday, 29 July, where the guns were safely delivered to Lord Saye's son John Fiennes, the governor of the castle. Brooke himself promptly collected an escort and rode urgently through the night from Warwick to collect them, arriving at Banbury at daybreak on Saturday. It is at this point that drama intervenes, and history merges with the cloak-and-dagger thriller.

The history of the secret, undercover activity of the Civil War has not yet been written and, by its very nature, is perhaps unlikely ever to be so. What is certain is that with allegiances fluid, the stakes high and many of the underlying issues far from straightforward, the public decision-making, military strategy, and endless marching and countermarching concealed an elusive network of intelligence-gathering, messengers carrying cyphered missives, plotting, spying and informing. Few of the surviving garrison accounts are without their quota of payments to 'scouts' and 'intelligencers', few newsletters without allegations of plots being hatched by undercover agents, few sieges without reports of spiked guns. It has become customary for historians to stress the inadequacies of the intelligence-gathering of both sides, but much, although primitive by modern standards, must have been competent, particularly where dependable, loyal individuals were involved. One such was Thomas Earle of Ailstone, near Stratford, a royalist agent enlisted in Lord Brooke's ranks as one of the escort for the Banbury magazine. Earle slipped away in the night half-way between Warwick and Banbury and hurried back to inform the Earl of Northampton. The Earl hastily abandoned plans to appear at Coleshill later that same day, assembled a small army, rode post-haste to Banbury and confronted Brooke's ponderous convoy of 'great gunns & other provisions of warre' shortly after it had left Banbury, about 9 a.m., and had just entered Warwickshire near Shotteswell. By a curious irony, this prelude to war therefore took place exactly half-way between the two future battlefields of Edgehill and Cropredy.

Several detailed contemporary accounts exist of this encounter of 30 July 1642 and, discounting minor discrepancies and evident partisan bias, remain consistent enough to allow a reconstruction of events. The Earl of Northampton blocked Lord Brooke's way, straddling Warmington Hill with a superior and more mobile force before dictating the King's demands: that Brooke surrender the armoury, refrain from further parliamentary musters and resign Warwick Castle to Northampton; and concluding, according to one graphic report, with the threat to 'make that place their graves that stood in opposition'. On Brooke's refusal a series of morale-boosting and provocative speeches by the two leaders raised tensions to such a pitch that violence seemed imminent. At some point proposals were made to avoid useless bloodshed by settling the dispute via a chosen number from each side or even a single combat by the two peers. There were passionate speeches, a skirmish or two between opposing guards, with both commanders 'being every houre ready to give fire to each other'. The accounts agree, however, that despite the aggressive rhetoric much of the day was spent in parleying, and that the outcome was a diplomatic compromise, that Brooke should return the magazine to Banbury and each leader pledge his honour to give three days' notice to the other before attempting to remove it.

Besides the intrinsic picturesqueness of the incident and its interest as the first known personal confrontation of the two long-standing adversaries, the episode is significant for several reasons. It marked the first military check to Lord Brooke's string of recent successes in securing the area for Parliament and gave notice that the two opposing sides were henceforth more evenly matched. It was in effect a tactical defeat for Brooke, it being admitted later by a parliamentary source that 'Lord Brookes conceivinge himselfe to bee too weake to encounter with the said Earle was forced for safety . . . to send them backe againe'. The parliamentary claim that Brooke declined combat solely to save lives, though doubtless a contributory factor, is unlikely to have been the decisive one, Brooke being pragmatic as well as zealous. But the episode does illustrate the reluctance of both sides at this stage to fire the first shots of the war, and their capacity to indulge in the courtly charades of drum-beat parley, rhetoric, the issuing of chivalric challenges to personal combat, and gentlemen's agreements. Above all perhaps, it is significant in offering the first clear indication of the voluntary participation of local inhabitants, no longer able to distance themselves from events, several accounts stressing that with 'the news thereof being carried backe to Banbury and townes adjoyning', 'the Countrey came

WARMINGTON, WARWICKSHIRE. A typical South Midlands village, whose hilltop site attracted frequent military activity throughout the war. Repeatedly occupied by troops, its vicar abandoned his parish to enlist as a cavalry officer. The churchyard contains a Civil War gravestone, unique in the district, of a Scottish officer killed at nearby Edgehill. (Photo: Banbury Museum)

THE SOUTH-EAST VIEW OF WARWICK CASTLE, 1729, from an engraving by Samuel and Nathaniel Buck. The great medieval fortress, regarded by the King as the major rebel stronghold in the Midlands, played an important role throughout the war. Already strengthened and provisioned before the war as a precautionary measure by its owner, the Puritan Robert Greville, Lord Brooke, it effortlessly withstood a siege by the Earl of Northampton in August 1642 and under its energetic commander, Major John Bridges, remained a major parliamentary garrison and staging post throughout the war from which many successful military expeditions were launched. (The County Archivist, Warwick County Record Office)

in very thick to [Brooke's] assistance', 'women also . . . bringing in Beere and Victuall in abundance, and six or seven cartload of harrowes to welcome their horses' and 'a cartload of bread and cheese'. The magazine was returned to Banbury, Lord Brooke hastily left for London to report to Parliament, while Northampton resumed the interrupted musters. Clearly, nothing had been decided, though the outbreak of war was for the moment averted.

Lord Brooke was absent in London about a week, mobilizing Parliament's support and receiving promises of the urgent dispatch of reinforcements for guarding the now threatened Banbury magazine. It is about now that, for the first time, there is clear evidence of a concerted royalist strategy to seize the initiative in the Midlands, and principally by defeating Lord Brooke in Warwickshire. No doubt it would be naïve to suggest that the King had devised a detailed grand strategy, but there is little doubt that the plan was to secure the Warwickshire base before marching on London, as is clear from 'a private letter from an eminent cavalier', who confided shortly after to a London friend:

> We were resolved upon the South, & to make Nottingham our Randevous, Leicestersh., Northamptonshire and Warwicksh. the Seat of our War . . . In those said Counties we designed to strengthen our selves, with the possession of Warwick and the Castle, Coventry and Northampton. . .

While the Earl of Northampton was, therefore, completing the much-postponed series of Commissions of Array on 1 August, the King prepared to move south to join his

Midland allies, after issuing a flurry of royal warrants directing political and military initiatives in Warwickshire. On 1 August he instructed Henry Hastings in Leicestershire to be ready to send aid to Warwickshire, his secretary, Sir Edward Nicholas duplicating the order to Hastings' father, the Earl of Huntingdon:

> His Majesty, understanding from your noble son Mr Hastings the insolency of the Lord Brooke and his adherents, hath given that the two troops commanded by Captain Nevill and Captain Sandis shall forthwith march into Warwickshire, to join with such forces as the Earl of Northampton hath gathered together; and . . . to draw the forces of Leicestershire to the borders of Warwickshire, to be there in readiness to assist. . . .[13]

This was followed a few days later by a further royal warrant, to William Dugdale, the royal herald who had been summoned to attend Charles at York in June, to exercise his official capacity as Rouge Croix to summon the castles of Warwick and Banbury to surrender, Lord Brooke's forces to disperse after laying down their arms and to name Brooke a traitor should he resist. At the same time, the King issued further directives to Leicestershire, to all its county authorities and his 'loving subjects', ordering the transport into Warwickshire of the arms and ammunition already collected, accompanied by a strong escort:

> To all Maiors, Sheriffs, Justices of ye Peace, Bayliffs, Constables, Headboroughs, and all other our Officers, Ministers and loving Subjects whome it may concerne, and to every of them.
>
> Whereas wee have given Order for sendinge into our County of Warwick Armes, powder, shott, and other Amunicion for the better strengthning of our Subjects there against any violence or attempts that may bee intended, or made uppon them. Our will and pleasure therefore is, that immediately uppon the sight hereof, you take up, or assiste the bearer hereof in takinge up, and bringinge in daylye a convenient number of horses, and all other necessaries for the carryinge of the said Armes, powder, shott, and Amunicion to such parte, or place within our County of Warwick, as the bearer shall directe. And that you appoint a stronge and sufficient Guarde of men, as well for conductinge the same by day through all Counties it must passe, as to watch the same by night, where it is to reste, for which such allowance is to be made as is usually and customary. Hereof wee require you, and every of you whome it may concerne, to use your utmost diligence, as you tender the good of our service, and will answere your neglects, and contempts at your perills. Given at our Courte at Yorke ye 5th August 1642.

These measures were followed on 6 August by further confirmation of the wide powers entrusted to the Earl of Northampton, authorizing him:

> . . . to imprest, raise, enroll and reteyne one Regiment of one thousand Foote furnished and armed, with full power and authoritie as Colonell them to commaund, arme, discipline, trayne and order in warlike manner, and with all possible expedicion to conduct unto such place as shalbee directed.

Banbury and the surrounding countryside were meanwhile living anxious, eventful days, 'in a great feare and uproare', as the news spread of imminent royalist attack. Defensive measures were hastily improvised in the town as the inhabitants watched the ominous influx of hundreds of sympathetic parliamentary soldiers flocking in from Northampton 'with their armes, Colours and Captaines', to be officially welcomed and fêted by the garrison commander John Fiennes, on 5 August. Substantial royalist forces were now massing nearby, augmented by help from staunch allies like the King's young cousin, 'a gentleman of wonderfull sweet and noble disposition', Lord John Stuart, stalwarts like Hastings and the Byrons, a group of Royalists from Oxfordshire under the Earl of Berkshire and even, apparently, forces from Yorkshire, all eager to strike a supposedly decisive blow against the rebels, while nearer at hand, Northampton's close ally Lord Dunsmore took time off from threatening known Puritans near Rugby to send in reinforcements of 'two load of ammunition for warre'. Rumours circulated that the King himself was on his way to take personal command. Equally effective in sapping the morale of a local population already weakened by a climate of rumour and occasional physical harassment by individual Royalists was the Earl of Northampton's psychological warfare. Parliamentarians alleged several 'plots' (and manufactured much righteous indignation at such treacherous methods), including the spreading of rumours that the town of Northampton was under imminent siege (resulting in the panic withdrawal of the Northampton volunteers from Banbury), deliberate exaggeration of royalist numbers, and even a forged letter, purporting to be from the leading Parliamentarian John Hampden himself, ordering Brooke's London relief force to turn back, on the false news that Banbury had, in fact, already fallen to the Royalists. So effective were such reports that, according to one account, one parliamentary captain took to his heels, 'so that men, Women and Children fled out of the town & the Ministers trembled, fearing to be abused by the Cavaliers'. Lurid tales of royalist atrocities circulated, no doubt with some basis of fact, as the whole area between Banbury, Daventry and Rugby was overrun by marauding bands of cavaliers: 500 troopers were reported terrorizing Rugby and Hillmorton, tiny villages like Grandborough and Woolscott were ransacked for arms, while outside Rugby, one of the very first armed clashes resulting in fatalities took place. A contingent of royalist horse under the young Warwickshire gentleman John Smith, of Skilts, brother of the Catholic Lord Carington of Wootton Wawen, and soon to be knighted at Edgehill for rescuing the King's captured banner, on their way to join the Earl of Northampton met rebellious countrymen at Kilsby armed with pitchforks and clubs, resulting in a dozen or more deaths. In a new, equally unpleasant twist, serving as precedent for countless similar episodes to follow, well-known puritan-minded clergy were harassed: James Nalton was violently assaulted in his church at Rugby, Simon Moore, the curate at Frankton, fled for his life to Coventry, and Royalists '. . . having taken Master [James] Sutton, [vicar of Fenny Compton], forced him on his knees to drinke a health to the confusion of all the Round-heads'. Outside Banbury itself the leading Oxfordshire presbyterian, the 'grave and reverend' Robert Harris, vicar of Hanwell, was evicted from his parsonage with his family and left 'to wander for his lodging' with his patron Lady Elizabeth Cope, of the leading puritan family of the district. Royalist gangs were searching everywhere for available arms. Lord Dunsmore was particularly active and according to Richard Newton, an inhabitant of Rugby, 'robed our towne of ther armes, & in pertickler my selfe . . .'. The people of Grandborough hastily removed all their sixteen weapons for safe-keeping to the moated house of the local wool drapers, the Burmans, at nearby Woolscott:

> . . . but the Troopers came so strong, they carried them all away, and where they will not deliver their Armes they kill, and take their horses away by force. Ours are taken away this night . . .

By the end of the first week of August the Royalists' war of attrition in the neighbourhood brought the desired result: Banbury's defences were sufficiently depleted and its morale sufficiently low for the Earl of Northampton to clinch matters by menacingly positioning three cannons on Crouch Hill overlooking the town, and after the usual parley the magazine was duly surrendered by Fiennes at about 4 o'clock in the afternoon of 8 August, under threat of razing the town by fire. The unscrupulous Lord Wilmot was reported by one parliamentary testimony to have contributed by preventing the citizens of his home town, Adderbury, 'from coming in to aide Banbury, and threatned he would hang up the men and send the souldiers to their wives'. For good measure, the Royalists threatened to demolish Fiennes's ancestral Broughton by more cannon moved up for that purpose, and Fiennes's later account to John Pym that he had no alternative but to surrender is probably the simple truth. According to a vehement parliamentary report, the town was stormed by the Royalists, with 'great bloudshed on both sides', even women and children using 'clubs, forkes, pikes and spitts' in a vain attempt to resist. The Earl of Northampton triumphantly carried off the captured guns to his home at Compton Wynyates. Once again, open war had for the moment been averted, but matters were deteriorating.[14]

CHAPTER THREE

THE OUTBREAK OF WAR

THE SIEGE OF WARWICK

Having now finally wrested the initiative from the admittedly absent Lord Brooke, the Earl of Northampton lost no time in acting. The next morning he transferred the captured cannons – or some of them – from Compton Wynyates to Warwick, 'where they planted them upon the side of an hill as neare as they could to the Castle', or 'on the Parke-hill', as one report specifies. The Royalists had moved so rapidly in this that 'his Lordship found an easie entrance into the Town' before the gate sentries were aware what was happening or, perhaps, because the town was less wholeheartedly behind Lord Brooke than the biased parliamentary reporting suggests. The whole town was gradually being placed on a war footing, with wide-ranging work on fortifications beginning, and soon to cause serious and lasting inconvenience to many of its inhabitants. But it was on the castle itself that Lord Brooke had been concentrating. Its walls had been repaired and raised, the Mount transformed into a strong defensive structure, the drawbridge strengthened, guns prepared and gunpowder bought, with the recent arrival of the Coventry magazine a welcome addition. Beds and bolsters had been made or acquired to accommodate increasing numbers of soldiers, and provisions stockpiled. For much of this work, as elsewhere in adjoining counties like Worcestershire and Oxfordshire, large-scale tree-felling had been taking place, for 'making a Platforme for great Gunns in the Castle' and other defensive structures, using the convenient timber resources from nearby Wedgnock Park which had also been stocked with large numbers of cattle and sheep as a precautionary measure by the prudent Brooke. There had been major calls on the services of local workmen, especially carters and labourers, digging and transporting huge quantities of turf for bulwarks from places like Myton Heath, while constant work at 'the quarry' suggests that not all the work was concerned with flimsy wooden structures. Carpenters were certainly particularly busy, however, some being drafted in from nearby villages and, like John Coppeland of Ufton, giving their services freely, with a simple and touching trust:

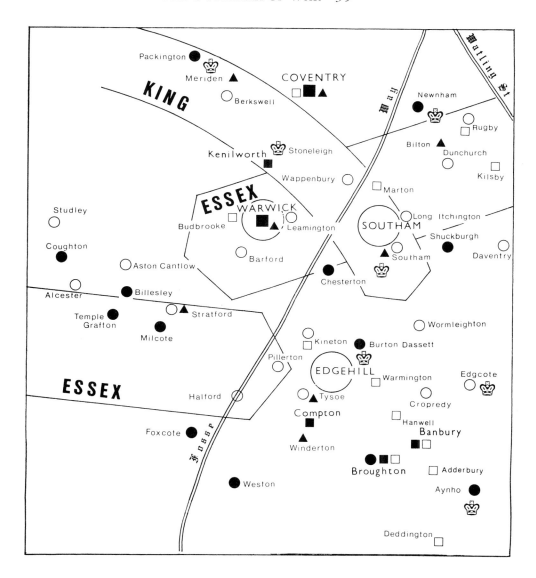

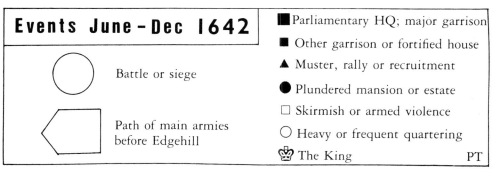

Events June–Dec 1642

◯ Battle or siege

⬠ Path of main armies before Edgehill

■ Parliamentary HQ; major garrison

◼ Other garrison or fortified house

▲ Muster, rally or recruitment

● Plundered mansion or estate

☐ Skirmish or armed violence

◯ Heavy or frequent quartering

♛ The King   PT

Fiftenne dayes worke unpayed for: Carpender worke at Warwick Castell bulle workes be for the Castel was beseiged by the Earle of Northampton. I was sett a worke by Sur Edward Paytoe, for which dayes workes I hear sett no prise, butt leave it to the discresion of the honorabel the Comittie to paye me as thaye shall thinke fitte.

Although only a handful of soldiers seems actually to have been in pay in August, armed and unarmed volunteers had been trooping in to the castle for some time, trebling the small garrison within a month, so that at the beginning of August, according to one possibly exaggerated report, 300 armed men, or 'a great company out of oure Towne of Alcester and from Stradford and from Brummychum side, and all the Country over', had materialized as a response to the musters and the 5s. per week promised wage. Most were in fact unpaid and ill-kept, for 'it is well knowne' (wrote one parliamentary reporter later), 'that for many moneths in the beginning of the Warrs that [Warwick] Garrison was in very greate distresse for pay . . .'. Drummers and trumpeters figure prominently in the accounts of the castle (and, indeed, for every garrison) for this period, however, suggesting that a proper sense of English pageantry had not yet been extinguished.

It seems possible that no one had seriously considered the likelihood that those defending the castle might refuse to comply with the King's demands, even though Lord Brooke had so far shown iron resolve, was known to have been fortifying the castle over the last six months, and had recently placed it in the charge of a staunch local Parliamentarian, Sir Edward Peto of Chesterton, aided by the redoubtable William Purefoy. Perhaps the Royalists hoped that a show of force would be sufficient to persuade the rebels to capitulate, as clearly 'two small Pieces of Cannon which were brought from Compton House' were ludicrously inadequate to demolish a stout medieval fortress. Interestingly, Peto was a kinsman of Sir Simon Archer, and had helped the Archer–Dugdale antiquarian enterprise of a history of Warwickshire; and Dugdale's duty as royal herald was to proclaim Peto and his allies traitors at the castle gates – an early and striking example of the way Civil War loyalties cut across civilized ties of friendship and shared gentlemanly values.[1]

As usual, there survive several slightly differing accounts of the siege of the castle which finally brought the Civil War to Warwickshire, but although clearly biased towards Parliament their incidental detail is such as to suggest overall reliability. Many incidents are common to several of the reports: the placing of a royalist cannon on the tower of old St Mary's church and the destruction of one of its pinnacles by a parliamentary cannon ball; the killing of a boastful royalist butcher carrying a shoulder of lamb down the street as he taunted the defenders; the accident which almost cost the life of either the Earl or, more probably, one of his sons, when a cannon exploded in his face. The position of each of the four defending cannons is specified: at the gatehouse, on the Mount, above the gate (on the platform noted above?), on Caesar's tower. The siege was to last two weeks, and must have been a desultory affair for most of the time, interspersed with moments of drama and with much plunder of the surrounding country to relieve the frustration of the impotent Royalists facing the impregnable walls with such inadequate armoury. For at least part of this time, the Earl of Northampton lodged, somewhat unprofessionally (and certainly dangerously, being in the direct line fire between the castle and St Mary's), at the nearby Swan Inn, kept by Mrs King.

The preliminaries began with the now customary recital of the King's Commission of

Array at the castle gatehouse, followed by the demand that the magazine be delivered and the defenders surrender and disperse, according to the terms of the royal warrant issued to the King's herald, William Dugdale, on 4 August. The whole ceremony was conducted by Dugdale, sumptuously robed in his official red and gold costume of Rouge Croix pursuivant:

> . . . all which being performed by the said Mr Dugdale in his coat of arms, with trumpets sounding before him . . . the castle of Warwick, being a fort of far more strength [than Banbury] and defended by a greater number of soldiers, under the command of Sir Edward Peto of Chesterton in that county, knight, most rebelliously contemned this summons; Sir Edward alleging that he was intrusted therewith by the Parliament, and would defend it accordingly. Whereupon he, and all his adherents there, were proclaimed traitors at the castle gates.

Seldom can the small country town of Warwick, little changed since Tudor times, have witnessed such a scene, reminiscent of some Elizabethan stage-set. For more than ever, the sense of players enacting some chivalric pageant on a darkening stage is clear; and this is not merely a false impression imposed by a modern viewpoint retrospectively on a now utterly remote incident. Contemporary commentators themselves spoke and wrote in these terms, the author of one account of the Banbury episode concluding, 'thus the poore Country is but the Stage whereupon these cutting Cavaliers do Act daily tragedies'. One of the major actors in the Civil War, the parliamentary commander Sir William Waller, in a justly celebrated letter to a former friend, now an enemy, was later to give poignant expression to this same sense of moving against a theatre backdrop, renewing Shakespeare's own image of only forty years previously of poor players strutting their brief hour:

> That great God which is the searcher of my heart knows with what a sad sense I go upon this service, and with what a perfect hatred I detest this war without an enemy . . . We are both upon the stage, and must act those parts that are assigned to us in this tragedy. Let us do it in a way of honour, and without personal animosities, whatsoever the issue.[2]

Over the following days the conflict developed into a series of sporadic and no doubt confused sorties and salvoes, causing some incidental damage to property, as in West Street where one inhabitant, Roger Fisher, later claimed £4 compensation for 'hurte done in my house by Battery from ye Castle'. By telescoping disparate incidents the surviving accounts, usually recalled some time after, succeed in rendering events probably more picturesque than the reality, as in the most complete, where an anonymous parliamentary sympathizer moves from the past to the present tense in the urgency of his reporting:

> This day seavennight in the morning, my Lord of Northampton, Earl of Darby, Lord Dunsmore and all their forces came to Banbury, & there they had small opposition, the ordnance was delivered [to them], & from thence with all speed went to Warwicke, to my Lord Brooks Castle. The town, unexpectedly to them in the Castle, let in my Lord Compton with all his forces; then, they were confident the castle would be delivered up presently. But there they found a man of courage, that brave man Sir Edward Peto, who upon the first message sent the lords an absolute answer he would not deliver the castle. They gave him 2 hours' time and sent again. Sir Edward sent an angry answer, that 'they might have taken his word at first'. The lords planted their ordnance against the castle & discharged one; Sir Edward in requitall discharged 2, and bid them 'as they liked that, shoot againe'.

Then Sir Edward made proclamation that all his friends should depart the town, and for the rest bid them looke to themselves. He hung out of the castle a bloody flag, and a flag of defiance with a crosse upon it in defiance of the Papists, and now shootes night and day with double muskets that kill 20 score; he shot through the house where the Lord Compton lay, which made him remove his lodging. The Lord Compton planting ordnance upon the tower of the Church, Sir Edward discharged an ordnance from the castle, which tooke off a pinacle of the tower & made the Cavaliers stir. Nevertheless they discharged the ordnance, (being one they tooke from Banbury), which broke all in pieces, and some say hurt the Lord Compton's sonne, whereupon they suspect all the ordnance that came from Banbury to be poysoned. A fellow of my Lord Northampton's going over the street with a shoulder of mutton in his hand held it up, and said, 'look here you roundheads, you would be glad of a bit!', presently fell down dead, being shot from the castle. There are not many yet slain, the castle stands untoucht, and Sir Edward now hangs out his winding sheet and Bible. The Lord of Northampton is gone out of Warwicke, it is supposed to meet the King who, they say, wilbe at Warwicke this night. The trayned bands are summoned upon pain of death to appear at Warwicke to guard the King's person. There are many gone. Some say Sir Edward promises if the King come, to deliver the castle, but I beleeve it must be upon very good terms. I heare there came fifty troopers last week to Coventry and there desired to come in; they took them in and disarmed them, and staid their horse. Our papists begin to stir; they disarme private men and take their arms out of the houses. They have taken Sir Edward Peto's horses out of the stable, 8 for the saddle; they kill my Lord Brooks Deer. But Sir Edward Peto is a brave resolute man, and hath got a greate deal of honour. We expect my Lord Say or some of our Parliament men to countenance us, for we are almost borne down with great ones.

Other versions add further incidental detail:

. . . And now some [Royalists] spare not to say that they will have the Castle flat on the ground by morrow breakfast time, but it must cost more then so. In the first place, they plant a peece of Ordnance on the Tower of the Church, and play against the Mount, where the besieged do save themselves by falling downe into the scratches and trenches which they had three made; and they also having a small hammer peece in Guyes Tower did play against the Tower of the Church, and smote downe one of the pinnacles, which made the cunning Balister to remoove from thence into the west street, and there he playde against the Mount as before, but with no successe, for the Defenders from the top of that Turret with their Ship-Muskets did give them neither rest nor safetie.

During the time of the siege the besiegers did breake downe the pale of Wedgnocke Parke, and daylie made havocke of the Lord Brookes Deare, killing red and fallow, male and rascal, young and old, fat and leane without distinction, and made Venison as plentifull among them as the meanest Mutton.

During the siege, efforts were made to strengthen the attacking forces, already fourteen to fifteen hundred strong if one account is to be believed, by the addition of what a parliamentary chronicler describes, possibly justifiably, as well-paid mercenaries, together with any available men from the surrounding countryside. Thus, the constable of Tanworth-in-Arden, John Court, was summoned on pain of death by the Earl of Northampton to bring in his local trained band. The group of rustics duly arrived in Warwick to lodge at George Willmore's, presenting their full array of weapons: three muskets with bandoliers, two pikes, some armour and a few swords. After the siege the constable asked that the arms be restored to him, and was told that they had been captured by the enemy. During the siege too, more indiscriminate plunder is widely reported, the Royalists besieging having 'possessed themselves of Warwicke Towne, and do daily commit great spoile and outrage against any that seem well affected to the Parliament'; they 'lie all up and downe the Countrey, pillaging in the little Townes; they steale Horse, Cowes, Sheepe, Cloathes and Victualls'. One obvious target for the

Cavaliers was Chesterton House and grounds, conveniently lying defenceless while their owner, Sir Edward Peto, conducted the defence of Warwick Castle, while the property of the absent Lord Brooke, as indicated above, was another prime target. One commentator gloomily noted: 'this was the first spoyle and disorder in this kinde that I heard of, but not the last'.[3]

THE KING'S INTERVENTION

L ord Brooke's precise movements during the siege of his castle are unrecorded, but parliamentary sources report that after a week in London 'in high indignation' at the loss of the Banbury magazine and subsequent events, he:

> raised a great and well-appointed troupe of horse that may couragiously encounter with the Lord of Northampton's forces . . . and is now (exasperated with the injuries and affronts offered to him) gone down . . . not onely to secure his much distracted Countrey from all divellish oppositions and machinations plotted by the malignants, but also, to the uttermost hazard of his estate and Fortunes, to defend his Castle at Warwick.

This particular force, authorized by Parliament on 15 August and apparently only one of several to be ordered to the Midlands, accordingly set out under Brooke, John Hampden and others via Aylesbury and St Albans, with a somewhat ambitious, multi-purpose task, 'to rescue Warwick Town and Castle, Coventry, Banbury, and to preserve the peace of the Country'. Brooke himself, presumably impatient to take command at Warwick, seems to have led a strong separate detachment which marched directly to Warwick without delay. Before the rest had gone far, however, in a little-known diversionary episode when stationed at Buckingham on 18 August, they sacked Bourton House, the home of Sir Richard Minshull, a prominent local Royalist who had recently left to join the King, before one of the units turned its attention to nearby Maids Moreton church, where the parish register records:

> In this Church of Moreton, the windows were broken, a costly desk in the form of a spread eagle gilt, on which we used to lay Bishop Jewel's works, [was] domed to perish as an abominable Idoll; the Cross . . . cut off the steeple by the soldiers at the command of one called Colonell Purefoy, of Warwickshire. He carried away what he could . . .

The elderly rector, George Bate, was later reported to have been 'nearly heart-broken with the insolence of the Rebels against the Church and King'. Although clearly partisan, there is no reason to doubt the general accuracy of these accounts, nor the participation of Purefoy in the events, since the unyielding Puritan would be subsequently charged with similar acts of iconoclasm in Warwickshire too. More justifiable military actions also delayed the parliamentary forces in their march north: in a timely initiative by the ever-wary Lord Saye an attempt to execute the Commission of Array in Oxfordshire was successfully thwarted by part of the army, and captured royalist leaders like the Earl of Berkshire, recently active in the Banbury magazine affair, were promptly dispatched to the Tower.[4]

The march of the parliamentary relief forces to Warwickshire in August 1642 underlines an important fact about the progress of the developing conflict: it is about now, during the siege of Warwick, that a clear attempt at both a widening and an intensification of the war effort begins to be apparent on both sides. As we have seen, while still at York the King had recognized the strategic importance of the Midlands by directing warrants and initiating moves designed to mobilize the area against Lord Brooke's successes. By now Commissions of Array had been planned or actually held in Warwickshire and in neighbouring counties, and various loyal petitions had been addressed to him from them. The approaching parliamentary forces for their part raised an awareness of imminent war in the areas through which they marched. In Oxfordshire, for example, Royalists claimed that such was the disturbance and fear aroused that a Commission of Array was an essential protective measure against 'certain disorderly Trains of armed Men', a point later reiterated by Anthony Wood. The university itself began to mobilize at:

> the report and bruit of diverse companies of soldiers that were daily sent downe from London by the parliament for the succoringe of Banbury and Warwicke, passing thorough the country'.

Excitement reached fever pitch as scholars trained in quadrangles, exercised in the Parks and paraded down the High Street, besotting students to the extent that books were abandoned in this 'greate disturbance to the youth of the citie'. The delay in the troops' arrival, though, was causing concern in some parliamentary quarters. One anonymous Warwickshire correspondent wrote despairingly to a friend on 8 August:

> . . . we fear the Parliament forces are too slow. Our Lord Brooke is not with us, we think him very long. I doubt they will doe us much hurt before he come . . . The yeomen of our Countrey stand out very well, but the Malignants draw abundance of the Rascalitie of the Countrey after them . . .

The following week, even the northern parliamentary leader, Sir William Brereton, voiced similar fears, predicting that Warwickshire would soon be lost, 'for the people begin to despair of the Parliament's assistance, because they see nor hear of no force coming down for their relief'. Parliament itself seemed prone to panic, instructing the Warwickshire authorities on 17 August to suppress rioting.

News of Parliament's relief force reached Warwick soon after the siege had begun and alarmed the leading Royalists enough to prompt urgent appeals to both Northamptonshire and Worcestershire for help, in almost identical terms:

> There are certain forces already upon the march from London towards these parts in opposition to his Majesty, his Royal authority and disturbance of the peace of this kingdom, whereby we are all in danger to be embroiled in a civil war, if timely prevention be not had. And do therefore desire that for the mutual strength of us all and speedy resistance of such powers, you will join with us . . . and forthwith raise and have in readiness all your forces, as well trained bands as other . . .

The Worcester reply was encouraging, stressing that the Commission of Array had been executed 'this day' (13 August) and accepting that 'when the danger knocks at our doors, the vicinity of counties involves a vicinity of interest, and that the danger is ours . . . .'.

Worcestershire seems to have been unable to offer material assistance, however, since two days later Warwickshire sent a further appeal even more urgent than the previous:

> . . . as those forces formerly mentioned are approaching nearer unto us and that great numbers of men from several parts of this county have, since we sent to you, gathered themselves in a warlike manner and are already entered in the city of Coventry (a place of great strength), there waiting their fittest opportunity . . .

It was against this quickening tempo of activity converging on Warwickshire that the King finally made the long-awaited move south from York, arriving at Nottingham and Leicester in mid-August, intent, it was widely assumed, on marching triumphantly on Warwick and, supposedly, ending the rebellion at a stroke. 'They say the King will be here on Wednesday, and bring a mighty strength with him', reports one correspondent; 'it is thought he . . . is resolved to march with his forces against Warwicke Castle, before which the Earl of Northampton lyes', surmises another; 'His Majesty is resolved to come in person to the said Towne of Warwicke and to desire the surrendering up of the same into his custody', asserts a third. Northampton now interrupted his command of operations at Warwick to travel to meet the King at Nottingham, on about 15 August, 'to draw His Majesty with his maine force to Warwicke Castle'. Warwickshire was evidently to be the chosen theatre of war, and the prospect of a seemingly inevitable clash between the converging forces filled correspondents with ill-concealed alarm:

> What they will do on either side when Mr Hampden and Mr Goodwin [leaders of the parliamentary relief force] cometh thither with 800 horse and 10,000 men from hence and out of Buckinghamshire, as he goeth towards Warwick, is not as yet known . . .

But by the time the King had reached Leicester there took place a pivotal event near Warwick. Lord Brooke's force had now reached the county, in time to confront a substantial royalist army of 5,000 horse and foot, led by an assortment of five earls and three lords, including Northampton, returning from conferring with the King, in what looks like a planned royalist attempt to force a showdown at Warwick. The rumours were probably correct in supposing that the King originally intended to lead this expedition in person; in the event, Lord Brooke arrived first, with the King still over a day's march away. The resulting confrontation, strangely ignored by historians, was as explosive a personal encounter between the two rival peers as any so far, and can in retrospect be seen as the end of the Warwickshire prologue to the real Civil War. It took place just outside Warwick, probably near Budbrooke, on Thursday 18 August, after the Royalists had been entertained and refreshed for the night by Sir Robert Dormer, Earl of Carnarvon, at Grove Park, on a day when at least one parliamentary regiment was unable to exercise 'by reason of foule weather'. If Dugdale is right in estimating Brooke's force on this occasion to be 6,000 horse and foot, two almost equally-matched small armies faced each other for the first time in Warwickshire. The anonymous reporter rose to the occasion in his graphic narration of the event as, for perhaps the last time, a scene of theatrical chivalry was re-enacted:

> The Lords, seing my Lord Brooks so well prepared, made a stand, and caused the Drum to beate a parly, which was answered by my Lord Brooks, and a Trumpet sent to demand the Cause, who was

met by a Trumpeter of the Kings partie, who gave information that they desired a conference with my Lord Brooks, wishing him to draw out a hundred Horse and fifty Musketiers for his guard, and they would doe the like; also that six men might be exchanged as Pledges for the security of either party, which was agreed on, and speedily effected . . . in the middle way, between both Forces.

The royalist peers then delivered what was in effect the King's final ultimatum, composed of five uncompromising 'propositions': that Brooke surrender immediately; hand over the castle; disavow the Militia Ordinance and, instead, proceed with the royal Commissions of Array; deliver up the county magazine to Northampton; and report to the King at Nottingham forthwith, to beg for pardon. Should Lord Brooke not comply, 'they vowed to make him the Subject of their that dayes fury'. The drama of what followed is vividly captured by the contemporary eye-witness:

These threats so farre incensed my Lord Brooks, that he was about to leave them without reply, but after a litle consideration he wheeld about, and boldly marcht up to them, speaking as followes: 'My Lords, I much wonder that men of judgement, in whose breasts true honour should remaine, should so much derogate from their Ancestors and noble Predecessors as to seeke, for private ends, the ruine of that Kingdom they should endeavour to support. Doth fond ambition, or your selfe-will'd pride so much bewitch you, that you cannot see the crown of all your actions? When the great Councel of the Parliament was first assembled, you were then Members; why did you not continue? Was it because your actions were so bad you were ashamed to own them? Had you done evill in some petty kind, Submission might have quitted you from that, and you have been still honoured, loved and feared. But by these actions, which tend both to the ruine of King and Kingdome and your selves too, you cannot make amends for former evills. As for these Propositions, take this in Answer: When that His Majesty, His posterity, and the peace of the Kingdome shall be secured from you that seeke the ruine of them all, I gladly shall lay downe my Armes and Power. As for the Castle, it was delivered to my trust by the High Court of Parliament, who reserve it for the King's use, and dare boldly say will so imploy it, and not, like you, imploy it against the King. As for the Commission of Array, you know it is unlawfull, and like your actions, destructive both the Laws and Religion of the Kingdome. For the Magazine of the County, it was delivered to him both by the Parliament and the Countrey; and although he was not an Earle, yet he dares be a truer Subject to his King, and a faithfuller servant to his Countrey; and being so, he was resolved to keep it till Northampton could show him greater authority for his delivery of the same. As touching His Majesties Pardon, as he was confident that he had not given any occasion of offence to His Majesty, so he needed not pardon, that being a duty belonging to offenders such as themselves; and he advised them to sue out a pardon with speed, for feare that, their offences being once knowne, they prove impardonable; for he doubted not but that in a short time His Majesty would finde who are his best friends . . .'

Lord Brooke's contemptuous final flourish has an almost Shakespearean eloquence:

As for their fury, he bade them spit their venome, for he hoped that Northampton should be translated to Warwick, and stand centry upon Warwicke-castle, to fright crowes, kites and buzzards.

The opposing parties then 'very fairely wheeled about and marched away, not once so much as taking their leave': matters could no longer be settled by debate.[5]

In the event, the King's own entry into Warwickshire proved no more impressive than his actions once there. Only lukewarm, unreliable displays of popularity were shown him, according to a caustic parliamentary commentator, as he travelled south from Leicester, crossing the Avon near Rugby before turning westwards through Kings Newnham, Lord Dunsmore's seat, for Stoneleigh. In one of those unverifiable but totally credible local traditions, without which history would be so much poorer, Charles when crossing Dunsmore Heath halted to dine under an oak near the ancient Fosse Way at Wolston, awakening memories of earlier Gunpowder Plot conspirators and the Marprelate Tracts nearby. The King remained at Stoneleigh for several days as the guest of Sir Robert Leigh, pausing to assess the situation at first hand, ruefully, exactly half-way between the two rebel centres of Warwick and Coventry, issuing himself a further, vain appeal to the Worcestershire Royalists to send urgent aid to the Earl of Northampton at Warwick, and reinforcing nearby Kenilworth. For some time Charles had been planning to make the stirring gesture of raising the Royal Standard, several northern towns having been rejected as geographically too remote for this, and it is possible that he intended to choose either Coventry or Dunsmore Heath for this symbolic act; certainly it was rumoured that his 'summoning of the country' to attend him there on 22 August was for that purpose. From Stoneleigh, however, issuing a warrant to the Earl of Northampton to raise a further body of a thousand volunteers, he first attempted to compensate for the Warwick fiasco by seizing Coventry, directing William Dugdale on 20 August to perform the same ceremony at Coventry as earlier at Warwick. The King's ill-advised and abortive attempt at Coventry on 20/21 August turned the city – still divided, although recently reinforced by further volunteers from Birmingham – almost overnight into a parliamentary stronghold which became the nerve-centre for rebel Warwickshire for the rest of the war. In sombre mood, sensing the onset of an unwanted but now inevitable war and with the Royalists still unable to make any impression on Warwick's stout walls, Charles discreetly slipped away, travelling, according to tradition, via a green lane from Dunsmore to take refreshment at Cawston Hall, 'the most beautiful Fabrick that there was in all these parts', the seat of one of his then staunchest allies, Sir William Boughton. After arriving in the evening 'weary out of Warwickshire', the windswept Royal Standard, somewhat mischievously described as 'like a May-pole, dyed red' and 'much of the fashion of the City streamers used at the Lord Mayors show', was finally raised at Nottingham rather than Dunsmore, on 22 August. Inauspiciously, it was blown down shortly after.

THE CORNFIELDS OF SOUTHAM

Matters in Warwickshire were now coming to a head. Although completely disorganized, substantial numbers of Royalists were roaming here and there, awaiting the long-expected parliamentary relief force from London. This finally entered Warwickshire, 'after a longe and tedious marche', on the morning of Monday 22 August, near Priors Marston, after quartering the previous night at Byfield wretchedly in need of rest and food: 'had we not bin suplyed with ten cart loade of provision and beare from Banbury', one soldier reported, 'many of us had perished'. News of the arrival of the enemy immediately became a more urgent consideration for the flagging Royalists at Warwick, and the siege of the castle was hurriedly abandoned the same day. With the lifting of the siege, Sir Edward Peto promptly sent search parties under the dependable John Bridges to ransack the town for useful booty, amassing, it was claimed, a quantity of arms sufficient to equip 500 men, stealing any horses they could find and arresting anyone suspicious or simply unsympathetic, like the shoemaker, John Thomas, who complained bitterly of 'beinge imprisoned 3 severall tymes at ye Castle to my great disadvantage, without ye least ground'. The claims of Richard Morrell from the High Street are fairly typical, and in the third item hint at widening ripples of social disruption:

> Item: a Mare taken by the Souldiers of Warwicke Castle imediately upon the Earle of Northamptons going away, being the 23rd of August £4. 4s. 0d.

> Item: Armes then taken, vizt. One Muskett, a half pike, A Halberd, one head peece, twoe brests & twoe backs of Armor £1. 10s. 0d.

> Item: the free quarter of a maymed Cavalier, & sometimes his wife and his twoe sisters for tenn weeks, for wch he was promised paymt by sevrll psons . . . but nevr receaved anything £2. 0s. 0d.

Not that all the inhabitants were necessarily impoverished by recent events. Mrs King, proprietress of the Swan Inn, having lost the highly profitable custom of the Earl of Northampton and his lordly allies, attempted to compensate by extorting £30 from the searchers. The Swan must have been a highly profitable establishment at this time: on one occasion (and unlikely to have been the only one) local inhabitants like William Bailey as far away as Henley-in-Arden were expected to contribute sums of money towards 'A breakfast att the Swanne for Warwicke souldiers'.

As for the Royalists, after hastily transferring the cannons temporarily to Kenilworth, many began assembling on Dunsmore Heath in large, indisciplined numbers increased by many of the unsuccessful besiegers of Coventry pursued by Lord Brooke, and plundering as far as Hillmorton, Rugby and Daventry as they awaited the expected conflagration. This was a time of much confusion, and it is impossible to reconstruct events or chronicle movements: the precise activities of neither Brooke nor Northampton have ever been established. One parliamentary pamphlet even claimed that Lord Northampton was captured, near Daventry. As we have seen, the King himself was indecisive, while militarily the absence of a coherent command structure, difficulties of communication, lack of organization and the personal bickering which was to bedevil both sides in the war all took their toll. In one episode typical of the confusion, the King's cavalry under the abrasive Lord Wilmot, which was to have guarded Northampton's retreat from Warwick under Sir Nicholas Byron, never in fact joined, either by mistake or, probably, rancour between the two commanders: Clarendon suggests that the older Byron was unwilling to take orders from Wilmot, who saw himself as having supreme command. In another incident reflecting poor professionalism, a royalist officer, Captain Legge, was pointlessly captured at Southam when, mistaking identical colours worn by a parliamentary unit, he rode directly into the enemy camp. He was promptly dispatched to London and imprisoned.[6]

The long-expected battle, the first in Warwickshire involving a deliberately-sought encounter between two sizeable armies in open country, finally took place near Long Itchington on the morning of Tuesday 23 August 1642, between the Royalists retreating from Warwick and Coventry, and the now considerably strengthened parliamentary forces from Buckinghamshire. Parliament too had been widening its recruitment and, in addition to Lord Brooke's major force others now joined, some from Northampton, and others from Leicestershire under the young Lord Grey of Groby, the son of the Earl of Stamford, whose men joined Brooke at Warwick, quartering at Whitnash and other nearby villages. As before, the half-dozen surviving accounts of events agree on essentials, and range from the sober report of two of the parliamentary commanders, John Hampden and Nathaniel Fiennes, to the much more circumstantial, racier account, so often quoted, of a parliamentary subaltern, Nathaniel Wharton. The Parliamentarians had arrived at Southam the previous night, intending to billet in the town, and had actually begun to arrange quarters and meals when the news spread that the town had recently quartered the Earl of Northampton's troops (possibly a reference to the Commission of Array held a few weeks previously), that many of the townspeople were royalist sympathizers, and that the vicar in particular was 'a man of very evill and dissolute conversation, and sustained in his house many Cavaliers at his owne charges'. As a leading ecclesiastical conservative and disciplinarian, the elderly scholar Francis Holyoak must indeed have appeared a notorious enemy to the proselytizing puritan ministers in the ranks of the parliamentary army, and the vicar was forthwith arrested and his house ransacked, incriminating saddles, muskets, powder and even a drum allegedly being found. No sooner had the excited soldiers resumed their interrupted rest than an urgent drum-beat alert warned them to prepare instantly to meet an approaching enemy force under the Earl of Northampton two miles away. Barricades were hastily erected in the town while most of the soldiers rushed into the cornfields north of the town 'in their armes ready for battell' to set up their positions, 'where they lay all night without meate or drinke', 'their beds being the ground, although it was a sharpe cold night'. The battle itself, beginning at 8 a.m. and lasting all the morning, ranged in a series of confused *mêlées* over a wide area between Southam and Long Itchington and beyond, with the Royalists assembled initially along the Itchen valley and the Parliamentarians on either Bascote or Snowford Hill. The discovery of cannon balls and skeletons at Bascote in 1815 is poignant proof of this late summer morning's affray.

There seems no reason to doubt the virtually unanimous parliamentary reports of a royalist defeat in the 'field much besprinkled with blood', nor many of the incidental details related: that many Royalist dead lying 'on heapes in the Corn-fields' were thrown into the Itchen to conceal the extent of their losses; that some hawked their weapons through the surrounding villages at 12d. apiece; and that most fled northwards towards Dunsmore Heath. Others, wearing Northampton's colours, were sent as prisoners to Warwick Castle. The discovery of bullets embedded in the stonework of Marton church during a later restoration substantiates the parliamentary reports of the long pursuit which concluded this 'very hot Skirmish on both sides'. The presence of the King, Prince Rupert and even, probably, the Earl of Northampton, reported in some accounts, may be dismissed as the wishful thinking of elated victors. Nothing had been resolved, no great victory won; but which of the ragged parliamentary soldiers who marched triumphantly into Coventry with Lord Brooke the next day to a rapturous welcome would have believed that?[7]

Southam is usually dismissed as a minor affray, but several interesting postscripts need recording. First, Southam sets one kind of precedent in noting the first Civil War casualty actually recorded in a Warwickshire church burial register, for 23 August: 'John Browne, alias Ripley, a souldier under Captain Jones in ye regiment of Robt. Lord Brooke', while an additional human note is the claim by a parliamentary clergyman that Brooke generously gave 'money out of his owne purse to carry the dead bodies of his Enimies to Southam to be buried.' Militarily, Southam offers a pointed reminder of amateurish and inadequately-trained soldiers and unreliable weapons, recorded parliamentary casualties alone including 'some twelve wounded by the firing of some Powder; and one shot himselfe through the foot with his Pistoll, and another his fellow through the back'. Even more interesting, though, in an incident which seems to have escaped the attention of military historians, is the suggestion of a rudimentary form of mine warfare about to be tested. The captured Royalist, Captain Legge, confessed to his captors that the Cavaliers:

> had undermined ten places in Southam-field, where they thought my Lord Brooke would have come with his forces. Whereupon my Lord sent thither, and found underminings, and therein great store of Powder layed under Faggots and Billets, with great wedges of Iron, all which my Lord caused to be carried away.

It is possible, therefore, that six months before the first mines were reported to have been used in the war, according to the note in Prince Rupert's journal, Rupert's engineer, Bernard de Gomme, had already joined the royalist forces at Southam and was preparing a new phase of warfare.

It is also about now that the extent to which the local population was becoming involved in the war effort first becomes clear. By now, all villages had been contributing regular sums of money to raise cavalry for Lord Brooke for several months, but other burdens now began to weigh. There was now, for example, widespread quartering of troops on totally unprepared small communities. Long Itchington alone gave free quarter to at least six troops of horse, three under Lord Brooke, each of which consisted of 150 men, at this time. Some villages, particularly those unfortunately situated, were clearly overwhelmed, like Dunchurch whose constable later complained: 'the whole number [of soldiers] wee cannot well remember, by reason of our frequent qrtering of soldiers (our Towne lying on the Rode way) . . . .'. Other unlucky villages would hardly be rid of soldiers of one side before troops from the other would arrive to find the village already emptied of provision. This was the case of Aston Cantlow in mid-September, where Parliamentarians 'could get no quarter, neither bread nor drink, by reason of the Lord Compton's late being there'. Nor was quarter confined to the more affluent households, immediately selected by officers and quartermasters for themselves. Significantly, a Southam account specifies a sum of over £5 paid to a Northampton captain:

> . . . for quarteringe of his souldiers in oure towne . . . att poore houses; [he] pretended the poore people should have [the £5], but he gave them none of it.

The abuse of quarter was already widespread, and the system whereby tickets later redeemable against cash payments were given to householders was often flouted. The Southam parson spoke for many when, after listing his claims for reimbursement, he pointedly concluded: 'And I never received pay for any quarter'.

Provisioning was itself a huge drain on the already meagre resources of many a hamlet and village, as extra supplies were imperiously demanded far and wide for ravenous troops. At first, no doubt, some were sent voluntarily, as already noted at Banbury and now again at Southam, where a parliamentary source boasted 'the Countrey round about brought in much provision of Victuall to refresh the Army'. Naturally, the nearest hamlets would be obliged to respond instantly, but more distant villages were by no means exempt, so that when Lord Brooke's forces were quartered at Long Itchington for the battle of Southam, not only Stockton but Wolfhampcote too sent in supplies. Similarly at Mollington, a good ten miles away, the constable, Richard Claridge, had been busy for a long time collecting the levy for Lord Brooke's cavalry, and now duly sent in the hamlet's additional quota of provision to his army at Long Itchington, just as Long Itchington, once the army had moved on, had in its turn to supply parliamentary quarters at Offchurch, Bascote and Hunningham as the war progressed. Although, therefore, it might be assumed that once troops had left the area the now deserted villages could return to a semblance of normality without further commitments, such was not always the case. Once Southam was vacated, for example, it still had to supply a further £5. 16s. 3d. worth of provision 'to the Lord Brooks Army to Coventry, after the battaile in our field, August 23rd 1642'.

Occasionally the civilian population is reported to have lent the soldiers more direct, physical support. At Southam, as later at Edgehill, at least one account claims that villagers 'took up clubs, and as any small company of [Royalists] passed, cudgelled them, and bid them go home againe'. Even more interesting, too, is the occasional suggestion of villagers banding together to protect their community from outside aggressors. Mary Temple's house at Frankton, a village apparently sympathetic to Parliament's cause, was threatened with siege by Lord Dunsmore and only saved, she claimed, by the protection of friendly neighbours.

As for plundering, this was becoming an almost daily fact of Civil War life, and often, clearly, much more than petty pilfering. Conspicuous royalist sympathizers like Francis Holyoak, the Southam vicar, could expect little mercy. Besides being targeted from now on for almost continuous free quarter by parliamentary commanders, costing him, according to his own estimate, over £80, he claimed to have lost horses, a silver bowl, rings, plate, linen, money, wearing apparel and other goods. Such parliamentary thefts were followed by more at Coventry, where 'our soldiers pillaged a malignant fellowes house in this city', and more substantial expeditions nearby. Lord Brooke himself, perhaps uncharacteristically yielding to retaliatory pressures, ordered Lord Dunsmore's mansion at Newnham Regis to be visited; the intended 'search' evidently deteriorated, for 'there hath been great slaughter made of his Deere by the Troopers and Coventry Soldiers, who have killed neare two Hundred'. In spite of Brooke's threat of severe martial law for offenders one day, the very next a band of his soldiers, according to an enraptured Parliamentarian's report:

> sallyed out of the City unto the Lord Dunsmore's parke, and brought from thence great store of venison, which is as good as ever I tasted; and ever since they make it their dayly practice, so that venison is almost as common with us as beefe with you.

One other prime target situated conveniently near, at Packington, was the estate of one of the King's Warwickshire Commissioners of Array, Sir Robert Fisher, for which, unusually, accounts from both sides may be compared. The parliamentary report specifies the booty as 'a cart loade of armes'; whereas Fisher's own emphasis is very different: not only four horses taken by Lord Brooke's men, but also:

> the dwellinge house, the lodge, and the newe house on the Hill rent, torne, and divers tymes plundred, [and] 200 Deere, 1,000 Couple of Conies, and great store of fyshe taken out of fower pooles . . .

Among the spoils of war taken from Sir Robert Fisher's that day, one more unusual prize stood out triumphantly among the captured weapons, 'his owne picture standing very stately in the cart'. Other entertainment much appreciated by the parliamentary soldiers was the harassment and taunting of politically-suspect clergy, one vicar being 'brought away prisoner, with his surplice and other relics' and another, the vicar of Walsgrave-on-Sowe, described bluntly as 'an old base priest', who was likewise 'led ridiculouly about the City [Coventry] unto the chiefe commaunders'. This improvised horseplay continued on the return journey back into Northamptonshire, where one morning:

> our soildiers sallyed out about the cuntrey, and returned in state clothed with a surplisse, hood and cap, representing the Bishop of Canterbury.

Naturally, such activities would have appeared morally justified where the victims were 'malignants', 'delinquents' or 'rebels', in the catch-all phraseology of the time, and little parliamentary sympathy would have been wasted on wealthy royalist magnates or supposedly ultra-reactionary country parsons in fat livings. The glee of the pious zealot is evident in much of Nehemiah Wharton's account of these post-Southam days. Nevertheless, lawlessness was spreading, plunder becoming increasingly indiscriminate, carried out by opportunistic looters on any available victim. While kicking their heels at Northampton shortly after, as they awaited developments, the parliamentary soldiers were not only mutinous but stealing among themselves, leaving allies swearing revenge on each other. Understandably, they had scant respect for their recently jumped-up superiors, complaining scathingly that 'a pewterer is their captaine, an Alehouse keeper their sergente and a cobler their ancyente . . . .'.

In considerable disarray, with long hours of inactivity interspersed with aimless sorties, training sessions, uplifting sermons, the catching of the odd spy, plundering expeditions, and amid growing rumours of royalist excesses to the north at Nuneaton and beyond by the 'diabolical Cavaleere' Prince Rupert, newly-arrived on the scene, the victors of Southam finally received new orders. The starving Parliamentarians recrossed Dunsmore Heath on 1 September, drinking stagnant water, eating pigswill when they could find it, and sleeping in churches as the only shelter, to regroup outside the Warwickshire border around Northampton, as they awaited the arrival of the new supreme parliamentary commander, the Earl of Essex, from London, to decide the next move. Parliamentarian hopes were high but tinged with anxiety. Mary Hervey wrote from Northampton to her cousin John Fetherston at Packwood on 2 September: 'this last night heere came in a brave troope of horse, and my Lord Brooke is now comeinge, they are gone out to meete him. I pray God he leave Warwicksheere safe . . .'. But less than two months later the King himself would arrive in nearby Southam and deliver a rallying speech to his army before the first full-scale battle of the war. Although no one could have known, the prelude to Edgehill was about to begin.[8]

CHAPTER FOUR

THE EDGEHILL CAMPAIGN

PRELUDE 1: ESSEX'S MARCH TO WORCESTER

Understandably, the Edgehill campaign is usually taken to have begun with the departure of the Earl of Essex from Worcester on 19 October. But long before engaging the royal army at Edgehill, Essex's forces had twice crossed the full width of Warwickshire, in both directions, and even once the battle was over neither army left the area immediately, as is sometimes implied by writers eager to pass on to the next 'campaign'. For the local population therefore, the experience was more widely felt, more continuous and more lasting than often imagined: long after the event, what 'Kineton fight' had meant to ordinary people was vividly etched into the folk memory of communities as distant from Kineton as Bilton in the east to Alcester in the west. The focus in this chapter will be on the nature of this experience, not on the events of the battle itself, which have already been adequately analysed elsewhere.

The Earl of Essex left London to a rapturous citizens' send-off on 9 September 1642 and immediately joined the Midland forces assembled at Northampton as supreme parliamentary commander, intending to march straight to Nottingham and capture the King. Those troops were, as has already been seen, largely untrained volunteers, indisciplined to the point of mutiny, threatening to desert, ill-equipped, ill-fed and unpaid, forcing their leader to appeal urgently to London for funds on 15 September. After a period of preparation and training, Essex, learning of the King's retreat towards Shropshire, was ordered by Parliament to shadow him. There seems less of a mystery about Essex's decision to march to Worcester than some have alleged, since the King's departure from Shrewsbury for (supposedly) Worcester was known to the House of Commons, and consequently Essex's move westwards was 'well approved of by the Parliament'. Essex was not to know for some time that the King was in fact making for Warwickshire rather than Worcestershire. Wisely rejecting an impertinent challenge from Prince Rupert to test his unready army against the Royalists on Dunsmore Heath, Essex ordered his army westwards, crossing into Warwickshire between Shuckburgh and

Hillmorton on Monday 19 September and quartering in and around Rugby in considerable numbers. One of the very first Warwickshire villages to see the arrival of the parliamentary troops was Wolfhampcote, as Essex's carriages rumbled into the county from Braunston on the heavily-used Daventry–Dunchurch highway, the same way they would take on their return journey six weeks later. A parliamentary news-sheet reported that Essex's men were acclaimed with joy by the country folk, and the next day there was a huge rally of the disparate parliamentary forces on Dunsmore Heath near Bilton Grange, lasting all day, at which Essex was joined by Lord Brooke and William Purefoy from Warwick and an eighteen-piece artillery unit, with neighbouring villages sending provision 'when the Earle of Essex kept Rendezvous upon our heath'. It is from this time that Prince Rupert's growing reputation begins to merge into that of the legendary folk hero, in the picturesque episode of the young prince heavily disguised as a pedlar, buying a merchant's stock of apples and selling them to Essex's men on Dunsmore Heath; other such tales would soon follow.

It is quite clear from the parish accounts that parliamentary quartering was so widespread at this time that hardly any village escaped its quota of soldiers 'on the Earle of Essex's first cominge downe', making the main route reasonably clear: Hillmorton, Bilton, Dunchurch, Wolston, Stretton, Ryton, Princethorpe, Wappenbury, Leamington, Warwick. Many units are discovered at some distance from this route, however, regiments of horse and foot lying as far north as Brinklow and others as far south as Southam, suggesting a far from unified marching front. Quartering on tiny villages often involved considerable numbers. Wappenbury was host to a whole company of seventy men under Essex for a day and night, with an additional troop of twenty of Lord Brooke's cavalry. Dunchurch likewise quartered a troop of sixty-four of Essex's horse for two days and nights, plus more of Brooke's, and such patterns were repeated throughout a wide area. Not all the local inhabitants were necessarily hostile to the huge invasion, especially those politically committed among the more affluent. At Bretford, a leading Parliamentarian, Richard Wilcox, recorded his own generous hospitality: 'Monsieur de Boyes, the Master of the trayne of Artillery under the Earle of Essex, for Himselfe & 8 others', adding pointedly, with perhaps a touch of pride, 'Monsieur de Boyes offered me payment, but I tooke none of Him'.

Once arrived safely at the parliamentary garrison town of Warwick, Essex's army paused to allow a forty-gun artillery train to catch up, once again fanning out to quarter throughout the neighbourhood: Barford, Bishops Tachbrook, Tachbrook Mallory and Leamington Priors received particularly large contingents of both Essex's and Brooke's forces. The condition of the lice-ridden men was described with grim humour by Nathaniel Wharton: 'backbiters have been seen to march upon some of them six on breast and eight deep at their open order'. Again, the resources of such villages (Barford was described by even the undemanding subaltern as 'very poor') must have been stretched beyond breaking point: in both Barford and, shortly after, Aston Cantlow, 'many of our soldiers can get neither beds, bread nor water'. Yet often, as we have seen, a village's commitments did not end with providing free quarter. Leamington Priors was particularly unfortunate, all available horses being requisitioned for Essex's carriages: first, for bringing them into Warwick all the way from Braunston in Northamptonshire, then continuing with them to Worcester, and finally drawing them back again all those weary miles to Kineton and eventually Daventry. How such villages managed without their horses at harvest time for what must have been several weeks on end is rarely mentioned, but years after, when they applied to the parliamentary authorities for compensation for losses, some inhabitants at least were not prepared to forget. One inhabitant of Whitnash, Nicholas Greenhill, for example, reported succinctly:

> Collonell Bridges Sent 8 Souldiers [from Warwick Castle] wch tooke 3 stoned horses, i mare & a sadle, wch being in the midst of harvest was to his prejudice   £5. 0s. 0d.

For Leamington, however, the absent horses were merely one grievance, for in addition Lord Brooke sent an urgent order to the village for a supply of cheese for Essex, quartered at the castle. And as a final unpleasant twist to the whole saga, once the troops had finally left the village was promptly selected for reprisal raids from marauding Cavaliers as a punishment for its enforced harbouring of the enemy. Here, Samuel Clarke, Lord Brooke's own protégé, the puritan minister of Alcester who often lectured at Warwick, was understandably a prime target, and suffered heavy losses. Other communities too, especially those unfortunately situated, like the tiny Ashow, between parliamentary Warwick and royalist Kenilworth, suffered considerable losses by being plundered by both sides almost simultaneously.[1]

As for the soldiers, their lot was if anything even less enviable than that of the destitute villagers as they resumed their march to Worcester. The weather had now turned wet, and major rivers like the Avon offered only few crossing points, like ramshackle wooden bridges and hazardous fords. Some groups of soldiers, taking a more southerly route, headed for Stratford and its surrounding villages, taking a short cut across the ford below the kitchen garden at Charlecote and camping in the great meadow, later renamed the Camp Ground, before continuing through Stratford, Binton, Salford, Dunnington . . . . Others marched due westwards from Warwick, through Wootton Wawen, Snitterfield, Henley, Aston Cantlow, Great Alne, towards Studley and Alcester, quartering in all of these villages. Typical is a complaint of one resident in the hamlet of Edstone, at having to receive '20 of the Earle of Essex souldiers when he wentt to Worcester, at Diett, and 10 lodged with mee all night'. No doubt the wet weather played its part in the evident lack of urgency on this march: one of Lord Rochford's company of foot soldiers loitered in Binton a whole week. Approaching Alcester, meanwhile, other pressing considerations delayed progress still further, as is clear from one soldier's candidly naïve report:

> We lay at a place called Colfon [Coughton] in Warwickshire, and there lived a great Papist, one Frogmorton [Sir Robert Throckmorton], who hearing of our comming fled away from his house, and his whole Family, which the Souldiers did plunder, and found abundance of Images and Pictures, which they brake and committed to the fire. They likewise burnt many popish Bookes, some of them being almost as big as we could lift with one hand, printed in parchment, and others were throwne into a great moate. In the house we found 3 or 4 Murthering peeces, brasse pots, and a great sheet of lead about 500 weight, which was hidden under ground. The Souldiers dranke up his Perry, Sider and Beere almost all, they did lye on his Fether-beds all night, and in the Morning cut them, emptied out the feathers, carried the tikes away with them, and also silke hangings for Beds . . .

This particular act of deliberate vandalism must be one of the first recorded in Warwickshire where, unlike earlier cases affecting the property of grandees like Lord

Brooke and Lord Dunsmore, there was no suggestion of active militancy on the part of the victim. Throckmorton was wealthy, 'a great Papist' whose family had long ago been implicated in the Gunpowder Plot and, more recently, in other Catholic scares, and that was more than adequate justification. The zealous Parliamentarians' plundering techniques had evidently become bolder since, a few weeks previously in Buckinghamshire, Nathaniel Wharton had confessed that 'every day our soldiers by stealth do visit Papists' houses'. Coughton Court now became a parliamentary garrison, exacting the usual supplies from nearby villages, like the 'one Hogshead of beeare to Captaine Smyth, with the Caske, to the Garrison of Coughton', or flockbeds, bolsters, sheets and blankets from Sambourne, Alcester and other places. The roads had now become quagmires: 'this day we had such foul weather that before I had marched one mile I was wet to the skin'. Understandably, the troops were loath to leave quarters 'when they lay about Alcester', one resident complaining, 'I was not without Souldiers for five weeks, at my very great Charges'. With the inclement weather the nature of the soldiers' thefts in Alcester reflects the most basic human needs of food, warmth and comfort: 'a paire of Shooes, besides wood and linens', 'postes and pales, railes and wood burned by the Earle of Essex his Armye . . . .'.

To make things worse, matters of more military urgency now intervened as the parliamentary soldiers finally approached Worcester. A body of Cavaliers under Sir John Byron had arrived in the city a few days previously bringing a valuable consignment of money, plate and volunteers from Oxford, pursued by a parliamentary force under Nathaniel Fiennes, marching via Butlers Marston and intending to rendezvous with Essex at Worcester. Before the two parliamentary forces could join, however, Fiennes's detachment was ambushed and badly mauled at nearby Powick by Prince Rupert, so that with night falling on dead and wounded, and panic breaking out among the Parliamentarians fleeing back towards Essex's forces approaching from Pershore, the two armies met, with the soldiers singing psalms through the night to keep up morale, for 'we had small comfort, for it rained hard. Our food was fruit, for those who get it; our drink, water; our beds, the earth.'

Supremely confident for his part, Rupert taunted Essex by parading his forces in Pitchcroft Meadow outside the city and sending him another personal challenge:

> I shall be ready, on his Majesty's behalf, to give you an encounter in a pitched field, at Dunsmore Heath, 10th October next or, if you think it too much labour and expense to draw your forces thither, I shall as willingly, for my own part, expect private satisfaction as willingly at your hands . . . by a single duel.

Understandably, the staid, middle-aged parliamentary commander once again ignored the challenge. Had he accepted, there can be little doubt that the course of English history would have been profoundly changed. Before finally entering the city, the restless troops had to listen to a long admonitory discourse from the gentlemanly Essex, his longest recorded speech to his troops, reminding them sternly of the righteous warrior's code of conduct, as set out in his own *Lawes and Ordinances of Warre*, while the downpour continued the whole day, '. . . and the way so base that we went up to the ancles in thick clay'. The demoralized troops finally trudged into the city by Sidbury Gate on 24 September and relieved their long pent-up generalized resentment against everything, from the weather to the 'base, papistical, atheistical, abominable' town and, in C.V. Wedgwood's graphic summary, 'arrested the Mayor, sacked the cathedral and tore down the sweet-toned organ that had been the joy and pride of the region'.[2]

With the King apparently static in Shrewsbury, the Parliamentarians remained in Worcester three weeks, during which time notable Catholics like Sir William Russell at Strensham were plundered 'unto the bare walls' and the cathedral and other buildings mindlessly vandalized, in spite of Essex's efforts to enforce discipline. The sacking of the cathedral, consistent with the victimization of clergy sympathetic to the King already noted, is a reminder of the deep religious divisions underlying this stage of the conflict, indicative of the wave of anti-Catholic iconoclasm sweeping the country and a foretaste of things to come. Though the Midlands were never to experience the scale of ecclesiastical destruction carried out elsewhere, a contemporary royalist account of events at Worcester Cathedral is worth quoting:

> All the Bishops beards, noses, fingers and arms, and all, if they had white sleeves, are broken. King John and the other Kings that lie interred there have not passed better in this quarrel, than with cracked crowns. In all the corners of the Church are the droppings of these unclean birds visible. A grave man, . . . with tears in his eyes, told me that with those eyes he saw divers of [Essex's soldiers] ease themselves in the Font and upon the Communion-Table, calling to them that chearfully looked on, to 'Name the child! . . .'.

Although partisan accounts are clearly suspect, there is a note of total authenticity here, in private correspondence, and the details accord well with those of other such episodes, like the Coughton one already quoted or Dugdale's description of very similar activities at Lichfield. Both sides, far from denying vandalism, frequently boast of it.

In mid-October, however, Essex's troops were disturbed in these proceedings by news that the King had finally embarked on his expected march south, and had reached Warwickshire:

> . . . on Wednesday last our Army marched out of Worcester, the King having before wheeled about behinde us from Shrewsbury, by Killingworth [Kenilworth], towards Southam.

A last opportunity to avert war was squandered when, on 18 October, the Earl of Essex sent the King at Packington, where he was the guest of Sir Robert Fisher, a conciliatory petition from both Houses of Parliament confirming that His Majesty would be welcome at Westminster, if he came peacefully. Charles not only refused to accept the petition but even denied safe conduct to its bearers, provoking a protest from Lord Brooke, Pym and others at this 'most high indignity and scorn', insulting thus the 'submissive, dutiful and earnest desires of peace . . . of his loving and loyall subjectes'. Confident now of its strength, the entire royal army rallied on Meriden Heath before resuming its leisurely march towards London. The following day, 19 October, Essex set out from Worcester to intercept. The countdown to Edgehill had begun.

PRELUDE 2: WORCESTER TO KINETON

It might be assumed that Essex, aware that the King was already well advanced on the road to London, would now act decisively and urgently to intervene. Why he did not remains one of the still unsolved mysteries of the war, but the fact is that, while the King's army itself advanced slowly, accomplishing less than 10 miles a day since leaving Shrewsbury, Essex's progressed even more slowly. Among the reasons usually suggested for this are the atrocious state of the roads after the recent wet spell, inadequate logistics, the appallingly cumbersome baggage and artillery trains which an army had to drag in its wake, and sheer amateurism – all valid factors which, however, applied equally to both armies. Certainly the state of the roads was abysmal, as already indicated on the march to Worcester. Prior to the Civil War at least twenty-four Worcestershire parishes reported to the county authorities that their roads were out of repair, even by the undemanding standards of the day. Only a little to the south of Essex's route, at Shipston-on-Stour, both the main Stratford road and the ancient stone bridge on the Banbury road were reported to the county authorities as being 'in decay', while a little to the north the vicar of Alvechurch complained about the 'ill and negligently repaired highways' which had trapped him 'twice fast set in the mire when riding about my lawful and necessary occasion of tythes'. Three years later, when the royal army passed through Worcestershire on the King's final march north before Naseby, the state of the roads is hinted at by Charles's instructions to the county authorities, which included demands for huge numbers of horses, at least five to draw every cart. Certainly Essex would have found no better conditions as his army crossed back into Warwickshire, the roads near Warwick itself still being impassable a century later and the main Stratford–Long Compton–Oxford road noted as atrocious even in 1790.

Everywhere, over the entire region, travellers' comments are unanimously scathing: the Adderbury and Southam section of the Coventry to Oxford road was 'indifferent', near Rugby 'deep and unpleasant', and near Shuckburgh 'very heavy'. At Chipping Campden the road was likewise 'very heavy', and at Four Shires Stone, at the southernmost tip of Warwickshire, 'a morass way'. Even the heavily-used Dunchurch highway was described in 1675 as 'usually very bad' and was notorious enough to inspire the poet-traveller John Taylor to a doggerel commentary:

> The way to Dunchurch foule with dirt and mire
> Able, I thinke, both man and horse to tire . . .
> Through plashes, puddles, thicke, thinne, wet & dry,
> I travel'd to the Citie Coventry . . .[3]

For Essex, therefore, the lack of draft horses was, despite the demands on transit villages like Leamington Priors, as we have seen, a crucial handicap. Clarendon reports that Essex's train 'was so very great that he could move but in slow marches', and there is moreover a suggestion of local obstructiveness, a later parliamentary account blaming 'the malignitie of the Cartars of that Countrie [who] did so neglect and retarde the service, that [Essex's] Carriages came the first day no further than Spetchley . . . but two miles from the Citie'. The result was that even when Essex reached Kineton four days later, much of his artillery, with its escort and valuable officers like John Hampden, were left a day's march behind. In addition, for Essex the political moderate, there must also have been the rebel's reluctance, in an unprecedented situation, to strike the first blow against his king, with the hope that matters even now would resolve themselves without further bloodshed, while his awareness as a soldier of the recent near-fiasco at Powick must have been a further burden.

Essex's extremely leisurely progress offered the more mobile of his units much spare time, an opportunity they quickly seized on for more plundering as they dispersed in all directions as they re-entered Warwickshire. It is here, once again, that the convenient arrows of military historians are clearly misleading. The army in 1642 consisting mainly, it is well to remember, of amateurs having volunteered for a variety of reasons few of which would have been genuinely ideological, was, as already demonstrated, a cumbersome, ill-disciplined, many-headed monster, whose ramshackle progress in any given direction bore little resemblance to arrows. Strategy was rudimentary, professionalism patchy and the lure of plunder imperative. There were virtually no maps or signposts. Roads were rutted tracks or quagmires, so that foot marchers and cavalry would often prefer to cut across this unenclosed, virtually hedgeless landscape peopled with the labouring poor toiling at their strips, trampling the corn as at Southam and deviating to loot whenever a promising hamlet or a known Catholic's wealthy estate came into view. None of the soldiers, of course, knew that they were marching to the battle of Edgehill, or where they would find shelter at night. In a telling comment to Prince Rupert, one royalist commander complained that 'troops are sent out without any manner of forecast or design, or care to preserve or quarter them when they are abroad'. No wonder that urgency was a low priority, quarter often for days or weeks at a time and troops scattered over a wide area, making rapid reassembly impossible. This was the reality at Edgehill and after.

As they re-entered Warwickshire the Parliamentarians' broad front extended from at least Alcester and Great Alne in the north, with John Fiennes quartered as far north as Studley for three days and nights, to Ilmington, some 15 miles to the south, with Stratford and the neighbouring villages all heavily quartered in between. In flagrant disregard of their commander's recent proclamation 'that no soldier should plunder either church or private house, upon pain of death', there was much deliberate pillage, at least two major Catholic landowners presenting prime targets nearby: Margaret Sheldon at Temple Grafton, of a branch of the great Sheldon family of Weston in the extreme south of the county, suffered losses on this occasion totalling £400; and the wealthy Richard Canning, of Foxcote Manor, Ilmington, when 'I had my house broke a little before the battle at Edge Hill'. Canning, along with his royalist neighbour, the rector of Ilmington, Dr Thomas King, was subsequently to be victim of repeated acts of plunder, in addition to suffering sequestration of his estate when he took up arms for the King, being forced to pay £100 in ransom, and finally being captured at nearby Lark Stoke House, home of his royalist neighbours the Brents, stormed by Warwick garrison troops in 1645. It is worth noting, however, one rare – indeed, almost unique – example of impeccable conduct by the parliamentary troops in Studley, where George Hunt insisted on recording for posterity that 'they used themselves well, & payed some smale tribute', even adding, generously, that he would claim 'nothinge for Divers other

Parliamt soldiers yt did nothinge, only quarter for one meale & soe passe away . . .'. At Morton Bagot, near Henley-in-Arden, Ann Canning was less lucky, reporting:

> There Lay att my house my Lord St. Johns, Lt. Coll. Essex & Major Andrewes, wth most part of theire Regimt, they payinge for nothinge but 2 sheepe . . . This Regimt Left behind them a lame souldier att my house . . . wch stayd wth me 8 or 9 weekes, & when he went away hee tooke a brasse pistoll, a new paire of bootes, a new shirt with many other odd thinges . . .

Essex's army, now joined by units from Lord Brooke's forces near Warwick, continued eastwards intent on relieving Banbury, now threatened by the King's advance. As usual, the passage of the troops did not pass unnoticed. There was renewed quartering, plundering and provisioning as far north as Henley, and at Stratford, where Essex left a defensive detachment. Snitterfield's vicar, Edward Nicholls, later volunteered to affirm on a solemn oath that he had lost half his hayrick to Essex's horse 'the Friday before Kinton fight', while twenty good sheep disappeared from the pastures of John Tewe and Thomas Boddington at Charlecote. Yet more villages were obliged to supply horses for Essex's carriages: Snitterfield had to provide them not only for the 10 miles to Kineton but, after the battle, for the further 20 miles to Daventry. Villagers' complaints of their horses being 'spoiled' by such service are among the most recurrent of grievances. Finally, the scattered parliamentary units converged ponderously on a whole cluster of unsuspecting south Feldon villages. Halford, Pillerton Priors, the Tysoes, Radway and Kineton were all heavily invaded 'upon ye Saturday before Kineton fight', with the usual provisioning demands on the neighbouring villages. At Halford, for example, John Baron received fifty men and horses, while the conspicuous Royalists William and Thomas Halford suffered nearer two hundred, or 'a great part of the Earle of Essex his army, before and after Kington fight'. Similarly, at Tysoe a whole of troop of soldiers quartered on the wealthy Francis Clarke alone, 'a Captaine and his Troope of horse whose name I know not' at William Bickerton's at Pillerton, and Essex's life guard at Chadshunt under Captain Draper. Essex himself, who always insisted on travelling with his shroud and coffin (though their presence is not recorded here), quartered at Kineton, the village constable later proudly reporting: 'The Earle of Essex with his whole Army at the Battell lay here from Saturday untill Tuesday night'.[4]

Unavoidably, the district experienced its first plunder and destruction during this long weekend, Kineton alone losing stolen coal, wood, and farmyard equipment such as ploughs, harrows, sheepracks, hurdles, pails, ladders and gates, with the odd hovel or cowhouse for good measure, to fuel the camp fires in the now frosty autumn nights. The effect of the soldiers' presence indoors was evidently equally devastating. In a typical example from Tysoe, for instance, Thomas Calloway:

> . . . had taken forth of his house by souldiers under the comand of the Earle of Essex bookes worth xxs., ten Cheeses worth xs., five yards of flannell worth ten shillings, two Coates worth xxs., provision spent in his house worth xxs., and seaven sheepe taken forth of his ground worth iiii pounds . . .

Solitary widows were no more exempt than anyone else, Hester Wootton of Tysoe losing:

> . . . twelve Cheeses worth viiis., halfe a pigg worth six shillings, foure yards of new Cloath worth xiiiis, a flaggon and foure sawcers worth iiis . . .

As villages to the east and west had already learnt to their cost, quarter and theft were usually inseparable. Ralph Ellis of Butlers Marston was not only obliged to provide quarter for twenty men and their horses for two days, losing thirty loads of carefully garnered hay in the process, but also 'lost att Kineton Fight by the parliament Soldiers 73 sheepe att 10d.p. sheep'. In view of such experiences, all solemnly recorded in the parish accounts, nothing appears more credible than the less 'official' traditional folk memories, like that of Essex's soldiers hammering on Oxhill church door during divine service, or those from Upper Tysoe of the theft of the housewife's newly-baked bread from the oven or her husband's hiding valuables by lowering them down the well in a pot until the soldiers had passed.

Meanwhile, several other parliamentary units had converged on Edgehill from other points of the compass: Lord Saye's from his ancestral Broughton in the south-east, where a tradition persists that troops slept on the eve of the battle, Lord Grey of Groby's from Leicestershire, quartering at Loxley, and Lord Willoughby of Parham's which, fresh from an encounter with Prince Rupert near Kings Norton on 17 October marched its

OXHILL CHURCH, WARWICKSHIRE. One of several churches near Edgehill reported to have been the scene of violent incidents. Oxhill's outspoken royalist vicar, Walwyn Clarke, was harassed by parliamentary soldiers for his frequent insults, and they are said to have hammered on the church door during a service, causing the parish clerk to rush out and be fatally wounded by a blow from a sword. Large numbers of Sir William Waller's forces camped in and around the village before the battle of Cropredy.
(Photo: Centre for Oxfordshire Studies)

800 horse and foot southwards, marking their passage through Henley-in-Arden's High Street by taking from John Horsley's (unspecified) premises his 'Case of Instruments belonginge to my pfession', and then liberally pillaging Stratford. Willoughby himself, apparently separated from his men for some unknown reason, billeted himself at Thomas Wilks's in Brailes, costing the yeoman over £2 on that single occasion as a prelude to much more substantial losses suffered later in the war. Also in the district was Sir William Waller who, whether at the battle or not, quartered at Tysoe with thirty of his men about this time, at the house of the wealthy William Browne. Spread out in this manner over a wide area and with several units still lagging far behind, aware that the Royalists were near but with no one quite clear what was happening, the scattered parliamentary forces dispersed to their makeshift quarters to await events.

THE KING'S CHALLENGE

The King's route to Edgehill was considerably more straightforward than Essex's, but is also less well documented, there being no royalist equivalent to the graphic pages of Nathaniel Wharton's journal or the parish books to suggest the impact of their troops in the local community. The King approached from Birmingham in a straight south-easterly direction, clearly intending to advance directly to London, or at least Oxford, and pausing at Sir Robert Fisher's at Packington. From Packington Prince Rupert ordered further supplies of arms and ammunition from the royal ordnance to equip his troop. The royal army, whose strength only recently, according to a parliamentary source, 'could not amount to the number of a just army', and was therefore 'obliged to shift from place to place since their inconsiderable numbers would scarce allow them to erect any garrison', was now much stronger. A mass rally was accordingly held at Meriden on 18 October, one royalist observer noting with satisfaction, 'the King came with the Foote to Meriden heath, where wee had the first appearance of an Armye'. The following day, as the Earl of Essex received the King's rejection of the parliamentary petition already referred to and set out from Worcester, Charles progressed to Kenilworth Castle, conveniently situated midway between the two hostile garrisons of Warwick and Coventry, with Rupert quartering at nearby Berkswell. The parish reports to the parliamentary authorities rarely itemize claims against the Royalists, but references by some local inhabitants, like those of Leek Wootton, to 'losses by the Kings army', probably relate to this time. The King then crossed the Avon, probably at Chesford Bridge, and proceeded to Southam on Friday 21 October, lodging, according to local tradition, at the Old Manor House on Market Hill. Charles's intention, according to a contemporary who had accompanied the royal party all the way from Shropshire, was to rest his army, since:

[we] received little rest since we came from Shrewsbury, and had not (by reason of ill provision of carriages and the uncharitableness of the country through which we marched) that supply of victuals which was necessary.

Coupled with Clarendon's comment about this hostile territory, in which the countryfolk concealed their provisions from the Royalists and 'the very smiths hid themselves, that they might not be compelled to shoe the horses', these observations suggest that the Royalists had their share of the same problems which beset the parliamentary forces.[5]

It was at Southam, only recently vacated by the parliamentary army, that the King, perhaps sensing the approach of a climax, decided to address his assembled troops in his longest, most eloquent and wide-ranging speech of the war so far (see Appendix B).

The manuscript of this major speech, not written in the King's own hand but apparently hastily drafted by a secretary, presents some minor variations from the version released for publication shortly after. The precise circumstances surrounding it remain obscure: why should Charles have decided to make it at this particular point in his march, outside an obscure Warwickshire market town 'in the bowells of oure kingdome'? Curiously, it has been virtually ignored by historians, in spite of its significant timing just before the first pitched battle of the English Civil War and the important clues it offers to the King's frame of mind at this decisive moment. Although the speech is an address to soldiers, it is clearly much more than a morale-boosting rallying cry and reveals a sombre, dignified monarch anxious to address wider issues, as well as to offer precise guidelines for the conduct of his recent recruits. He describes how his own attempts at conciliation have been mischievously thwarted by those prejudiced against him, rejects the false accusations of the disloyal, reiterates the justness and legality of his actions, and stresses his overriding concern for the continued freedom and happiness of his subjects. His present 'posture of defense' has been solely dictated by the need to defend the state from subversion and himself from personal danger, and in this he is supported not, as the rebels claim, by scheming foreigners but the 'prime gentry' of the land. He is particularly aware of the threat of a revolutionary coup, 'some greate violacon' by an 'innovated power.' Finally, turning to address his soldiers as individuals, he reminds them sternly – as the Earl of Essex had reminded his own forces recently at Worcester – of the importance of private morality and good conduct, before his eloquent peroration:

> . . . and wee doubte not but in tyme, just God will direct and protect us in all oure actions, and bring our weary labours to a good Conclusion, when all our sadnesse shallbee tourned into joy, the subiect possesse his free liberty uncontrolled, and the kingedome continue in firme peace for ever.

Although there is a hint of bitterness as well as resolve in its recital of grievances against the rebels, this is a speech whose tone is one of sorrow rather than anger as the King faces the realization that, in a phrase that recalls Sir William Waller's celebrated 'war without an enemy', 'whoesoever hath the victory, wee are sure to be the loser', for 'if such a warre must follow', many of his loyal men will die, having 'lesse assurance to preserve your lives now than ever you had'.

It is difficult, in the context of the two converging armies now separated by only a village or two since the last confident rally of the Royalists at Meriden, not to interpret this address, with its moving conclusion, as marking the final, reluctant acceptance on the King's part that war was no longer avoidable. Two days later it was Charles, often seen as indecisive and vacillating, who deliberately ordered his army to about-turn to engage the Earl of Essex's forces.

After leaving Southam the King continued southwards, with Prince Rupert making short excursions as far as Weston-under-Wetherley in one direction, to visit Thomas Morgan, a leading Catholic allied to the plundered Throckmortons of Coughton, and to Dunchurch in the other, where renewed royalist plundering was reported from Rugby, this time by the Earl of Northampton's regiment 'the day before Kineton fight'. After a day's march the Royalists dispersed to quarter in a spacious triangle of hamlets straddling the three county borders, with Rupert at Wormleighton at its northern apex and the southerly base extending from at least Ratley to Culworth, a good 10 miles or more. The villages in the central, Cropredy–Mollington area, all seem to have quartered substantial consignments of soldiers. With the King himself arrived at Edgcote on 22 October, a council of war was held and reconnaissance parties sent out to locate the enemy, while an attack on Banbury was contemplated and, according to one account, actually attempted but 'bravely resisted':

> The Townesmen . . . stood upon their Guard and fortified the Towne as well as they could upon a suddaine, by stopping up the passage with Loggs of wood, cutting downe trees, and laying them in the way with Cartes, Harrowes and other provision . . .

With all this activity few of the local inhabitants of the entire area from Stratford to Banbury and well beyond could have been unaware of the dangerous trend of events, all the more so that on this Saturday before Edgehill the King's own baggage train, presumably lagging behind the main force, was ambushed and comprehensively plundered by the enterprising Captain John Bridges, soon to become the governor of the Warwick Castle garrison. Acting on Lord Brooke's orders, and in league with 'divers well affected Country men [who] were Assistants to the Souldiers', Bridges swooped on the procession when it was imprudently 'comming by Warwick', presumably on the way from Kenilworth to Southam. Local participation in the exploit is confirmed by several entries in the churchwardens' accounts of nearby Offchurch, undated but almost certainly referring to the incident:

> Item: Paid to John Cox & Nicol. Gibs & Edward Arnold for goeing wth the Kings
>   Carriadge   £1 4 0
>
> Item: Paid for 2 fatt henns for the Kings Cart takers   £0 1 0

The captured booty, later alleged to contain items of almost fabulous value and reportedly including the King's engraved cutlery and jewels by the 'apronfull', was instantly transported back to Warwick and 'unladen out of the Carts in the outward and inward courts' of the castle. Prizes were distributed to encourage the garrison, but 'it being a time of trouble and some confusion' the consignment was left unguarded and immediately pilfered to such an extent that a cellar in the castle was set aside to house it and popularly dubbed 'the pillage house'. The picturesque details of this episode, Bridges' alleged embezzlement and his wife's cupidity in the affair, were later the subject of protracted legal wrangling still progressing through the courts over twenty years later, and are scattered profusely through the archives of the period. Undeterred, the King shortly afterwards ordered the manoeuvre which precipitated the battle, riding, according to tradition, from Edgcote to Edgehill along the minor road through Cropredy, Mollington and Warmington.

EDGEHILL. The battlefield today, looking west towards Kineton. (Photo: Banbury Museum)

The King's decision to postpone the planned attack on Banbury and to wheel round towards Warwick was dictated by news from parliamentary soldiers captured by Rupert as he rode into Wormleighton on the evening of 22 October. They gave the first accurate information of the precise whereabouts of Essex's army, at Kineton, intending to march to relieve Banbury from the royalist threat. This news was confirmed in the small hours of the morning by a further report that the Parliamentarians were marching 'with all Expedition' towards Banbury. The royalist army was therefore given orders to occupy the commanding position of Edgehill, and by daybreak on that Sunday morning, 23 October, the ever-eager Rupert had begun to assemble his cavalry on the escarpment, then bare of trees, the rest of the Royalists joining during the morning. Meanwhile, Essex's forces had indeed reached Kineton the previous night, and were continuing towards Radway; his army was incomplete, some units lagging behind as far as Evesham. Essex was clearly in no hurry to fight, and it would have been suicidal to charge the assembled Royalists uphill. He was in fact on his way to worship in Kineton church, about 8 a.m., when 'unexpectedly an Alarme came . . . that the [royalist] Enemy was advancing within two or three miles'. The Royalists continued to deploy, many moving downhill to Radway and beyond, so that by about 2 p.m. less than a mile separated the two armies facing each other, roughly equal in numbers, on a broad front between Radway and Kineton, on 'as fair a day as that season of the year could yield, the sun clear, no wind or cloud appearing'. The stage was set.

At some point the King precipitated matters by riding through his troops at the head of a retinue of officers and nobles, and preceded by a conspicuous scarlet standard, 'to encourage them to their Duty, . . . and spoke to them with great Courage and Chearfulness, which caused Huzzas thro the whole Army'. The royal progress halted while the King made a brief speech:

> Friends and souldiers, I look upon you with joy, to behold so great an armie as ever king of England had in these later times, standing with high and full resolutions to defend your king, the parliament, and all my loyall subjects. I thanke your loves offered to your king, with a desire to hazard your lives and fortunes with me, and in my cause, freely offered, and that in my urgent necessitie. I see, by you, that no father can relinquish and leave his son, no subject his lawfull king; but I attribute all this unto God, and the justnesse of my cause: Hee that made us a king will protect us. We have marched so long in hope to meet no enemy, we knowing none at whose hands we deserve any opposition; nor can our sunne-shining through the clouds of malignant envie suffer such an obscuritie, but that some influence of my regall authoritie, derived from God, whose substitute and supreame governour, under Christ, I am, hath begotten in you a confidence in my intentions. But matters are now not to be declared by words, but by swords. You all think our thoughts; endeavour to defend our person, while I raign over your affections as well as your persons. Now, therefore, know, my resolution is to trie the doubtfull chance of warre, which, with much grief, I must stand to, and endure the hazard. I desire not the effusion of blood, but since Heaven hath so decreed, that so much preparation hath been made, we must needs accept of this present occasion and opportunitie of gaining an honourable victory, and some addition of glory to our crowne; since reputation is that which doth guild over the richest gold, and shall be ever the endeavour of our whole raigne. The present action of this battell makes me speak briefly, and yet lovingly and royally unto you, our loyall armie. I put not my confidence in your strength or number, but confide, that though your king speaks unto you, and that with as much love and affection as ever king of England did to his armie, yet God, and the justnesse of our cause, together with the love I bear to the whole kingdome, must give you the best encouragement. In a word, your king bids you all be couragious, and Heaven make you victorious.

The speech clearly adopts a more urgent, practical tone than the previous Southam one, and it was probably its noisy reception which provoked Essex into opening fire directly towards the King's position, and a long but ineffectual preliminary artillery duel followed, forcing Charles to retire to a further, though still exposed, position, traditionally identified with Bullet Hill. Both sides were inexperienced, but the Royalists must have felt they held the moral high ground with the King's presence. Their morale, too, was high because of the recent victory at Powick and, not least, they had a virtually impregnable position. The fighting began in earnest in the early afternoon when Prince Rupert, after passing through his regiment giving precise tactical instructions, ordered a cavalry charge along the open ground following the main Knowle End–Kineton road, on the right-hand flank. Rupert's accelerating charge was brilliantly successful, unnerving Sir James Ramsey's parliamentarian wing who quickly turned 'and ranne away disorderly', with later allegations of prearranged treachery and desertion. Among those narrowly escaping death was Colonel Sir William Waller, soon to become one of Parliament's most competent generals, who lost a horse killed under him. A similar royalist success was recorded by Lord Wilmot on the opposite, left-hand flank, brushing aside Lord Fielding's regiment in another cavalry attack towards Kineton. The difficulty of halting and reassembling victorious cavalrymen intent on plunder and destruction, however, was the price paid for this initial success, and the royalist infantry in the centre was now left vulnerable to parliamentary counter-attack. They had advanced towards the parliamentarian ranks under the veteran Sir Jacob Astley, uttering

PRINCE RUPERT AT EDGEHILL, BY STANLEY BERKELEY. The Civil War was a favourite theme for Victorian painters and illustrators. Berkeley's spirited interpretation, an engraving based on an oil painting exhibited at the Royal Academy in 1884 as 'Prince Rupert, His Last Charge at Edgehill', is typical, but avoids the sentimentality and glamour of many period treatments. Although Rupert bears little resemblance to the now well-known portraits, and the snow is imaginary, the stark landscape matches the known facts of the Royalists' headlong charge across the meadows towards Kineton.

his celebrated prayer: 'O Lord, Thou knowest how busy I must be this day. If I forget Thee, do not Thou forget me!'

A prolonged and confused *mêlée* lasted through the afternoon, with the advantage swinging alternately between the two sides, both 'continuing to fire at one another even till night'. There was much heroism and much carnage in the hand-to-hand fighting, graphically described by Clarendon, during which the King ordered the young princes to be escorted to safety up the hill, Charles himself remaining bravely in the thick of the fighting. At one point Sir William Balfour, a dour Scots' veteran, made a brisk successful counter-attack uphill against the royalist gun positions, while in the centre the Royalists had been forced to give ground, the King's standard-bearer Sir Edmund Verney, the Knight Marshal of England, being killed and the standard seized from his lifeless hands. The Royalist Captain John Smith, involved in the incident at Kilsby already reported, was knighted the following day for heroically recapturing the banner. The royalist cavalry eventually began returning from Kineton, barely in time to save their severely harassed colleagues from likely annihilation by the Parliamentarians, during which time other parliamentary units were still arriving from afar, including John Fiennes's, Hampden's and Oliver Cromwell's. As dusk fell and a cold autumn night set in, exhaustion overtook both sides as the two dismembered armies camped on the field for the night, more or less in their original positions, tradition insisting that to leave the field of battle was to admit defeat. Both the King and Essex spent the night on the field. Food and fuel was short, dead and dying men and horses were scattered over the fields. The Parliamentarian Edmund Ludlow wrote after, that when finally he was given meat by villagers, 'I could scarcely eat it, my jaws for want of use having almost lost their natural faculty'. The contemporary eye-witness accounts often graphically describe the bitter cold, the horror and the desolation of this, the first major encounter of the war. Both sides claimed victory; but Essex had failed in his plans to block Charles's route to London and prevent the capture of Banbury, and the King's cavalry, unlike Essex's, was virtually intact. The following morning the Royalists further mauled the demoralized Parliamentarians straggling away in all directions north and west. Essex had, in fact, lost, and admitted it by marching away towards Warwick.

THE IMPACT OF EDGEHILL

The impact of Edgehill is an entire subject in itself, for the reverberations of the campaign extended in space well beyond the immediate locality and in time, far beyond the days or the month of the actual events. It was, in effect, a national

KINGSMILL MONUMENT, RADWAY CHURCH, EDGEHILL. A well-preserved example, unique in the district, of a near-contemporary memorial to an Edgehill casualty, the royalist captain Henry Kingsmill, of a Hampshire family with Warwickshire connections. The monument, erected in 1670, originally stood outside Radway old church, and was removed to its present location when the Victorian replacement church was built in 1866. See p. 65 for inscription. (Photo: author)

rather than a purely local conflict. The soldiers themselves, after all, far from being exclusively local men, had included substantial numbers of volunteers from all corners of the kingdom, the Royalists counting large Scottish and Welsh contingents in particular, as well as many others from Cheshire, Shropshire and the Marches, and named individuals from Exeter, Shoreditch and Hampshire, while the Parliamentarians included, as we have seen, a large body who had marched much of the way from London via Northampton, Warwick and Worcester and back, collecting further recruits on the way. There was also more than a sprinkling of foreigners. Many of these must have reported back their experiences at home, even if no more dramatic than those of the London carter Francis Pare, who lost his stock of four horses and two servants at Edgehill, or Robert Bennet from Exeter, who lost his seven 'good horses' worth at least £82. Equally, although the casualties included many anonymous local recruits, there were many from farther afield, bringing their quota of grief to distant homes, like Richard Chaloner, 'a bigge lad' from Myddle in Shropshire, who 'was never heard of afterwards', or Henry Kingsmill from Hampshire, commemorated in the moving tribute at Radway, erected years after by a proud mother:

> Here lyeth expecting ye second comeing of our blessed Lord & Saviour Henry Kingsmill Esq. second son to Sr Henry Kingsmill of Sidmonton in ye county of Southton Knt whoe serving as a Captain of foot under his Matie Charles the first of Blessed memory was at the Battell of Edgehill in ye yeare of our Lord 1642 as he was manfully fighting in behalf of his King and Country unhappily slaine by a Cannon Bullett, in memory of whom his Mother the Lady Bridgett Kingsmill did in ye forty sixth yeare of her Widdowhood in ye yeare of our Lord 1670 erect this Monument.
> 'I have fought a good fight I have finished my course henceforth is layde up for me a Crowne of righteousness'.

The Hampshire Kingsmills were connected with the Lucys of Charlecote and staunch Royalists. The young Cavalier had ridden a white horse on the hillside that day, conspicuous to the parliamentary guns.[6]

But it is with the local impact that we are most concerned, and this was dramatic, prolonged and physical enough to provide the ultimate, ineradicable proof in a spate of new, permanent place-names: King Charles's Road, Bullet Hill, Battleton Holt, King's Leys, Graveyard Coppice and, farther afield, Saddling Lane in Tysoe and the mysterious Prince Rupert's Tent near Mollington. No one in the vicinity could have remained unaware of events, alerted by the frenzy of activity, the depletion of village resources and, according to at least one parliamentary account, the firing of the ancient beacons:

> All the Beacons all about the Countreys thereabouts were set on fire, and great preparations were made in all places to assist [the Earl of Essex], and much company came with all speed from Warwick, Coventry and Oxford-shire to assist.[7]

Above all, however, the sounds of the battle itself carried far and wide in the still autumn air, clearly audible to the fidgety parishioners at Alcester, almost 20 miles away, listening with half an ear to their Sunday afternoon sermon. Richard Baxter, the visiting minister, was later to recall vividly, 'As I was preaching, the People heard the Cannon play, and when sermon was done the report was more audible', and to confess that next morning he could not resist saddling his horse to ride to see the battle-field for himself. Local stories of churchwardens rushing excitedly out of doors during the service exclaiming 'They're at it!' are perfectly plausible, as are many reports of innocent civilian casualties. At one church a tailor is reported to have run off 'to see the fun' and was mortally wounded, at Pillerton the village shoemaker ran off to see the battle, received a sabre cut and returned clutching his entrails, while at Oxhill it was the turn of the parish clerk to be the hero, killed by a blow from a heavy cavalry sword when Essex's troops hammered on the church door. Parliamentary reports of huge numbers of casualties among innocent onlookers at the battle are clearly wildy exaggerated, but are likely, nevertheless, to have a basis of unpalatable fact:

> . . . well nigh three parts of those who are slaine on our side were Waggoners, Carters, and poore unarmed people that stood in the Reere to see the sight, some of them old men, women and Children, a poor piece of valour for such a boasting enemy . . .

The news of the battle spread quickly. The accounts of the borough of Leicester, some 40 miles away, include payments of 6s. to men to ride to Coventry to send reports of what had happened.

Kineton, in particular, lived bitter, long, unforgettable days, with continuous disruption from quartering, plunder, destruction to property and worse, for once the battle was over, according to a royalist sympathizer:

> the Earle of Essex left behind him in the village 200 miserable maimed soldiers, without relief of money or surgeons, horribly crying out upon the villiany of those men who corrupted them,

and some of these, in persistent parliamentary reports, may indeed have fallen easy victims to Prince Rupert's ruthlessness. Few nearby villages can have been without their share of wounded, and 'charges with a maymed soldier after Kineton fight' becomes a recurrent item in the parish accounts at this time. Long after, memories remained vivid. Hester Whyte, in 1646, petitioned Parliament for relief for having cared for the sick and wounded after Edgehill, using her own meagre resources, before losing her husband two years later at the siege of Banbury:

> [She] did ymediatly after Kineton fight take upon her ye care of 2 of ye Parlyamts souldiers there maymed whoe contynued at her house in great misery (by reason of theire woundes) for ye space of three months at ye least, she being constrayned many tymes to be up night & day with them, wch was not only a greate trouble to her but, in respect of her tendernes to ye Parlyamts freinds in that case, a great charge alsoe, she laying out her owne moneys to supply their prsent necessytyes. And· further . . . her husband [Daniel] was kylled in the Parlyamt service at ye seige of Banbury Castle: Anno dni 1644, wherby she is left destitue [sic] and comfortles. Your poore petitioner therefore humbly prayeth . . . your help to releeve her whoe in ye tyme of her abylytie willingly afforded both her paines & cost for ye help of such distressed.

As always, estimates of precise casualties vary, but they were evidently substantial and left a permanent mark on the landscape, for not only were there the Edgehill gravepits themselves, containing in the estimate of one local antiquarian vicar 1,200 bodies buried, according to Dugdale after 'strict enquiry from the adjacent Inhabitants', by the villagers themselves, but others who died in nearby villages or whose corpses were carried away for burial. One wounded soldier reached Newbold Pacey before succumbing, the parish register noting: 'A Souldier wounded in that great battell betwene ye King and the parliament Oct. 23 was buried Oct. 29'. Local burial registers are surprisingly silent on Civil War casualties, but one notable exception is Warmington's:

> The Battell was fought by our Sovraigne Lord King Charles and Thearle of Essex the three and Twentieth Daie of October beeing Sabbath Day Ano Dom 1642, ptely beetweene Radwaie and Kington. Richard Sannes Captaine of a Foote companie, a gentleman of Worcestershire, was buried in Warmington Churchyard the Four and Twentieth daie of October Ano Dom 1642. Alexander Gourdon, a Scotsman, was buried the Five and Twentieth Daie of October Ano Dom 1642. Also Seven others were buried in Warmington Churchyard shortly after, whose names I know not; and it is reported that one or two more were buried within the fields and precincts of Warmington aforesaid.

In the hilltop churchyard the Scottish soldier's worn headstone still carries its simple epitaph: 'Here lieth the body of Alexander Gourdin, Captaine, Buried the 25 Day of October Anno Domini 1642'.[8]

Naturally, with attention focusing on the high drama of the battle, few observers thought to comment on more mundane matters like the disruption caused to farming, but this must have been severe for at least a short period. The battle-field was rich farmland, partly ploughed, part open, with ditches and a hedge or two crossing it and sheep farming, barns and enclosures nearby, and occasional incidental comments juxtapose the battle with the concerns of those attempting to safeguard their livelihood and uphold the norms of civilized behaviour. Richard Gillet, the servant of John Danvers of Upton and the area's High Constable, later recalled accompanying his master during the battle, 'to get his sheep in safety, and did meet some souldiers that had plunderd two horses or mares which he did consider were some of his neighbours, and did Inforce the said souldiers to leave the said horses . . . .'.

It might be thought that once the dust of the battle had settled the countryside would quickly resume its former peace. Nothing could be farther from the truth. For one thing, there was no immediate withdrawal, the ragged armies remaining facing each other all the next day before slowly and chaotically dispersing. Standard accounts usually state that Essex's forces 'fell back to Warwick' and the King to Banbury, but as, in fact, few units of either side remained intact, the parliamentary forces in particular had been dismembered, the cavalry had ranged far and wide, and there were mass desertions, it will be suspected that the reality was somewhat different. With Essex and all his commanders 'and many others' arrived in Warwick 'upon Munday night', disciplining the rest at Kineton must have been impossible, and the whole district was anything but quickly vacated. The parliamentary army in particular was in a pitiful state. Those fit enough to do so either deserted in such numbers that Essex was obliged to write wheedling letters to call back to duty those he diplomatically described as having 'gone to visit friends', or scattered haphazardly in all directions, cold and hungry and therefore plundering, loitering in all the nearby villages for weeks: Kineton, Halford, Pillerton, the Tachbrooks and many others, as well as Stratford and Warwick and beyond. The harrying of Rupert's cavalry seems not have prevented more looting as they fled, nor their abusing the hospitality of Giles Eliot, the Tysoe alehousekeeper, nor their quenching their thirst, according to tradition, at the tavern at Whatcote. The sick and wounded lingered even longer, left to their own devices in alien billets, dependent on the compassion of the cottager's wife when not being attacked by hostile villagers as they sought relief. Offchurch was only one of many villages full of wounded, receiving relief from the churchwardens' petty funds. Some, unable to fend for themselves, were dragged off to the rudimentary surgery at Warwick; so many parliamentary wounded resulted from this first major encounter of the war that the carts recently captured from the King's train were requisitioned 'for the releife of maimed souldiers which were to ye number of 3 or 4 hundred sent to Warwicke to be cared for and cured of their wounds', and almost as many were transported to Coventry. A year later hundreds were still being cared for in Warwick Castle, petitions being sent to Parliament by Richard Lacy, the bailiff of Warwick, and John Bryan, the garrison chaplain, for help in relieving them. Not all of those fleeing were infirm or destitute, however. Forty-three sheep mysteriously disappeared from William Elliott's pastures at Bishops Tachbrook immediately after the battle, while Clement Throckmorton claimed that the high-handed governor of Warwick Castle, John Bridges, had imprisoned him for refusing to hand over £330 left in a tavern in Haseley or Hatton by soldiers fleeing from Edgehill, which he had claimed by right as lord of the manor.

Though it would be quite impossible to chart the many routes taken by the parliamentary soldiers after Edgehill, when 'Essex stole by other roads as many of his army as he could', it is abundantly clear from the parish accounts that not all took the road to Warwick; some, indeed, are found in diametrically-opposed directions. Once the immediate aftermath of the battle had passed there was once again the task of transporting surviving goods from the neighbourhood, involving a further supply of villagers' carts. Wealthy parliamentary gentry like Anthony Stoughton of Warwick could not be expected to object to lending aid, and having already assisted Kenilworth parliamentary garrison on 12 September and helped Essex's forces when marching to Worcester now did so again when carts were needed to retrace the road in the opposite direction, to Northampton. But many inhabitants of much more modest status were called upon, not only for the long-enough Warwick–Daventry transit in November, like the Snitterfield case already mentioned, but for much longer journeys, like an inhabitant of Wappenbury who was obliged to supply three men and five horses 'wch went to Dunstable wth the Earle of Essex his Cariages psentlie after Kyneton fighte'. It is doubtless on one such journey that incidents like that traditionally associated with Willoughby occurred, inconsequential enough to suggest authenticity, when parliamentary troops passing through the village fastened a rope round the ancient cross with the intention of pulling it down, and were only dissuaded from doing so by a plea from the vicar. Plundering expeditions too were becoming routine, often more ambitious and highly organized by those with the means to make them. In one such typical of others, the mansion of the influential catholic landowner William Sheldon, at Weston, Long Compton, was pillaged shortly after Edgehill by a parliamentary troop of horse from Warwick, while a similar contingent from Kenilworth, now in parliamentary hands, even had the leisure to drive an entire herd of Sheldon's cattle well over 20 miles back to their garrison to replenish their stock. Essex himself had time to issue warrants to seize the goods of prominent local Royalists, and Richard Chamberlaine of Temple House, Nuneaton, Thomas Morgan at Weston-under-Wetherley and Richard Knightley at Offchurch were all plundered, according to the later testimony of Benjamin Ash, an officer in Major Peter Burgoyne's company at Coventry. On another occasion, the thirteenth-century chapel at Burton Dassett, lovingly restored as recently as 1632 by Lady Mary Wotton of Northend before fleeing the district at the outbreak of war, was wrecked. As for the Royalists, they would doubtless have conducted themselves similarly, had they not been able to focus their immediate efforts on capturing the local prize of Banbury. As it is, Sir Peter Temple's house at Burton Dassett was plundered by a royalist troop, many deserted and 'the greatest part of them stragled into the neighbouring villages to get victuals', some according to Clarendon, being assaulted by hostile villagers. Others collected as much parliamentary booty as they could and entrusted local activists, like William Loggins of Butlers Marston, with the task of scavenging for much-needed arms and useful salvage from the strewn battlefield.[9]

With its dramatic escarpment sweeping down to the Kineton meadows as the soldiers huddled round the hillside campfires in the frosty night, Edgehill has inspired more than the usual crop of picturesque vignettes. Some are clearly apocryphal, like the story (curiously, from a parliamentary source) of Cromwell hiding from the battle in Burton Dassett church tower and escaping by swinging down the bell-rope and fleeing across the fields. Some remain mysterious to this day. Is the earthwork near Preston-on-Stour the burial-mound of Edgehill horses, as is said? Others are much more authenticated: the Welsh, 'so brave, that they had no Arms but Pitchforks and suchlike Tools, and many only with good Cudgels, yet they went down the Hill as eagerly to fight as the

ARLESCOTE HOUSE, EDGEHILL. Largely rebuilt after the Civil War, the house is traditionally identified as that to which the King sent the two young princes for safety during the battle of Edgehill. A pane of glass carrying a scratched seventeenth-century signature, 'Charles' (not *in situ*), said to be that of the future Charles II, survives. (Photo: Banbury Museum)

best armed'; the Earl of Essex among his men on the moonlit battlefield, who 'about midnight . . . when the mone went downe . . . came out of the fild into a howse and refreshed himselfe by the fyer syde'; the extreme cold, so that 'having nothing to keep me warm but a sute of iron, I was obliged to walk about all night, which proved very cold by reason of a sharp frost'; the celebrated old physician William Harvey, reading his pocket Virgil while protecting the young Princes under a hedge; the young Prince Charles scratching his name on a pane of glass in nearby Arlescote House; old Sir Jacob Astley's memorable prayer . . . But among such stories few are more picturesque and human than the rarely recorded one of a poor corporal of dragoons, Jeremiah Stone. Wounded at Edgehill – though not seriously enough to prevent his stealing a bag of money from a dead comrade – he made his way to Warwick and lodged at the Anchor tavern at the beginning of November, entrusting his money to his hostess for safe-keeping during his convalescence. A fortnight later he was sufficiently recovered to reclaim his money, whereupon the landlady and her husband denied ever having received it, and reviled him 'as farre as the uttermost of her vaine Rethoricke could stretch'. Swords were unsheathed and violence committed before the soldier was arrested, tried and condemned as a common criminal. The innkeeper, however, perjured himself twice in court: 'I would, quoth he, the Devill would fetch me away now presently, Body and Soule, before you all, if I sweare unjustly.' The narration only now deviates from what had been an entirely credible report. Suddenly, the innkeeper was:

> . . . carried forth visibly over the Market place, so that his Body was never seene againe, Nothing being left behind but a terrible stinke as a witnesse [of] an uncleane Person. The Bench being all amazed, rise; th Hostesse, hearing of this unhappy disaster, confest the Fact, and restored the money to the souldier.

Told by a shoemaker who swore on oath to have been an eye-witness, this story is of the very stuff from which the Grimm brothers would weave their *Household Tales* a century and a half later.

In so many ways, therefore, the Edgehill campaign constituted a unique experience as 'the first large field of bloud in these civill warres'. Certainly traumatic at local level, it provided a climax to the string of interconnected dramatic events that summer at Warwick, Coventry, Southam and Banbury, shattering the peace of the broad Warwickshire acres in many a village from Dunchurch to Alcester for many weeks, presenting substantial material losses to many, and unquantifiable fear and insecurity to as many others. The local community could not easily or quickly forget these events, for the establishment of royalist garrisons at Banbury and Broughton in the immediate aftermath, to challenge the parliamentary ones at Warwick, Kenilworth and Coventry, added to the fortification of many private houses like Compton Wynyates and Coughton, meant that south Warwickshire had in effect become a militarized zone. There was, too, an unpleasant first anniversary. On Sunday 22 October 1643 the vicar of Stoneleigh, Edward Mansell, was interrupted in his preaching by rowdy troopers led by Corporal Bowyer of Warwick garrison. They discharged pistols at the church porch and windows and broke into the service, insulting the vicar in his pulpit 'to the great affrightment of all the People'. Significantly, parliamentary comment does not deny the events themselves, though naturally it puts a different gloss on them.

But perhaps the most startling evidence of the unique extent to which the experience of Edgehill stamped itself on the collective memory is afforded by the almost instant creation of a supernatural dimension to the battle. Barely two months after, shortly before Christmas, detailed accounts of ghostly noises and apparitions were reported by countrymen and travellers, and were soon substantiated on oath by a local JP and parliamentary minister and publicized both nationally and in private correspondence:

> There are now divers reports of strange sights seen, and strange noyses heard at Edgehill, where our last battle was fought; in the place wher the Kings army stood, terrible outcries; wher the Parliaments, music and singing psalms . . .

The King himself, by this time at Oxford, was sufficiently perturbed to send an investigating team which in its turn corroborated the stories. At parish level many other traditions grew up, but are known only locally and are now fast disappearing. At Brailes, for example, one story, already largely forgotten, relates to sounds of fleeing soldiers heard clashing at the lonely Traitors Ford. As Edgehill is directly linked with this spot by the ancient, long-disused trackway known as Ditchedge Lane such a legend, like many others of its kind, may indeed relate to a real incident now irretrievably buried in the folk memory.

Many further sightings of ghostly figures at Edgehill have been alleged over the centuries since that winter of 1642, and the subject continues today to exert a powerful hold on the imagination, from occultists to the modern poet-historian, Gladys Mary Coles:

After Edgehill, 1642

1 Villagers Report 'The Late Apparitions'

A December Saturday, star-clear
at Kineton. Three months since the battle,
the village collects itself – Christmas
perhaps a demarcation, a control
in the blood-letting. Yet on the ridge
of Edge Hill, the night resounds,
armies grinding one against the other
re-enacting the action, re-dying the deaths.

Shepherds hear trumpets, drums –
expect a visitation of holy kings with retinues.
Instead, the spectral soldiers strike,
icy night skies crack with cries,
steel clashing and the sput of muskets.
A knot of Kineton men watch, witness;
Samuel Marshall, the Minister, says
the Devil's apparitions seize the dead.

2 A Ghost Speaks

I am unplanted, my world this waste –
the heath where bone was split, undressed of flesh,
where arteries unleashed their flood, the colour
of death. What is the colour of honour? The blue
in which we dissolve into air? the white of ashes?
Can I be woven into braids of her hair, my lady,
or exist in the quick of my son's fingernails?
I, who carried the Standard, once drove the plough,
turning up earth, the harvest of worms. Now I envy
the seeds in the furrow, their dark cradle.

My blood is this Midlands field, this hacked hedgerow
where I lie, hearing the drumbeat of the dead,
corpses strewn rotting, graveless.
I glide up and down these rows of human manure,
the faces of soldiers like fallen cameos.
Here is Sir Edmund Verney, Thomas Transome –
they look skywards, lolling near my own wistful face.
Sir Edmund is grimacing slightly as he did in life,
Thomas Transome's skull a broken eggshell.

The brittle linnet flies from me. Dry leaves relinquish
their hold on twigs. A hare sits motionless, watching,
listening to last groans forever in the wind.

I see a troop of Horse on the skyline – Parliament's.
They charge our pikemen; now they vanish
like moving cloud-shadows across the field.
I cannot follow the clouds; I am chained to my carcass
hovering, as others are, above their unburied selves.

3 A Dragoon Observes Colonel Cromwell

Like a falcon from the gauntlet, he throws off these deaths.
He tells us 'Smile out to God in Praise', for his is the sword
of the Lord. I see his horse, piebald with blood. [10]

In retrospect, Edgehill seems to constitute a watershed. Before it, war might always have been avoided; after it, both sides were aware that no quick or painless solution was possible, and settled down to a long struggle. For the civilian population the war had finally come, stark and clear. In many Midland counties local administration was breaking down as anarchy spread to the civil courts. On 4 October the Warwick Quarter Sessions started late when the two long-serving, elderly JPs, Sir Thomas Holt and John Lisle, were delayed from arriving at Shire Hall, only to have the proceedings violently disrupted when within the hour:

> . . . the Lord Rochford entered Warwick with 800 [parliamentary] soldiers, and the noise of the drums and trumpets (which came with him) so disturbed the court that the court was instantly adjourned to the Swan, which was so filled with his Lordship and his soldiers that nothing could be done there.

The court would not resume until 1645. As Anthony Fletcher writes, 'violence was beginning to overlay customary standards of civilized behaviour':

In the six months following Edgehill the noise of war could no longer be ignored. It reached some families suddenly and ferociously with the arrival of plundering troops, others more surreptitiously with a knock on the door by a constable demanding money or supplies . . . Garrisoning of towns and manor houses and mustering of volunteer companies, minor skirmishes and simmering factionalism were the characteristics of the local war in this period.

Not surprisingly, the contemporary ballad-writers now turned to the war as their principal subject in countless street-rhymes and doggerel verses, typified by this 'Godly exhoration to this Distressed Nation' lamenting the England of November 1642:

> When as the Kingdome is divided
> And by the sword of the cause decided,
> When people for meer trifles quarrell,
> And make a Pulpit of a barrell;
> When people run from place to place,
> Unreverently Gods church deface;
> When dire destruction runs before,
> And brings bad tidings to our door;
> When 'arme, arme, arme' is all the crie
> To add griefe to our misery;
> When armed men each day we meet,
> In every lane and every street;
> When as our streets are chained streight,
> And Ordnance plac'd at every gate;
> 'Tis time for us to crie and call,
> 'Good Lord, have mercy on us all!'[11]

CHAPTER FIVE

WINTER TRIALS

THE CAPTURE OF BANBURY

With his army scarcely more intact than Essex's, but feeling himself the victor at Edgehill, the King issued graciously-worded pardons to the rebel rank-and-file from both Edgehill and Aynho immediately after the battle, and published a lengthy and wide-ranging political 'Declaration to all his loving subjects after his late victory', justifying his recent actions and refuting once again Parliament's accusations of wishing to reinstate catholicism and deny Parliament's traditional freedoms. The short march to Aynho took him via Middleton Cheney, crossing the ancient Banbury Lane, near which a field called Kings Stile traditionally marks the spot where Charles refreshed himself with cake and wine supplied by Chacombe Priory. At Aynho the King spent the night at the great house, 'a very fair, goodly building wherein the King himself lodged after the battle of Edgehill', where the pointed absence of its owner, John Cartwright, already marked out as a parliamentarian troublemaker, was ominously commented upon and noted for future action. But the King's attention was now focused on the capture of Banbury, the original project already ordered on 23 October but postponed when Essex's challenge at Kineton could no longer be avoided. It was indeed time for him to check Banbury's insolence. Its long-standing puritanism, its sullen and disloyal inhabitants who had recently opposed the Earl of Northampton over the magazine and now the King himself, its intolerable demeanour as the rebellious Fiennes's family stronghold and its present parliamentary garrison were all an affront. Adding insult to injury, the town had only the previous week injudiciously sent to London a 'great butt' filled with plate and money collected in the town for Parliament's use.[1]

Although the King's decision to delay his advance south in order to capture Banbury has always been criticized as inept, it made some sense militarily. Far from being a 'Place of very little Consideration', it was a strategically-important position near the major supply route from the south-east along Watling Street to Northampton, Daventry and Coventry, the route already used to good effect by successive parliamentary convoys, besides being an important road junction in its own right. Later, the parliamentary chronicler Sprigge certainly had no doubt of:

> the commodiousnesse of its situation . . . . as lying but eighteene miles North from Oxford, and in such a convenient place as gave it a command into divers other Counties, viz. Northamptonshire, Warwickshire, etc., from out of which it gathered large contributions for Oxford,

while another Parliamentarian made the same point more succinctly, 'Oxford cannot want while Banbury flourishes'. The parliamentary commander Whetham went further, stressing that control over Banbury was not only vital for Oxford but opened up 'liberty of Trade to London from many parts'. While deciding to besiege Banbury Castle, however (considered by some of his advisers, according to Clarendon, inadvisable with winter coming on), the King sent a force to capture Lord Saye's Broughton Castle which, after initial resistance, surrendered:

> From [Banbury] some part of the army being directed to quarter at the Lord Say's house, repaired thither, but were foolishly denied by the persons trusted there, who soon apprehended their folly and submitted; and received a Colonel of the Brigadoes into the house, who according to his Majesty's command, took care to prevent any disorder there by the soldiers, though they found much arms and one of his Majesty's own waggons of munition there.

While there is no clear evidence, it has usually been supposed that the destruction of buildings in the service court, the second gateway and bridge, and the repairs to the main gatehouse in 1655, were occasioned by this siege.

Although this action too was criticized as pointless, in context it also made sense. While very different from the impregnable Warwick, Broughton was nevertheless a stoutly-built moated fortress and, as such, as Compton Wynyates was to prove, might easily have been transformed into a valuable garrison at a time when success at Banbury was not assured. Clearly too, it presented a significant boost to royalist morale, impaired by battle casualties and widespread desertions, less because of the useful arms find than through its symbolic value as the rebel leader's principal lair. It is unclear to what extent it had been fortified by Lord Saye. One contemporary source says it had not, and the traditional story of sacks of wool being suspended by hooks to protect the walls from enemy shot certainly seems to suggest a degree of amateurish improvisation. However, in spite of the Royalists' denials of 'disorder', the Cavaliers seem to have had the satisfaction of plundering comprehensively, as Saye himself certainly claimed the following week. Having the previous year 'ploughed up a good Part of his ancient Pasture Grounds to raise Portions for his Younger Children, and to pay his Debts', it is reported:

> . . . his house have [sic] been pillaged, neere Banbury, and his Parke broken open, and all his Deere droven out, with other great spoiles to his nurseries and young trees.

Long after, Lord Saye was unwilling to let the matter drop, petitioning the House of Lords in 1645 that, having initially lent £1,000 to the parliament cause, he had subsequently sustained very great losses throughout the war on his Oxfordshire and Gloucestershire estates, beginning soon after Edgehill, when the Royalists seized all his 'very great Crop of Corn and Wood, his stock, household furniture, to a great Value', while 'defacing, tearing and burning his principal House at Broughton'. He had received, he stressed pointedly, no reimbursement from the parliamentary authorities, even though he had been reduced to selling his plate and borrowing. The Lords recommended speedy compensation . . .[2]

With the restless Rupert frustrated by the King's more cautious elders in his ambition to mount a potentially-decisive lightning strike against undefended London, this period added another strand to the growing Rupert myth. A picturesque contemporary story relates how the young Prince, chafing at the delay at Banbury, was overtaken by a heavy shower when riding alone near Warwick. Entering a tavern to shelter, he exchanged clothes with a cabbage-net seller and sold his wares in Warwick market before returning to the alehouse to restore the borrowed clothing, having systematically reconnoitred 'many passages in the town' in his disguise. Finally, he revealed his identity to the astonished company and promised retribution on the King's enemies before riding off.

The capture of Banbury Castle itself, on 27 October, proved a valuable windfall after Edgehill, with important consequences for the entire district for the rest of the war. Although, as usual, contemporary accounts vary considerably in detail, all agree that, whether through treachery, cowardice or both, it proved surprisingly easy and painless. One typical parliamentary account reports that the King 'had free entrance without any opposition' through the betrayal of the commander, in spite of the Earl of Essex's promise that relief was forthcoming within hours, while another speaks scathingly of the surrender's false pretext of being 'not sufficiently provided for a siege'. Whitelock also agrees that it surrendered 'without blows', adding interestingly that two foot regiments and a troop of horse defected to the King. Clarendon's well-known royalist account substantially agrees, claiming that although the parliamentary garrison was certainly strong enough to defend it, the defenders surrendered 'upon the first shot made' and 'fairly and kindly delivered the place', with half the garrison defecting. The usual charges of 'treachery' – in retrospect suggesting nothing more evil than the fluid loyalties of uncommitted pawns in an unwanted conflict – were repeated more than once in the days following, as in this private letter:

> I shall not need to relate particulars, you have heard of the misery of a poore Towne which was betrayed by those that were appointed to keep it, . . . but we were forsaken by those we trusted, and now have experience what it is to bee under the command of such mercilesse Cavaliers.

Almost as important as the capture of this strategic point was the Royalists' psychological victory. Clarendon comments that they 'had again recovered their appetite to action', and that in the public perception, 'the King's army was looked upon as victorious'.

As winter approached the King moved south to Woodstock and finally, on 29 October, to Oxford, where the court was established, leaving the Earl of Northampton as 'Our Governour and Commander in Chieff in our Towne of Banbury for the safety and security of Our sayd Towne and the Countyes adjacent'. On reaching Woodstock one of his first acts, on 28 October, was to order the total destruction of Banbury Castle in case 'the Lord Say putt in some to defende yt':

> Wee finding that the Castle of Banbury is and hath been of late made use of not onely as a Receptacle for Rebells and disturbers of ye peace of this Our Kingdome but for ye imprisoning of such of Our

good Subjects as have faithfully served us, have therefore given Order for ye present demolishing and slighting of ye said Castle. And Wee doe hereby Declare and Order that all such persons of ye said Towne . . . or elsewhere as shall assist in ye present demolishing . . . shall have for their paines the materialls of the said Castle, and free liberty to carry and dispose of ye same for their proper benefit.

This order was evidently countermanded, presumably because a reassessment of the situation concluded that Banbury was too valuable an acquisition to be dispensed with: situated in enemy territory, it would neutralize parliamentary influence over a wide area and provide a valuable protective outpost to Oxford itself. The permanent garrison which the Royalists now established at Banbury proved indeed, from this date until its recapture by Parliament in 1646, the major strategic asset for the Royalists north of Oxford, dominating an important regional crossroads, constantly threatening parliamentary movements and, not least, providing a vital tax-gathering centre in the three counties it overlooked. The Royalists therefore settled in, first searching the town. The semi-official royalist account, possibly written by the gentlemanly Dugdale, makes the proceedings sound innocuous enough:

His Majesty sent some of His principall Officers to discover and bring away all such Armes and Ammunition as were found in the Towne, and to take up upon Tickets all Woollen cloath, stockings, shooes and victualls for the accommodation of His souldiers, forbidding all manner of plundring, and permitting only one Regiment to enter and remain in the Town that night.[3]

Certainly the King himself attempted repeatedly to minimize the suffering caused to the local population, distinguishing clearly between innocent civilians and rebellious activists. Even the latter were to be treated humanely, the seizure of their goods being strictly limited to such as contributed to the war effort, as the following signed warrant to the Earl of Northampton makes clear:

Right trusty and well-beloved Cosen . . . We greet you well, and do hereby give you full power and authority for us . . . to search for, seize upon, and take into your custody all such money, plate, arms, ammunition, and horses . . . remaining in the custody of any person or persons . . . maintaining the war against us . . . Straitly charging you not to take from or seize on any goods herein specified, but of or from such person or persons only as have contributed to the war against us, and not to take from such persons any other their goods or household stuffs, but of such kind herein mentioned . . .

The problem, never resolved by either side, was of course one of enforcement in the near-anarchy that reigned in the various regiments and the flouting of such orders by even senior commanders like Prince Rupert who did not necessarily share such a code of conduct. As it was, the activities of the Banbury Royalists soon became as notorious as those of the Warwick Parliamentarians. One of their first chosen victims was from the disaffected Cartwrights of Aynho. In the absence of the lord of the manor, John Cartwright – such was the logic of war – his elderly mother Mary had her house at Astrop destroyed and was physically assaulted before being imprisoned in Banbury Castle for nine months. In the weeks and months following, too, plundering became an almost continuous activity, often carried out by flying cavalry units at considerable distances. Horses were particularly sought after: at Hillmorton at this period William Bromitch lost three worth £13 to Prince Rupert's men, John Compton three worth £16 and a further three worth £15 to Sir William Compton's soldiers. James Pettiner's shop at Hillmorton was also broken into twice by royalist raiders, losing £40 worth of unspecified goods. Rugby too, already frequently victimized by Lord Dunsmore's troops on their home ground, was comprehensively ransacked. One inhabitant, Richard Newton, identified the culprits as both the Earl of Northampton himself and his son, Sir William Compton, the new governor of the Banbury garrison, who between them plundered him 'thertene tymes', causing him losses totalling £304. The parliamentary commander Colonel Whetham's later description of the Banbury garrison as a 'den of theeves' seems hardly an exaggeration.

CONSOLIDATION AT BANBURY

The capture of Banbury was unquestionably a major royalist achievement. Its consolidation and maintenance were, however, far from painless, and the Earl of Northampton spent what were to be the last weeks of his life confronting a whole series of interrelated problems, military, financial and organizational. Militarily, the problem had an almost reassuring familiarity. Although the Earl of Essex had now moved south, via Northampton, Woburn and St Albans, to London, there remained a constant threat to the Banbury Royalists from the two equidistant parliamentary garrisons at Warwick and Northampton. More unforeseen and more unmanageable, however, was the permanent financial burden of maintaining the garrison, compounded by repeated demands from the King for contributions to equip the growing royal armies, to say nothing of the considerable expenses of the court at Oxford. The Banbury garrison certainly proved costly. Northampton claimed that the district allotted him for the collection of 'contributions' was inadequate to support the four regiments needed to garrison Banbury satisfactorily. The most he could raise was £450 per week, whereas maintaining his troops, he claimed, cost £536. Ignoring this, the King persisted in making imperative demands on Northampton and his other trusted allies:

> Whereas in this time of so general distraction we are forced to expect the support and supplies of our subjects towards the maintenance of their Religion, Laws, Liberties and Peace; and whereas we have appointed you our governor of our town of Banbury, and have remitted to your care the defence and securing both of that place and the country adjoining: We do hereby further require you to use your utmost industry with our well-affected subjects in our counties of Northampton and Warwick to persuade them to contribute horses, arms, ammunition, plate or money to us for our assistance and defence . . .

By Christmas the royal finances, as well as the condition of the army, were both precarious enough to oblige the King to address a personal plea to his assembled lords at Oxford to help prevent the army from disintegrating and enable the war to be pursued:

> till such time as we shall gaine power to enlarge our quarters, [since] . . . common reason tells us that our excursions being stopt and our dragooners so farre impoverished, it will be a means to increase mutines.

The gravity of the situation, however, was such that the Earl of Northampton, acting as spokesman 'in the name of all the lords', had no alternative but to deny the King, reminding him 'with what willingnesse and allacrity we have exhausted our Treasure to the ruine of our present Estates, having disbursed all the Coyne that wee could rayse upon our Lands or credits', and pointing out that effective parliamentary authority in much of the district had meant that since the outset, 'we have received no Rents, our Tennants being injoyned the contrary'. Northampton was, in fact, experiencing great difficulty in collecting contributions and rallying tenants to the King's cause, to such a degree that he was soon forced to bargain for their loyalty by making concessionary offers to waive the age-old rights of lord of the manor to any joining him at Banbury who might later die in his service: 'I myself, nor my heirs or assigns, shall or will take any benefit thereby'.

As for the army, the King was clearly not exaggerating when he described its condition as 'very deplorable'. The faithful Sir Lewis Dyve, already wounded at Powick Bridge but present at both Edgehill and the capture of Banbury, addressed emotional pleas to Prince Rupert for urgent measures:

> May it please Your Highness: Our troops are in extreme necessity, many of them having neither clothes to cover their nakedness, nor boots to put on their feet; and not money amongst them to pay for the shoeing of their horses; the sight whereof hath made me so sensible of their misery, as I have taken the boldness to become an humble suitor to your highness . . . to move his Majesty that some speedy course may be thought upon whereby to relieve their wants. Otherwise it will be a hard matter, if not impossible, to hold them long together in that condition they are now in . . .

Matters had not impoved a fortnight later when the King, almost apologetically, sent Banbury unpaid, ill-equipped and ill-fed reinforcements under Colonel Herbert, the royal pleasure being that the Earl of Northampton 'take care of them . . . as you shall be able to afford them for the present'. Adequately provisioning the troops in winter was a constant headache; at Christmas the King had added a post-script in his own handwriting to a letter ordering the fortification of Banbury: 'I desyre you to Vitale the Castell with all expedition, and for this service if the country will not fech it in, you must make your Horse doe it'. That the country people were less than cooperative is clear from a further royal message to Northampton on 10 January:

> We understand that divers inhabitants in the country near you who have obtained from us protections, pretend thereby to be exempt from allowing any provisions or contributions for support of our Army. Wherefore we will you to let them know that the protections given them are to preserve them from plundering, not to exempt them from . . . maintaining of our Horse and foot in a requisite and fitting Proportion. And therefore you are not to spare any of them upon any such pretence . . . and to punish those that are refractory.

Nor was the royal army supplied with even that most basic, defining commodity of the soldier, ammunition. Colonel Herbert's reinforcements were to use Banbury's meagre quota, 'if your store of ammunition will afford . . . a convenient proportion'. Any available metal was liable to be requisitioned to be melted down to resupply depleted magazines. Even the church bells at Deddington, lying idle since the tower had collapsed in 1634, did not escape the King's spies, and Charles directed an order on 21 January 1643 to 'our trusty and well-beloved subjects the Parson, Churchwardens, Constables . . . and . . . parishioners':

Whereas information is given us that by the fall of your steeple at Dadington in this our county the bells are made unserviceable for you till that shall be rebuilt and they are new founded, and that the metal of them may be fit for present use, both for own and public occasion: we hereby require you to send the same to our magazine here in New College, and some such trusty persons with them as may see the just weight, and the nature of them taken by our officers there, to the end that we may restore the same in materials or monies to your church, when you shall have occasion to use the same. And to the end we may the better effect this, we hereby command the commissioners of our train to remember us hereof when it shall be opportune. And for full assurance hereof to your whole parish, we are graciously pleased to confirm this by our own royal signature.

The order was promptly complied with, the King's commissioners noting, ten days later, that:

. . . two of the Bells are now brought in to the Officers of the Artillery from Dadington, which are directed speedily to be weighed and valued. And whereas there yet remained three Bells more, whereof one onely is hanged up fitt for use, and the other are not; it is thought fitt that these two other Bells shal be sente in also for the King's service, and weighed and valued also; and ye sheriff of the County is desired to send these two other Bells speedily, and the Parishioners shall have satisfaction from the King for these foure Bells, to be paid unto them either in Bills or money when their steeple shal be fitt to receave them.[4]

The fortification of Banbury Castle, described as being 'old through time', was also an urgent necessity if impending parliamentary attacks were to be repulsed, and in this Banbury's corporation was evidently less cooperative than Deddington's churchwardens had been over the bells. On 20 December the King had ordered Northampton to discipline the mayor and his officers for their incompetence or dilatoriness and to warn them of the consequences of incurring the royal displeasure:

Whereas we understand that the works for the strengthening and defence of our town of Banbury are much foreslowed by the great neglect and backwardness of the Mayor thereof, forbearing to summon in a sufficient number of Labourers for that purpose: and that likewise many other necessary duties and supplies for our Garrison there are either wilfully omitted by the said Mayor and his subordinate officers or otherwise not furthered and attended in such sort and manner as is requisite for the advancement of our service, and for the security, defence, and supply of our said Town and Garrison: Our pleasure and command therefore is, that you forthwith call for the said Mayor and his subordinate officers, to whom you shall declare our will and command to be that they immediately summon and cause to come in such a number of sufficient labourers with shovels, mattocks, and other tools as you shall appoint, and find requisite to go in hand with and to perform and finish the works requisite for defence of our said Town. And that the said Mayor and his other officers fail not from time to time to fulfil and perform their respective duties, and to cause such supplies of all kinds to be brought and furthered in unto our said Garrison as shall be needful, and to be in all things conducing to our service and the good of our said Town, aiding, obedient, and readily assisting to your directions. Whereof you are to charge the said Mayor and all other the officers and other Inhabitants to take notice and to be duly observant henceforth, as they and every of them tender our displeasure, and our calling of them to an account for their neglect and contempt, for their defaults aforesaid, as well as such as shall be hereafter discovered against them.

A week later the King returned to the subject, ordering Northampton to demolish whatever buildings were necessary to complete satisfactory fortifications, and adding a further warning to the mayor:

Whereas we understand that there are divers houses, buildings, and other obstacles in and near our town of Banbury, which do hinder that our Ordnance from the Castle of Banbury cannot do the service requisite for the defence thereof and for repelling such forces as may come into the said town. Our will and command therefore is, that you forthwith cause all such Houses, Buildings and other Obstacles to be with all diligence pulled down and removed, whereby you may better defend our said Castle, and prevent such attempts as may be made against it. And we further hereby require you to command the Mayor, Aldermen, and all other officers in our town of Banbury and the liberties thereof in our name to be aiding, assisting, and obedient unto you in all such things as you shall think fit for the security of our said town and the advancement of our service there. Wherein if any of them shall fail or be negligent we require you to send them hither to us in safe custody to be proceeded against according to his or their demerit.

The following week, with the enemy still threatening, the King had no qualms about ordering the Earl of Northampton to take even more drastic action at Banbury if necessary:

Our express will and command is that you forthwith take and seize upon all the provision of victuals, of what kind soever now remaining in the town of Banbury, and dispose the same into the castle for the supply of such soldiers as you shall leave there; and when you shall receive certain information that the rebels intend to march again to that town, we command you to set it on fire and to burn it down, and to retire with your Horse to some place of safety thereabouts.

These near-panic measures were justified by the continued threat from parliamentary forces, not all of which had evaporated after Edgehill. A myth has grown up that Civil War activity was largely confined to the summer months. How far this is from the truth was recognized by Warburton: 'winter did not bring its usual suspension of hostilities'. Indeed, there was an almost continuous cycle of activity in and around Banbury during the winter of 1642/3. In particular, Northampton was well established as one of Parliament's most important garrison towns, while at Warwick the enterprising Captain John Bridges was always ready to attack. In one typical foraging raid, militarily insignificant but none the less satisfactory for parliamentary morale, the old Earl of Bristol's personal baggage train was intercepted 'as they were passing to the Kings Garrison att Oxford'. At a later enquiry Bridges denied that any 'treasure' was found other than four trunks and '2 little deale boxes', the subsequent events being related with some realism:

The same having been opened before the Souldiers . . . there was therein Two Tobacco boxes and a snuffe boxe tipt with silver, and a boxe with some single pence and halfe pence, but otherwise neither money, plate or Jewells or any other thing valuable. Therein was alsoe some clothes and Bootes . . . and some few course Linnens with a great Cheese. The boxes & the pence were given away to some standers by, the bootes and the Cheesse to the troopers. The souldiers had likewise given them for their encouragement tenn pounds in money and the Intelligencer tenn shillings, and thereupon the trunkes were imediately nailed upp againe, and laid in a greate compasse window in the Castle for divers yeares, during which time this defendt would gladly have parted with them, . . . beinge informed (the trunkes being old and full of holes) that the rain had beaten in att the windows, and the water thorough the holes runn into the Cloathes, and . . . a greate parte rotten . . .

The King, meanwhile, was sufficiently alarmed at more ominous rumblings of parliamentary activity as to issue instructions on 9 December to the Midland counties to give immediate notice of enemy movements in the locality, and to settle winter quarters at a council of war. Oxford was girdled with a circle of protective garrisons, the outer ring comprising Banbury, Brill, Wallingford, Abingdon, Faringdon and Burford, with additional northerly regiments at Woodstock, Enstone and Islip strategically placed near the main routes to Chipping Norton and Banbury. The threat to Banbury now seemed acute. On 13 December the Earl of Northampton wrote to Prince Rupert requesting help to ward off an impending attack, wrote again on 22 December from Deddington thanking him for his reassurance and pleading with him to 'make all ye hast you can to us', and warned the King that rebels were approaching Banbury with 300 horse and peasants brandishing pitchforks. On 23 December a resolute parliamentary force from Northampton took advantage of the Earl's temporary absence and, joined by mutinous sailors (one of whom wounded their commander on the shoulder with a blow from a poleaxe), actually entered the town and bombarded the castle with cannons all day on Christmas Eve. Other parliamentary units almost succeeded in routing the Earl of Northampton's returning force near Deddington, retreating only before a last-minute intervention by Prince Rupert and Sir Charles Lucas who, marching all night, finally 'chased the Enemye from Banburye [and] marcht back thorow the towne'. Rupert returned to spend Christmas at the court at Oxford, but on Boxing Day received yet another appeal from Banbury to help prevent the rebels from regrouping. A further one came the next day, recounting parliamentary outrages in Northamptonshire and requesting help in dispersing the enemy and to 'encourage the country to rise on his Majesty's behalf against them and, I am confident, to a considerable number'; and yet another similar appeal the day after. A few days later, on 4 January, Northampton reported to Rupert the unwelcome arrival of parliamentary reinforcements from Leicestershire under the nineteen-year-old Thomas, Lord Grey of Groby, the son of the Earl of Stamford, at Daventry with two pieces of ordnance intending to march on Banbury. A distraught inhabitant of the town wrote to a friend at this time of the effects of the continuous military activity on the life of the neighbourhood:

> I pray God in mercie look upon us, and put it into the heart of our King and Parliament that there may be an accommodation for peace, for otherwise our countrey will be wholly ruinated in a short time. Wee cannot enjoy any thing that is our owne. The towne of Banbury, for the most part the chiefest men, are wholly undone all alreadie, and wee in the countrey cannot long subsist. For wee have great Taxes layd upon us, and if wee will not pay them, our selves and goods are both taken away. I prayse God I have my libertie yet, but doe not know how long I shall enjoy it, for I am in great feare of my selfe.

The expected parliamentary assault on Banbury was averted by the arrival of royalist reinforcements from the King under Colonels Herbert and Wentworth, together with musketeers from Woodstock, with the result that the Royalists could resume their plundering expeditions in order to relieve their near-destitute troops. In January it was reported that while Northampton's ally Henry Hastings was robbing carriers in Derbyshire, Northampton himself and Prince Rupert between them stole at least twelve hundred horses from the plough and countless wagons, filling them with plunder which was then promptly resold at local fairs in Northamptonshire and Warwickshire:

> . . . leaving in many villages neither beds to lie on, nor bread to eat, nor horse, cow, nor sheep – and this he did to some of his friends, as well as those he esteemed his enemies.

One item of immediate practical value was the reported theft by the Earl of Northampton of sixty wagons of cheese. The plundering continued as far as Daventry, which was similarly treated, if the parliamentary reports are to be believed. The Royalists arrived to find the enemy withdrawn towards Leicestershire with only a minimal guard remaining, so that:

> . . . coming sudainly upon the Towne, the forces there being very carlesse in sending forces and keeping their watches carefully as they ought, [the Earl of Northampton] entred the Towne without any resistance, the Souldiers all taking flight. At which the Cavalliers were not a little glad, expecting to inrich themselves with the pillage . . . and fell to plundering, sparing none that had any thing to loose, and tooke the Carts and Wagons they found in the Town and loades them with the Pillage they had taken . . .[5]

STRATFORD AND THE SHAKESPEARE CONNECTION

Such, then, were a few of the problems facing Banbury's garrison that winter, at the precise time that the Edgehill ghost stories already referred to were circulating, with embellishments. One parliamentary report gleefully alleged that it was now the turn of the new Banbury garrison itself to be demoralized by similar hauntings: 'the Cavaliers in the Castle are frighted at the sight of a great man that walkes in a surplice . . .'.

Naturally, however, the harassment of the inhabitants and the general dislocation to life in the Banbury neighbourhood did not exempt other districts from similar disturbances and violence as the war spread. Stratford, for example, an important regional market attracting commerce from well outside the county borders and situated at a strategic crossroads, could not long expect to escape unscathed. It had, indeed, already suffered from quarter and plundering by Essex's forces crossing the district both before and after Edgehill, with the usual fall-out of sick and wounded being cared for long after, besides having to tolerate a detachment of Essex's army which had been left behind there as a precautionary measure. Such activities had no doubt exacerbated tensions in an already deeply divided town, with an absentee royalist vicar, Henry Twitchet, who had already deserted his parishioners for the King's garrisons, an aggressively parliamentarian schoolmaster, John Trapp, who later became chaplain to Warwick garrison, and prominent parliamentary sympathizers like the Puritan William Combe, owner of the College, the largest house in Stratford, and naturally at odds with a mayor, bailiff and corporation, all royalist in sympathies. Many Stratford inhabitants were later to be accused of royalist 'delinquency', and it certainly seems to have had its fair share of bellicose Royalists, if later court testimonies are to be believed. In one case an ex-Warwick Castle soldier, Thomas Sharpe, attacked by a royalist collarmaker, William Greene, with a club in a Stratford street with cries of 'Have at you, Parliament rogue!', told the court that such incidents were not uncommon in the town. Greene was, he claimed, 'an inveterate Malignant who hath sevralle tymes raysed the rabble people of the said Towne against the Parliament souldiers'. Perhaps the pious Puritan Thomas Spencer was not alone in imputing Stratford's Civil War misfortunes, as well as the succession of disastrous fires which had ravaged the town, to divine retribution for its general depravity . . . .[6]

It is against this turbulent background that a small parliamentary force from Warwick Castle arrived in Stratford on 7 January to neutralize the politically unreliable borough, only to be refused entry by a hostile official reception committee:

> The Towne did oppose their entrance. Uppon which, comming to a parley, they demanded all the Armes in the Towne; which, when the Bayliffe and Aldermen had refused to deliver up, they went away in discontent, threatning to come againe with a greater number, not onely to disarme the Towne but to plunder it also.

The threat was no idle one. Five weeks later a more substantial parliamentary force under Colonel Hans Behr descended purposefully on Stratford for a week on the first of two recorded visits. Militarily, Behr's visit would merit only a minor footnote in the history of Civil War Warwickshire, were it not for the unique dimension given to it by its Shakespeare connection. Less than thirty years after Shakespeare's death Stratford was still peopled with those who had known him well, with family friends and close relatives, with Greenes, Ardens and Hathaways, as well as his sister, Joan Hart, still living in Henley Street, and his own daughters, Susanna Hall and Judith Quiney. Behr promptly billeted himself, his servants and two horses on the wealthy Thomas Nash, son of Shakespeare's friend Anthony Nash of Welcombe and married to Shakespeare's granddaughter, Elizabeth Hall, who had inherited the poet's own home, New Place. As the largest house in the town centre, New Place had occasionally served as lodging to eminent official visitors to the town in peacetime, and once war had broken out had been chosen by parliamentary commanders as an almost regular lodging whenever they were passing through the district. Already Nash had been forced to entertain Colonel John Fiennes and his brother Nathaniel and the Edgehill stalwarts Sir Philip Stapleton, Sir William Balfour, Sir James Ramsey, as well as Lord Brooke (and later Sir William Brereton), so that Behr's choice of lodging was to that extent automatic. The political affinities of the inhabitants of New Place – who included, as Nash himself obligingly noted for posterity, 'my mother in law Mrs Hall, [Shakespeare's daughter, Susanna] who lives with me' – are not entirely clear and, given Behr's uncontestable authority when choosing quarters, largely irrelevant anyway. Although Susanna had, like her husband the eminent physician Dr John Hall, puritan leanings, the younger Nashes seem to have been Royalists. Thomas Nash was listed on 24 September 1642 as the largest of Stratford's contributors to the King's cause: 'Thomas Nashe, esqr, in plate or money paid in at Warr. – – – £100' (though he was in the same month one of the largest contributors to the fund for distressed Protestants in Ireland, too), while the signal honour accorded the Nashes by Queen Henrietta Maria's visit to them in July 1643 (see below, Chapter 7) must have clear political significance. Whatever Behr's reasons for quartering at New Place, Nash later claimed £10 in compensation for 'keepinge a Constant table with extraordinary firinge' for those six days, and as Shakespeare in his will had bequeathed his granddaughter Elizabeth all his plate, Behr and his officers may well have eaten from the poet's tableware in the poet's own house. Nash also records 'a scarlet Peticoat of my wifes, with two faire laces, taken by [Behr's] men', and two cloaks. Of the many other householders reporting items stolen by Behr's men some of the most substantial losses were incurred by the Stratford chamberlain, Thomas Horne, from his house in Henley Street. Horne, used to keeping the borough accounts meticulously in his official capacity, carefully listed every item of a bill totalling almost £50 for this single week:

> They dranke 5 hogsheads of beere at 16s the hogshead; bread 10s; meate 33s; had from the butchers beside bacon, foure porke, butter & cheese 29s; fire xxs; fresh fishe, salt, tobacco & pipes.
>
> £9. 3s. 6d.

> In horsemeate for 57 horse 4 daies & 4 nights at 6d day & night £5. 4s. 0d.; eight strike of beanes; 20 strike of ots at 18d. a strike; candles in the howse & Stable.
>
> £8. 0s. 0d.

> Two hogsheads of beere £1. 12s. 0d.; bread 10s. 0d.; meate for them from the butcher 15s. 8d; other houshold meate for them, bacon, porke & Sowce 6s. 8d; butter, Cheese & eggs 6s. 8d; fire 6s. 8d; 64 horses day & night at 6d £1. 12s. 0d; candles in the howse & Stables 2s. 6d; a strike of beanes & ots 2s. 0d.
>
> £23. 4s. 6d.

Horne also appended a note requesting sympathetic consideration in respect of 'a soldier dangerously wounded, left without meanes', and another similar casualty, 'gone away nowe, sound & whole', whom he had lodged. As usual on these occasions, the town's losses were not confined to mere board and keep for, among many other typical claims, Edward Welles notes: 'Tooke away by the pliamt soldier 2 flaggons, 2 pewter Chamber-potts, and paid them to have a bible againe and other goods: 16s. 0d.'[7]

Hardly had Behr's cavalry left in mid-February than a 300-strong force of Cavaliers under the Earl of Northampton arrived to quarter in Stratford, and began 'fortifying and entrenching the Towne'. It is unclear what progress was made in this, though the 'quantity of wood lying upon ye River of Avon neare Stratford' belonging to Sir Edward Peto which the King ordered Northampton to seize on 2 January may have been earmarked for such work. In the event, Stratford was spared the disruption caused to Warwick, an authoritative royalist source blaming this on indiscipline among the royalist commanders, presumably the personal jealousies to which Clarendon refers more than once, with the result that the town was 'too long neglected through an unreasonable desire of command in some . . .'. As ever, Captain John Bridges was keeping matters under close surveillance from nearby Warwick, and it is probably to this time that an undated record of a typically opportunistic raid refers:

> I haveing notice of great sadles [being] sent to Stratford uppon Avon by George Wincoate, a sadler in Warwick, to be sould to a partie of the Kings Armie that were there or expected to come there the same day, I sent a partie of souldiers after them, and tooke them upon the roade.

Shortly after, Lord Brooke himself, now given supreme command by Parliament in Warwickshire and Staffordshire, marched with new forces and armoury from London in a wet February, arriving at Warwick via Northampton and Coventry late on the night of Friday 24 February, to be told of Stratford's occupation by the Royalists. Clearly, Brooke could not countenance the establishment of a royalist garrison at Stratford as well as Banbury, and acting with characteristic decisiveness decided 'to give them an Alarum'. Finding the time to make the humane gesture of visiting one of the royalist prisoners, the young Earl of Lindsey, in bed in the second chamber in Guy's Tower,

Brooke promptly 'went into Towne, and from house to house did call up the Cartars to goe away with his Cariages', and marched towards Stratford with a strong force at daybreak the next morning. At 8 a.m. near Ingon, however, their approach was sighted by an alert royalist sympathizer who, 'espying us 2 miles on this side [Stratford], crossed the Fields and gave the enemy advertisement'. A running battle ensued parallel to the Warwick road between Snitterfield, the Welcombe hills and Clopton Bridge, over land rich in Shakespeare associations, as the Parliamentarians pursued the outnumbered Royalists 'so fast as our Carriages and the plowd Lands well softened with the raine would permit us'. The Royalists, among whose commanders was the abrasive Colonel Gerard Croker, fled towards Banbury.

As the parliamentary troops entered the town, a mysterious explosion partially wrecked the new Market Hall or Town Hall, a stone's throw from Shakespeare's New Place, recently constructed with Cotswold stone after two years of wrangling over building and design costs and valued at £340, and evidently being used to store the town's magazine. This was probably an accident, though parliamentary reports were quick to suggest deliberate sabotage by a treacherously laid 'Traine of Pouder' intended for their commander:

> . . . in the Hall 5 Barrells of powder . . . within an Houre after blew up the town-house, . . . no doubt designed to have surprized my Lord [Brooke] and all his chiefs, presuming they would have sate in councell there.

Captain John Needham was charged with disarming the town:

> By order from ye Lord Brooke I went to Stratford, disarmed ye towne, tooke awaye theyr Ammunition (all wch did amount to ye value of two Cart loades) and delivered them at War. Castle to be disposed of by Col. Bridges.

The process of 'disarming' a town, particularly one suspected of harbouring royalist delinquents, was clearly wide open to abuse, as Lord Brooke himself was the first to realize in issuing widely reported orders at this time 'to be made in severall places that no Souldier should offer violence to the people of the Towne, or spoyle them of their goods'. Naturally, weapons were legitimate booty, and although Needham's claim of two cartloads seems exaggerated, a moderate quantity which had escaped Behr's attention was confiscated. From High Street alone, a musket and case of pistols were taken from one of the aldermen, Richard Castle, a sword and pistols from Shakespeare's lawyer, Thomas Lucas, a 'birding peece' and rapier from Edward Rogers, a carbine from John Whiteland, two drums from Henry Bridges . . . Besides the confiscations from individuals, part of the town's armoury yielded a richer haul: 10 muskets, 7 calivers, 4 pikes, 4 corslets, 10 swords with belts and bandoliers, 10 helmets. As usual, useful non-military items were also gathered *en passant*: shoes from Peter Holland in High Street, clothes and linen from Nicholas Ryland in Sheep Street, saddles and beer from Richard Ingrams in Bridge Street and much else, on 'the morning the towne hall was blowne up'.

Once again, however, the most evocative entry in the litany of homely items stolen by the soldiers is one with strong Shakespearian connections: domestic objects taken from the Maidenhead inn, the eastern part of the Henley Street birthplace, the so-called

Woolshop formerly belonging to Shakespeare's father and considered by some authorities as likely to have been the poet's birthplace. This property had been kept for several years by widow Jane Hiccox (friend of Shakespeare's widowed sister Joan Hart, who lived next door at the present birthplace until her death in 1646), with her two orphaned children, as tenants to Shakespeare's daughter Susanna Hall. Picked out in bold lettering in the original manuscript as if to draw attention to a particularly shameful deed, the widow's losses 'from the howse called the Maidenhead' almost certainly include items once, if not still, belonging to the Shakespeares:

> Tooke away by the Lord Brooks soldiers when hee came to Stratford and drove away the Kings forces there, as followeth:

> 17 silver spoones, 2 silver boles (a bigger & a lesser), a double silver salt in old money £3. 7s., & divers other things in a trunke, to the value of   £20. 0s. 0d.

One more Shakespearian link to the Civil War, of a different nature, relates to Lord Brooke's surgeon, James Cooke, of Warwick, and probably dates from this time. Attending a detachment of parliamentary soldiers left to guard the strategically-important entrance to the town over the ancient Clopton Bridge, Cooke was invited to New Place by Susanna Hall to view her husband's medical records, from which he later published a selection of these unique case-histories of a seventeenth-century physician. Among Hall's cases were those of the Stratford schoolmaster, John Trapp, who 'by much study, fell into hypochondriak melancholy' before redoubling his parliamentary activities, of the Countess and Earl of Northampton, whom he rode the 40-odd miles to Ludlow to attend in 1622 and, to show his political neutrality, Lord Saye's daughter.

Shakespeare's New Place served, no doubt, as quarter to other troops periodically throughout the Civil War, though these occasions are seldom reported. Colonel John Okey, the commander of the New Model Army's dragoons, was there shortly after Naseby in June 1645, and more parliamentary soldiers imposed themselves again on the poet's granddaughter Elizabeth in April 1647, shortly after her husband's death, one of them being implicated in deer stealing from the estate of the prominent JP, Greville Verney, at Compton Verney. In July 1643, however, as we shall see, New Place was host to a much more illustrious visitor. As for Captain Needham, once he had accomplished his Stratford mission and returned to Warwick, he was soon promoted governor of Kenilworth garrison, where he was involved in large-scale tree-felling to fortify the castle, disafforesting many coppices 'in the Kings wood lying betwixt Kenellworth and Stonly'.

A lurid postscript to the skirmish at Stratford, related by an outraged Parliament-arian, swung the focus of action back to Banbury soon after. A royalist soldier, Captain Twist, wounded at Stratford and left there on parole by Lord Brooke, was rescued by Banbury colleagues and transported towards Oxford. Discovering this, Elizabeth Phillips, wife of a Banbury magistrate who had long ago fled the town, sent a messenger, William Needle, to inform Parliamentarians quartered at Bicester of this breach of honour. On the way the hapless Needle was captured by royalist scouts, forced to confess his mission, taken prisoner back to Banbury and interrogated by the castle governor, Colonel Hunks. On his evidence the incriminated Mrs Phillips was imprisoned too, on 10 March, 'notwithstanding good Bayle was offered for her enlargement' and in spite of having ten children, one unweaned, to care for. Her shop was ransacked, £14 stolen from it, her home plundered and she herself reduced to beg. The following day both prisoners were summarily tried at a hastily convened council of war, sentenced to death and brought to be executed on 14 March in Banbury market place. The mother's sentence was commuted to imprisonment, but not before she had been abused and led round the square with her children in derision. Needle was promptly hanged. The account is an emotional one, clearly an act of pious martyrology by a patently prejudiced reporter. There is little reason, nevertheless, to doubt its overall accuracy, and it conveys something of the insecurity and lurking horror that increasingly stalked ordinary people in these troubled months.[8]

CHAPTER SIX

THE GRIP OF WAR: SPRING 1643

THE MIGHTY FALLEN

Although 1643 brought no major battles to the region comparable to Edgehill or Cropredy, it was a period hardly less dramatic for the combatants and certainly no less disturbing for the civilian population. War was now a fact of life and its consequences, tragic, debilitating or merely unsettling, were felt everywhere, at all levels of society. Although peace negotiations were conducted at Oxford between the King and the parliamentary commissioners, and military operations in theory suspended until mid-April, garrisons were now scattered throughout the region and soldiers were never far away, liable to interrupt traffic on the highways or burst into the village to billet themselves, ransack houses and extort supplies, producing the fear and turmoil already described at Banbury and Stratford in the opening weeks of the year. Events had now, seemingly, a random momentum of their own, sometimes producing a chain reaction with unforeseen consequences for a given locality weeks or months later.

With his success at Stratford and Warwickshire as a whole now virtually secured for Parliament, Lord Brooke immediately returned to Warwick and prepared to undertake the next task assigned to him, that of securing Staffordshire too. He lost no time in setting out from Warwick, some of his men helping themselves to free footwear from John Thomas's shoemaker's shop as they did so. By 28 February the Earl of Northampton reported from Banbury that Lord Brooke was marching north-wards, and immediately after that he was besieging the Royalists in Lichfield Close. By the time this letter was delivered at Oxford to the King's secretary, Sir Edward Nicholas, Lord Brooke was dead. Having reached Lichfield the previous day, in one of those grotesque ironies of war the leader who had given so much to his cause and dominated Midland politics for so long was killed by a stray shot through the eye as he sat in an open window, fired by a boy perched on one of the cathedral's towers. The youth was later reported as having 'afterwards escaped over the wall of the Close in the night time'.

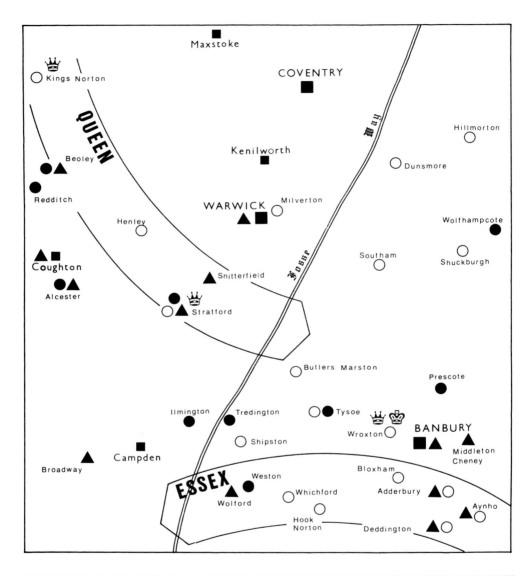

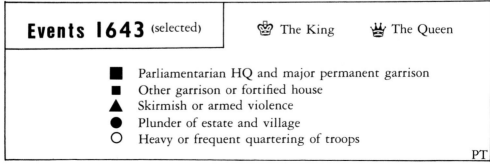

Events 1643 (selected)   ♔ The King   ♕ The Queen

■ Parliamentarian HQ and major permanent garrison
■ Other garrison or fortified house
▲ Skirmish or armed violence
● Plunder of estate and village
○ Heavy or frequent quartering of troops

PT

The departure of Lord Brooke for Lichfield was followed by one of those dramatic missed opportunities which, if seized, would without doubt have changed the entire course of the Civil War. The Staffordshire campaign had so substantially depleted the Warwick parliamentary garrison that the castle could now, the Royalists believed, be captured, the Earl of Northampton reporting to the King at Oxford:

> I have just now received Intelligence . . . from Warwick that there is not now left above thirty Soldiers in the Castle, diverse being runne away since my Lo: Brooke went, & very few left in Coventrey; and the Townsmen & Souldiers at greate varians, but kept under, being disarmed.

Moreover, the unreliable parliamentary governor of Kenilworth Castle, Hastings Ingram, apparently in charge at Warwick too during Brooke's absence, was reported to be willing to betray it to the King. Such plots were a recurrent feature of the war; a very similar one involving the seizing of Windsor Castle at night through the forest, with the capture of the Earl of Essex, was planned at exactly this time. It is far from clear whether Ingram, who had recently escaped from imprisonment by the Royalists at Oxford and been placed in charge of the parliamentary stables at Kenilworth, was indeed a double agent or merely an unreliable turncoat, but he was shortly after incriminated by a letter found upon the Earl of Northampton's body and arrested by the parliamentary authorities. The King immediately ordered preparations for the seizure of Warwick, using the assistance of his chief 'fireworker', Bartholomew La Roche, later to be knighted for his services, with an assortment of explosives. Prince Rupert, writing to the Earl of Northampton at Banbury on 2 March, reported:

> It is His Majesties pleasure that there be something attempted upon the Castle of Warwick. Therefore you are to send as many Musquetiers as you can horse, with the Prince of Wales his regiment of horse and your own. This bearer, La Roche, will bring Petards and all things necessary for them. You must march to morrow in the Evening, to be there before break of the day on Saterday.

As it happened, Ingram's loyalty was not tested, a hastily-convened war council at Banbury at 8 p.m. the following day unanimously concluding that Bartholomew La Roche's provision of explosives from the meagre supply available was inadequate to guarantee success, and pointing out that a bungled attempt would be disastrous on several counts:

> We received your Highness's directions by Monsieur La Roche, and we find that he is not provided for the certain effecting of an attempt upon Warwick castle; so that we have thought fit, by a general consent of us all, to present your Highness with our opinions before we go on, to which end it is deferred one night more. First, there is [sic] two doors to be forced one way, and three another; one of which must be done; and he hath but two petards. So that he himself saith, if one should fail, the design was not only lost, but it would give warning to secure themselves for the future. Next, the failing might bring a greater durance upon those now in prison than yet they suffer. Besides, we conceive the not gaining it would be some loss of honour, both to his Majesty and those who should go about it. Notwithstanding, we are ready to venture our lives as your Highness shall think fit, but if there might be two pieces of battery, that if one way failed it, the other would be certain to do the work. However, we are ready to perform your Highness's directions and commands, which we crave may be sent speedily.

Four hours later, at midnight, Rupert — who was actively engaged in making last-minute preparations for his assault on Cirencester — replied somewhat ambiguously, but in effect authorizing Northampton to use his discretion as to whether to attack Warwick or not:

> I have acquainted the King with the hinderance you have in your desire. He was pleased to command me to tell you that your Lordship should send one of your Scouts to enquire if Ingrom be in the Castle. If he be, you may safely go on with your designe; for knowing but of your coming, he will make but little or no resistance. If after this you should think it feasible to raise the siege at Litchfield, you have also that power to do it.

In the event, Northampton made the fateful decision to march instead to confront the parliamentary forces now massing to assault Stafford, a change of tactics with momentous consequences for the Royalists. Northampton arrived direct from Banbury, took the initiative and routed the Parliamentarians, but was himself killed. Within weeks, two separate yet closely related incidents at only a few miles distant from each other had deprived each side of the major military and political personality who, perhaps more than any other, had initiated and directed the course of the Civil War in the Midlands. The loss to both sides was incalculable. After an interim period of shared command, among which William Purefoy was prominent, Brooke was eventually replaced by the less impressive, more controversial figure of Basil Feilding, Earl of Denbigh, of Newnham Paddox. Northampton was succeeded by his twenty-year-old son James, who immediately requested his father's command in a letter to Prince Rupert:

> I thought it my Dutie, affaires standing as they do and I untimely having an unwisht for honor fallen uppon me by ye unfortunate death of my fath. Earle of Northampton, to let your highness understand how his military commands at this present stands. Hee was raising a regiment of horse, and had allready raised three troupes besides his owne, two of whiche were here [Stafford], present at the battell, the other was sent back from Henley in Arden to Banbury, for ye securitie of that garrison whereof ye Earle of Northampton was governor; his foot regiment, excepting some commanded men, being left there for ye defence of ye towne and Castle. If it shall please his Matie and your highness to confer those commands whiche were my fathers on mee, none shall bee more willing to do his Matie service (according to my weake abilities) with Life and fortune . . .

To his widowed mother the young Earl, barely out of his teens, wrote bravely:

> Deare Mother, On Sunday last we got the day of the Rebels; but our losse (especially your Honours and mine) is not to be expressed, for though it be a generall losse to the Kingdome, yet it toucheth us nearest. But Madam, Casualties in the world will happen, & in such a cause who would not have ventured both life and fortune? Pray'e Madam, let this be your comfort, that it was impossible for any to do braver than he did, as appeares by [the rebels'] owne Relation . . . His Armour was so good that they could not hurt him till he was downe, and had undone his head-peece. Pray'e Madam, be comforted; and think no man could more honourably have ended this life . . . to be partaker of heavenly joies. We must certainly follow him, but can hardly hope for so brave a death.
>
> Thus humbly craving your blessing, I shall remaine till death your obedient Sonne, Northampton.[1]

The opportunity to capture the prize of Warwick Castle had now passed, a letter to Prince Rupert from Lady d'Aubigny at the end of March confirming that 'the designe of Warwick hath been long discovered'. Nevertheless, the parliamentary authorities were now seriously alarmed at their apparent weakness in face of the loss of Lord Brooke, their financial plight which had forced many units to be disbanded, and the proliferation of royalist garrisons. The mercurial Rupert seemed everywhere; he had struck directly across Warwickshire at the end of a snowy January, quartering successively at Southam, Butlers Marston and Shipston-upon-Stour to take Cirencester by storm at the beginning of February, and after lightning forays in the south was now back at Oxford ready to take the initiative again. A group of Coventry Parliamentarians headed by William Purefoy wrote in sombre mood on 14 March to the Earl of Essex at Windsor:

> Our danger is the more by reason of our weakness, occasioned by late disbandings of many men for want of money & supplies sent to Killingworth [Kenilworth] & Maxstoke Castles, and two companies to Lichfield . . . we are assured that there are mortar pieces as well as battering ordnance intended against us . . . If we should be besieged, we should be in great defect of a commander of experience.

As the peace negotiations at Oxford dragged on intermittently, Prince Rupert set out at the end of March to clear a passage north to the Queen in Yorkshire, inflicting ferocious assaults on Birmingham and Lichfield. He moved north briskly but in easy stages, quartering at Chipping Norton, Shipston-upon-Stour, Stratford and Henley-in-Arden, a march rapid enough to reduce the opportunities for widespread plundering, though parliamentary news-sheets reported extensive pillaging at both Shipston and Henley. In a clearly desperate attempt to denigrate the charismatic Rupert's reputation as a military leader – though not necessarily inaccurate for that – a mischievous parliamentary reporter described Rupert's second arrival within two months at the little royalist town of Shipston, long associated with the bishopric of Worcester and adjacent to the Earl of Northampton's extensive south Warwickshire estates:

> Prince Rupert came hither with 7 Colours, and upon the Green at the Towns end kept his Randevow . . . There attended him two Lords, the one supposed to be the Lord Digby, the other the Lord Denby; with foure small field-pieces and some horse, most of which had Cases for Pistols yet but one Pistoll a peece. His Dragoones were double armed all most all, with a Musket before; and behind him, an Irish-Whoore (which seems rediculous, but is a truth) furnished with a strong-water bottle. His foot men [were] thus armed: with Pikes, halfe Pikes, Pike-staves, Holbeards, Brown-Bills, Hedge-bils, Welch Hookes, Clubbs, Pitch-Forks, Cowl-staves, with Choping-Knifes and pieces of Sithes fastened into them. Thus this ragged Regiment marched halfe clad with miserable poore ragges. This Towne being formerly visited with Prince Ro: and part of his matchlesse Regiment before his Last passage to Cicester [Cirencester], were known to bee true Malignants, and therefore favoured each other at that time. But now, the Prince Ro: pleased their Malignancie and Plunderd most, if not all of them.

Leaving Shipston, Rupert moved north through Stratford and Henley-in-Arden, reportedly 'pillaging the Countrey extreamly' with his force of almost two thousand, even though many of Henley's inhabitants at least were presumably sympathetic to the royalist cause, being later accused of being much given to:

> unlawful meetings of idle and vain persons . . . for erecting of May poles and May bushes and for using of Morris Dances and other heathenish and unlawful customs, the observation whereof tendeth to draw together a great concourse of loose people.

From Henley Rupert proceeded to his notorious storming of Birmingham and Lichfield, while more interesting evidence is provided of the indiscipline of widely scattered troops by a successful parliamentary attack on part of his rearguard near Warwick, evidently in no hurry to join their commander, at a time when Rupert himself was already in Staffordshire:

> Hearing that Prince Roberts forces were coming within 3 miles of Warwicke, [Col. John Bridges] saylyed out with a party of horse and fell upon the rere of his men and tooke 2 carryeges laden with provision, and tooke 6 commaunders and some other common soldiers which are now prisoners in Warwicke.

Rupert himself, after taking Lichfield successfully, quickly returned to Oxford via Coleshill, 'Merryden Heath' and Henley again, in late April. As spring advanced with mild, 'fair, calm and growing' weather, further royalist excesses were reported, this time from the Warwickshire–Worcestershire borders. In yet another typically aggressive initiative by Bridges at Warwick acting upon information from captured enemy scouts, dozens of musketeers were sent through the night to flush out Royalists from Evesham quartering in Alcester. A running battle ensued in which the Cavaliers were routed but managed to call up reinforcements from Prince Maurice's main force near Evesham and pursued the Parliamentarians back towards Warwick. Failing to overtake them in time the Royalists returned to Alcester and relieved their frustration by plundering 'every house in the Towne of what ever was portable' and even, according to one parliamentary account, 'carrying away all the men they could find there into slavery'. Shortly after, more violent skirmishing was reported from the Alcester district, again provoked by Bridges at Warwick, commended for his enterprise: 'Warwick Castle sent to discover what they could abroad, and in that way they doe much remarkeable service'. Finally, in this dangerously exposed corridor between the royalist Cotswolds and parliamentary Warwick, it was the turn of Ilmington to experience the violence that so many other small communities had witnessed:

> On Sunday May 28, about three of the Clocke in the morning, about twelve Scouts of the Kings side meeting by chance in an open field neer this Towne with twenty of Warwicke Castle . . . had a short skirmish, and most of the Cavaliers were either taken or kild, . . . the rest fled to [Chipping] Camden and raised the Troops of Cavaliers there. Whereupon the furious Cavaliers came downe to Ilmington, and because the men of the Towne did not come forth to helpe theire fellowes Pillaged and Plundered the most part of the Towne . . . before ten of the Clocke that morning; so that the poore Towne, who medled not with either Party, was indamaged by them at least three hundred pound, and no destinction made between either friend or foe.

Such incidents, naturally, were in themselves militarily insignificant, even pointless. They reveal the poverty of the conflict in the region in the spring of 1643 which, following the deaths of the two leaders, had already degenerated into a formless chaos of isolated skirmishes lacking any obvious overall strategy. The focus of the present work, however, is not on military strategy, but upon the impact of the conflict on the small communities and the usually passive individuals who had the misfortune to lie in the path of apparently random forces. The reporting may, as usual, be biased and the accuracy of detail suspect, but these deficiencies cannot conceal the human and social effects. Militarily such incidents brought little, if any, gain, but to the community or the individual they could be catastrophic.[2]

WARWICK UNDER MILITARY RULE

Perhaps as a direct result of this increasing royalist activity, as well as Parliament's own self-confessed weakness, a strenuous effort was now made to strengthen Warwick. Lord Brooke had long ago fortified the castle, as already indicated, and work had no doubt been continuing for some time on strengthening the town itself. Certainly, by the spring of 1643 work was well under way, and some indication of the importance attached to the project may be gauged from the size of the geographical area forced to finance it. From 25 May 1643 to 10 August 1644 alone a total of almost £250 was collected in regular levies exacted not only from the wards of the town itself but also from over fifty townships and villages in the surrounding countryside. These included Ashorne, Ashow, Alveston, Barford, Bearley, Bishops Tachbrook, Budbrooke, Charlecote, Claverdon, Cubbington, Hampton Lucy, Harbury, Haseley, Hatton, Henley-in-Arden, Hillmorton, Honiley, Hunningham, Leamington, Leek Wootton, Lighthorne, Loxley, Milverton, Moreton Morrell, Newbold, Norton Lindsey, Offchurch, Packwood, Preston, Sherbourne, Shrewley, Snitterfield, Southam, Stratford-on-Avon, Tachbrook Mallory, Tiddington, Ufton, Wasperton, Weston-under-Wetherley, Wellesbourne, Whitnash, Wolverton and Wootton Wawen. Such contributions, it must be remembered, represented only one of many other financial burdens thrust on small communities for a range of other causes, and not surprisingly some villages found difficulty in meeting these demands. A Corporal Richardson was sent out from Warwick with a strong escort on several occasions 'to fetch Default money' from Leek Wootton, Leamington and Radford.

While a precise reconstruction of the Warwick fortifications is made impossible by the random nature of the entries in the parish accounts, it is possible to piece together the overall picture, and it is quite clear that virtually the entire town, as well as many outsiders, were implicated and that ordinary life was severely disrupted over a long period. Work concentrated on the creation of 'bulwarks' comprising a defensive trench or trenches to be filled with water, and a bank, possibly surmounted by wooden or stone fencing, encircling the whole town. The bulk of the work relates, therefore, to the manual labour of ditching and banking performed by quantities of carters and labourers hewing and hauling stone from nearby quarries with teams of oxen or horses with wagons, cutting and transporting turf from places like Myton Heath, and felling trees. One inhabitant alone, Roger Fisher, lost '33 Timber Trees . . . for ye States use' and then a further sixteen, a loss he estimated at £30 10s., besides structural damage done to his property in West Street by stray cannon balls from the castle guns. For such a task Warwick's own male population was evidently inadequate, warrants being sent out 'to bring in the Countrey to the worke', as well as orders given to the town's constables 'to warne the wards to the worke' and to attend the building sites themselves. A few conveniently available royalist prisoners from the castle were also used. Picks, axes, spades and mattocks were much in evidence, Robert Southam being paid 6d. per day 'for lookeing to the picks and spades' on one occasion, Richard Morrell for sharpening them on another, while 'Iron Crows, sledges and wedges for the Digging' and mending of wheelbarrows hint at the laboriousness of it all. The fortifications obviously entailed the additional complication of constructing and erecting numerous gates, drawbridges and 'barricadowes' at the town's main entrances, with guard posts permanently manned by soldiers and civilians needing constant supplies of candles and 'fire' 'for the town guard' or 'ye soldrs use at watching', not to mention frequent beer. For all such essential items regular payments were made by all the inhabitants to successive constables: William Hind, Robert Hodgkins, Thomas Dadley, John Boyes. Some traders could be adversely affected; for example Widow Lee claimed compensation for loss of her unspecified (alehouse?) 'out trade and garden' in Saltisford.

More substantial inconvenience, however, was caused to those who had the misfortune to live in the path of the projected bulwarks. In Saltisford, William Hadley 'had a baye & a Cutt end of Housing pulled down & 3 apple trees Cutt downe to my loss, at ye least £6'; John Corpson 'sustayned 40s. per yeare Losse in Regard the Bul-works were digged through my Ground'. Similarly, two days were spent in demolishing Mr Prescott's barn, 'that the worke might passe', while another making a claim was Richard West, 'by Reason of the Fortificon [sic] being Drawen through my back side and some pte of my house pulled Downe'. Widow Smallwood's fence was destroyed, Mrs Wagstaffe's barn pulled down and Stephen Glendall's orchard dug up. 'Poore Widow' Brotherton's case was typical: her house was 'removed', the site being filled in with two loads of stone, before, apparently, being re-erected a little way off, since bricks, stone, glass and even lime for pointing walls and chimney were specified on 5 June 1643. Another widow, a Mrs Eades, had a different but equally unsettling experience, the circumstantial detail of her voluble account reflecting her report to the constable:

> She had a very great Elme tree grew in her back syde, wch did much shelter her home from ye vyolence of ye wynd, wch at ye time of makeing ye Bulworks was cut downe & taken away by ye souldrs, whoe made her pay for the Chypps thereof (haveinge noe satisfacon for ye tree). And synce, it hath cost her xxxs. in repaires, by reason of ye wynd, & wilbe a contynuall charge.

Even the Warwick bailiff, John Yardley, at one point imprisoned by the Warwickshire parliamentary committee as politically unreliable, was not exempt from military necessity, claiming compensation later for substantial losses sustained:

> . . . the Bullwarks being made thorough his ground: pte thereof taken out, beside the trenches, sixe bayes of building pulled downe by the Soldyers of the Garrison, a great pte thereof burnt, a tylekilne and other howses Destroyed of good value. . . . Divers trees with Lopps cutt downe & used about the Bullwarks, a great pte of the ground turved, and quarreys of stone digged for the making of fortificacons.

He estimated his losses at £80 'at least'. As the trenching progressed, pipes were prepared to flood the new moat, 'trunks' being 'Layd at the [Leicester's] hospitall in the works to convey the water', and 'in the workes at Stephen Glendall's orchard'. Unfortunately, precise locations for all these projects are seldom specified, but bailiff Yardley's property was situated on or adjacent to the Market Place and other random references to the Leicester hospital, North Gate, barricades and drawbridges at Saltisford, 'West Chapel' and a sallyport being constructed at Linen Lane clearly retrace the line of the medieval town walls. And finally, when all was completed and the summer grass grew long on the raised banks, men with scythes were needed. . . .

Placing Warwick on a war footing meant often, therefore, severe disruption to the life of the community and substantial losses to many individuals. It would be misleading, however, to suggest that the operation was a tragedy for all; the machinery of war, as the twentieth century knows to its cost, means profit for some as well as loss to many. Quantifying profiteering by artisans, traders and farmers in the Civil War is clearly impossible, but random evidence, as well as an awareness of human nature, suggests that not all inhabitants were ruined by the war. Locally the production, sale and transport of livestock, materials and foodstuffs must have increased dramatically to fit new demands, and to revert specifically to the Warwick fortifications alone, carters, carpenters, candlemakers, tanners and shoemakers must all have experienced a welcome boom. Even an army quartering on the town or merely passing nearby could be good for trade, even if it only meant the Warwick chemist supplying extra 'oyles and plaster to the Pothecary to ye Earle of Essex' when the town was full of the Edgehill wounded. The livestock dealer Thomas Fish was one named tradesman in Warwick whose affairs seem to have thrived in the early months of the war. He proudly refers to his 'business' involving 'beafe bought for Provision for the Castle of Warrwicke by mee Thomas Fishe' and 'hides sould by mee for the use of the State', volunteering the information that 'some of the Hides . . . were sold before I undertooke the business and some of them after', implying steady success. Fish evidently bought animals from locals named Hawkesforth, Westcott, William White and Henry Palmer, selling the meat to the castle, the hides to the tanner and glover 'at the Bridge' and the tallow to unnamed candlemakers. In six months or so Fish received well over £300, a considerable sum, for such trade. Similarly there was a brisk trade in coal to supply the cavernous rooms at the castle, from at least September 1642, bought from what looks like a profitable business run by Thomas Little, Thomas Hunt, Francis Neale 'and the rest of theire Neighbours' in one contract, through Nicholas Judd 'and his partners' in another. The coal was presumably transported from the north Warwickshire coalfields at Bedworth which had been supplying south Warwickshire from at least Elizabethan times, and was sold at Warwick at 9d. or 10d. per cwt in sizeable quantities: 27 loads on 19 September, 9 on 11 October, 5 on 17 October, 38 cwt on 8 November, 11 more loads on 22 November, and so on.

As the parliamentary garrison at Warwick became a permanent feature and as the royalist threat failed to materialize the inhabitants of the countryside began to experience a presence almost as oppressive as that of the Cavaliers at Banbury. The seizure of goods being transported on the highway and the arbitrary waylaying and imprisonment of innocent wayfarers became the stock-in-trade of many a garrison commander hard-pressed to feed, equip and maintain the loyalty of his men, and John Bridges, now in sole command at the castle, found such activities a lucrative pastime. Bridges had from the outset been seldom less than enterprising and had achieved some notable early successes, as when he had neatly turned the tables on an over-zealous High Constable of Worcestershire, 'very active for pressing men for the late King, and having gotten together a great many psons and pent them in Churches for that purpose'. Bridges had swooped down from Warwick, rescued the men and imprisoned the constable. But he and his men could put the same talents to less worthy use, as a spate of despotic incidents at Tysoe about this time testifies. Ralph Wilcox, for example, reported that:

In January 1643, his sonne being at Warr. markett was taken to the Castle, and his horses, and he payd to Collonell Bridges for the release of them £20.

Other inhabitants of Tysoe suffered from similar experiences, including widow Rose Mister:

In May 1643 her man was going to Stratford market wth Corne. Collonell Bridges souldiers tooke him to Warr. Castle, where to Free her man, two mares and one quarter of barle she payed to Collonell Bridges £6.

Henry Middleton too:

His sonne, going towards Stratford Market with two horses and a quarter of barley, was taken by Collonell Bridges his souldiers to Warwick Castle and Imprisoned, where he payd to Coll. Bridges for his liberty Six pounds, and for his horses and barley eight pounds.

Horses were particularly prized and, once stolen, any attempt at recovery was likely to be hazardous, as both John Mister and the husband of Anne Malms, again both in Tysoe, found. Both were promptly imprisoned, and released only when ransom was handed over. At Coughton, Bridges' other garrison seems to have been kept only intermittently, but when in residence it naturally followed the Warwick example and acted in the same high-handed manner. The Captain Smith already noted extorting beer, bedding and other goods from Alcester to supply the garrison was quite prepared to take the law into his own hands, one inhabitant of Studley, William Petford, complaining volubly that:

. . . in Januarii, Rydinge peaceably on ye way, [he] was suddenly opposed & wounded by one Smith, wch was of Colton [Coughton] Garrison under ye Comand of Col. Bridges; ye wch wounde was so farre tedious yt hee Lay under ye surgeons hands some 20 weeks or more, in all wch time hee was Carried to bed, . . . beinge not able to dresse himselfe or any way able to helpe himselfe.

There is no doubt that such behaviour by soldiers, reflecting the example set by commanders who were accountable to virtually no one, was the rule rather than the exception, and that the reported incidents which have strayed into the nation's archives document only a small proportion of those which actually took place. The parliamentary governors at Kenilworth – successively Ingram, Needham and Hawkesworth – were all equally autocratic, while the most notorious reign of all, as will be seen, was George Purefoy's at Compton Wynyates. Victims who, although innocent themselves, had the misfortune to be related to known enemy activists, like the wealthy Francis Clarke of Tysoe, could be ruinously plundered:

Taken away the 25 of March 1643 by the souldiers of Killingworth [Kenilworth] comanded by Leivetenant Wagstaffe: 9 geldings and mares, six beastes, and the most pte of the houshold goods and wearing Apparell, to the worth of £300 & upwards.

To such hapless victims such incidents could produce an escalating toll of ruin, even ending in personal tragedy, as in the case of the wealthy Royalist Thomas Peers, of Alveston, near Stratford, in February 1643. Although the reporting is not impartial, the details suggest a fairly accurate account of the ruthlessness of the extortion procedures adopted:

himself, his trusted subordinate Colonel Anthony Greene and William Compton, closed ranks sufficiently to defend itself so well in the 1644 siege.

In the midst of this climate of suspicion, intrigue and rancour at Banbury the chance to engage the real enemy must have come as a welcome relief: this came with the royalist burning of Banbury on 3 May and the skirmish at Middleton Cheney three days later. Although the outcome, a decisive victory for the Royalists, is not in doubt, events leading up to the battle are confused. One parliamentary version claimed that the Royalists had been summoned by the King to a mass rally at Oxford, and that on leaving Banbury they set fire to many homes as a general act of revenge on a notoriously unsympathetic population:

> What should induce them to that inhumane Act cannot of any certainty be gathered other then this: their inveterate spleene to the place for their good will to the Parliament, which hath also had the ill hap to bee the place where the first bloud was shed in the war, and hath been full of troubles and distractions ever since.

More specifically, perhaps, 'they did not pay the mony assessed upon them towards the mayntenance of the Kings Army'. This version argues that parliamentary forces from not only Northampton but Buckinghamshire too marched on Banbury, intending to help its citizens and avenge the incendiarism, but it also introduces a dramatic complication. The Royalists had devised a well-planned plot involving a forged letter, purporting to come from the Earl of Essex, ordering the Parliamentarians to march south to Reading, who were then trapped by 'the Kings forces, [who] had provided for their coming, and had strengthened themselves and lay in ambuscado in the way'.

The royalist account gives a different emphasis, but is not incompatible: on learning of the parliamentary approach via Culworth the Earl of Northampton sent his forces to Bodicote about noon on Saturday 6 May, engaged the enemy and pursued them back to 'Middleton Cheney Towne field' where the main encounter took place that afternoon. There were substantial parliamentary casualties, including over two hundred killed, according to one royalist account, forty-six of which were buried at Middleton Cheney the following day. Many prisoners were taken, while others escaped 'in small companies into by-lanes and hedges', and there was a considerable booty of much-needed arms and ammunition for the Royalists. Many of the parliamentary prisoners subsequently escaped from Banbury Castle, it was alleged, while their keepers were drunk, telling of 'inhumane cruelties of the Cavaliers as would make even a souldiers heart to tremble'. The extent of the damage in Banbury is impossible to gauge; Beesley is wise to dismiss claims of up to two hundred houses burnt as a wild exaggeration. It seems likely, however, that there was substantial damage, and the provocative remark of a royalist commentator, that 'this most wicked rebellious Towne of Banbury, which hath so often provoked [the King]', was saved from being 'burned to the ground' only by 'His Majesties exceeding mercy & clemency', may indeed be a convoluted admission of as much. In the aftermath the Royalists themselves also admitted to solving one other problem: the Earl of Northampton punished parliamentary Northamptonshire by dumping many of the wounded on its villages, rather than encumber the already overstretched Banbury garrison with them, to bring home to them 'the miserable effects of their disloyalty and disobedience'. The young earl was evidently quickly learning the arts of this particular war. Militarily insignificant as it was, this encounter makes clear once again how the deeply divided people of a district could not avoid being implicated in this war. Besides those rendered homeless and others forced to lodge and care for the wounded, some bitterly complained of 'thus being drawn out, to lose their labour', while many Northampton gentry made their own political gesture, according to a royalist account, by redoubling efforts to reinforce the King's forces with new volunteers armed with the captured parliamentary weapons.

Despite this morale-boosting success things were far from healthy at Banbury, however; it is about now – dates are uncertain – that a serious family feud between the young Earl of Northampton and his two teenage brothers Charles and William Compton developed, or resurfaced. The quarrel affected the garrison's command structure and added to the general anarchy, besides implicating the elderly countess (the late earl's widow) and the King himself who at one point engineered a short-lived reconciliation between the brothers in the garden at Christ Church. At this distance in time the underlying causes of a tortuous family dispute are irretrievable; but it must be remembered that the three brothers were boys thrust overnight, by their father's premature death and the peculiarity of war, into positions of military and social power, that the problems of maintaining a garrison in the conditions already outlined would have taxed experienced commanders three times their age and that the isolation of Banbury, staffed with unreliable and unscrupulous officers, deprived the young Comptons of wise and disinterested counsellors.

The origins of the quarrel remain obscure; some at least of the accusations are clear. The twenty-year-old earl's orders to his younger brothers 'not to intermeddle' with his management of the garrison were constantly flouted, it was alleged. They had torn up his warrants, they had exceeded their rights regarding quartering and collecting contributions from the villages, they disobeyed or abused his officers who were simply carrying out their orders, they were guilty of 'countenanceing the disorders of the souldiers', and on one occasion, when called 'a knave [who] had cheated ye Country', one had responded by surrendering his commission, 'refused to March wth ye Regiment upon Orders' and preferred to go absent-without-leave to Oxford. Heated exchanges are hinted at as accusation and denial alternate. The dispute simmered for over a year, until the fall of Compton Wynyates, Cropredy and the first siege of Banbury all renewed occasions for animosity and destroyed a fragile truce. The parliamentary capture of the family home at Compton Wynyates in early June 1644, for example, was alleged to have been a direct result of insubordination. The brothers consistently disagreed over promotions policy, supporting opposing candidates to a point where rival cliques were formed sporting cudgels adorned with identifying coloured ribbons, neither camp recognizing the authority of the other. A new treasurer of the garrison was considered 'a Gentleman of abilities and fortune whoe haith merited Highly' by the elder brother, and of suspect integrity by the younger, and vital sums of money were diverted from the scant resources of the treasury, illegally, in an attempt to pacify unpaid, mutinous soldiers. Issues were doubtless aggravated by personal rivalry. James had seniority, but William was (at least for a time) the nominal governor, and some of the personalities involved were long-time family retainers in the Compton household. This extraordinary dispute continued to sow bitterness on all sides until it resurfaced with renewed intensity at Daventry in the fatal confusions of the pre-Naseby days.

Family quarrels are apt to appear faintly comic to the detached observer, and a few decades later elements of this saga might easily have found their way into a mock-heroic poem by Pope or a Swiftian political satire. But this richly human document tells an almost unique inside story, complementing what can be pieced together from sources like Nathaniel Wharton's celebrated journal of the realities of garrison life at the height of the Civil War, but this time from the commanders' viewpoint. Apart from the human interest at the heart of so much triviality, the quarrelling offers an insight into the amateurism of the times when a family feud could come close to destroying a potentially effective military unit and the care-worn King himself be expected to take time off from high affairs of state to adjudicate in the bowers of college gardens.[4]

CHAPTER SEVEN

SUMMER PASSAGES

THE TREDINGTON HORSES

Although 1643, as already suggested, brought no major battles to the region under discussion comparable to Edgehill the previous year or Cropredy the following, the spring had been far from uneventful. There had been a succession of what are usually dismissed as minor skirmishes, like those already described at Stratford and Middleton Cheney, increasingly oppressive military regimes installed at Warwick and Banbury, a quantity of disturbing incidents of random plunder, as at Shipston, Stratford and Ilmington, and the harassment, vicious treatment and arbitrary imprisonment of travellers or supposed delinquents, as at Studley, Tysoe and Alveston. The mere collection of 'contributions' was apt, as we have seen at Long Compton and Brailes, to involve the threat or actual perpetration of violence. Each of these individually minor events caused disruption to the life of the community and sometimes tragedy to the individual, as at Alveston. The easy, frequent assumption that, so long as major battles took place elsewhere, a particular district was largely left in peace in a merely episodic war ignores the constant interference in the lives of ordinary people by the local garrison, the mounting disruption to trade and the knock-on effect of distant events. Military offensives well outside a given region often had an unpredictable local impact, and the summer of 1643 was to prove as unquiet a period for the Warwickshire Feldon as the spring had been, even though the main theatres of war were elsewhere.

Particularly feared by the common people, with good reason, was the passage of 'foreign' troops through their district on some long-distant mission. Released from the web of local loyalties, the soldiers could be even more harsh and unprincipled than when nearer home and, lacking the local knowledge to enable them to distinguish friend from foe, their plundering was apt to be even more indiscriminate than usual. Horses were particularly prized and therefore particularly vulnerable, and cavalry units far from home could easily degenerate into bands of horse dealers. In one particularly blatant example, Sir Thomas Aston's royalist cavalry, which had already improverished largely loyalist

Worcestershire on its way north in January 1643, ran amok as they careered southwards again in June, smarting from a humiliating defeat in Cheshire, provoking angry complaints from the inhabitants of the Bromsgrove–Droitwich area and an official petition to the King's Commissioners from the people of Armscote and Blackwell in the parish of Tredington. The text is worth quoting in some detail for the light it throws on a typical village experience and the sheer human interest of its narrative:

> According to our late Information, uppon Satturday the Third of June instant [1643] we were plundered and bereft of 40 of our best horses . . . Uppon our diligent and chargeable search and Inquiry, we have found out our horses in the Regimt of Colonell Sr Thomas Aston att their quarters about a place called Black Burton neere Burford in the County of Oxon. But soe incomisserate and unreasonable are theis Plunderers That (not content with the wrongfull takeing our said horses, beating and abusing us for onely requesting to buy them agayne, and att their departure wilfully trooping away neere a quarter of a Mile over a furlong of our Beanes & Pease in a body of 7 or 8 score horse, when a fayre high way of 30 yards broad lay all along by the said furlong). But when our Messengers and servants whom wee ymployed in seekinge after our horses wth 4 or 5 dayes expence of tyme found them in the said Regimtt att Black burton aforesaid, The soldiers there . . . (in contynuance of theire mischeivous practises) did imprison & threaten our said Messengers and servants & rob them & pick their pocketts and take away & deprive them of all their moneyes wch they tooke wth them for their necessary expences. Soe that we dare pceed noe further in pursuance of our said horses Except you wilbe pleased honorably to afford us yor assistance and aide herein . . . And we shall allwayes pray for yor happinesse both here & hereafter.

That horse theft was one of the commonest crimes of all in the Civil War, and that some cavalry units were admitted by even their own side to be little better than common thieves (Colonel John Fiennes's regiment was a particularly notorious local one, condemned by Sir Samuel Luke, the parliamentary commander at Newport Pagnell, as 'the horse drivers – you may see how the country suffers') was scant consolation to the inhabitants of these two hamlets for such a catastrophic loss at midsummer, and the sense of despair and outrage is palpable. Those same horses which were such a vital component in the villager's husbandry were regarded as infinitely expendable by the cavalry officer scouring the countryside for ever-increasing numbers of them. Many districts must indeed have been literally emptied of them. For example, Luke noted in November 1644 that 'they have no horses to plough and sow the land', and tiny Warwickshire villages like Cherington seem to have been as 'clean stripped of horses' as elsewhere. Any roving young trooper took it upon himself to collect as many as he could find, secure in the knowledge that they could be sold for a good price. Samuel Coxe, a former trooper in Captain Wells's Warwick company, was still only twenty-four when he admitted having several years previously stolen eighteen horses from 'Mr Stanford's at Salford', several more from Dr Jenkin Bowen, rector of Welford-on-Avon (pointedly, one harvest time), and thirteen or fourteen more at Ilmington on another occasion. As in the Tredington incident above, where the victims were forced to plead to buy back their own horses, extorting inflated ransom for the animals was a popular practice. Officers of William Purefoy's Warwickshire regiment, who included Captain Benjamin Lovell, former rector of Preston Bagot turned captain of horse, were particularly adept at this pastime, as the case of John Eades in Tysoe well illustrates:

> In September 1643, he had taken from him foure mares by Collonell Purefoys souldiers: on[e] by Capt Halfords sergeant cost him to have her againe xxxs.; on[e] by Capt Lovehils Lieuetenant cost

him to have her againe of Capt Lovehill foure nobles; on[e] mare cost him to have her againe xxxs vid; and on[e] mare Capt Atwood had would not let him have her under ten pound, but she was well worth five pound.

The distress caused by such wanton acts cannot be quantified, but the anger of individual victims at the loss of even one, perhaps much-loved, mare is occasionally felt in the recital of details. At Bretford, for example, an unforgiving William Poole was not prepared to let things rest and insisted in carefully identifying the culprits he hoped to bring to justice:

> One of them yt tooke this mare was one Stacie, sonne in lawe to one Stringer of Tachebrooke. Another, one Powers, whose brother lives in Killingworth [Kenilworth]. Another, one Yates, who was once a scout-master in Warrwicke. And John White of Auster [Alcester] Rode the mare awaye.[1]

THE QUEEN'S PASSAGE

The Midlands were intermittently the scene of further agitation in the summer of 1643 caused by two more protracted events of a totally different nature, namely the passage of Queen Henrietta Maria from York to Oxford in June and July and the parliamentary relief of the besieged city of Gloucester in September. Both events originated and concluded elsewhere, and need not have touched Warwickshire. In the event, however, both attracted intense military activity to the region, thus ensuring that the threat of violence – even though it never substantially materialized locally – was never totally absent from the lives and concerns of ordinary people.

Charles's consort, Henrietta Maria, had left England in February 1642 for the Netherlands, where she had spent a year raising funds by pawning the Crown Jewels, amassing a substantial quantity of much-needed arms and even recruiting some important professional volunteers for the King's cause. After a hazardous sea-crossing she had disembarked at Bridlington and, after a prolonged and busy stay in York spent in congenial court politicking, was now eager to deliver her valuable cargo to the royalist headquarters at Oxford and be reunited with the King. She was in buoyant, girlish mood at the prospect of the forthcoming adventure of the long march south and elated at the opportunity of stiffening Charles's resolve to prosecute the war even more vigorously, writing in mid-May from York: '*Il y a fort longtemps que je n'ay été si gaye et si satisfaite que je suis*'. Although Yorkshire and the north Midlands were unsafe, with the Fairfaxes, Brereton and Grey of Groby posing ever-present threats, the recent death of Lord Brooke at Lichfield had left Parliament in some disarray and with the Earl of Essex still in London unable to assemble an effective army. With the recapture of Lichfield by Prince Rupert in March as part of a plan to clear parliamentary 'obstructions' from the Queen's intended path and so escort her triumphantly to Oxford, the Banbury–Daventry area under royalist control and staunch allies like Henry Hastings and the Earl of Northampton eager for action to neutralize any threat from the east, it was decided she might venture south without incurring undue danger as long as the obvious hazards of the direct route via Leicester, Coventry and Warwick were avoided and some secrecy maintained: 'she does not say which way she will come, hoping that secrecy and speed will constitute her surest escort'. Having contemptuously rejected the Fairfaxes' offer of a safe passage to Oxford on condition that she travel without soldiers, money or arms, she accordingly left York on 4 June 1643, having forewarned the young Henry Hastings 'to be in readiness lest I should have any occasion to use your troops'. Riding at the head of a substantial army and picnicking in the open air with her young officers (and, according to rumours maliciously picked up and inflated by parliamentary news-sheets, entertaining an unhealthy affection for one of them), she entered the Midlands via Newark, Nottingham and Ashby-de-la-Zouch before striking due west to Burton. Whether this deviation was a deliberate ruse or an improvised change of plan in response to some imagined threat remains unclear, but the fact that Parliament was unable to block the Queen's march was due less to royalist strategy than Parliament's inability to mount the coordinated offensive which would have been necessary to confront the well-protected and belligerent Queen, revelling in styling herself *sa Majesté généralis-sime*. Certainly the precise route she would take was the subject of intense debate on both sides. Even before she left York a long westward detour via Worcester was being advised by royalist commanders, 'there being no question but the Queene must for many reasons come by Worcester . . . to avoid Essex and those forces at Coventree, Northampton and Warwick'. It is equally clear, however, that she herself was the effective decision-maker, informing Charles unambiguously that only once one stage of her journey was completed would she determine the next: '*nous prendrons une résolution sur le chemin à suivre*'.[2]

By the time that she had reached Ashby, however, and her indisciplined troops sacked Burton, rising tensions are manifest on both sides as parliamentary scouts began reporting accurately on both her movements and those of the Royalists, including Prince Rupert, preparing to meet her and assembling in the Daventry–Weedon area. Warwickshire itself was now, once again, becoming aware of the very real threat from the converging forces, fuelled by panicky and at times fanciful reporting from both sides. Parliament's alarm was tempered with pride at what it hoped was a popular uprising in its favour:

> All the inhabitants in Warwickshire from the age of sixteene to sixty are up in Armes, and have encamped themselves on Dunsmore-Heath to stop their march that way to Oxford. Yet she having the Westerley parts open, may go from Ashby to Lichfield, from thence to Dudley Castle and so to Worcester, from whence without any obstacle she may go to Oxford, unlesse Sir William Waller prove a block in her way.

A scornful royalist report put a very different gloss on the alleged local agitation:

> Lord Grey and Colonell Cromwell being reconciled, had drawne their joynt Forces towards Dunsmore heath; and causing a report to be spread abroad that the Queene was comming with an Army of outlandish Papists to destroy the religion of the Land and bring in Popery, occasioned very great multitudes of seduced people to come thither to them, in hope to intercept the Queene in Her passage thither. But on the first report of Prince Ruperts coming . . . this great cloud dispersed. The brave Captaines made as much haste as any . . .

A further, entirely plausible, royalist account adds the significant detail that the motivating force behind the alleged solidarity of the people was the influential Puritan William Purefoy, who had persuaded the parliamentary committee at Coventry to issue 'warrants read in all Churches thereabouts' instructing them to report to Dunsmore Heath for service 'upon paine of death', 'to oppose that accursed Popish Army of the Queenes'. The reporting is highly emotional, but likely to be substantially accurate. Certainly warrants were issued from Coventry on 10 June to the High Constables of south Warwickshire ordering all village constables to force recruits to report for military service at Warwick 'for the present defence of the County of Warwick', and as usual this created an opportunity for renewed pilfering in the district: one inhabitant of Kenilworth 'had a mare taken by a soldier when ye Randesvous was at Dunsmore when ye Queene came by'. But the uncertainty over the Queen's route meant that the parliamentary soldiers were sent far and wide as a precaution. Most evidently marched east as far as Churchover, presumably to cover the Watling Street sector, one inhabitant duly complaining that 'when Collonell Barker & Collonell Purifry wth the rest of Coventry armie went to meete the queene there men tooke from me a Beaver & a Bible'.

Purefoy's commitment to the puritan cause, however, took an even more dramatic and colourful form at this time, for it was while the Queen was approaching that there occurred the most serious incident of ecclesiastical vandalism which Warwickshire was to suffer in the war, and directly attributed to him. He had already been identified, as we have seen, as the commander responsible for the attack on a Buckinghamshire church in August 1642 (see above Chapter 3), and his regiment may well have been implicated in the two major acts of cathedral desecration in the Midlands at Worcester and Lichfield.

As an implacable Puritan hostile to political compromise or religious toleration, as well as a military leader of formidable energies, Purefoy was automatically a target of royalist vituperation, who saw in him an upstart from 'the dregs of the People, . . . a man of a mean and desperate Fortune' whose fanaticism had 'seduced' Lord Brooke. The judgement may be unreliable, but evidence does suggest a fervour akin to fanaticism in the future regicide. As for the events of 14 June 1643 at Warwick, accepted sorrowfully by the civilized Dugdale and never denied by the Parliamentarians, they are worth quoting in detail:

> In St. Maries Church in Warwick and the Chappell (commonly called the Earles Chappell) adjoyning to the Quire of that Church are diverse faire Monuments of the Beauchamps, anciently Earles of that place, which Family long flourishing there had been great Benefactors & beautifiers of that Church . . . But such is the barbarousnesse of the pretenders to Reformation, that upon Wednesday the 14th of this instant June, the Souldiers, by the appointment and encouragement of one . . . called Colonel Purefoy . . . did beat downe and deface those Monuments of Antiquity; and not content with this, by the same Command they break down the Crosse in the Market-place, not leaving one stone upon another, Purefoy all the while standing by, animating and encouraging them until they had finished their so barbarous Work.

An equally malicious royalist account ends with a deliciously-barbed conclusion:

> Sir Wm Purefoy, Collonel and Governor of Coventry, fought resolutely against the Crosse in the Market place at Warwick and against the antient monuments in the Earles Chappell in St. Maries Church there, for which he had £1,500 given him, but when he should have fought with the Enemy hid himself in a barley field,

while further reports add that after assembling 'all his party', Purefoy and his men 'brake all the Chappell windowes' and the reredos. Naturally, such reports were written to extract maximum propaganda value from the events, but their substance has never been seriously challenged. The moderate Dugdale accepted them without question, noting with commendable restraint shortly after the war, 'the beauty of this goodly Chapel and Monument, through the iniquity of later times, is now much impaired', while thirty years later, when the restoration of the Beauchamp Chapel was undertaken long after the passions of war had subsided, the shameful episode was recalled again:

> The stately Tombes and Monumentes long since erected in that beautifull Chappell . . . have been much abused and defaced, and the costly windows of rare Workmanship in Glasse . . . were shamefully broken and shattered.

There is no evidence to suggest a clear connection between this vandalism and the Queen's approach or Purefoy's attempts to mobilize the neighbourhood, but the whole desperate episode must surely take its place in the general apprehension and frustration felt by the Parliamentarians at this time at the consort's unimpeded march towards them.

One particular parliamentary commander watching events with growing alarm was Cromwell, struggling to fend off royalist attacks in Nottinghamshire with mutinous and unpaid soldiers and quarrelling with Lord Grey of Groby, while warning Parliament of the Queen's approach and demanding urgent counter-measures. The Earl of Essex ordered reinforcements for Grey, 'for the giving check to the enemy in his insolency, and seeing the Queen is on her march with 1,200 horse and 3,000 foot, as credibly informed by Col. Cromwell's letter', and according to a later report by his supporters, gave Grey and Cromwell 'many strict commands to have fought with the Queens forces and stopt her passage, . . . for which designe they had a competent force; but notwithstanding, it was not done . . .'. Whatever the reason, the parliamentary response was inadequate and uncoordinated. Cromwell was left frustrated and impotent and Essex himself brilliantly routed by Rupert, at Chalgrove, and his forces scattered to the winds. Opportunities had indeed already been missed. The Royalists had earlier split their convoy from York, the main consignment of arms for Oxford – forty-six cartloads by one reckoning – being dispatched to Newark and transferred there to Henry Hastings's care for the transit to Banbury, which it had reached in early May, long before the Queen had set out from York. At Banbury the charge had been transferred to the Earl of Northampton, who had conveyed it safely to Woodstock on 13 May through an area liberally sprinkled with protective royalist units: Deddington, Adderbury, Bloxham (where there were even 'some small fortificacions' constructed), with 'the Kings forces quartered all there betweene Banbury and Oxford'.[3]

With his successful elimination of the threat from the Earl of Essex near Oxford and its crowning success, the death of the parliamentary stalwart, John Hampden, Rupert was now free to devote himself to the pressing matter of the Queen's approach, and as she turned due south again through Lichfield to Walsall he was given overall command by the King to guarantee her safety through the last, potentially dangerous stages of her journey. Obediently Rupert swiftly marched north from Buckingham through Farthinghoe and Daventry to Lutterworth in Leicestershire, evidently unaware that the

Queen was travelling south on a parallel track almost 40 miles west. Only then was he informed of the decision, evidently taken by the Queen herself, to continue south to Kings Norton, relayed to him by a letter from Lord Falkland on 10 July, that the consort 'will be this night at Kings-Norton in Worcestershire'. At this stage, with the Queen lodging (though this is not recorded) either, according to one tradition, at the manor-house identified as the later Saracen's Head inn, or with the Middlemores at Hawkesley House, later in the war besieged and destroyed, the safer route via Worcester was still the King's preferred option, his secretary informing Rupert of Charles's anxiety over a more direct route:

> . . . and therefore lays it to your Highness's consideration, whether you will not advise the Queen to come by Worcester, lest if she come by Stratford-upon-Avon, the Earl of Essex may force her to fight before it would be possible that his Majesty can come up to her.

The anxious King added an urgent postscript reminding Rupert that Essex was moving towards Brackley, 'which makes me very confident that the best way for my wife will be Worcester, for otherwise it will be impossible for her forces to eschew fighting'. Telling evidence that the risks were all too real was provided by yet another lightning exploit of Colonel John Bridges, who was able to pounce from Warwick on part of the Queen's convoy of provisions and arms on the way between Burton-on-Trent and Banbury, the Royalists being laden with so much recent plunder, as the Queen herself told Charles, that they could hardly march effectively, let alone defend themselves against a resolute attack: *'ils ont tant pillé, qu'ils ne sauraient marcher avec leurs paquets et ne les veulent point quitter . . .'*. It seems likely, in the absence of further surviving letters which would clarify the situation, that it was the intrepid Queen herself who decided to ignore good advice and march directly to Stratford, on 11 July. There was little enough secrecy: as she approached, property at Edgbaston was plundered 'by the Queens Army' (undated, but probably on this occasion), and the Warwick garrison was put on alert and efforts redoubled to block up the town's entrances against the possibility of a surprise attack from her Cavaliers, one Robert Morrell requesting payment 'for beare for Laborers that blockt up the towne when the Queene lay in Stratford . . . the 11th of July 1643'.

Of the unique occasion of Henrietta Maria's visit to Stratford, tantalizingly little record survives. Only tradition – though a firm and venerable one dating from at least 1733 which has been widely accepted – lodges her at New Place with Shakespeare's granddaughter Elizabeth, still only in her thirties and married to Thomas Nash, the wealthy royalist son of one of Shakespeare's friends. It is plausible to suppose that the theatre-loving Queen pointedly ignored the Puritan William Combe, owner of the largest house in Stratford, the College, preferring its second largest house, the old home of a dramatist whose plays she had often enjoyed at court performances at St James's and Hampton Court in happier times, and a copy of whose second folio was in her husband's possession. Living at New Place, too, was the poet's daughter Susanna, 'good Mistress Hall' who, although thought to have puritan leanings, was 'witty above her sex', and whose husband, the eminent physician Dr John Hall, had once cured the Earl of Northampton, a personal friend of the Queen since the days he had accompanied Charles to Spain to promote the royal marriage. It was at Stratford, evidently long vacated by the parliamentary forces, that Prince Rupert finally joined the Queen, having doubled back through the night from Lutterworth across Dunsmore Heath again via Southam and lodging in Stratford, according to tradition, in Bridge Street. Much conjecture has naturally been lavished upon the romantic Stratford interlude, one aristocratic biographer of the Queen evoking a scene of unparalleled splendour, with the town streets thronged with welcoming, good-humoured citizens as Cavaliers (dismissed malevolently by one Parliamentarian as 'a most filthy, wicked crew') strewed flowers before her cavalcade. Perhaps it was like that: the only surviving evidence, from the chamberlain's accounts in the unpublished borough records, does suggest lavish official celebrations with peals of bells being rung and a banquet whose highlight was a huge presentation of cakes:

Monyes disbursed and payd when the Queene Majestye laye in the Towne:

Payd to 6 foote men for their fee	£1. 10. 0d
Pd to the cochmen and porters for their fee	£1. 10. 0d
Pd for 4 quayles	£0. 04. 0d
Pd for 3 heens, 1 coke, 8 chickins	£0. 05. 4d
Pd for cakes presented to the Queene	£5. 00. 0d
Pd for 6 malt shives for them	£0. 06. 0d
Payd to the buchers for meate	£3. 18. 6d
Pd to Wm Hopkins for beare	£0. 15. 8d
Pd for 1 quarter of oates and 6 strike of beanes	£1. 02. 0d
Pd to Mr Bayliffe of Warwicke for their fortifications	£3. 00. 0d
Pd to John Copland for bread, cheese and beare	£0. 12. 6d
Pd to the bell-ringers	£0. 02. 0d
Total:	£18. 06. 0d[4]

After spending two nights in Stratford, during which time Prince Rupert was able to take time off from his official duties to make a short excursion across the river with a coachful of ladies to pick fruit in the gardens of the virtually abandoned Milcote House, the Queen left on 13 July, the royal party being observed, according to a Lucy family tradition, from Charlecote's turret windows as it passed towards Kineton on that summer afternoon. Parliamentary scouts assumed, inaccurately but understandably, that the Queen was 'expected at Banbury eyther this or tomorrow night':

All the Kings-forces which lay quartered at Adderbury and Deddington are advanct to Banbury . . .
It is certainely reported that the King is at Banbury, and if the Queene come not this night the King intends to goe to Stratford upon Avon to her, and that the greatest parte of the Kings forces are there.

The King had in fact planned what he considered a pleasant surprise for Henrietta Maria, and the reunion finally took place near Kineton that same afternoon, on the site of the battle of Edgehill whose great cavalry charge Rupert must have recalled with particular pride. Curiously, although commemorative medals were struck and fulsome verses composed for the occasion, there survives little record of what must have been a spectacular and highly emotional ceremony, even though a parliamentary commander had noted the previous week that there was 'much preparacion for [the Queen's] entertaynment' and the event must indeed, as the royalist account boasts, have been witnessed by 'great multitudes' of country people from the surrounding district. It is even uncertain precisely where in the 'Vale of Kineton' the reunion took place. The parliamentary account is terse, and notes tartly that 'the common Souldiers [were] very unruly':

> On Thursday, July 13, the King came to Banbury, where he made no long stay, but went and met the Queene below Edgehill, neere unto the place where Keinton battle was fought . . .

The royalist reporter is not prepared to leave it at that, but is more rhapsodical than informative. After stressing the obvious, that the royal family met each other 'with most chearfull countenances', he becomes relentlessly unctuous:

> The place made happy by the meeting of these excellent Personages, whom the unplacable malice of seditious men had so long divorced, was Edge-hill, a place before sufficiently famous for the good successe which God there gave His Majestie, . . . but farre more gratefull to posterity in being the place designed for this blessed enterview. A sight so acceptable to all sort of people, great multitudes whereof attended to behold the meeting, that with their loud and joyfull acclamations they added much to the solemnities of this happy day, and made it little lesse triumphant than their day of marriage . . .

From Kineton the royal couple and the young Princes, still accompanied by Prince Rupert, rode the short distance to spend the night at Wroxton Abbey as guests of Sir Thomas Pope, already specially honoured in November 1642 by receiving the King's protection. Pope had recently been appointed the King's receiver for the Banbury–Bloxham district in order to maintain Prince Rupert's forces, who were now charged with guarding the eminent visitors from look-out posts on Warmington Hill. The next day the King and Queen continued to Woodstock, where they paused briefly until news of Oxford's most recent outbreak of plague was sufficiently reassuring to allow the prepared bonfires to be lit for their final triumphant entry into the city, on Friday 14 July. As the celebrations and revelry got under way the royal couple were greeted by news of the resounding royalist victory over Sir William Waller on Roundway Down, which had taken place exactly at the time of their Kineton reunion; it must indeed have seemed to them a providential conjunction. That the completion of these last stages of the royal journey should have passed without enemy interference was due essentially, however, to parliamentary ineptitude and the virtual occupation of the south Midlands by royalist units. Few villages within a vast triangle bounded by Rugby, Stratford and Aynho could have been unaware of the military activity caused by the Queen's passage, and as her route was uncertain, as we have seen, quartering must have been more indiscriminate and unpredictable than usual. Certainly royalist regiments are reported as being widely scattered over this area, particularly near the obvious main routes. Daventry, Weedon, Lutterworth and Holdenby are specifically mentioned one week, 'Daventry, Shugborough and the townes adjacent' the next, as Rupert's forces anticipated the Queen's arrival via the direct route from Ashby. Then Banbury, and villages along its various axial routes, like Warmington, Adderbury, Deddington, King's Sutton and Aynho, must have witnessed almost continuous movement, quarter and plunder as her more oblique approach from Stratford became apparent. But even villages not obviously on the road to anywhere, like Tysoe, are mentioned, as the parliamentary commander Sir Samuel Luke sums up the situation as it seemed to his scouts about 17 July:

Divers of the Kings forces lye at Tizur [Tysoe] in Warwickshire, and a troope of horse at Adderbury, and 300 in Banbury, and 4 drakes, and all the townes betweene Banbury and Stratford upon Avon are full of the Kings soldiers.

If no major battle was fought in the Midlands in the summer of 1643 this was little short of a miracle. With the bellicose Queen journeying south, the King's protective army dispersing north to meet her, Parliament's supreme commander approaching to within a few miles of Oxford to intervene and, above all, with the two ablest commanders, Cromwell and Rupert, loitering in the wings spoiling for a decisive fight, the converging forces presented all the ingredients for a spectacular showdown. That such an explosive combination produced nothing more than the picturesque midsummer cameos of the Queen partaking of cakes and ale at Shakespeare's table or embracing the King under the brow of Edgehill is indeed one of the quirks of England's history.[5]

'THE TURNING OF THE WHEEL': THE RELIEF OF GLOUCESTER

A good example of the unpredictable local reverberations created by distant events is provided by the last of the major, well-defined military events to affect the south Midlands in the summer of 1643, the parliamentary campaign to relieve the besieged city of Gloucester. Once Prince Rupert had successfully completed his mission of escorting the Queen to Oxford he immediately left to resume the possibly more congenial task of attacking Parliament in the south, a campaign culminating in his triumphant seizure of Bristol on 26 July. This was a spectacular prize for the Royalists, and when it was quickly followed by the surrender of other important southern towns, the King's power appeared at its height, John Corbet, the parliamentary chaplain at Gloucester gloomily conceding that 'the king's country reached from the utmost Cornwall to the borders of Scotland'. The Royalists were so confident that there was talk of capturing both Coventry and Northampton before marching on London, but the King first turned his attention to the only remaining major obstacle to his domination of the entire West Country, the puritan city of Gloucester, 'the most considerable Garrison in all that part of the Realm'. With Sir William Waller's army having recently been routed at Roundway Down and the Earl of Essex squabbling with the parliamentary authorities in London, the King's optimism seemed justifiable as he summed up the position: 'Waller is extinct and Essex cannot come'. The beginning of the King's siege of Gloucester on 10 August, however, unexpectedly galvanized Parliament into action. It immediately issued a proclamation declaring London's solidarity with Gloucester and within three weeks a hastily-assembled scratch army was ready to march to relieve Gloucester under the Earl of Essex.[6]

The direct route from London to Gloucester via royalist Oxford – itself surrounded by other royal garrisons – was clearly out of the question, so that a northerly, curving route was planned which would allow additional parliamentary contingents from Aylesbury and Northampton to join along the way, as well as others from Leicestershire under the young Thomas, Lord Grey of Groby. After a mass rally at Hounslow, Essex finally set out on 26 August, informing the authorities at parliamentary Northampton a few days later, 'I am marcheing for the releife of Glocester'. He marched his army at first due west to Maidenhead in order to mislead the Royalists into supposing that he intended to take the southern route to Gloucester, leaving Oxford far to the north, before swinging abruptly north to Beaconsfield and Aylesbury – so that the Royalists 'suspected rather that he would give some alarum to Oxford'. News of the departure of the expedition soon spread, one well-informed observer being the ever-watchful Colonel John Bridges, governor of Warwick Castle. Bridges had recently entertained at Warwick a demoralized Waller who, after his disastrous defeat at Roundway Down, had limped back with the remnants of his army through Evesham, having narrowly escaped drowning near Gloucester, and ironically being hailed as 'William the Conqueror' by citizens unaware of recent events as he rode into Warwick. The details of this dramatic and curious episode remain obscure, and there is little trace of Waller's passage through Warwick-shire to Northampton and London, but Waller's conduct was to sow lasting dissension between him and his superior, Essex, incensed that he had inexcusably 'left the West to take care of itself [and] marched to Warwicke' intent on surrendering his commission. At Warwick Bridges evidently provided a valuable morale-boosting information service between Gloucester and Essex's expedition, being informed of the situation at Gloucester by spies slipping through the cordon of besieging Royalists, while at the same time relaying to Massey at Gloucester news of the approaching relief forces from Essex's dependable scoutmaster, Sir Samuel Luke. Thus, on 27 August, Luke's *Journal* notes that a messenger 'went to Warwick to Major Bridges with lettres from his Excellency [Essex]', while the parliamentary chronicler John Vicars was able to note from the besieged city about 29 August, 'this night we had intelligence from Warwick of speedy releife coming by his Excellency'. Determined not to be excluded from any military venture within reasonable distance, Bridges offered Sir Samuel Luke every assistance:

> If in any thing I have a capacity to serve you, if you please to honor me with your commands, you shall find ready and chearfull obedience from your affectionate and humble servant.

Meanwhile the parliamentary expeditionary force continued north to a further rendezvous at Baynards Green, near Brackley, on 1 September, with Essex establishing his headquarters at Aynho, the London units at Souldern, and with Grey and his Leicestershire forces at Adderbury. The now substantial army was therefore in effect camped within what the Royalists had long considered their home territory, the north Oxfordshire approaches to Banbury, an area now deliberately reinforced by a cavalry detachment under the competent local commander Henry, Lord Wilmot of Adderbury, fresh from his recent triumph at Roundway Down, whom the King had sent 'to wait about Banbury' for precisely this eventuality. With at least one intelligence report reaching the parliamentary authorities claiming that the King had an army twenty thousand strong in the Oxford area, besides other detachments reported to Sir Samuel Luke recently at Adderbury, Aynho, Brill and Bicester, it is far from clear why, even if such reports were exaggerated, apparently little or no royalist attempt was made to intervene before the various parliamentary units could rendezvous and merge. Even when it materialized, the royalist response was surprisingly lack-lustre in spite of their numerical superiority, as Essex himself later reported:

> The first time the enemy appeared before us was at Aynho on the hill, with a very great body of horse; which Colonel Middleton faced more than a whole day with but two regiments, . . . and skirmished very often with them.

Sporadic fighting continued in which the Royalists withdrew along the Oxford road, where Wilmot was positioned near what a contemporary source refers to as a 'pass' – presumably either Nell Bridge or Clifton Bridge over the Cherwell, or one of the crossing points of the Cherwell's tributaries. More skirmishing continued the following day, 2 September, the Royalists claiming that the Earl of Northampton's 'two noble brothers' (in his absence) engaged Grey successfully at Adderbury, the Parliamentarians that the Royalists were driven back from Deddington 'in great confusion' as far as Banbury, taking horses and prisoners, with 'the Enemy not daring to stir out of the Castle'. Few casualties were reported, and the Parliamentarians were able to continue unscathed and unmolested westwards to Hook Norton, 'at which Village our whole Brigade was quartered'.[7]

Militarily these were clearly minor events, and in no way impeded the parliamentary army's task of relieving Gloucester, accomplished successfully shortly after in spite of Prince Rupert's attempt to bar the route near Stow-on-the-Wold. What was of more concern to the local population, however, was once again the unruly presence of the soldiers in the neighbourhood, many of whom quartered, apparently aimlessly, for days on end before moving on. The strict chronology noted by the contemporary reporters is not always borne out by the accounts of the parish constables through whose territory the troops passed, and leaves much unexplained. For one thing, the passage of the expeditionary force seems to have been accompanied by other, related activity in the region, one example being the influx of a large body of parliamentary cavalry who quartered in Milverton between July and September 'by the space of 11 weekes together when they went as a Convoy wth Ammunicon from London to Gloucester', costing the town over £300. Nor will it be expected that the actual relieving army confined itself to the most direct route to Gloucester quite as rigorously as the reports suggest. Such a route would have avoided Warwickshire altogether, but as we have seen, Civil War troop movements rarely meant a disciplined and unified advance. In the event, units of Essex's army strayed deep into Warwickshire, thefts of horses being reported from Brailes and Willington by Essex's men 'goinge to raise the seige of Gloster about the latter end of Aug. 1643', while a group of Essex's life guard, accompanied by their servants – a party of sixteen men with their horses – quartered on the wealthy Royalist Richard Randall in Wolford. Deviating even more inexplicably from any obvious route towards Gloucester, and evidently quite unhurriedly, were groups of soldiers from Aylesbury and Northampton who quartered in Bilton, near Rugby, for three or four days. Meanwhile, the reinforcements brought by Essex's colleague Lord Grey of Groby were an even greater nuisance. Having approached from Leicestershire via Stratford on his way to link up with Essex and establish headquarters at Adderbury, Grey quartered virtually his entire force, in groups of tens and twenties, for a seemingly interminable three days and nights, in Ascott and Whichford. Grey himself, with officers and men comprising a party of 200 men with their horses, billeted on the unfortunate royalist vicar of Whichford, Dr Richard Langston, 'in harvest time', as the village constable pointedly adds in a hint at the price exacted by war on the rural community. In what looks like a calculated insult the parson had his bible stolen by the soldiers. Adjacent to Whichford, however, was an even more irresistible target for parliamentary soldiers, the home of the wealthy catholic landowner, William Sheldon, at Weston, Long Compton. Already plundered at Edgehill and later to be plundered again, at Cropredy, Sheldon now lost five more horses and £300 worth of goods from his mansion. His loyal servant, Thomas Savage, himself an active Royalist and according to his enemies, 'a scout or Intelligencer to the Kings party', compensated for this outrage by warning the besieging Royalists at Gloucester of the Parliamentarians' approach, and joining the siege himself.

Not surprisingly, given the heavy presence of troops in the district at this time, local passions were exacerbated to a degree where armed skirmishes could involve the villagers themselves. In one incident, at Little Wolford in August, a cavalier attack on the manor house of the conspicuous local Parliamentarian Hastings Ingram, was probably prompted by the presence of Essex's forces nearby. A neighbour reported that the occupants were forced to flee for their lives:

> About August 1643, one Hastings Ingram Esquire taking up armes then for ye Parliamt, I did furnish him with 4 souldiers whereof one was my eldest sonne; wch souldiers did stand out in his house wth him in their defense against part of ye Kings army till he was forced to yeald & they to fly the house, being fired over their heads.

In a largely royalist neighbourhood where substantial numbers of inhabitants were tenants of either William Sheldon or the Earl of Northampton, and where the Royalist Richard Randall, as we have noted, was forced to provide quarter for parliamentary soldiers on their way to Gloucester, Ingram must have enjoyed considerable notoriety, as he conceded himself in a later letter to the Earl of Denbigh. It was his known parliamentary sympathies alone, he claimed, that had forced him to adopt a lower profile than hitherto: 'For my pte, thr malignitie & power agt me was ye occasion of ye layinge downe my armes'.

Over the centuries the soldiers have not usually had a good press. But before condemning the indiscriminate pillaging by both sides which was such a notable feature of this war, the appalling conditions in which they were expected to serve must be remembered. The notion that campaigns were restricted to the summer months is a myth, and clothing, including shoes, was pitifully inadequate. Food was often non-existent for days on end and pay, when it materialized at all, was meagre and almost invariably long in arrears. Not surprisingly, sickness and death were common, outbreaks of plague prevalent – Banbury's garrison was particularly affected – and for those lucky enough to survive, desertion and open mutiny were a common option used both during and after the war, decimating whole regiments. Conditions akin to those already noted on the parliamentary march to Worcester in September 1642 were repeated on this march to Gloucester a year later, compounded by an exceptional spell of severe weather as the troops crossed the bleak expanses of heath along the high ridge separating Warwickshire from Oxfordshire, from Bloxham through Hook Norton,

Rollright and Adlestrop towards Stow-on-the-Wold, 'where the winds blow cold'. If the London sergeant Henry Foster's testimony is to be believed – and his reporting is all the more eloquent in its restraint – Essex's troops were literally starving. Having eaten little since Souldern, where 'we were very much scanted of Victualls', arriving near Cornwell to camp without shelter 'upon a great Common about halfe a mile from Chipping Norton':

> . . . our Regiment stood in the open field all night, having neither bread nor water to refresh ourselves, having also marched the day before without any sustenance, neither durst we kindle any fire, though it was a very cold night.

Other reports paint an identical picture, of:

> . . . cold lodging without any refreshment, for the Souldiers could not the day before, in all their hard march, get any considerable modicum of bread and beere . . . we lay all in the open field, upon the plowd-land, without straw, having neither bread nor water . . .

One eye-witness speaks of 'famine' one day, approaching Chipping Norton, followed by 'tempestuousnesse of weather' the next, whereby:

> . . . the whole Army had for three dayes march before extremely suffered through a Country that the Enemy had already destroyed; and that night, through the violence of cold and rain, divers of their horses died.

Little wonder that a short while after the conscientious Essex should bitterly complain to his parliamentary superiors at Westminster of 'not being able to stay [with his army] to hear the crying necessity of the hungry soldiers'.

With Essex's successful relief of Gloucester, the turning point of the war for many historians, the last of the major campaigns to affect the Midlands in 1643 came to an end. But that meant little respite for local people from the activities released by that campaign, for the entire region, from the Midland plain south to the Cotswolds and Chilterns, was now full of armed detachments quartering and plundering at will, haphazardly-scattered garrisons living off the country and indisciplined cavalry bands roving with impunity. The whole saga, with variations, was in fact to be repeated.

THE GLOUCESTER CONVOYS

When Essex successfully raised the siege of Gloucester in September 1643, no one, least of all the inhabitants of Warwickshire, could have foreseen that there was to be a protracted sequel affecting many of them, once again triggered by decisions taken in far-off London. The city of Gloucester had suffered much during the long siege and desperately needed money and materials to repair its defences and provision its long-suffering defenders and inhabitants. In reporting his success Essex had reminded Parliament that substantial supplies were essential to the city's survival, a plea soon given added urgency by the Royalists' clear intention to blockade the city, hoping to starve the garrison into surrender over the winter. The activities aroused by the siege of Gloucester had in fact no time to subside, for the immediate result was to send back a substantial part of the royalist forces into Worcestershire, where a mocking parliamentary journalist reported them aimlessly 'roving up and down, since their hopes of Gloucester were frustrated', as far as Warwick. Colonel John Bridges at the castle was only too willing to accept this renewed challenge and redoubled his energies to an extent where it is difficult to keep track of his many, usually highly successful, sorties at this period as he 'sent out severall parties of Horse from the Castle at severall times'. While his colleague Colonel Joseph Hawkesworth continued to supervise the fortifying of the town, causing in the process the disruption already noted, Bridges himself cleared the environs in skirmishes resulting in fatalities and many wounded, 'now under the Surgeons cure at Warwicke that wrote this Newes'. Bridges operated tirelessly throughout the neighbourhood. At one moment, in early October, he burst successfully upon Evesham Royalists who had positioned themselves on the hills above Broadway, allegedly to intercept deserting Welshmen eager to return home. At the next moment, a fortnight later, learning of a contingent of enemy cavalry riding from Oxford to royalist Chipping Campden, he dispatched 'a considerable partie . . . in the midst of the night' and took most of 'the Kings Cormorants' prisoner back to Warwick. Again, shortly after, he is reported raiding Broughton Castle, taking more prisoners and a stock of a thousand sheep from the park, before switching his attention to the opposite side of the county where, learning from a parliamentary unit keeping watch at Studley that:

> . . . a company of ragged Welsh-men were come into Worcestershire and intended to fortifie themselves in Coughton house, . . . he sent thither about 80 Musqueteers, who possessed themselves of the House and fortified it, . . . and intends to make that House a strong and compleat Garrison.

Once again the local habitants fell prey to indiscriminate pillaging by this kind of parliamentary outpost contentedly living off the country, one inhabitant of Studley, George Strayne, reporting:

> . . . theire quartering & beere, strong waters & tobacco, they spent & tooke away that time [October 1643] amounteth to ye value of £5. More, they tooke from mee 2 Loades of Cole & 2 of Wood to make fyers at theire mayne Gards, & Heye & Oates & Straw Carried out to theire Horses, Wth Ducks & Sheepe, Geese & other thinges then tooke from mee.

As the second winter of the war set in the weather at times made life as uncomfortable as the war itself. In what must have seemed to many simple villagers an act of divine wrath, Hampton-in-Arden's church spire was destroyed by lightning during a violent storm on the last day of November. Meanwhile, sheer amateur bungling continued to bedevil the disorganized Royalists when a half-hearted attempt to recapture Coughton came to nothing, as Dugdale reports laconically at the end of November:

> Forces from Worcestershire went towards Coughton house, but could not agree about their comands, and soe returned without doing anything.[8]

Among other parliamentary units similarly kicking their heels that autumn was the regiment of Bridges' close colleague, Colonel William Purefoy, scavenging in the district when not otherwise engaged. On one doubtless typical excursion in September 1643, Tysoe – like all its neighbours now paying regular weekly sums to the local military tax-gatherer, Captain Thomas Wells at Warwick, in this case £12 per week as from 11 June – was particularly victimized by a trio of Purefoy's captains, namely John Halford, Anthony Otway and a Warwickshire vicar, of Preston Bagot and Lapworth, now turned cavalry officer, Benjamin Lovell. As usual, horses were the prime target, as in the case of John Eades's losses already noted, but no pretence was made of selecting plunder only of military significance. In addition to his five horses, for example, Ralph Wilcox at Tysoe lost bedding, pewter, brassware and clothing, while John Middleton lost linen, shirts and even a bible. Shops were broken into, Edward Boreman losing £2 worth of 'money and wares' from his, while even the barber's was ransacked:

> [Edward King] had taken from him by the souldiers in Collonell Purefoy's Regement the 14th day of September 1643 a new broad cloath coate, a paire of bootes, a paire of layd spurs and a box of Barbers Instruments worth £2. 10s. 2d.

As always, the precise recital of such details is a human reminder of how memorable to the victim were that day's events, although trivial to anyone else. These inhabitants might have been forgiven for finding unconvincing the usual justification for the existence of garrisons, repeated by Captain Wells at this time to another village nearby, that they offered protection to the locality against the enemy.

Meanwhile, the Earl of Essex's plea for the urgent relief of Gloucester, from Tewkesbury on 10 September, reinforced by a letter from the city governor himself, Colonel Edward Massey, drew an unusually swift response at Westminster. Within days Parliament voted to reward Massey financially for his heroic defence of the city and to send a substantial convoy of supplies via the usual dependable London–Northampton–Warwick route. The supplies themselves amounted, even initially, to an enormous cargo: 100 barrels of powder and an equivalent quantity of inflammable match, 600 muskets, swords, belts and bandoliers, 100 cases of pistols and 100 carbines, with further large quantities being added shortly after. The whole convoy, with wagons, horses newly 'pressed' for the occasion and considerable numbers of newly-raised recruits as an armed escort, as well as many other companies of troops joining along the way, must have comprised one of the most impressive military processions ever to snake its way across the English counties. Given the importance of an event which exercised the attention and energies of so many over such a long period of time it is perhaps surprising that there remain so many unsolved – perhaps insoluble – mysteries about it. The precise route taken, timing of the various stages, how much its escort and actual composition changed during its passage, to what extent the contents were deliberately dispersed for safety, the amount of disinformation surrounding it and, not least, quite why it was allowed to reach its destination at a time when the parliamentary forces were severely stretched by other major commitments: these are all unclear. Naturally, however, the mystery is partly explained by the secrecy of the parliamentary authorities and the need to take last-minute decisions at local level, for as will be seen, not even Massey knew by which route the promised supplies would come, nor when.

Once the supplies were assembled (many from the magazine in the Tower of London) and recruits raised, under Colonel Constance Ferrer, the immediate military task was clearly to secure the proposed route for such a valuable consignment, threatened at the outset by royalist garrisons at Newport Pagnell, Towcester and Banbury, and at the other end at Chipping Campden, Evesham and Worcester. In a further, potentially ominous development for parliamentary hopes, Prince Rupert arrived to make his headquarters at Towcester at the end of September, from where his forces began scouring the region as far as Banbury and Northampton. As news of the parliamentary project to relieve Gloucester became an open secret, the Royalists began their own preparations. There was a mass rendezvous at Banbury on 13 October as a prelude to an attempt to seize Northampton, and both Evesham and Towcester were strengthened in November, Sir Gilbert Gerard writing to Rupert from Evesham on 13 December proposing to intercept the parliamentary convoy whenever convenient. The Banbury–Daventry–Northampton triangle became once again the scene of much skirmishing throughout the autumn, involving forces under Rupert and the Earl of Northampton, with Rupert lodging at the Crown Inn at Banbury on 14 October. Once again, however, the Royalists unaccountably failed to seize the initiative through poor coordination and leadership: the attempt on Northampton came to nothing amid lurid accounts of treachery involving Banbury Royalists, an arch-deserter from Parliament, Colonel John Hurry, and Robert Palmer, a royalist spy from Compton Scorpion stationed at Northampton. Even worse, potentially invaluable Newport Pagnell was almost casually allowed to fall into parliamentary hands at the end of October by 'mistake, . . . which spoyled all', as Rupert's secretary noted despondently.[9]

In all this Warwickshire had not so far been implicated. It became so at some unspecified date when the convoy seems to have reached Northampton intact, almost unnoticed, but was then unable to proceed towards Warwick for lack of sufficient numbers of troops to escort it. The parliamentary commanders decided to confront the major threat to the convoy, and to their fledgling eastern association, posed by the strategically-situated Towcester, the key royalist garrison in the area and now being reinforced by Rupert as a winter garrison. For the expected assault on Towcester General Philip Skippon called on reinforcements from far and wide to converge on his new parliamentary garrison at Newport Pagnell, drawing on Lord Manchester's forces from East Anglia, Colonel Nathaniel Whetham's at Northampton, his own London Trained Bands, and contingents from Warwickshire. The Warwickshire forces had in fact already begun moving south long before, in October – whether in anticipation of an attack on Towcester, to assist the convoy or simply to counter the general royalist threat in the region is not clear. The fact that the Warwickshire soldiers were led by the two stalwarts Colonels Joseph Hawkesworth and William Purefoy suggests, however, that their colleague John Bridges, the governor at Warwick Castle, had continued liaising with Essex's able scoutmaster, Sir Samuel Luke, at St Albans. On 24 October 'a gentleman of quality' in Banbury, Edward Londisdale, wrote an urgent warning to the Earl of Northampton that five columns of enemy cavalry had rendezvoused at Hillmorton on the outskirts of Rugby, while the parish accounts confirm heightened activity in the village as provisions were sent to Purefoy's quarters at Rugby and record thefts by Purefoy's soldiers marching towards Northampton and, specifically, by Coventry and Warwick troops when they 'went against Grafton House', near Towcester. The conduct of the soldiers on such expeditions, and the feelings of the outraged victims of their passage, is well caught in the circumstantial account of Thomas Clarke of Wolfhampcote:

> Uppon the 24th Day of October 1643 in the night tyme came a party of Captaine Hawkesworths souldiers from Warwick, and brook open my stable door and plundred or took away with them five Mares and one gelding, & imploied two of my best mares then worth £24 in service against Grafton house; where they were both shott & lamed. And after that they came to Warwick againe, Captaine Hawkesworth would not let me have my black mare again unles I would give him £3 in ready money, or another Mare then worth £2. 10s. and 10s. of money, the wch I was forced to doe before I could have any Mares againe. And thother Mare cost me two qters of barley for her keeping & healing, and when they came home to my house the said Mares were not worth, in the judgement of any understanding man, six pounds. Soe that by this meanes I am dampnified to the value of £20.

In the event, the planned attack on the recently-strengthened Towcester was abandoned by Skippon as too dangerous, the Parliamentarians deciding instead to assault nearby Grafton House, which was successfully stormed and burnt, with a valuable haul of important prisoners, arms and ammunition, on Christmas Eve. If the Towcester campaign had been planned as a diversionary tactic by Parliament it succeeded; the convoy had by now slipped through to Northampton, and was now awaiting its next stage. On 31 December Essex wrote to the convoy commander Colonel Ferrer from St Albans assuring him that the Committees at Northampton and Coventry had been directed to afford him 'all assistance . . . for the safe conduct of the forces and ammunition under your charge', and instructing him to contact them 'for advice touching the time and way that is best for your march'.

Meanwhile, the part of the entire campaign most to affect Warwickshire villages was about to begin. By mid-December Warwick and Coventry forces had assembled and marched eastwards into Northamptonshire under Behr, Purefoy and Barker to meet Ferrer's convoy at some undisclosed rendezvous near Northampton. By January 1644 Massey's plight at Gloucester was becoming desperate. Not mincing his words he told the House of Commons bluntly that 'if he had not present help sent him, his distress was such that he should be forced to deliver up the city to the enemy'. Parliament responded by instructing Lord Grey of Groby on 7 February to 'cause the Convoy for the Garrison of Gloucester to march thence' [unspecified], suggesting either that Grey's reinforcements had now arrived from Leicestershire or that the convoy, which seems to have been stationary near Northampton during the whole of January, was now reassembling in villages much nearer Leicester before making the final dash for Warwick. By 12 February the convoy, or parts of it, were passing through the Willoughby district, accompanied by large contingents of Northampton, Newport Pagnell and Warwickshire soldiers, as well as Behr's unpopular Dutch or German mercenaries. For the Royalists this was another period of frustration and missed opportunities, in spite of their regional strength. The King had withdrawn the Towcester garrison for an abortive attempt on Aylesbury before redeploying them in Gloucestershire with little effect. A new proposal submitted to Rupert on 3 February to seize Warwick Castle, by a lightning strike from Banbury using a gun and explosives, was not pursued when Rupert left Oxford to take up new responsibilities in Worcestershire, while the feasibility of an equally dramatic attack on Coventry was allowed to slip by. Certainly the parliamentary authorities considered Coventry 'in imminent danger' on 4 February, so much so that precautionary steps were hastily taken to conduct a census to ensure that in the event of a Gloucester-type siege provisions would be eked out fairly among the citizens:

> The Kings side prevailing, the City was in danger of being besieged, and ye people were Numbred in order to ye making and managing provisions, . . . and the number was 9,500 persons.

Banbury garrison, weakened by the Earl of Northampton's absence in the Cotswolds, did not attempt to intervene in the convoy's progress either. There had, in fact, been no serious or concerted attempt to block the elusive convoy since Sir Gilbert Gerard's proposal to intercept it on 13 December or Sir William Vavasour's similar eagerness. The result was that, by 15 February, at least twenty-eight cartloads of the parliamentary ammunition had arrived and 'lay at Warwicke under a convoy of 1,000 horse and foote', while more was on the way. The successful completion of this stage of the journey had been greatly helped by the trivial matter of an efficient military postal service, the London authorities having posted a man every Wednesday at 'Mr Danbys house at Northampton' to exchange letters and information with Purefoy, his Coventry alderman colleague Colonel John Barker and, inevitably, Bridges at Warwick. Ironically, the day the convoy reached Warwick the King made a further appeal to the Midland counties for their assistance.[10]

Once safely arrived at Warwick, about 15 February, the convoy halted for another lengthy period to allow a reappraisal of the situation both in London and locally, and while Parliament considered the formidable logistical problem posed by the forthcoming last, potentially most hazardous stage of the entire journey. As a result, important modifications were made to the plans: the supplies were now to continue by horse rather than wagon, a speedier and above all more flexible mode allowing smaller, more manageable quantities to travel at different times and, if needs be, by different routes. From now on it is no longer possible, strictly speaking, to describe the convoy as a single entity. Orders were therefore issued for a large number of horses, some to be provided locally, specifically from Gloucestershire, complete with saddles and paniers, for which the owners were to be compensated; while a further, unspecified, quantity would come from Warwickshire. The bulk of nearly two thousand, however, were ordered from various parliamentary cavalry regiments, not only locally, from Warwick and Coventry, but from farther afield, from Staffordshire, Nottinghamshire, Leicestershire and Northamptonshire, and even from Newport Pagnell and St Albans. Eight drakes (small cannons) were also ordered, four to be brought from St Albans. Conversely, the quantity of gunpowder to be transported was now halved and new, different, totals were given for guns, match and brimstone. Clothing for 1,200 men, principally coats, shirts and shoes, was added and, finally, £2,200, presumably in money bags. Although Colonel Ferrer was still in command of the convoy itself, there was as yet no overall commander for the whole expedition by 22 February, when Essex was instructed to appoint one. Shortly after Colonel Hans Behr, who had already marched his troops into Northamptonshire to fetch the convoy to Warwick, was named. Estimates of the total complement of escorting troops vary, almost from day to day, but on 19 March, when 'the necessity that the town [Gloucester] is in' was again stressed, numbers given are 3,150 horse and 3,500 foot. Of these, 1,000 horse and dragoons were already waiting at Stratford, 'to carry in their knapsacks and on spare horses powder and provisions into Gloucester'.

Apart from the sheer logistical nightmare, Parliament faced two other overriding problems, the one yet to be confronted, the other only too ever-present. The Royalists had by now, somewhat belatedly, deployed a formidable array of troops throughout the Cotswolds and Severn valley, awaiting the next parliamentary move. Although estimates of numbers are notoriously unreliable there is wide general agreement in this instance of roughly six thousand men, reported on 1 March by the parliamentary chief intelligence officer, Sir Samuel Luke, to comprise the following companies: the Earl of Northampton at Stow, Sir Gilbert Gerard, Colonel Washington and Colonel Sandys at Evesham (the town reportedly 'verie strongly fortified'), Sir William Vavasour at Tewkesbury, Colonel Veale at Painswick, Sir Walter Pye at Pershore, Lord Chandos at Sudeley and Lord Molineux at Chipping Campden, plus some smaller garrisons. Massey himself gave Essex a similar picture ten days later. As though this was not enough, the King ordered Prince Rupert to march with all speed towards Worcestershire on 2 March (though this never materialized), Lord Wilmot was sent to Chipping Norton, and the Earl of Forth, nominally the supreme royalist commander, was also ordered into Gloucestershire on 4 March to take overall charge of the campaign. Evidently no chances were to be taken. Vavasour, who had been eager to block up Massey since December but had been frustrated by politicking in Oxford, was patrolling the Gloucester district, reported successively at Berkeley, Newent and Tewkesbury, to prevent a surprise parliamentary approach from the west, writing to Rupert from Newent on 17 February:

> Coll. Sandes sendes mee word yt he heares yt ye Convoy is cominge towardes Gloster. I hope ye Lo: Wilmoet will secure ye Hills; I shall endeavour to prevent theire cominge ye Low way. . .

Other allies, like Colonel Nicholas Mynne and Sir John Winter, were covering the approaches to the Forest of Dean. The royalist build-up was certainly impressive enough to alarm the new Midlands parliamentary commander, the Earl of Denbigh, who reported his anxieties to London from Coventry on 29 February over:

> . . .the great forces drawn towards these confines and about Gloucester purposely to intercept this convoy; a number too considerable and much superior to our forces intended for this expedition, as you will find by the enclosed paper of the enemy's quartering advantageously for that end.

In the face of this apparently insuperable barrier Parliament needed above all a strong, united and efficient military command structure. This was precisely what was lacking. There was continuous bickering between the rival commanders appointed by different authorities, insubordination and a widespread undermining of the authority of the conscientious, if militarily mediocre, Denbigh, already politically suspect because of his family's known royalism. The remoteness of London's decision-making committees from a volatile local situation added to the confusion: at one point the Earl of Manchester believed the whole Gloucester expedition had been cancelled. The ablest commander, Cromwell, was only marginally involved; when apparently about to join with the Warwickshire forces to escort the convoy and even, at one moment, falsely reported to have stormed Banbury on his way there, he was given instructions to remain near Buckingham until further notice to create a diversion. Obediently, he demolished the small royalist garrison at Hillesden on 4 March, while remaining in contact with Behr should his services be required at Warwick. At the heart of Parliament's problems was the uneasy relationship between Denbigh and the Coventry committee, headed by the prickly and much older Purefoy, 'growne so stiffe by opposing the Earle of Denbigh', a royalist journalist sneered, 'that the Brethren and Sisters are much broken', while relations between the courtly diplomat Denbigh and the German mercenary Behr were acrimonious. Moreover, there were many other urgent demands on Parliament's limited resources at this time which made their prospects look bleak. Cheshire and Shropshire were unsafe, Tamworth and Newark needed immediate relief and a major battle was looming in Hampshire. Had Parliament only known, however, similar confusion over tactics, strategy and personalities existed in the royalist camp, Sir William Vavasour complaining to Rupert after a brief visit to Oxford on 1 March, 'I find such uncertaintyes att Court'. Having warned more than once of 'ye stronge preperatione wch was made for ye relievinge of Glocester' and received assurances that the Earl of Northampton would shortly 'wyne with mee wth at least a 1,000 Horse, Dragoones and foot' at his camp at Berkeley, he was naturally aggrieved to receive 'not above 350 Horse only'. Vavasour concluded by reminding Rupert of Gloucester's strategic importance, 'for if ye Convoy should pass, all south wards would be indangered, but if wee cann but stop them but 3 weekes or a month'.[11]

Meanwhile, in Warwickshire things appeared to be coming to a head by the end of February. 'Severall reports of what distresse that Valiant Commander Colonell Massey is in for want of Ammunition at Gloucester' continued to circulate openly, and as though in direct response a rendezvous at Warwick was set for 27 February, for contingents from 'all the Garrisons betweene Newarke & Warwick', presumably for imminent departure. Massey himself wrote to Bridges at Warwick on 28 February, 'at nine of ye clock in ye evening', asking to know 'yor resolution of march, and the word signall, and way by wch you meane to march', and adding pessimistically, 'yor ptie will be too slender, I am afraid' to confront the enemy 'verie stronge about Stowe, Broadway, Cambden, Evesham, Upton and Teuxbury'. Nevertheless, he concluded in good heart, 'Yet if I have yor tymelie and certaine notice, I shall endeavoure to divert the enemy in these parts, and keepe them on the other side of ye river'. The following day Colonel William Purefoy was ordered to report to Warwick to take command of the Warwickshire forces under Behr, Denbigh confirming to Essex that 'Col. Purefoy is this day gone to Warwick to command the forces of this county in this present expedition'. By the beginning of March Lords Grey, Manchester and Willoughby had all brought in further reinforcements to assist the convoy 'as yet at Warwick', and by 4 March Behr felt confident enough to announce, 'I intend to morrow (god willing) by breake of day to advance to Stratford upon Avon wth my whole troope'. The convoy – or part of it – finally left Warwick on 5 March:

> . . . it was advertised by divers who came from Warwicke Fryday March 8 that the Earle of Manchesters Forces and the rest which were designed for that service went thence with the Ammunition for Gloucester on the Tuesday night before, about ten of the clock at night, and that they carried a great part of it upon horses, and some the Troopers carried behind them, in case they should have beene met withall by the Cavaliers . . .

Behr, it was reported, 'intendeth this night to quarter at Stratford-upon-Avon, where he will remayne untill he be advertized of the enemyes condition'. Behr was at Stratford, already under virtual parliamentarian occupation, on 6 March, intending 'to march tomorrow morning', but on this occasion got no further. Although he reported to Sir Samuel Luke that the Royalists had withdrawn to Winchcombe, he was himself forced to retreat back towards Warwick under a determined royalist assault soon after leaving Stratford. Although this setback is denied in some wild parliamentary accounts (one of which even has Rupert, in reality in Cheshire or Shropshire, 'forced to swim over a river'), it was admitted by more sober reporters:

> Coll. Beare [Behr] went out in a silent way from Warwick with about 200 horse load of Ammunition, and being come to Stratford, sent before a party to discover, who before they were aware, fell into an ambush of the enemies, and had hard work to get off. They lost fourty men; we fear they went not forward.

Further confirmation comes from other parliamentary sources like John Vicars and the reliable Sir Samuel Luke, as usual relaying news from Behr and Bridges to the Earl of Essex, who reports, with some delicacy, on 20 March, that finding the way blocked by Royalists, the Parliamentarians 'held it convenient to retreate for the safety of the ammunition'. The King's secretary even reported on 17 March that the convoy 'is now retired back between Warwick and Coventry'. There must have been considerable confusion. One of Behr's captains, James Burkin, wrote to the constable of Wasperton, half-way between Warwick and Stratford, on 27 March, admitting that 'divers of our horses have miscarried in our march', and instructed payment of £4 to Adam Hanks for the theft of one of his horses. Given the importance of this clash to both sides it is curious that details have remained so meagre, but it is evident that Behr had already been quartering in Stratford for several days when the attack took place, on about 10 March, and that the Royalists were not numerically strong enough to press home their advantage, the bulk of their forces being still deployed much further south. Notwithstanding, Massey boasted to his superiors that 'though closely besieged', he could defend Gloucester, with God's assistance, for six months more. Not surprisingly, the authorities in London were no longer sure of the position at Warwick, writing to Purefoy, Bridges and Ferrer on 15 March for clarification:

> We desire you forthwith to take an exact account of the money, ammunition and arms that were brought by Colonel Farrar and are now at Warwick, for the service of the garrison at Gloucester, and how many men are there under Col. Farrar that came with the convoy and are to serve at Gloucester.

Parliament was continuing to detail even more forces for the expedition. On 6 March Newport Pagnell soldiers were reported marching towards Banbury and a royalist agent in Aylesbury, Sir John Culpepper, reported more *en route* for Warwick on 19 March, while Parliament added a further four hundred Newport men the following day. Ten days later it confirmed that it had ordered the whole process to be repeated, writing to the Northampton committee:

> Considering the necessity of relieving Gloucester, [we] have given order for the same proportion of forces to be sent to Commissary-Gen. Behre to Warwick that were with him before for that purpose,

and therefore desire you forthwith to send thither for your parts that proportion which you sent before . . .

Denbigh and Behr had made a brief expedition into Leicestershire at the end of February to attempt to retrieve the situation in the east Midlands. Parliament now recalled Behr to Warwick, 'to attend the opportunity of relieving Gloucester', while Denbigh was pleased to report to London that at least two consignments of supplies had successfully reached Gloucester without Behr's help, 'by means of small parties' of '40 horse with panniers'. On 6 April, further reliable confirmation of the success came via:

> . . . a Serjant of Colonell Massyes, Governor of Gloucester . . . by whom we have certain intelligence that the monyes formerly assigned by the Parliament for that Garison, and part of the Ammunition (the rest remaining still at Warwick) is arrived safe at Gloucester.

The same day, London instructed Essex to enquire of Behr 'whether the relief of Gloucester can be effected with the force he has' (given the demands of the simultaneous Shropshire and Nottinghamshire campaigns), and to instruct Purefoy 'that if he see the way open to Gloucester . . . with safety, then to go . . . and join with Col. Massey to do service there'. It is clear that about this time more supplies did indeed leave Warwick, perhaps at several times, with Purefoy, Ferrer, Purefoy's Coventry colleague, Colonel John Barker, and a troop of Bridges' Warwick garrison, and the fact that Denbigh alleged that these forces left without his permission was an additional cause of friction. At the end of April 1644 the Earl of Denbigh, while accepting that Gloucester was 'now relieved in all respects', was still complaining bitterly of having been left in the lurch by this unprofessionalism, warning that if such conduct continued, 'I know not what can be expected but ruin to these parts'. The supreme commander Essex was also highly critical of the entire parliamentary war effort; in an unusually emotional, lengthy analysis to his superiors on 8 April he concluded bitterly, 'Newarke is not taken, Lyncolnshire is lost, Gloucester is unsupplied, and the last week there was but a step between us and Death and (what is worse) Slavery'. A final ironic twist came in May when Colonel Ferrer was accused of not delivering all the money entrusted to him for the Gloucester garrison.

The Royalists, however, had even less cause for congratulation. As the much-needed supplies continued to elude them and slip into Gloucester, and news of their defeat at Cheriton in Hampshire became known, they began to withdraw their forces from the Cotswolds, tacitly admitting failure, and allowing Massey to break out and even, impudently, to attack royalist Evesham. Contemporaries, including many Royalists, saw in the whole Gloucester episode the turning-point of the war, as Denbigh himself noted perceptively at the end of February:

> The enemy hath set up his rest so much upon this business that they use no other language than this: that if they cannot resist this convoy, they give themselves for lost, and despair for the future of any good success in their affairs.[12]

It would be easy to dismiss the whole lengthy saga of the Gloucester convoys as a purely military operation, and an unimportant one at that, and that is indeed how it has usually been treated on the few occasions historians have referred to it. The repercussions on the local population, however, cannot be so easily ignored. At the most obvious level, many direct effects may be easily imagined; the presence of large numbers of marauding troops throughout the district for weeks on end, and being relayed by others as soon as they had moved on, must have transformed many small communities into virtual garrisons – as Banbury, Coventry and Warwick already were. 'There are about 2,000 horse billeted in the town and countrey adjacent to Warwick, and have been these ten dayes', notes one parliamentary reporter who goes on to estimate numbers of Royalists in the locality as nearer six thousand. On more than one occasion Stratford was said to be quartering about another thousand. It would be quite wrong, however, to suggest that only the larger centres of population suffered. An examination of the parish accounts for a specific neighbourhood, with their often very precise numbers of quartering soldiers, is proof of the involvement of small villages. As already indicated, the regiments detailed to escort the convoy marched both east to Northampton to fetch it, and then back again, retracing their steps a few weeks later. On their outward march they are briefly recorded in mid-journey passing through Hillmorton, 'when they came to meet the carriages from Northampton', on 18 December – the same district, it may be recalled, which Colonel Hawkesworth's soldiers had already quartered and looted on their way south to Towcester barely two months previously. It is on the much more protracted return journey, however, that their unwelcome presence was felt to the maximum. In a broad diagonal swathe cutting through Warwick and extending from Churchover in the east, on the Leicestershire border, west to Bidford on the Gloucestershire border, few villages were unaffected as from early February and throughout March parts of the convoy or its escort, comprising not only its Northampton, Aylesbury and Newport Pagnell regiments, but also the additional Warwickshire ones, streamed back across the county. Village after village records, sometimes for precise dates, their presence, numbers and thefts, as the entire neighbourhood suffered a virtual military occupation for weeks on end: Willoughby on 12 February, Rugby 2 March, Eathorpe 6 March, Grandborough 18 March, Thurlaston 22 March, Dunchurch 23 March, Sawbridge and Wolfhampcote 23 March. Behr himself quartered at the long-suffering Dunchurch, but many of his companies, far from keeping to the main routes, dispersed, often for long periods, to remote hamlets, presumably waiting for orders which the complicated logistics of the operation must have rendered problematical, acting as sentry units, and certainly in no hurry, in mid-winter, to move on, particularly when the captains had found comfortable lodging. Such was the case, for example, at a cluster of hamlets south of Princethorpe – Eathorpe, Marton, Wappenbury, Hunningham – invaded in early March by Behr's troops comprising about a hundred men in each, under Captains Potter, Stevens and Goddard. Some of these remained as long as two weeks, ordering provisions from nearby Bourton-on-Dunsmore and Draycote:

Provision (viz): A Flitchen of Bacon wch cost Foureteene shillings and Tenn pence. A Mutton worth Seaven shillinges. A Veale worth Seaven shillings. A Quarter of Oates eight shillings & eight pence. Sent to Eathorpe (a village not farr distant from us) towards the mayntenance of Captayne Goddardes companye under the Comand of Colonell Bere [Behr].

At nearby Weston-under-Wetherley the Northampton captains Redman, Clarke and Combes had found even more impressive lodging, at the great Tudor mansion of

Thomas Morgan, the prominent Catholic who had entertained Prince Rupert there before Edgehill. In this single fortnight's stay they took provisions and goods later estimated at £40, before moving on, at leisurely pace, to Snitterfield. At each halt, guard posts were set up, necessitating particularly imperative demands for food, drink and fuel, often in the houses of some hapless villager, like Richard Low's at Napton-on-the-Hill, when Major Lidcot's Northampton soldiers were billeted on the town; to his chagrin thirty-four men with their horses took over his property, 'the guard beinge at my house'. John Bradshaw at Hillmorton had a similar experience in March:

> When Colonell Beare [Behr] his souldiers Quartered at Dunchurch, I having a house lying Vacant there without a Tenant, they kept sentery therein and burnt mee up 7 doors, besides settles, a well Corbe, pailes & railes, to ye value of £2.

When not actually billeting soldiers, each village sent provisions to their less fortunate neighbours who were. Supplies for Behr's troops went from Napton to Dunchurch, from Ufton, Whitnash and Bishops Itchington to Offchurch and Lillington, from Luddington and Drayton to Stratford. The picture of confusion conjured up cannot be entirely due to defective archives, it must have been real enough. Some companies, like Major Abraham Pont's at Whitnash, stayed three weeks, while others moved on relatively speedily only to return again and again, to the understandable exasperation of the villagers: Rugby complained bitterly of Captain Stevens's company quartering there on three successive occasions during March 1644, and Leamington Priors of Captain Bailey's 'one and Twenty days at severall times'. Also particularly dreaded by community and individual was to have their land chosen as rendezvous, inevitably resulting in grass 'spoyled' or 'eaten upp', crops ruined, stables broken into and livestock stolen or killed. Typical was George Medley's complaint regarding his property, unfortunately only too conspicuously placed on Warwick High Street or High Pavement:

> Lost by the Keiping of Rande vows at 3 severall times by Warwike Shire regiement under the comand of Colonell Purfrey going with convoys to Gloster, in the spoyle of my grass: £2

Such rendezvous often affected tiny communities rather than towns, as Behr's at Newbold Pacey-Ashorne. As before, if by this time any countryman was foolish enough to leave his horse unattended, it would be an automatic pawn in the usual extortion process, as at Draycote in March:

> A Gray mare plundered & taken away from Thomas Woster of Draycott aforesayd gent, worth Five powndes, by pte of Captayne Goddard his troope, who also himself was privie to the same and yet would neyther deliver the sayd mare againe nor give other satisffaccon for her.

Occasionally, horses were returned, though often in pitiable condition; one taken by Major Pont from Whitnash 'upon the Expedition to Gloucerster was upon Service 3 weekes'. The loss of a single horse could, of course, be a personal tragedy to its owner, involving much fruitless expenditure of time and energy. John Green at Tachbrook Mallory contacted the influential Thomas Boughton, 'now at Parliament', about his stolen horse; Boughton was sympathetic but firm:

[Boughton] ingaged himself . . . to restore my horse to me at Aucester [Alcester], where I attended, but Could not have him; his answeare was, he wanted horses for his men. The price of the horse: £4.

From each village the litany of losses is conscientiously itemized, sometimes relatively minor, like Henry Garrett's at Wappenbury, who lost all his portable 'howshold stuff' and servants' clothing to Behr's soldiers, sometimes more substantial, like Margaret Sheldon's at Temple Grafton, already plundered before Edgehill and now victimized again:

She lost all the houshold goodes wthin her house, togeather wth all her Corne, plate, apparrell, money and prvision both wthin doores and wthout, to her totall ruine; plundred by Collonell Beares souldiers under the commaund of the Earle of Manchester; wch said goodes amounted to the sume of £400.

The more moderate commanders were themselves in no doubt about the harm done by the soldiers in such activities, not least to public relations and the war effort generally, at a time when recruitment of men, civilian sympathy and the provision of ever more horses were more important than ever, and as large sums of money were being demanded of villagers to support the Earl of Denbigh's forthcoming campaign in the north Midlands. On 2 April Denbigh alleged, no doubt justifiably, that the conduct of Behr's troops especially had seriously damaged his recruitment campaign, and he returned with even greater emphasis to the subject a few days later. Behr's men, he complains:

. . . lying here upon free quarter, and the disorders of his soldiers . . . divert the country from bringing in horses to complete my regiment and hinder the people from enlisting in my regiment of foot; of both these I have had sad experience, being forced to abate much of the proportion of horse the country was willing to bring in, upon their just complaints of the insolent behaviour and plunderings of Commissary Behre's forces, of their unjust taxes of horse, money and provisions, and the unequal distribution of his men in their quarters, sometimes 20 or 30 of them having defrayed themselves for diet and provender at the charge of one poor family.

Behr had, Denbigh continues, blamed 'the miscarriages of his men' on others, and had recently:

. . . so plundered and wounded the people near some towns belonging to me, where my officers were then raising my own company of foot, and so disaffected them, that I could not raise any considerable number, though amongst my own tenants.

Not long after, such popular resentment against the armies and the exactions of both parties would create the so-called Clubmen movement of militant neutralism in parts of the Midlands.[13]

Although, curiously, there was to be no major showdown over the convoy, with the Cotswolds and Vale of Evesham seething with soldiers, it brought in its wake several minor skirmishes. On one occasion, on about 19 March, Colonel William Purefoy, presumably intent on clearing a way forward, sent out an assault party against the Earl of Northampton's company quartered near Chipping Campden, 'to beat upon their quarters'. Large numbers of Cavaliers were taken prisoner, including officers, a victory confirmed by Daniel O'Neale, one of Rupert's cavalry commanders patrolling near Broadway, who promptly promised a retaliatory strike:

> Puphery iss quartered att Camden this night [with] 5 troopes [and] 2 of Dragoones; this morning he came from Warwyck . . . [Colonel] Sands & Collonell Westons regiments are drawn between him and Warwyck, [and] I am now going towards him on this siyd . . . I hope wee shall make him pay for our losse . . .

More interestingly, a deliberate policy of creating diversions and a heightened state of alertness (and therefore aggressiveness) for the various garrisons throughout the region meant a number of provocative sorties to take the enemy by surprise and unnerve him, and these could take place literally anywhere, far from the convoy's actual path. In this category are Cromwell's exploits near Oxford in late February, when from his base at Padbury, obedient to his instructions to act 'in the best way for a diversion', 'Col. Cromwell faced Oxford last week with 1,500 men & drove all the cattell from the very wall to his quarters', 'and left them naked of provision'. 'Colonell Cromwell hath uncattelled them about Oxford', boasted one jubilant parliamentary reporter.

A more violent local drama indirectly caused by the convoy was the Adderbury–Chadshunt skirmish of 3 March 1644, when the Warwick garrison forces decided to

CHADSHUNT CHURCH, WARWICKSHIRE. When most rural building was of wood, the village church often attracted violence as companies of soldiers took refuge from the enemy within its stone walls. As at Alcester, Canons Ashby and elsewhere, Chadshunt church was briefly stormed in such an incident, and nearby cottages fired. The Newsham monument in the nave was probably mutilated by soldiers, though not necessarily on this occasion. (Photo: author)

profit from the Earl of Northampton's absence near Stanway awaiting the convoy and the departure of other Banbury Royalists for Newark, and attacked Royalists recruiting and collecting contributions in the Banbury district. A small cavalry force under Major Abraham Pont and Major Joseph Hawkesworth dashed through the night from Warwick to break into the royalist camp at Adderbury, surprised the sleeping Cavaliers 'before they were drest' at about 4 a.m. on this Sunday morning, and 'took them Dormant', as one Parliamentarian mocked. Many prisoners were taken back to Warwick, but about a hundred of Sir William Compton's cavalry from Banbury, alerted by an escapee from Adderbury, caught up with the convoy half-way to Warwick, 'goinge downe Edgehill and in Radway field'. While half of the Parliamentarians with the prisoners hurried on to Warwick to alert their garrison, Hawkesworth's rearguard 'faced about neere Keynton [Kineton]', engaged the Royalists 'at the end of a lane' and lost twelve killed, before being forced to retreat and barricade themselves in Chadshunt church. Baulked of their prey and not wishing to linger and confront the inevitable parliamentary reinforcements from Warwick, the Royalists set fire to the hamlet before riding off to Banbury. Fortunately, the parliamentary account concludes:

> . . . by Gods mercy, with little helpe the fire was stayed; two or three houses was [sic] burnt, and some rickes of Corne and Hay, and the rest preserved.

Shortly after, Hawkesworth received a substantial pay rise, from 39s. per day to 51s., and promotion to major, probably as recognition of his courage in this incident.

Chadshunt church escaped serious damage, but only just. As it was, the mutilation by parliamentary soldiers of the plaque to Walter Newsham inside the church, of a family later accused of 'frequenting enemy garrisons', may well date from this time. This kind of incident, in which fleeing soldiers sought refuge in churches that were then liable to be stormed by the pursuers, was becoming more common. A similar incident was reported at Alcester later in the year, as will be seen. Added to episodes like those already noted at Stoneleigh and Adderbury, where preaching clerics or even the mere presence of the sacred texts on the lectern could spur soldiers or civilians to violence, they stress the role of churches in focusing discontent and anger. On 18 April, a similar but more widely reported clash took place at Canons Ashby when a small party of Parliamentarians sent from Northampton somewhat impudently to collect taxes in the Earl of Northampton's home territory, was confronted by a large royalist cavalry force from Banbury. The outnumbered Parliamentarians fled into the church, which was promptly broken into 'by fastning a pettard to the Church-door, which instantly forced it open'. The parliamentary soldiers barricaded themselves in the tower until the Royalists set fire to the church and they were 'smoaked down' and captured, together with their arms and the £7 so far collected. Casualties included one Cavalier killed by masonry dropped from the tower's parapet. Often, such incidents were not clear-cut single engagements: they had a tendency to provoke retaliatory strikes, as in this case. The Canons Ashby prisoners were taken back to Banbury, where they were herded into 'ye parsons barne' before being rescued the following week, on 27 April, by a much stronger assault party from Northampton who, adding insult to injury, drove back a royalist unit into the castle, took many prisoners and booty, and rescued some hapless locals who had been pressed unwillingly into the royalist forces, before returning well

CANONS ASHBY CHURCH. Violence at churches was a frequent feature of the Civil War. At Canons Ashby, as at Alcester, Chadshunt and elsewhere, the church was damaged when fleeing Roundheads barricaded themselves in the tower before being 'smoked down' by Royalists using fire and explosives.

satisfied to their Northampton base. The incarceration of prisoners in a barn suggests that more orthodox prison accommodation was as overflowing at Banbury as it evidently was at Warwick at the same time, where Dugdale notes:

> This night about 60 prisoners broke out of ye Lady Hayles her house in Warwick, wch ye Rebells had made a prison for them; whereof some came to Worcester, some to Dudley Castle and others to Bambury, his Matyes garrisons.

This particular Banbury rescue was led by Major Lidcot, only recently returned from escorting part of the Gloucester convoy through Warwickshire. With Banbury's royalist garrison reportedly so weakened at the end of March 'that it is thought a small force would take it', the King ordering Sir William Compton to reinforce it with a quantity of 'Iron shott being moved from Evesham to Oxford', and the energetic governor of Northampton, Colonel Whetham, free to use his initiative in local matters now that Gloucester was relieved, Banbury was in fact shortly to become once again the focus for determined parliamentary action. This particular skirmish, and a further one on 11 May, were merely trials for the much more sustained assault soon to come.[14]

CHAPTER EIGHT

THE PITY OF WAR

LANDLORDS AND ESTATES

By the summer of 1644 the war was at its height, and the mounting toll of disruption, hardship and personal tragedy was affecting, albeit unequally, all aspects of life and permeating every level of society. Although this did not ultimately, in the view of most historians of the period, amount to a 'revolution', the deep economic, social and financial wounds took many years to heal. England was still predominantly a rural society, and one of the most obvious victims of the war was landed society and the tenantry. Financially, some of the losses sustained by private landowners were, of course, voluntary, as in the military spending indulged in by many to equip and maintain private regiments and garrisons, and their many gifts of plate or money for the war effort. These, although difficult to assess, should not be underestimated. As already noted, Henry Somerset, the Marquis of Worcester, claimed that he had contributed the truly phenomenal sum of almost £1 million to the King's cause by the end of the war, and many other substantial figures have been claimed for other major landowning peers and gentry. Naturally, however, it was the war's sheer destructive capacity which created the greatest – and least calculable – losses, and here the private landowner, both big and small, was particularly hard-hit, since the management and very maintenance of estates soon became well-nigh impossible as the war dragged on. The economic and financial impact of the war and its long-term consequences have been the subject of an increasing number of regional studies, and an excellent general analysis, supported by many precisely-documented examples, is provided by Christopher Clay in Joan Thirsk's monumental *Agrarian History of England and Wales*. Some illustrations for the region under discussion have already been given in previous chapters, and the present one will limit itself to supplementing these, before passing to other aspects of the war's effects.

At the one end of the social scale, the major landowning peers certainly increasingly felt the impact of the war. Both sides penalized the other's large estates, and often those

of unfortunate neutrals too, by visiting them with heavy fines, taxation, sequestration, plunder and actual confiscation, and, as has already been pointed out, in
disputed areas which changed sides or were a border district between the two camps
landowners could find themselves paying heavy taxes to both sides, either successively or even simultaneously. The resulting financial losses, cumulatively, could be
huge. After the war the Earl of Northampton estimated the family losses at over
£60,000, and cited the devastation at Compton Wynyates and Castle Ashby, lying
'almost waste':

> . . . which in these times of distraccion have bin plundered and almost pul'd downe, and of late
> uninhabited, are daily fallinge into greater decay, and his Parkes and Chase lying unfenc't and almost
> waste.

As noted earlier, Lord Saye likewise petitioned for large war reparations on similar
grounds.

In the absence of the landlords, either as 'delinquents' taking refuge elsewhere or,
perhaps, actually in arms, their estates were being tended by stewards or agents of
varying competence, honesty and loyalty, powerless to prevent the deterioration of the
resources in their charge, dwindling revenues from tenants unable to pay rents, actual
damage to property, the felling of trees for fuel or fortifications, the disappearance of
livestock and plunder by passing regiments or lawless marauders. Estates unfortunate
enough to be situated in war zones or near garrisons, even friendly ones, suffered
particularly. Sir Thomas Pope's, it was reported after the war, 'lying between Oxford
and Banbury [were] consumed by the King's garrisons'. Pope, it was alleged, had
resorted to evicting tenants, turning traditional copyhold tenures into fixed-term leases
and re-letting at no doubt inflated prices. Such patterns were repeated, with local
variations, across the region, although the impact of the war on these landowners and
their tenants has never been subjected to detailed analysis.

Besides the cases of the Earl of Northampton and Lord Saye, one of the most
graphically documented locally is that of Lionel Cranfield, Earl of Middlesex, whose
loyal bailiff, Robert Fawdon, has left a vivid account of his despair over the estate at
Milcote, near Stratford. Cranfield's case is an almost classic illustration of many of the
aspects enumerated above. Milcote's geographical situation near the Gloucestershire–
Warwickshire border meant that it was taxed by both county committees for Parliament,
while being forced to pay royalist contributions to both Chipping Campden and
Evesham. Situated at one end of the contested Cotswold route, it was of course
exceptionally vulnerable to local skirmishing and the almost continuous passage of
troops and convoys. Like some other local mansions, Milcote had, by the end of 1643,
become a shadow of its former prosperous self, virtually abandoned by its elderly owner
and occupied by the morose steward alone. It had already had its quota of pillaging
troops and vagrants, the theft of livestock by Essex's soldiers before Edgehill and the
plunder by Behr's from Stratford a few months later, other livestock confiscated for
non-payment of taxes and occasional occupation by soldiers. Tenants, themselves near
subsistence level and, no doubt, not unwilling to take advantage of the situation, were
unsympathetic to their lord's problems, threatening to surrender their leases and
demanding rent reductions because of the dangers of living in an area at a military
crossroads. 'The tenants would put all on your honour', Fawdon reported gloomily to his

master. Such a situation was indeed far from untypical. At Hardwicke, near Gloucester, the bailiff of a church estate received no rents for three and a half years, the war having:

> . . . caused the tenants to throw up their leases, it lying between Gloycester & Worcester, and they forced to pay contribucon to both garrisons, besides Free quartering continually to the one partie or the other, whereby the said tenants were disabled to pay their rents.

At Milcote, meanwhile, Fawdon's appeals to both the parliamentary authorities and the Oxford Royalists apparently fell on deaf ears:

> Here is so many great impositions upon your honour's lands on both sides that I can hardly get any money to keep your debtors from driving, for never was there such taxes upon these parts, lying between the Garrisons. I have been at Coventry and Warwick, but no good to be done but either pay or drive the grounds.

At sheep-shearing he dared not attempt to send the wool to market for fear of highway robbery, 'for here it is much eyed, and I cannot conceive any safety in sending it away, having so many dangers to pass through'. Royalist soldiers had taken over Milcote for several days after Edgehill, stealing sheep and cattle, and now there were more troops quartered on Cranfield's other nearby estate at Sezincote, near Moreton-in-Marsh, heralding almost, it seemed to the distraught steward, a new dark age: 'God of his mercy amend it; or the soldiers will have all; for they are the masters of all'. Other estates had been taken over wholesale either by friend or foe, and some, like Wedgnock and Broughton, stocked with livestock stolen from miles around and consequently attracting violence to the area as soldiers either raided or defended them, devised retaliatory strikes and encouraged outraged locals to take the law into their own hands, as at Broughton in July 1643:

> Divers active Malignants had gotten great store of their own cattell together, and all that they could steal from their neighbours, and had driven them into the Lord Sayes Pastures and into some grounds belonging to Master Fynes [Fiennes] neer Banbury, making them their Commons, and intending from thence to supply Oxford with provision; which divers of the well-affected and resolute Country-men, observing and seeing a convenient opportunity, gathered together and went into the said grounds, tooke those that were stolne, and restored them to the right owners, and kept the rest for their owne use.

Similarly, Broughton attracted Bridges' attention on more than one occasion for the same reason:

> Serjeant-major Bridges, Governour of Warwick-Castle . . . sent out severall parties of Horse from the Castle at severall times, which brought in from within two miles of Banbury out of the Lord Sayes grounds a thousand sheepe which the Banbury Garrison had stolne from the poore inhabitants of the Countries and places adjacent, and also surprised an hundred of the enemies horse, taken a Serjeant-major and some other officers . . .

Clearly, profitable estate management could not long survive such conditions, and even estates which were not sequestrated and were placed in less exposed geographical situations than Milcote or Broughton saw a substantial loss of revenue over the war years. Robert Sidney, Earl of Leicester, one of those genuinely torn between loyalty to the King and rejection of the King's policies, watched the rents on his Warwickshire

WESTON HOUSE, LONG COMPTON. The great Tudor home of the wealthy Sheldon family was one of many local mansions repeatedly damaged and plundered by marauding troops during the war, some being destroyed completely. Weston survived relatively unscathed, though its owner, William Sheldon, a royalist sympathizer and a catholic, was forced to flee. It was eventually demolished in 1827 (see p. 139).

estates at Temple Balsall and Long Itchington fall to half their pre-war value. That these great landowners almost invariably survived the war in spite of all and, indeed, recovered remarkably quickly, should not be allowed to minimize the almost unendurable hardships of those years when their estates were ruined and their houses either brutally garrisoned or actually destroyed. One of the worst cases was that of the prominent Catholic William Sheldon, of Beoley, Worcestershire, and Long Compton. The family had risen to prominence under the Tudors by a combination of judicious marriages and property-buying, had acquired a string of South Warwickshire and Worcestershire estates and built a palatial mansion at Weston, near Long Compton, where the King had been entertained in 1636. Periodically charged with recusancy and implicated in papist scares, it was inevitable that Sheldon should be accused of active malignancy and suffer sequestration. He vigorously denied the charge, 'being never in arms, but sequestered on sinister information', a claim later accepted by the parliamentary authorities, in spite of his having been present in Worcester garrison at the city's surrender in July 1646. The Coventry committee even went as far as ordering Sheldon:

> . . . to be protected from Wrong or Violence. These are to Charge and Command All Officers and Souldiers whome these may concerne to forbeare to molest, imprison or to offer any Vyolence to the said Mr William Sheldon . . . or to Plunder or Pillage his houses, or to take his horses, Beasts, Sheepe, Cattle or other goods upon any pretence whatsoever, Provided that the said Mr Sheldon Shall not beare Armes against the Parliament.

These belated measures brought little comfort to Sheldon, who had been constantly harassed and pillaged from the beginning. His own remarkably restrained account of his woes, far from being exaggerated, actually omits details acknowledged by independent parliamentary sources, and one can only sympathize retrospectively with this humane and cultured old man, whose family had pioneered local tapestry-weaving and who had himself purchased a copy of Shakespeare's First Folio in 1628, and for whom the war years represented an unforgettable nightmare:

> In September 1643 my house at Weston in Warwickshire was ransacked, and my cattle and goods taken away by souldiers, to a great vallew.
> In December following, my house at Beoley, in Worcestershire, was burnt to the ground, and all my goods and cattle there plundered by the souldiers to a very great vallew, besides the incurable loss of my . . . court rolls consumed in the fire.
> Immediately after, all my flock of cattle for my provisioning of housekeeping was taken from us at Weston by A party of souldiers, by means whereof I and my wife were inforst for our refuge and safety to go to the city of Worcester; and after a short stay there, finding the inconvenience of living in A garrisson, removed to a small Farme house in the parish of Clifton upon Teme . . . where wee remained about 8 months, until all our goods and horses were also taken Away by A party of souldiers and the house threatened to be burnt. Whereupon my wife and my selfe not knowing whither to goe by reason of Sir William Waller's souldiers had then lately before taken away all our provision and stock of cattle at Weston, compounded with the committee of Warwick Shire, were fors'd to returne back to Worcester. And after A short stay there and long before the said city was besieged, wee returned to Weston.

The great Tudor mansion at Weston was fortunate to escape serious damage on this occasion, surviving until it was almost casually demolished in 1827. But other houses were less fortunate. As we shall see, as the war progressed, so the almost wanton destruction of England's country mansions increased.

Further down the social scale, the comfortably-off yeomen was no more immune to the effects of the war than the lord of the manor, particularly if he were unfortunate enough to be related to known delinquents or the politically unsafe, as could easily be alleged on the flimsiest evidence. The case of Silvester Warner of Wolston, of a rich merchant family with long-standing foreign trade, is no doubt typical of many others not so clearly recorded. With a brother a prominent Royalist and sons whose estates were sequestrated he must have presented a sitting target to parliamentary soldiers who plundered him. Warner petitioned the authorities with an emotionally-worded plea: men from the Coventry garrison had seized all his household goods, horses, hay and corn, valued at £300, pretending that they belonged to his brother. He earnestly hoped that this 'vast sum' might excuse him from further taxation at least for one whole year, 'by wch tyme his hope is that God will either take him out of this world or make him more able to undergo these burdens'.

Similar cases of middling yeomen who saw their modest fortunes plummet as the effects of the war began to bite are not hard to find, even though they are usually recorded only accidentally, as it were, when a protest or petition is involved. One such case was that of Thomas Warde of Allesley, evidently far from rich but affluent enough to possess a few horses, a small estate and perhaps three or four tenants. With the renewed scouring of the country for horses to equip the Earl of Denbigh's spring campaign of 1644 his plight was desperate enough for him to plead for Denbigh's protection and permission to keep 'a couple of nags or mares of small value . . . for my selfe and man to ride about my occasions'. His distress is voiced in an account all the more eloquent for being sober and unsensational:

> I have not received any rent this three quarters of this yeare, and I am not able to subsist. I have allowed fifty pounds a yeare out of a hundred for the weekly tax, and now my land is throne up into my owne hand, and noe body will take it of mee. I must be forced to stocke it my selfe, which land lieth seaven miles beyond Warwicke, and I must goe very often hither my selfe, which I cannot doe without my lordes protection.

Minor gentry hoping to remain uninvolved and who took the trouble to seek protection from the local military commander found it an untenable position. George Raleigh of Farnborough claimed to have been plundered by Major Bridges' forces from Warwick long before he committed himself to the Royalists, and 'not wth standinge he hade my Lord Brooks ptection'. Once he had opted for the King his situation worsened: besides being forced to send provisions to at least five different parliamentary units within the space of a few months during the summer of 1644 – Waller's, Fiennes's, Cromwell's, Northampton and Aylesbury regiments – his house was plundered, with boots, shoes and stockings being taken, his woods were decimated and sheep racks and large quantities of timber taken to assist in the siege operations against Banbury Castle, and a start was evidently made on dismantling his very house: 'Taken away by Capt. Hawksworths Soldiers . . . from his manor house of Farnbrow About 60 Casements wth windowes, Barres, bolts & other Irons: £20 . . .'.[1]

The legacy of the war was of course not necessarily short-lived. It could sometimes be perpetuated across the centuries in minor, unexpected and little-explored ways. At Shenington, near Banbury, for example – and presumably similar cases could be unearthed elsewhere – from at least 1650 until well into Victorian times tenants of property belonging to Oriel College, Oxford, were legally required by a specific clause inserted in the lease to pay 'over and above [their] rent . . . all charges, taxes, military payments, contributions and free quarter for soldiers'.

THE POOR

It would be inexcusable, however, to give the impression that the wealthy alone suffered. Naturally, those who had most had more to lose, but apparently trivial losses to those who had next-to-nothing were an even greater catastrophe, since they were without the assets, health and resilience to recoup them. The theft of one cow or one horse could be a greater tragedy to the person who had little else than the theft of several prime herds to the lord of the manor. As we have seen, the working farmer or small husbandman was particularly hard hit, a target for continual plunder by the troops desperate for the very things which were essential to the farmer's own life: his horses, his livestock, his carefully-stored foodstuffs. Horses were crucial to husbandry, for without them the farmer could neither plough, harvest, store nor market his produce. Early on in the war, in February 1643, Prince Rupert's seizure of horses was already causing serious problems for some Oxfordshire villagers, so that 'the inhabitants are constrayned to joyne 3 or 4 of them to make upp a teame', and this situation became desperate in many places as the war continued and the whole countryside was ransacked for horses. As for quarter, taxation, forced labour and the provision of food and drink, all these depressed tenants' ability to pay rents and affected virtually every villager. Although the major commanders quartered on the more substantial householders as a matter of course – Behr on Thomas Nash at Stratford, Grey of Groby on Dr Richard Langston at Whichford, Sir William Waller on William Browne at Tysoe – these cases were hugely outnumbered by those of lowly villagers who had little option but to accept whatever demands for quarter and 'diet' were made of them on vague promises of later compensation. That such demands were often totally unreasonable we have on the unimpeachable authority of the Earl of Denbigh, who charged Behr not only with 'insolent behaviour and plunderings', but with '. . . the unequal distribution of his men in their quarters, sometimes 20 or 30 of them having defrayed themselves for diet and provender at the charge of one poor family'. Apart from husbandmen, village labourers, carpenters and carters could not expect to go unmolested for long, harvest was disrupted and the requisitioning of horses and carts affected everyone. Even a brief examination of the parish claims for one or two villages reveals the lowly status of many, if not most, of the claimants. Among the sixty inhabitants of Brailes submitting complaints of quarter and plunder few were wealthy. Most were modest husbandmen; Nicholas Bishop a labourer, Thomas Eddon a shoemaker, and many others, twenty years later, still had only one or two hearths to their name. There is little doubt that a close analysis of the social spectrum of a representative cross-section of parishes would corroborate this general point.

Although evidence is not entirely conclusive, the plight of the poor probably worsened considerably during the war, as the administration of justice and poor relief at parish level broke down, following the suspension of the county Quarter Sessions from 1642 to 1645 and of court leets which no longer met on many manors. Cases of destitution could no longer be dealt with, and poor levies remained unpaid in many parishes, often specifically, as at Priors Marston, 'by reason of the late troubles'. There were frequent disputes over unpaid levies, as at Temple Grafton and Wellesbourne, they went unpaid at Newbold-on-Avon, in Priors Marston for four years, in some of Stratford's neighbours for six, and at Balsall for ten. Many JPs now devoted more time to raising troops or meeting demands for 'contributions' made by both sides, while constables, treasurers for maimed soldiers and overseers of the poor now collected not only for the needy but also for the troops. Perhaps not surprisingly therefore, almost three times as many cases of poor relief were dealt with at the resumption of the Quarter Sessions as before the war, and many of these, one way or another, were caused directly by the war.

The war certainly dramatically increased the incidence of vagrancy: over three times as many cases involving resettlement of vagabonds were dealt with for 1649–60 as for the pre-war decade. In 1651 official anxiety was expressed over the 'multitude of poor impotent people and other that . . . wander up and down and thereby become rogues and vagrants', and soon such fears became so ingrained that Warwickshire tradesmen saw a threat to their livelihood in this proliferation of vagrants, producing a petition blaming 'the late distractions' for the crisis:

The trade of the Kingdom in general and this county in particular is much decayed, and the petitioners impoverished by reason of a swarm of idle, loose persons hatched up together in the time of the late distractions destitute of a fixed being and going under the name of Scotchmen, wandering up and down the kingdom to vend wares and bear[ing] no burden of payments in any public charge whatsoever, lodging in barns, stables and the like, by means whereof many villanies have been committed and much further danger may be justly feared; and if they should be suffered to trade here (having served no apprenticeships to any trade) will inevitably destroy the petitioners in their estate and trade.

The petition had the desired effect. At Easter 1662, the Warwick Quarter Sessions court ordered:

. . . that the several high constables within this county do forthwith upon sight hereof direct their precepts to all the petty constables within their divisions that they . . . cause a strict and watchful eye to be had over Scotchmen, and others who wander under the names of Scotchmen as petty chapmen to vend linen cloth and other commodities, and to cause them to be publicly whipped and punished as rogues and vagabonds if they shall presume to travel without licence or passes, and to be sent home to the several places of their last dwellings or places of birth, according to the form of the statute in that case made and provided.[2]

For the destitute, the elderly or handicapped, the situation was often critical. At Leek Wootton, regularly plundered by the Royalists, one inhabitant, John Hankhorne, pleaded to the parliamentary tax authorities, 'I am a poore Tenant which have nothing but upon the rack rent, being tenant at will', while the constable recorded of another, 'Thomas Barnet is very poore and hath nothing but what he getts by his dayly labour'. The situation in most parishes cannot have been very different. In the most populous of all, Brailes – which not so long ago had been receiving assistance from other parishes under the old Elizabethan Poor Law, because its own resources were inadequate to relieve its many destitute, and with a substantial proportion of indigent cottagers 'soe extreame poore that they have neither lands nor tenements, goods or Chattels' – lists of inhabitants in arrears of taxes and others assessed, significantly, at 1s. were regularly returned by the constable. Elsewhere there were cases like that of the destitute widow Ellen Raphes of Stretton Baskerville, lame and over eighty years of age, whose house was for some reason pulled down during the war, or the many war widows like Mary Hemming, whose husband Robert was killed at the siege of Worcester, Margery Browne of Pillerton, whose husband Thomas was killed at the siege of Banbury, and Alice Higgins of Warwick, whose husband William died 'of divers hurts', leaving seven unprovided children. The plight of those afflicted by age, poverty and lameness could be desperate. Thomas Flower of Frankton petitioned for relief on the grounds that he had been 'several times plundered by the Scots and other armies . . . fallen into great want and poverty, being near one hundred years of age', and Christopher Mills, already a poor man before having to quarter troops and have wounded soldiers foisted on him, then broke both legs in severe weather and pleaded for relief, fearing that he could not otherwise survive. His 'humble petition' is moving not only in the recital of his distress but in the degree of abasement deemed requisite on these occasions:

. . . Humbelly Shewing unto yr good honors tht yr pore petissioner hath at all times From the beginning of the wares bine willing to billit and quarter yr souldiers, as he hath bine Commanded; and is behind For theier payment neare threescore pounds, to the utter undoing of yr pore petissioner his wife and Children, being lame this twelfe month and not abell to helpe hime selfe; and for the not payment is soe farre indebpted that he is everye Daye in Danger of being layed in prisson for the money that he oweth. Beseeching yor good honores to pittie my missorabell Distressed estate and be ameanes to healpe me to some of my money, and I and all mine shall be for ever bound to praye for your honors eternall happines.

The Coventry parliamentary committee accepted his petition in June 1646 and instructed its treasurer, Thomas Basnet, to release £3 for immediate relief. The collection of taxes in the villages, often performed by soldiers accompanying the constable as a precautionary measure, was evidently strict and spared no one. At Exhall, near Alcester, the constable reported no arrears 'except one . . . poore man yt owed more than hee was worth', and Widow Lumley, who was duly forced to pay up by the usual effective procedure of seizing goods:

> At Exhall ye sd Captaine [Benjamin Lovell] did for arreares distrayne of Widdow Lumley, her sd arrears beinge Five groates. Ye distress taken was a payre of Sheetes, which sd distress was restored uppon ye payment of yd sd moneyes.

The Coventry authorities were not insensitive to cases of hardship, however:

> It is ordered by the Comittee that Mrs Comsby shall have 50s abated of her Rents, in regard Mr Barrowes hath testifyed she hath a hard Bargayne.

Other well-documented effects of the war include masters refusing to take back apprentices after serving on the wrong side, levies unpaid for making essential repairs to the local bridge so vital to the life of the community, and an alarming increase in the number of beggars. Occasionally, specific acts of violent intimidation are recorded, like that involving Maurice Walsingham of Coughton, elected to the office of High Constable only to be 'grievously wounded by divers of the king's soldiers and thereby disabled to execute the same office'.

But perhaps the largest single group of those suffering the direct consequences of the fighting comprises the wounded soldiers themselves, disbanded, unpaid for often long periods, without a trade, and a burden to the community to which they returned. Their petitions for relief dominated the parliamentary committee's proceedings for many years after the war. One such, doubtless typical of so many, was that of Paul Spooner of Nuthurst, near Tanworth-in-Arden, who:

> . . . haveing binn A soldiar three yeares and upwards in the pliamt servis wass wounded and . . . is utterly unable to stand, or any waise to get one peny to helpe him selfe; and now beeing disbanded hee hath not any more pay to reseve, nor any meanes of his owne, or freinds that are Able to releive him; his mother beeing A poore old wyddow, and no other meanes to Leive upon but what shee gets by spinning for iid. a day att whose poore Cottage howse, wch standeth upon the wast in the hamlet of Nuthurst; the inhabittants of the said hamlet beeing all togeather unable to Alow him any mayntenance, ther beeing in the said hamlet but two freeholders and foure other dwellers That rent small Tenemts; And no les Then seven poore Cottagers, and all of them reseve allmes . . .

Many such desperate cases were of soldiers who had served throughout the war on a fraction of their full pay, like those formerly under Captain Hunt who submitted their request through their corporal in 1646 and were careful not to prejudice their case by demanding too much:

The peticoners most of them served under ye said Captaine from ye very beginning of ye warrs for halfe ye pay which other troops had, and could never have lived had they not beene helped by their freinds and beene supplied with horses & Armes att their charge. They are farre more in Arreares then any other Troope . . . And yet never discredited them selves by muteny or offering any dishonor or abuse to this Honoble. Comittee, but have patiently waited, hoping in tyme to receive some satisfaccon towards their great arreares . . . Humbly prayeth yt yor Honors so soone as possibly you can will please to afford them some money towards their Arreares.

The most graphic cases are the 'humble petitions' of the disabled:

Yor petr. [Edward Wisdom] hath beine a soldier in the parl ment service the space of 2 years, and at the first seige before Banbury Castle was shott so dangerosly that hee is beecom unable to follow his Caling and (being now disbanded) hath not any meanes to subsist . . .

[Robert Field] was a Volunteer at the beginning of these present warres, [and] came with Coll. [William] Colmore at ye first Entring upon this Citty [Coventry] for ye Parliament, & was afterwards Listed under the said Coll. [in Capt. Thornton's company] & being (amongst others) commanded to storme ye Castle of Banbury was in ye sayd attempt of storming shott through the legg and had his leg then broken to peeces. It cost [him] for a horse litter to bring him home xiiis., & for one to attend him xxxvs., over & above the vis. wch he payd to his Chirurgien for his paines . . .

Consider too the case of a sergeant, Thomas Arne, a member of the parliamentary garrison at Warwick for over four years, who:

. . . beinge sent out uppon a partee, was shott in the face by the Enimie, wch shott deprived him of the sight of his left eye. And afterwards beinge at the first siege before Banbury Castle, by reason of an other shott in the face yor peticioners other eye was much endangered, and hee is at continuall charge for the preservation of the sight thereof.

Among the most interesting pleas are those in which a military doctor, William Green, petitions the authorities for reimbursement of his professional expenses:

For Dressing & Cureinge [i.e. treating] of Will Rosset, beinge very daungerousely wounded with a shott through the thigh, wth a fracture of the head of the bone; beinge unable for 8 weekes to stirre out of his bed & chamber, & after prooved tediouse & troublesome.

We desire you to pay to Mr Wm Greene twenty shillings for his cureing of Job Marston, being shott through both the thighes.

In a possibly unique case from this district the Coventry 'surgeon' then submitted his bill for expenses and accompanied it with a note of the actual medicines used, listed with the bogus erudition of the day and providing poignant insight into these desperate cases, few of whom could have long survived:

For dressinge & Curinge [i.e. treating] the wounded souldiers at Astly . . . being three, 2 whichof weare daungerously wounded, the one deeply wounded under the Emunctory of the heart & wounded in the arme, the other wounded through his side into the over lobe of the lungs & runne through the arme with a broade sword; wch occasioned the spendinge of many medicines, Inward & outward, also much paynes & attendance . . . I was forced to goe over to them 9 or 10 severall times. I do very well desire seven pounds besides Inward medcines:

Inward Medicines

	£	s	d
Imprs. a Cordiall potion	0	2	4
It. a vulnerary drinke	0	3	8
It. 2 suppositories	0	0	6
It. a sanative pectorall drinke	0	3	4
It. a pectoral trochiske	0	0	4
It. an openinge Electuary	0	1	4
It. a pectorall Lincture	0	2	1
It. a Cordiall potion for 2	0	4	8
		18	3
Total to be pd	7	18	3

In all cases these petitions are endorsed by a scrawled note instructing the committee's treasurer, Thomas Basnet, to pay the modest sums requested. As only the successful petitions seem to have survived, the overall scale of relief provided for what must have been an avalanche of requests is impossible to calculate.

To quote a limited number of random cases is no doubt scientifically inconclusive. But the sheer quantity of such entries in the Quarter Sessions records and the graphic pages of the military and parish accounts constitute a cross-section of vividly-recorded cases illustrating the effects of the war on named individuals – the tip, clearly, of a very considerable iceberg of unrecorded cases. There is little doubt that overall, the end of the first Civil War already saw a substantial increase in numbers of poor people of all categories, and whether this increase was caused directly or indirectly by the war is perhaps academic. And this increase coincided with the breakdown of the system of poor relief at parish level, as the authorities themselves recognized in 1647 by admitting that relief had been affected, 'for want of due execution of such wholesome Lawes and Statutes as have beene formerly made'.[3]

CHARITABLE INSTITUTIONS: ALMSHOUSES AND SCHOOLS

One little-explored social consequence of the war concerns those poor inhabitants fortunate enough to have been hitherto protected from the full rigours of poverty by the local almshouse. Charitable giving, whether by individual benefactors or communally, inevitably tends to be one of the first casualties of severe social upheaval, and although, once again, evidence is only fragmentary, there can be little doubt that the war was directly responsible for the decline of many a charitable institution, if only temporarily. Certainly the governors of Christ's Hospital, London, had no reservations on the point:

In respect of the troubles of the times, the meanes of the said Hospital hath very much failed for want of charitable Benevolences which formerly have beene given and are now ceased; and very few legacies

LEICESTER'S HOSPITAL, WARWICK. Ancient almshouses were frequently requisitioned for military use, damaged and survived the war only precariously. At Warwick the hospital's life was disrupted as its revenue disappeared and occupying parliamentary troops took over the chapel and supervised the construction of the town's fortifications through its grounds. (Photo: author)

are now given to hospitals, the rents and revenues thereunto belonging also very ill paid by the tenants, who are not able to hold their leases by reason of their quartering and billetting of soldiers and the taking away of their corne and cattell from them.

For Warwickshire there is meagre but incontrovertible evidence that whether or not charitable giving itself dried up, the war directly affected the well-being of those in the two ancient institutions at Warwick and Stoneleigh. At Warwick, where work on the town fortifications continued unabated throughout 1643 and 1644, with a fresh order on 4 September 1643 for more 'gates and barricades in and about the Burrough', the general disruption previously referred to in Chapter 6 soon reached the almsmen at Lord Leicester's foundation. Although the conscientious Rice Jem, Master since 1635, conceded in May 1644 that 'the wrongs done by the soldiers are not now so great as at the first' – implying serious, if unspecified, damage earlier in the war – 'yet now they have taken the Great Chapel to their use [and] make continued incursions to the House, to the fear and trouble of the poor old men'. Situated at a strategic vantage point at the town's edge, on or very near the line of the medieval walls, its tranquil surroundings were threatened with the same 'works' as the rest of the town as plans were formulated 'to draw a bullwark all along the garden', to include pipes 'layd at the hospitall in the works to convey the water'. Although new pensioners continued to be admitted on the death of inmates, the hospital's revenues, derived from increasingly precarious tithes and leases in Napton, Harbury and many other places, declined in the war, and securities were, as the warden himself pointed out, 'in these tymes [of] litle worth'. By July 1644 Jem was seriously worried that the local committee's tax demands could not be met, 'must needs fall short, and the poore Hospitall soe nobly founded quite fall to the ground; the wch thing I would be loath to see, and live'. Touchingly, the warden referred more than once to his presumably unavailing attempts to enlist help by appealing to the Governor of Warwick, the Coventry parliamentary committee and even Parliament in London, to relieve 'this poor distressed Hospital'.

At Stoneleigh, home of the King's Commissioner of Array, Sir Thomas Leigh, who had entertained Charles before Edgehill, the ten ancient almshouses maintained by the Leighs fell victim to a classic Civil War situation, namely the sequestration of both the family estate and the vicar's living in 1643, thereby handing the Royalists an impressive propaganda coup. Although such consequences were clearly unintentional, the royalist news-sheets were able to manufacture much moral indignation at the inhuman parliamentary measures of those 'resolved to rob Hospitals' and who 'doe not allow one farthing for the present livelyhood of these poore wretches'. Such inhumanity is, sadly, only to be expected, the royalist pamphlet concludes bitterly, of those prepared to condone a murderous assault on the vicar of Stoneleigh in his pulpit as he was recently preaching a charity sermon on behalf of the paupers of the parish, prevented by the war from leaving the village to beg of others. The truth, no doubt, is less lurid, having to do less with ethics than the reality of war: the accommodation offered by charity institutions, including many schools, was in wartime an unacceptable luxury liable to automatic requisitioning for military use. One royalist journalist noted, significantly, that the King had decreed places in these institutions for the relief of his wounded soldiers, only to have the plans thwarted by Parliament, since 'many of His Majesties Almes Houses and Hospitals are under the command of the Rebels'. Even if nothing more dramatic happened to them, many almshouses must have served as makeshift military camps and, dependent on dwindling income from lapsed endowments and rents, must at the very least have fallen into serious disrepair. Such was the case at Rugby, where after the war a charity commission ordered repairs to the long-neglected school buildings and almshouses, 'so ruined that . . . they will take at least £63 10s 0d to be put in Repair'. Others simply fell victim to the general destruction of war, like those at Hereford, reportedly set on fire deliberately by the Royalists in September 1645, presumably lest they should serve as an enemy garrison.[4]

If the enquiry is extended to the schools themselves, those other charitable institutions often at first associated with almshouses, major problems face the local historian and prevent a simple answer to the question, 'How were they affected by the war?'. In the case of the large majority documentary evidence is either pitifully meagre or lacking altogether. But the subject has been hampered not only by the scantiness of the surviving records, but also by inadequate local research and an assumption, common until recently, that educational provision was synonymous with the ancient grammar schools – ignoring the vast numbers of unendowed common schools in market town and village, the very existence of which was, until very recently, unrealized. These were often ephemeral, uninstitutionalized and makeshift, but must nevertheless have been of inestimable value to generations of villagers who learnt to read and write in the schoolmaster's house, the church, or, as in John Evelyn's case, at the church porch. Until further painstaking research complements that pioneering work already achieved for part of the area under discussion, one must fall back on isolated cases for which surviving evidence is suggestive. Although there is no reference to a Warwickshire school as clear-cut as that to Grimston's in Norfolk, where the war reduced the school to decay and forced the master to flee, it is reasonable to suppose that many schools must have lived a precarious existence during the war years. Without any established educational system to protect them, dependent on endowments and individual benefactors with goodwill and energy, and at a time of severe social upheaval and mobility, individual and collective hardship and offering tempting accommodation for passing regiments, all schools other than the soundly endowed privileged few were vulnerable. Staffed by either unimpressive or politically-suspect clergy or freelance masters or dames ekeing out a living from the fees they charged, many must have disappeared. Little enough, indeed, is known about how even the major grammar schools survived – how many closed for a time, like Shrewsbury, lost valuable books, or sustained structural damage. For Warwickshire the assumption must be that those under strong parliamentary protection, like Warwick, Stratford, and Coventry, staffed by dedicated and influential Puritans, survived relatively unscathed and escaped the physical damage caused elsewhere, as at Pontefract and Ashby-de-la-Zouch, or the complete destruction, as at York. The pioneer Leach found nothing more to say about these three major schools other than that they 'seem to have gone on quietly during the war'. Leach's conjecture is reasonable, for Warwick's master was Thomas Dugard, a humane, godly scholar who remained at his post throughout the war, while John Trapp at Stratford, of Dugard's circle, also had impeccable political credentials: both were familiars of Lord Brooke. The enlightened parliamentary committees at Coventry and elsewhere had every reason to protect such schools and no doubt did so.[5]

Other endowed schools deprived of such protection were, however, much less secure. Rugby, for example, unfortunately situated at an important military crossroad from the outset, from Nathaniel Wharton's 'good quarter' there in September 1642 to Crawford's in March 1645, seems to have suffered from a combination of a weak master, Raphael Pearce, and the pressures of war. Both the master's salary and the fabric of the school were affected. When defensive constructions were improvised on school land, tenants withheld rents because their land had been 'spoyled by the workes', the school building was 'stopped with straw to keepe out rain and wind', and the school's tenant at Brownsover, William Howkins, released only a derisory 2s. 7d. of the master's annual salary of £12, because of his 'Taxes and quartering soldiers', reducing the schoolmaster to selling timber and scavenging for fuel for himself and his family. The town certainly suffered exceptionally heavy quartering: Cromwell's colleague Lawrence Crawford rested there 'with a strong force' on his march from Northampton to Banbury on 30 March 1645, though whether this was at the old manor house on the site of the present school house, as a plausible tradition claims, is not known. Although Cromwell himself is not mentioned in the parish accounts, the schoolmaster, like so many in the town, was continually called upon to provide free quarter for the soldiers, the first as early as August 1642.

The case of the ancient grammar school at Brailes is quite different, though equally suggestive. Situated in a remoter corner of the county next to the churchyard of a straggling, overgrown village which had declined from its prosperous market and guild status in the early Middle Ages, the school had already entered on hard times. It had survived the Dissolution, but had suffered from much subsequent property speculation as its lands had been sold off piecemeal since Tudor times and it experienced difficulty in recruiting a competent schoolmaster on a fixed salary of £8 1s. 8d. which had become insufficient after a century of inflation. Care is therefore needed not to attribute its problems exclusively to the effects of the war. But with a notable catholic family, the Bishops, suffering sequestration, as patrons, a royalist vicar, Gerard Verrier, soon to suffer a similar fate; and virtually all the village lands owned by either the Earl of Northampton or William Sheldon, both sequestrated Royalists, it was clearly in no state to withstand the new pressures of war, all the more so that it was now deprived of the patronage and supervision of the royalist Bishop of Worcester which must to some extent have protected its interests hitherto. Its fortunes during the war are not documented, but by the time of the Wase enquiry shortly after it is clear that problems were mounting as it found itself unable to adapt to the new post-war world. The new vicar, William Richardson, ejected at the Restoration for ideological reasons but then reinstated, had discontinued the traditional practice of teaching in the school, that task being consigned to a succession of parish clerks or their nominees 'approved by the parish' but, according to the leading trustee William Bishop, of doubtful competence, being 'but meanely qualifyed for learning'. This fact, coupled with the war itself, had allegedly devalued traditional learning, elementary English replacing Latin. It had no proper governors or eminent visitors, possessed no library or manuscripts and was generally, it was implied, but a shadow of its former self. Brailes school did in fact survive, but the probability is that the war effectively accelerated its decline.

Of other local grammar schools virtually nothing is known, but the teaching in many must, at the very least, have been interrupted, particularly after the end of 1643, when the commissioners scouring the country to impose sequestration orders on catholic estates were told to extend their activities to 'inquire after malignant schoolmasters', thought to be many. Those offering unusually spacious accommodation, like former hospitals, must sometimes have been taken over by commanding officers, as Brackley's Magdalen College was by the King just before Cropredy, while difficulties of one sort or another may reasonably be conjectured in many cases. Can the new one at Hampton Lucy, ambitiously teaching Hebrew, as well as the universal Latin in 1635, and taught by Christopher Smith, the vicar of largely royalist Cherington in sequestrated William Sheldon territory over a dozen miles away, have long survived? How did Alcester's fare, 'situate in the field on the South side the town, towards Arrow', in the constant quartering, skirmishing and plundering which took place in and around the town, and whose master, Mr Maris (Morris?), was advised after the war to seek legal redress to recover his salary arrears of £20 per annum, recently unpaid through the sequestration of William Fortescue's land in Weethley? What, above all, of those schools unfortunately situated in areas heavily and almost continually quartered by the ravenous troops, fought over and besieged, like Adderbury, Chipping Campden, Chipping Norton, or actually on battlefields, like Southam, whose vicar was the prominent Royalist, Francis Holyoak, or Long Itchington, whose vicar was until 1642 the same Raphael Pearce of Rugby? Were these affected, as was Thame's, which had to close for a time following war damage? Was Banbury school's demise hastened or caused by the use of its St John's

Hospital premises in the churchyard as an overflow military prison and the devastation of successive sieges? No documentation has so far come to light to answer these questions unambiguously, but such schools must, at the very least, have experienced severe difficulties.

The many petty village schools were no doubt equally, or even more, precarious, dependent so often on the benevolence of individuals. Here reading, and sometimes writing and arithmetic, were taught in unorganized, improvised accommodation, and were important enough in time to attract criticism for stealing pupils from the endowed schools. By their very nature ephemeral, they must have become even more so during the war. If the tiny school at Compton Wynyates, to which old Richard Newman walked across the fields in Brailes as a boy in the 1520s, had survived into the 1640s, its perilous situation on the Earl of Northampton's estate must surely have made it one of the war's very first casualties. Some schools, naturally, were situated at 'crossroad' villages, like Shipston-on-Stour and Henley-in-Arden which became automatic camps for passing regiments. At Shipston, where a school apparently existed long before the well-documented Pittway foundation of 1706, the school is unlikely to have survived in a village forming part of the Bishop of Worcester's estates, referred to as royalist in sympathy and whose schoolmasters seem to have been members of the local royalist Croft family. Similarly at Henley, which must have experienced disruption in the heavy quartering it suffered and incidents such as that 'when an alarum came into the towne', Richard Bannister's position as schoolmaster was affected (though details remain obscure) when Beaudesert parsonage, held by the conspicuous Royalist John Doughty, was sequestrated. At tiny Combrook, near Kineton, the recently-founded school was also vulnerable to politics, and immediately Compton Wynyates was captured by Parliament, the autocratic new governor at Compton, George Purefoy, diverted the £8 p.a. salary of the schoolmaster, Edward Langley, to his own use, reducing Langley to 'teaching ye towne children gratis in ye free Scoole'. Finally, a more classic case presented itself at Swalcliffe from the very outset of the war, where the royalist vicar–schoolmaster, Thomas Merriott, was charged with using 'reproachful terms' against Parliament. Learned author and scholar he may have been; he was nevertheless harassed by the parliamentary authorities, plundered and imprisoned at Compton Wynyates for a time when the house was captured by the Parliamentarians in June 1644, had his living sequestrated and later died in poverty. His schoolteaching must have been an early casualty. The Swalcliffe example is simply one documented case among so many which must have arisen in an area where so many clergy, who traditionally doubled as village schoolmaster, were politically harassed, undermined and became the subject of parochial dissent before being finally ejected as delinquents or malignants. In some cases, no doubt, they were relatively painlessly replaced, but in far more, particularly where replacement ministers themselves became the centre of controversy, educational provision in the village must have suffered. But the fact remains that virtually nothing is known of the fate of these village schools, known to have been in existence pre-war, at places like Ashow, Berkswell, Bourton-on-Dunsmore, Brinklow, Harbury, Kenilworth, Leamington, Stockton, Tysoe, Warmington, Whitnash and Wilnecote. On these and on so many others the records have so far remained tantalizingly silent.[6]

COMMUNICATIONS AND TRADE

The widening ripples of social disruption affecting everyone are hinted at in a very different, mundane yet crucial local feature, the village bridge. There is only scanty evidence of its fate in the Civil War, but what there is suggests the mounting toll of the conflict. In mid-seventeenth-century England bridges were few and far between – London itself had only the one – and because they were heavily used and, often, already ancient, were in constant need of repair. Traffic was so heavy on some that on occasions, as at Deritend in Birmingham, orders could be given for the bridge to be chained and padlocked to force travellers to cross by the alternative ford, in order to save the bridge from unnecessary wear and tear. Many bridges were ramshackle wooden structures, likely to be swept away in stormy weather, like Offchurch's, but even the stone ones were already notoriously defective before the war. At Brownsover, the 'ancient stone bridge . . . leading to Lutterworth' was described as 'ruinous and in great decay' in 1638, Shipston-on-Stour's 'in decay' in 1633 and again in 1635, Barford's, 'lately repaired' in 1641, was again 'in great decay' by 1649, Bidford-on-Avon's 'in very great ruin and decay' in 1638. It is clearly impossible, therefore, to prove that the spate of bridge repairs recorded after the war was directly due to war damage, though it is reasonable to suppose that the constant, unprecedented military use by convoys and whole regiments of already dilapidated patched-up structures was disastrous. More pertinent, however, is the deliberate tactic of bridge-breaking adopted by both sides in the war in an attempt to gain time and prevent enemy pursuit. The most celebrated episode of this was the King's march from the Cotswolds to Bewdley and back in June 1644, which was accompanied by a systematic campaign of bridge destruction in Worcestershire, when Bidford's also was a victim, according to Sir William Waller. The most celebrated Warwickshire case was Clopton Bridge, Stratford. On 28 November 1645 Parliament ordered Colonel John Bridges to demolish 'one principal arch' of this bridge, 'for the securing of this county from the incursions of the enemy's forces', the historic bridge being allegedly 'the only pass that the enemy hath or can have all this winter between Oxford and Worcester, Hereford, and the other garrisons in those parts'. Stratford's bridge was far from being the only one so damaged, however. Those at Salford, in Aston, Birmingham, at Bretford and Halford on the Fosse Way, at Thurlaston and Barford, and Nell Bridge, between Aynho and Adderbury, were either 'plucked down for the safety of the county' or to gain a temporary tactical victory. The most well-documented case is perhaps Halford's, apparently destroyed by the Royalists almost two years before Stratford's in a vain attempt to prevent the Gloucester convoys moving south in February 1644. On 1 March Sir William Vavasour wrote to Prince Rupert:

> Wee have broken off three Bridges betweene Warwicke and Campden, wheare ye Genlls. Regiment lyes. They ashure mee yt the convoy canot pass but by Banburye, soe yt wee shall have fayre [battle] fieldes, if wee had forces enough.

The parliamentary commander, the Earl of Denbigh, confirmed that Halford Bridge had indeed been 'cut down', and that the Royalists:

. . . intend to do the like to all the other bridges which lie in the way; and to make the passages more difficult they are cutting trenches in all the fordable places of the River Stour.

The precise damage done to Halford bridge is, in fact, unclear. A year later, a few pack-horses of a large parliamentary convoy from Gloucester to Warwick were reported to have crossed the narrow bridge, yet in 1650 the county authorities were enquiring 'how it became broken down', and were informed, evidently incorrectly, that it had been broken by parliamentary decree, like Stratford's. Nor does it appear which other bridges over the Stour may have been affected.

Clearly it is impossible, given the scanty and random nature of the available evidence, to quantify to what extent such activities affected civilian traffic. But there can be little doubt that, whether intact or not, local bridges were places for the innocent traveller to avoid if at all possible. They were a natural focus for military activity, attracting guard posts, ambushes, and frequent skirmishes, as at Powick in September 1642, Stratford in February 1643, Halford itself more than once, and Nell Bridge, near Adderbury, also at several times. One typical incident, probably associated with the Halford incident of March 1645, resulted in fatalities at Newbold-on-Stour, the Tredington burial register recording, 'Two men killed at a skirmish betwixt the Kings Maties soldiers and the Parliaments above Newbold church bridge.' Occasionally, as at Cropredy, bridges attracted a full-scale battle.[7]

The dangers associated with bridges were however only one aspect of the wider general hazards of travelling at all, as many incidental contemporary accounts reveal. The most mundane journey on private business a parish or two away now made the prudent think twice, like John Fetherston at Packwood: 'the tymes are so distracted and dangerous that I dare not adventure to ride to the sayd debtors, nor they to come to me'. Quite apart from the increase in lawlessness on the highways – the word 'highwayman' dates, significantly, from this period – the roads themselves, as already noted in John Ogilby's telling comments, were atrocious. Roads like the notorious and heavily-used Dunchurch highway, already mentioned, were so waterlogged after showers that, as at Oxford, traffic could be stopped until the water had subsided. After one skirmish in Northamptonshire a troop of horse floundered in the mud and, reportedly, never extricated itself. In midwinter, carters could prove unobtainable, as the Earl of Middlesex's estate steward reportedly sombrely from Stratford to his master in London in December 1644:

I doubt I shall not gett Waggons or Carts to carrie these goods (if the way be open) for now the Season of the yeare makes the waies soe bad that I feare they will not goe.

Specific evidence exists from Cheshire and Somerset of the further deterioration of roads during the Civil War through abnormally hard use, and the fact that parochial obligations to repair them were unenforceable, that highway surveyors' appointments lapsed and bridge committees did not function all compounded the problems facing the would-be traveller, even if the local bridges and fords remained theoretically passable. The general decline in trade and commerce experienced in the war years was no doubt due in part to this vicious circle of events triggered by the war itself.

In the circumstances it may seem surprising that local markets and fairs survived, as they generally seem to have done from the incidental references to those at Banbury, Rugby, Warwick, Stratford and elsewhere. Yet the age-old country practice of going to market was, as already hinted, fraught with new dangers, as even at times of relative peace when no local siege was taking place or when the nearest garrison was at some distance, the innocent wayfarer was likely to lose his goods, his horse and even his own liberty, as in the cases from Tysoe already reported. Transporting goods was potentially risky: Colonel John Barker, the Governor of Coventry, noted on one occasion taking £225 from 'severall drovers, being suspitious psons'. As we have seen, John Bridges at Warwick was adept at the same practice, while the Earl of Middlesex's steward, Robert Fawdon, was fearful of highway robbery for his consignment of newly-sheared wool from the Milcote pastures near Stratford and alarmed at the depressed market for his master's livestock of 'Fatt Cattell' of which:

> . . . I am in daly feare, and of others also, and heer we can sell no kind of cattell neare the vallew, for the cuntry never was in soe great miseries & feares as att present since these sadd times began . . . I feare the safetie of the passage, for I know that some waynes and Waggons weer pillaged this Last week by the way.

Many country folk must have simply stopped going to market, fearful of the open road, the general lawlessness and the violence which the market itself might attract. Visitors to Banbury market were evidently being screened at a royalist checkpoint at one stage, when John Danvers of Upton House and his servant Richard Gillet went 'on a market day':

> . . . and at their Entrance the souldiers did disarme the said Mr Danvers, but at his returne home the same day the said souldiers did deliver the said Mr Danvers his sworde againe.

If soldiers did not actually burst in upon the market place, they might well, as at Adderbury in the spring of 1645, be loitering on nearby highways, 'lurkeing for people going to the Fayre'. Interestingly, there are occasional hints that as the war dragged on local market-goers increasingly resented this kind of interference from the soldiers. A report of October 1644 states that Worcestershire Royalists 'marched towards Aulcester in Warwickshire [Alcester], but it being the Fayre-day they durst not enter the Towne'. Evidently less inhibited, 200 royalist cavalry under the Earl of Northampton reportedly plundered Rugby market on Saturday 27 September 1645, besides committing many other outrages in the district, including the abduction of five men from an unspecified church 'in sermon-time' the following day. Rugby fair was evidently considered potentially dangerous enough to persuade the parliamentary authorities at one point to send troops to 'secure' it, while Stratford was reported to have been totally 'undone' by repeated royalist plundering:

> The King's forces . . . have undone the richest market town of the bigness in all the country, for besides good store of plate and other commodities which they took from gentlemen, they have taken all the shopkeepers' cloth and other rich wares, to a very great value.

But perhaps the clearest evidence in the Midlands of the decline of the market comes again from the Earl of Middlesex's bailiff at Milcote, who wrote to his master on 7 May 1643:

> I was on May day at Stow Fair, that usual great fair for sheep, where thousands used to be sold; and I am assured there was not 100 sold that day there.

The fair at Evesham was, in fact, cancelled in September the same year because of fears aroused by the mere presence of so many royalist regiments in the area in the aftermath of the siege of Gloucester.

Trade generally was, in any case, already seriously reduced, not only by the direct effects of the war but also by measures deliberately taken by both sides to restrict or even halt cross-country commerce, lest it should benefit the enemy. The cases of some individual merchants are well attested. Those needing to travel for their livelihood were particularly vulnerable, as permits were increasingly required to move even short distances, and these could be withheld, or only grudgingly accorded, by the local commander. Two Dudley traders provide typical cases. Henry Finch, an ironmonger, was held up at Birmingham as he was fetching goods from East Anglia, by Colonel 'Tinker' Fox, the parliamentary governor of Edgbaston garrison much derided by the Royalists for his supposedly lowly origins, until he could produce a warrant from the Earl of Denbigh, and Margery Davies, a haberdasher, received a parliamentary warrant in June 1644 with a stern caution, giving her:

> . . . full power and authority to carry, sell and vent all such hatts as she shall make, to Coventry . . . provided she carrys nothinge with her prejudiciall to the state, or doth not convey any of her hatts to the enemyes garrisons.

Nor were the high and mighty necessarily exempt from the demeaning process of requesting travel permits, which could easily be refused. When Sir William Compton wrote from Banbury Castle in March 1645 to Sir Samuel Luke at Newport Pagnell for a six-day safe-conduct pass for his mother and her servants to visit Moulsoe in Buckinghamshire on family business, Luke replied courteously, but a trick was suspected and nothing came of the application. Where the applicant was known to be an ally, a protective *laisser-aller* might be issued, a useful precaution in the prevailing anarchy, as in the case of Sir William Waller's authorization for the Parliamentarian Richard Lucy, dated 31 January 1644:

> To all officers & Souldyers or whom soe ever else it may Concerne: These are straightly to charge & Comand all & every of you to permitt the Bearer hereof Mr Rich. Lucie wth his servants & horses to passe through yor severall Courts of Guard aboute his necessary occasions to Warwicke, & to repasse thence to London wthout any lett or molestation, & for soe doeing this shall be yor sufficient warrant.

The picture, although confused, is one of increasing interference with the transport of goods. Trade between Coventry and the royalist north was disrupted by both sides, retaliatory or copy-cat seizures of carters' goods are widely reported, while the King issued a proclamation to several Midland counties on 17 October 1643 'to restrain all Trade or Commerce with the City of London and some other Cities and Townes now in Actuall Rebellion'. The King also prohibited the free passage of cloth to London in 1643, and although the Warwickshire parliamentary authorities were ordered in May 1644 to allow cloth from the west Midlands to pass through to London unimpeded, this was reversed the following year when all trade between London and the counties of

Worcestershire and Herefordshire was ordered to be stopped by military action to prevent the profits from helping the royalist war effort. The specific case of cloth illustrates the general plight of traders' livelihoods, now seriously at risk. Such was the overriding importance of clothing the soldiers that convoys of cloth which ventured on to the highways were regularly waylaid. In the first week of May 1644, in what must have been one of the last acts of the royalist garrison at Compton Wynyates before the house was captured by Parliament, Dugdale reports laconically, 'A loade of Clothe, etc., drawn by 6 Oxen and 2 Horses, taken by a pte from Compton garrison, at Wellesbourne, within 4 miles of Warwick'. A much more spectacular raid occurred almost a year later, barely three miles from the same spot, at Halford Bridge, on 6 March 1645, when Sir William Compton's Royalists from Banbury were busy collecting contributions near Ilmington. A detachment of the Banbury scouts routed a small party of Parliamentarians, only to discover that they were the advance party of a much larger parliamentary contingent escorting a huge convoy of clothing 'of great value' travelling from Massey's Gloucester garrison towards Warwick via Chipping Campden. Hastily calling up their main regiment, the Royalists successfully ambushed the convoy of heavily-laden pack-horses as it had begun negotiating the narrow Halford Bridge, evidently either repaired or less than effectively damaged the previous year:

HALFORD BRIDGE, WARWICKSHIRE. Bridges were few and far between, and often attracted violent incidents. Like Stratford's and many others in the district, Halford's ancient pack-horse bridge on the much-used Fosse Way carried much military traffic, was deliberately broken to impede enemy movements and was the scene of several lethal ambushes. (Photo: author)

Sixe or seaven of their packs got over the narrow Bridge at Hawford Mill; the other 72 Sir Charles and his Souldiers seized, three or foure whereof the Souldiers presently opened, and found to be broad Cloath of 20 shillings a yeard. In those packs which the Souldiers opened were wrapped in the Cloathes Mony, Plate, fine Linnen and rich Apparell . . . Sir Charles slew 12 Rebels in the place, tooke neare 70 of them Prisoners, and almost six score Horses. . .

The Royalists claimed the booty to have an estimated value of £10,000: 'they in Gloucester say they are undone, and cry they have lost many thousands of Pounds'. The sober parliamentarian reports vouchsafe for the accuracy of the royalist account, admitting the loss 'in the conveying of some clothiers packes of great value . . . taken betweene Campden and Banbury', but blaming the disaster on 'the misguidance of the officer that commanded'. An interesting postscript to the incident was provided eight years later, when the Earl of Northampton petitioned against penalties imposed on him by the clothiers for his brother's theft. Far from denying that it took place, he defended the action as a legitimate military one, the traders' consignment being not an innocent one, 'but as it was defended by a convoy under whose protection they had placed themselves'. The King himself had, moreover, approved the seizure in order to clothe his troops.

With such actions being commonplace, it was little wonder that areas dependent on a particular trade felt that the situation had reached crisis point. The clothiers of Worcestershire, along with those from many other counties, protested that trade was dead and petitioned the King for a relaxation of the trade ban, pointing out that:

. . . their Trading chiefly consisteth of Clothing, that their Weekly Assessment and other Taxes were so heavie (and want of Trading so great, by reason they were prohibited from comming to London, where they heretofore vended their Cloth and other commodities) that they were utterly unable to pay the money assessed on them, and the poore not able to subsist any longer. . .

The petition was apparently granted but, according to an enraged Parliamentarian, was ineffective, for shortly after:

. . . having His Majesties Protection, the Clothiers and Chapmen issued forth their Commodities. But being met withall by the Kings Forces upon the way, the Carriers had all their Horses and Cloth taken from them; and his Majesties Protection made onely a stalking Horse for their Insolencies and Robberies.

The countryside was, in any case, so severely depleted of horses by theft and requisitioning that the movement of goods other than military was becoming well-nigh impossible. One particular royal order which has survived, dated 15 June 1643, must have been one of many such; it authorized two officers:

. . . to impresse and take upp in the citty of Worcester or in any towne, parish or village within ye Severall Counties of Gloucestr, Worcester, Warwicke and Oxford As many Horses, Carts and Carters as shalbee requisite and useful for the draweinge and carriinge of all such Ordnance as are now to be brought from ye saide citty of Worcester to this citty of Oxford.

Although some trades, like shoemakers and tanners, prospered as a result of increased demand (Alan Everitt has pointed out, for example, that Northampton benefited so much that the town's great shoe industry grew out of the war), many other traditional ones were adversely affected, either directly, by military action of one kind or another, or indirectly, by the general knock-on effects of the war, trade depression and punitive extra taxation. It was against the latter, in the form of the hated excise, that a band of Warwick butchers led by John Lathbury protested. The decline in the numbers of buyers at the town's market had forced them to lower their prices to an uneconomic level, 'at a great under rate', yet they were still expected to meet the exorbitant demands of the excise in spite of being far from affluent:

> . . . for ye most parte of them [are] of very meane estates (not being able to mayntayne themselves, wives & children), some of them being very aged, and allsoe ye greatest parte (having families wch consist of 6 or 7 in a family) whose wholle subsistence meerly relyeth upon their trade for their support . . .

The building trade, in particular, must have suffered a disastrous slump through the diverting of stone and increasingly-scarce timber to military use. Like Arden, Wychwood Forest was severely depleted during the war, and it is probably significant that a detailed study of domestic building in the Banbury region has pinpointed a conspicuous gap in activity for the period 1640–5.

There can be little doubt that cumulatively, the weight of the isolated strands of fragmentary evidence from the parish accounts and the wider testimonies of national archives is such as to substantiate the claim made by a social historian writing over sixty years ago that the Civil War caused 'serious dislocation of industry and trade'.[8]

THE SUFFERING COMMUNITY

The increasing dislocation of ordinary life described above gives at times a picture of near-chaos, of a virtual breakdown of law and order as the war came to dominate all aspects of life and military rule prevailed. Accounts, invariably subjective and often biased – though not automatically to be dismissed for that reason – suggest a community already deeply divided at the onset of the war, even more so as the war reached its height. A letter dated 13 May 1644 by a Parliamentarian describes the continuing recruitment of yet more soldiers, large-scale interference with local farming, extortion and side-changing:

> Most of the inhabitants in those parts [Warwickshire] doe now grow sensible of the miseries which they have a longtime indured by reason of the violent and outragious courses of the Cavaliers, and as a manifestation of their affection to the cause of Religion and Liberty undertaken by the Parliament, many of them doe daily repaire to the Castle at Warwicke and to divers other places, so that within lesse then this moneth past there have beene foure or five compleat Troops raised as an addition to the Garrison at Warwicke Castle; and they might have many more men . . . if they could but get horses for them. One Captaine Chamberlaine, with divers others . . . have lately raised a Troop of Horse . . . and about a week since . . . came to Admington to gather contribution Money . . . whence they tooke many Cattell which they drave away with them. But upon the Composition of the owners,

who paid them the Money they required, they restored the Cattel unto them. Many Souldiers come daily from the Kings Army to Warwicke Castle, and divers unto Colonel Massie at Glocester.

The petitioning process of the early stages of the war, already described in Chapter 2, was continuing unabated, both from interested groups and individuals. One, by the 'Gentry, Freeholders and Inhabitants of the county of Warwick' and dated 21 August 1644, addressed both Houses of Parliament as part of a concerted campaign to consolidate the power-base of the controversial young Earl of Denbigh, who had already met much local opposition, particularly from the Coventry-based parliamentary committee. After a preamble acknowledging the Earl of Denbigh's great service to the county and pledging continued support for his 'noble proceedings', it comes to the point: the major grievances of taxation and mismanagement by the county committee. Taxes are unjustly high, being 'double, if not treble, at the least' those of larger and richer neighbours like Northamptonshire. Moreover, no upper limit has been set by a committee with 'unlimited power to Tax, Assesse and raise what sum they thinke fit', resulting in many anomalies. The petitioners therefore request the weekly assessment to be reduced and then fixed, and for more competent financial management to be adopted, with accounts properly kept and submitted to a committee – by implication unrepresentative and incompetent at present – enlarged by the addition of 'Gentlemen of quality, known estate in the county, and approved integrity'. The petition then rehearses the familiar complaints of Warwickshire's exceptional suffering, 'the losse suffered by free quarter, frequent plunder almost throughout the whole County, and diverse other insupportable burthens, hard taxes and other grievances', and warns Parliament that the effect has been to produce 'a generall discontent upon the whole people, and thereby most are disabled, others discouraged, to doe that service for the Parliament which otherwise they might.' It recommends that 'all just complaints and grievances whatsoever' be in future submitted to the Earl of Denbigh. It ends by drawing Parliament's attention to two specific examples of implied mismanagement, though without detailing precise charges: the government of the town of Warwick (under the autocratic rule of Colonel Joseph Hawkesworth), and of the newly-installed garrison at Compton Wynyates (under the equally abrasive Major George Purefoy), and suggests that part of the county committee sit henceforth at centrally-situated Warwick rather than the inconveniently distant Coventry. Twenty Warwickshire gentlemen presented the petition, reportedly signed by over three thousand inhabitants of the county, in person to the House of Lords on 21 August, the Lords 'well approving' it, the Commons promising to consider it when pressure of other business would allow. Some of the petitioners were reported to be returning home 'very merry and well satisfyed' the following week, but others were still 'residing in town' on 1 October, and increasingly anxious to return home to safeguard their properties from an increasing incidence of plunder encouraged, they alleged, by Denbigh's absence in London.

There seemed little, on the face of it, to object to in the points raised. Warwickshire's parliamentary committee, however, though reluctant 'to foment differences', was sufficiently stung by these 'aspersions cast upon them' to respond angrily a month later in a lengthy 'remonstrance', bearing all the hallmarks of William Purefoy. The committeemen begin by condemning the petition as being both a 'most improper' procedure and lacking in credibility, devised by people masquerading as well-intentioned neutrals but in effect 'secret enemies of the state': they who have done nothing for the war effort themselves have no right to criticize others whose actions 'saved the county from the cavaliers' at the outset of the war, in the summer of 1642. They then move on to rebut specific charges. The committee's composition is defended. Members are all disinterested local men who have themselves paid the penalty of their devotion to the cause in suffering personal loss, and who have striven to implement Parliament's laws justly and impartially as far as possible in difficult times. There may have been odd instances of unjustified confiscation or misconduct, but these were in exceptional circumstances, either when quick decisions had to be made, where a town was known to be disloyal or when actual resistance was met with, as when a soldier was killed doing his duty. If plundering took place, it was for similar reasons. The committeemen reject unfair comparisons with other counties, like Northamptonshire. The Warwickshire regiments have conducted themselves well, the Earl of Denbigh's perhaps less so, but even they could not protect every village or remain permanently at hand when duty sometimes calls outside the county borders. In conclusion, if occasional errors and misconduct have been committed, these were few and invariably in the cause of duty.

The intensity of these local rivalries between a Denbigh camp and a Purefoy one has been well analysed by Ann Hughes, and one sympathizes with the county committee, assailed with unprecedented burdens, who nevertheless managed, as she has pointed out, to create out of the chaos of war a reasonably efficient military and financial organization.[9] It would be easy to dismiss the controversies pinpointed by this petition as academic. But that they were anything but is proved not only by the wealth of illustrations of community and individual suffering already given but by the specific nature of the grievances recited: that assessors often imprisoned rather than confiscate goods; that villagers had to suffer the free quarter of soldiers collecting taxes, a double injury; that soldiers were being paid by one county, Worcestershire, while feeding off another, Warwickshire, and stayed far beyond the term agreed; that whole herds of livestock were distrained at a time from some villages; that unruly and insolent soldiers had plundered indiscriminately; that horses taken supposedly for army service had, in fact, been sold for individual profit; and that no redress was given for damage. None of these complaints is unfamiliar to a reader of the parish accounts, buttressed as they are by a spate of further petitions from villages and individuals alike. Far from diminishing, the conflict was intensifying and widening for so many, bitterly complaining, like Barton-on-the-Heath in a rating dispute later with Long Compton, that their taxes had been unjustly raised 'in these late unhappy wars'; praying earnestly, like Cubbington, 'that no more troops may be quartered upon them, as those already sent have consumed all their provisions', and complaining, through one inhabitant, Thomas Parsons, that 'the town where I live is deep rated for the weekly assessment, and we send provision often to Warwick and Kenilworth, horse-meat and man's-meat, and do so very often entertain soldiers'; overburdened, like Rowington, with abnormal numbers of immigrants seeking security which it could not support and witnessing actual violence when plundering soldiers stripped Lawrence Bird's home of its contents and 'did beate yor pet. his wife & children, and comitt great outrage'; plundered and over-taxed, like Alcester, to the extent that it was left to a humane gesture of one soldier, Captain William Acock, to entreat his commander, the Earl of Denbigh, to spare it futher harm; or visited, like

Stratford and Banbury in particular, by outbreaks of plague exacerbated, if not actually caused, by the influx of soldiers. To such villages the war was not some remote ideological debate, but a recurrent nightmare. Lillington's distress at not being able to supply the Earl of Denbigh with even the two horses demanded of them shines through the uncertain grammar of its constable, William Robinson, and his band of village representatives each appending his mark:

> Whereas your good Lordship, out of your especiall care & opon onavoydable necessity, have issued out your warrants for the raysing of a company of horse for ye safe guard of ye County, whereby wee are enjoyned to send in to your Lordship two horses: howsoever wee are wonderfully willing to satisfy your Lo: expectation, yet such is our present weake state, not onely by former losses sustained and taxes imposed but also most chiefly by the late heavy burthen of 4 troupes, consisting of about 220 psons opon free quarter, who besides the eating of our pvision in our houses and barnes, & spending our seed pvided for ye grounds, have much impoverished us by spoyling some of our horse & exchanging others; that we are utterly onable to comply with your Lo: as otherwise. We could heartily desire our late losses amounting to £200 & opwards more than the yearly pfitts of our Lo: opon extreme racke, we all of us being poore tennants & most of us deeply engaged by reason of our great debts. The pmises considered, in all humility we prsume to become humble peticioners to your good Lo: desiring what favor your honr can afford us, and wee shall never cease to pray to the Almighty for the prospy of your Lo: & noble family.

Few Warwickshire village constables could not have drawn a similar picture in the summer of 1644. As David Underdown has written:

> Much of the distress cannot be quantified – the emotional scars of bereaved widows and parents, the psychological scars of families divided by the war, the physical scars of the maimed, the financial scars of the ruined . . . War taxation; the quartering of soldiers; plundering; the physical devastation of town and countryside: these were universal realities for the population of all regions, royalist and parliamentarian alike.[10]

CHAPTER NINE

THE HEIGHT OF THE WAR: SUMMER 1644

THE COMPTON GARRISON

Much has already been said of the hardships inflicted on the community, but of all the crosses borne by the long-suffering villagers none was worse than that of having to endure the presence of a local garrison. The quarter and plundering associated with periodic troop movements, though intolerable when they occurred, were random and intermittent, dependent on the vagaries of orders and tactics decided elsewhere. But a neighbouring garrison, once established, was a permanent affliction. Not only did it automatically invite the constant threat of attack and perhaps prolonged siege, with unforeseeable local repercussions and widespread devastation, but even in lulls of activity when the flames of war were flickering elsewhere a local garrison meant an oppressive presence of ill-disciplined troops kicking their heels under an arrogant commander accountable to virtually no one. The Parliamentarians' description of Banbury's royalist garrison as a 'den of theeves' seems perfectly justified by the parish accounts, and some garrisons, indeed, became notorious even with their own side. To Clarendon's disgust the royalist garrison at Chipping Campden 'brought no other benefit to the public than the enriching the licentious governor thereof, who exercised an illimited tyranny over the whole country'. Of the major garrisons affecting south Warwickshire and north Oxfordshire, none fits Clarendon's description better than the Earl of Northampton's seat at Compton Wynyates, once it was seized by Parliament in June 1644. The great medieval fortresses of Warwick and Kenilworth were recognized as virtually impregnable, and after the initial months of the war were largely left alone by the Royalists to dominate their immediate neighbourhood unchallenged. Banbury's two sieges did indeed affect a wide region, as will be seen, ending the Royalists' notorious reign. But Compton was equally centrally situated for the region under discussion, and was not only besieged at least twice, in June 1644 and January 1645 and threatened at other times, but was manned for two interminable years by a strong parliamentary force under a particularly unscrupulous commander, Major George Purefoy, an arrogant

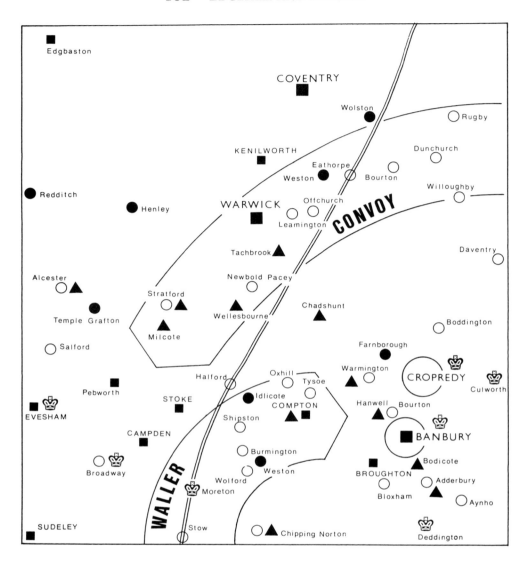

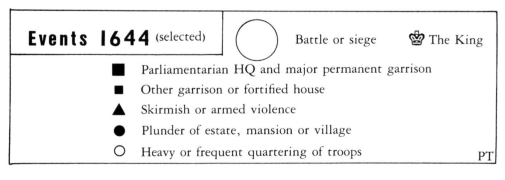

Events 1644 (selected)   ◯ Battle or siege   ♛ The King

- ■ Parliamentarian HQ and major permanent garrison
- ▪ Other garrison or fortified house
- ▲ Skirmish or armed violence
- ● Plunder of estate, mansion or village
- ◯ Heavy or frequent quartering of troops

PT

young kinsman of the indomitable Warwickshire Puritan, Colonel William Purefoy. The impact on the local community of the new Compton garrison, curiously ignored by historians, is difficult to exaggerate. It was clearly considered almost as important as Banbury itself by both sides – judging on the one hand by the initial succession of royal warrants issued from the court at Oxford guaranteeing its protection and, on the other, once taken by parliamentary troops, by the substantial taxes levied on neighbouring parishes to support it, the scale of the fortifications and repairs undertaken to maintain it as a viable base, the royalist attempt to recapture it and, above all perhaps, by the vastness of the area deemed necessary by Parliament to support it. From Alcester in the north-west to Bicester in the south-east and comprising literally half of Oxfordshire, dozens of parishes in the two counties were bled to support it financially and supply it with provisions. Compton Wynyates (invariably referred to as Compton House in contemporary sources) was in effect strategically placed for both sides as the farthest frontier post between their respective areas of influence, in what was effectively a buffer zone for much of the war.

Until its capture by the Parliamentarians in June 1644, surprisingly little emerges of the activities of Compton's royalist garrison. It was situated at the heart of the extensive Northampton estates, all sequestrated, and being managed by a loyal steward, William Goodman of Winderton, Brailes, himself a substantial yeoman, and there seems to have been little plundering of the largely loyal surrounding villages by the resident garrison. The assumption must be that, situated in a fold of the hills remote from the main arteries of the region, it was considered by both sides to be a secondary outpost to Banbury. The Earl of Northampton himself was, of course, almost permanently absent on active service, and although he maintained a small garrison there which had evidently constructed some 'workes' in the grounds, the house and park were probably not fortified to any great extent. Why Parliament should have suddenly turned its attention to Compton is not entirely clear, but as already indicated, the parliamentary relief of Gloucester released many regiments for service elsewhere, and there was a general build-up of activity throughout the south Midlands throughout May and June. Parliament had ordered a major attempt to defeat the King by sending both Essex and Waller towards Oxford and then Stow-on-the-Wold, the King had moved into Worcestershire, Sudeley was captured by the Parliamentarians and Banbury came under renewed threat. The entire district was throbbing with intense, if somewhat haphazard, military activity, and random pillaging exploits continued unabated. In the first week of June Royalists looted Sir Robert Dormer's mansion at Rousham, took twenty-five horses, plundered the village and emptied all the ale they could not drink or carry away 'in waste on the ground'. One of the parliamentary units sent northwards from Gloucester to counter the renewed threat from the King in Worcestershire was William Purefoy's cavalry, and his arrival coincided with a spate of provocative royalist raids from Compton House. In what must have been one of the very last exploits of the royalist garrison, a parliamentary regiment marching towards Burford was attacked, while another royalist party from Banbury fell upon Essex's rearguard lingering at Chipping Norton, taking many prisoners and a consignment of the parliamentary soldiers' letters destined 'to their friends in London', causing much mirth among the Cavaliers. Stung into action within days of arriving on the scene, the elderly Purefoy hurried from Worcestershire via Bidford and Stratford, joined with Bridges' forces at Warwick, called up whatever reinforcements could be spared from an already depleted Coventry, marched to Compton and on Saturday 8 June, summoned the garrison to surrender. The only surviving descriptions of the engagement are brisk parliamentary ones. The garrison at first rejected the summons:

> . . . whereupon [we] battered the house, and made approaches neer unto their Workes lesse then halfe Musket shot. The enemy plaid against our men all Friday and Saturday very fiercely. At last, after some houses were gotten by our Souldiers and some chimneys beaten down, the enemy next day cried for Quarter; and upon quarter for their lives, and to be civilly used, they surrendred the place.

A further parliamentary account adds more picturesque details: that besides about 150 prisoners, who included the governor of the house, Captain Matthew Clarke, and the Countess of Northampton's brother, many horses, 400 sheep, nearly 160 head of cattle and 18 loads of plunder were taken, besides over £5,000 'in ready money' inside the house and 5 or 6 earthen pots of money which had been hastily thrown into the fish-ponds. The Royalist, Dugdale, adding yet another interesting slant, alleged that the Parliamentarians 'drove the park and killed all the deer, and defaced the monuments in ye Church' – probably a direct result of the presence of William Purefoy as commanding officer. The young Earl of Northampton later attributed the disaster to the fact that his brother Sir William Compton, the stormy relationship with whom has already been touched on, had countermanded his choice of the competent Sir Charles Waldron, 'an experienced souldier whom I had apointed to goe to Compton house, he sending an other in whose hands the plaice was lost'. The assault on Compton House evidently took place in appalling weather, when the lush, low-lying hollow, its hillside spinneys and clayey pastures must have been sodden. Lord Grey lamented at Leicester on 9 June that 'the ways were never so deep at Christmas in comparison as they are now', the Earl of Manchester complained on 8 June of flooding at York in 'tempestuous rainy weather', while in Worcestershire, Sir William Waller's regiments were incapacitated on 10 June by weather 'so foul that the infantry and artillery could not march'. As usual, the besiegers found some comfort by taking free quarter in the surrounding villages, and the effect on the civilian population may be glimpsed by selecting one small community as an illustration. Virtually all the inhabitants of Brailes, a village which had so far escaped the worst of the war, received a small but important quota of soldiers billeted on them for the night or two of the siege, with additional provender demanded for their horses: four with Edward Walker, five with John Eddon, five with Philip Mumford, five with Thomas George, twelve with Thomas Eddon, six with Thomas Marshall, six with Philip Mills, six with the vicar, Gerrard Verrier . . .[1]

As soon as the house was captured and the new parliamentary garrison installed, the nature of the obligations on the local villages changed and became more burdensome still. Edward Walker, the Brailes constable, had to provide carriages to transport the booty from Compton to Warwick, a scattering of sick or wounded soldiers, sometimes with someone to care for them, descended on certain villagers, and virtually everyone was involved in working to establish the garrison. Those living nearest, in tiny Winderton, were naturally the first to have their lives disrupted. Robert Hunt had to provide hay and straw for litter and cart it the short distance across the fields from Winderton church to Compton, spend two days carrying wood and planks, release one of his labourers for three days to work on fortifications and another for two days at the moat, to spend another day thrashing beans for the garrison, to send sheets, cheese, lambs and to accept a wounded soldier for a fortnight. His neighbour Trubshaw Swarbricke similarly had to look after a sick soldier and his companion for five weeks, supply more straw, wood, hay, stone, turf for the fortifications, dung for damming the pool and lend his labourer for three days' unpaid work at the bulwarks. From Brailes, Alice Powell had to supply two blankets, a pair of sheets, a bed, bolster and pillow, together with a brass pot for the new governor's convenience, and Ralph Bushell likewise 'a wool bed carryed to the same garrison'. All this is not to mention the usual plunder, some of it considerable. Thomas Wilkes not only lost a mare and five lambs to the soldiers besieging Compton, but goods he estimated at well over £200, comprising 'mony, plate, household goods & all manner of waring clothes of my owne, my wives & 4 children'.

The great Tudor mansion was promptly stripped of its contents, William Purefoy taking charge of the plunder operations using carts requisitioned locally via hapless village constables like Richard Wilcox of Tysoe and Edward Walker of Brailes to convey the goods to Warwick. The position of the village constables, often unpopular enough in peacetime, was becoming increasingly untenable, expected to walk an impossible tightrope between incessant military demands from local governors, commanders or, indeed, any determined soldier, and the objections of his village neighbours to the unprecedented activities of military tax-gathering, horse-requisitioning and supply-gathering which were thrust upon him. Richard Wilcox was even forced to round up men for forced labour at the new garrison. Not surprisingly, the war saw an increase in the numbers of petty officials like constables and overseers of the poor refusing to take up office or, when in office, involved in lengthy litigation initiated by irate villagers.

An inventory of the stolen contents of Compton House was later compiled by the Earl of Northampton's trusty steward, William Goodman, who had in happier times supplied the family with meat and other provisions. This inventory, slovenly written as though in haste, has remained buried in the archives until now:

Houshold stuffe, apparell, Linnen & houshold provision &tc (besides mony, plate, cattle & other goods before certifyed) lost when Compton house was taken in June 1644, from Mr Wm Goodman

	£	s	d
Trunkes, Chests, presses with linnen apparell and other things in there, by conjecture in value worth about	50	0	0
Beding and hangings & curtaines & cushions & carpetts, worth about	20	0	0
One Cabinett Cupbord wth boxes, & other cubbords & tables & cheeres & stooles & formes &tc of that kind, worth about	05	0	0
Brasse pewter spitts, dripping pans, Andirons, grates, fire shovells & tongs, warming pan, furnesse of brasse or copper, Cesterne of lead, Jack for rosting &tc, about	12	0	0
hogsheades, barrells, Cabinett sellers for wine & strong waters, brewing vessells, tubbs, weeles, payles & dayrye vessells	04	0	0
Bread, beere, bacon, butter, cheese, some Corne in the house & other pvision, about	5	0	0
One brasse clock	2	10	0

	£	s	d
Guns, Crosbowes, slurbow, longbow & arrows, pistoles, swords, hangers, dagger, bills, speares &tc, worth about	7	0	0
vowlclothes, malt mill, pittcole, Charcole, & other fuell, about	2	10	0
One side sadle, one pillion, 3 or 4 sadles, bridles, [ ], &tc about the stable, about	1	10	0
Swine & poultry about the lodge	5	0	0
Sum total	114	10	0

p Mr Willm Goodman

This inventory, interesting though it is, is indistinguishable from those of countless gentry households of the period and, even allowing for the existence of others, 'before certifyed', which seem not to have survived, falls far short of what would be expected of such a large mansion. It suggests that the house had been largely emptied of the most valued family possessions as a precautionary measure. Among the prisoners taken in the house were John Philpot, rector of Lighthorne (who later claimed that far from ever being in arms he was 'very serviceable' to Parliament) and William Goodman himself. Goodman's loyalty to his 'good Lord & Maister . . . of about 30 yeares standing' cost him dear. He subsequently claimed on oath that on this occasion alone he lost almost 1,500 sheep, 24 cattle, 80 loads of hay, £140 in cash divided between money bags, a locked box 'in an inner Roome' and 'a Trunke in one of ye Chambers which was broken up by ye souldiers', besides his wife's purse containing more than £20, three or four gold rings taken from his maid, and a further £10 worth of his own gold. He himself was physically searched and robbed in the presence of the officer-in-charge, Major James Castle, notorious with his own parliamentary superiors for illegal extortion of ransom from the prisoners in Warwick Castle. Not content with this, the newly-appointed garrison commander, Major George Purefoy, ordered a large quantity of malt, wheat and peas from Goodman's Winderton farm. The unfortunate steward had already had his other estate at Prescote, near Banbury, plundered the previous October, when over 400 sheep, 25 cattle and 3 horses had been seized and driven to Warwick, besides suffering also at the hands of the Earl of Denbigh's indisciplined soldiers on another occasion. Perhaps Goodman's greatest trial, however, was yet to come, since his estate at Prescote lay literally astride land which that same month would experience the battle of Cropredy. Three years later, the sequestration authorities examined the details of his personal estate valued at £2,000, 'all which was seized uppon'. Goodman's case was far from unique, as others of the local gentry managing the Northampton estates were also harshly treated. One, William Calloway of Tysoe, was at one point imprisoned in Compton house and released only on producing 8 cwt of butter and 7 cwt of cheese for the garrison commander.[2]

Once again, however, it would be misleading to imply that such outrages were confined to the wealthy, able, it might be argued, to recoup losses. It soon became clear that those of very modest means and even the downright poor were to suffer too, as the new governor, George Purefoy, set about systematically terrorizing the entire neighbourhood. Swingeing taxes were imposed on all the nearby communities, to take effect from the date the house was captured, 9 June, with additional fines as punishment for villages considered 'disaffected' in the past. The inhabitants of the adjacent parish of

Tysoe, in particular, were appallingly treated, being immediately subjected to a stream of imperious ultimatums demanding men, materials and food supplies, addressed to the constable at first at almost weekly intervals. Two typical 'warrants' dated from successive weeks in June read as follows:

> Charging and Commanding [the constable] to send all such labourers to Compton as had laboured at the workes, wth an additional number, where [the constable noted] they continued untill his pleasure was to release them, and had no pay; also in the same warrant [I] was to send so much Bread as possible could be spared.

> To the most base, malignant Constable and Townes of Tysoe: Comanding to send to Compton one Labourer forth of every houshold in all the three Townes, and three Draftes out of each towne; to continue their all that weeke, upon paine of imprsonment and plunderinge.

During his short term of office as constable, Nicholas Tysoe later reported having received 'at the lest Forty warrants' from Purefoy demanding teams of oxen, carts and labourers for work, 'most of it done by the husbandmen wth[out] any pay'. Much of the unpaid labour was for improved fortifications, the scale of which is evident from the warrant quoted above and the length of service often exacted of husbandmen uprooted from their fields: 'Humphrey Tennant was labouring at Compton cutting Downe trees, thaching hayrickes and about the workes Forty Dayes and upwards'. A glance at these Tysoe indemnity claims, among the most detailed and circumstantial of the parish books, leaves the impression indeed that virtually every able-bodied man was for a time dragooned into Purefoy's service, seriously dislocating the life of that community in the height of summer. Little escape was possible in such close-knit communities, and arbitrary summonses were issued by the governor for named individuals to appear at improvised courts, 'charging the constable and other of the Inhabitants to appeare at Cumpton to Answere to such thinges as should be laide to their charge'. The whole episode is curiously reminiscent of the actions of a twentieth-century wartime commandant in enemy-occupied territory. The Compton barns were replenished free of charge with thirty loads of straw and new-mown hay from the Tysoe pastures pending the arrival of more substantial supplies from further afield:

> Item. Comanded by my warrants for ye use of my garrison 120 loads of hay, from ye townes neare adjoyninge to the same: as Tysoe, Brayles, Oxhill, Idlicott, Whatcott, Epwell, ye Pillertons & Eatenton; ye said quantity beinge burned in the barne whn ye enemy stormed ye Garrison.

Considerable quantities of utensils and food – bread, cheese, butter, bacon, salted beef are repeatedly mentioned – made their way to Compton from the surrounding villages, suggesting that the members of the garrison intended to make the most of their temporary quarters and live comfortably. Suppliers to the garrison, like William Elliot (presumably related to Giles Elliot, the Tysoe alehousekeeper), found that obtaining payment was another matter:

> William Elleott had owing of him by the Cooke for meate wch the Major prmised to see him satisfyed the some of twelve pounds fifteene shillings . . . and by the foote souldiers eleaven pound five shillings. The Major would pay none of this money, but putt him to take bisket and cheese for it, wch will not bring him above Five pound, so he looseth £7 15s 0d.

Bedding was particularly prized, with sheets, linen, blankets, bolsters, pillows and beds themselves being hauled across the countryside, as many a former ploughboy or shepherd turned soldier slept more comfortably than ever before in the great stately home on sheets supplied by rich and poor alike, from Sir Hercules Underhill in his mansion at Idlicote to the cottage of Widow Saul at Brailes. As usual, far from being military in intention, many of the thefts were quite indiscriminate. In one visit from the soldiers in Tysoe, one inhabitant's losses included a riding coat, waistcoats and petticoats, boys' hats and stockings, silver clasps for a bible and a pair of 'sifters tipped with silver'. And lest such robbery be ascribed to indisciplined subordinates, the victim in this case insisted on specifying, 'the Major being present himselfe'. Such episodes were repeated countless times throughout the district as Purefoy's marauders descended on village and hamlet in the Warwickshire Feldon and across the border into Oxfordshire. Alkerton, where the royalist rector and scholar Thomas Lydiat was brutally treated, was raided several times, Shutford was threatened 'upon paine of plundering, imprisonment and other extremities' to produce its arrears instantly, and 'expect not one houre longer, at your perils', and Over Norton likewise, with the alternative detailed in the clearest terms: 'I will plunder yor towne and hang yor Constable'. Purefoy constantly meddled with the elected village representatives; a warrant addressed to the inhabitants of Sibford Ferris instructs them, ungrammatically but unambiguously:

> You are uppon Thursday next, all excuses set aparte, to meete together and to Choose anewe Constables and two Tithingmen, for those that are now in place shall not continue any longer . . . He that shall refuse returne his name to me and I will take another course with them. Faile not therefore att yor utmost perill. Given under my hand att Compton this 30th December 1645. George Purefoy.

Regular complaints from north Oxfordshire parishes were later submitted to the parliamentary authorities that Purefoy had imprisoned their constable and tithingmen at Compton, together with any vicar whose views were alien to him, like George Moorcroft of Kingham, who 'suffered imprisonmt of his bodie xi daies, paying great Fees and Charges during the time'. Purefoy also followed the lead of Bridges at Warwick in apparently random kidnapping of innocent travellers in order to exact ransom. Robert Meese of Over Norton bitterly complained:

> One of his Sonnes being at Sandford on business was unjustly carryed prisoner to Compton, & after three or foure dayes stay there, was sent to his Father with ye Major's [Purefoy's] letter for £5 to redeeme the mare on which he rode. Which £5 was sent accordingly, but in Conclusion both mare and money were detain'd.

A further refinement on the process of extortion is illustrated by the case of Steeple Barton, whose village representatives failed to answer a summons to attend Purefoy at Compton because of the unprecedented military activity in their district, and were then not only imprisoned but forced to pay for the expenses of the officers sent to arrest them:

> The Kings garisons beeing so neare us, and the [royalist] soulldears beeing often with us, we could not go at the appointted time. So that they [Purefoy's men] did fet away our constable and other men so often that they had of us for marchals feese £1 15 0, bee sides our charges whils we were ther in prison at all times; which comes to: £30 13 6.

The character of the expeditions from Compton may be judged from a petition later submitted by Thomas Tasker, a poor labourer of the tiny neighbouring Oxfordshire parish of Epwell, to the parliamentary authorities:

> Yor Petitioner being a poore man and aged, in December 1644, in the middle of the night, a Partie of Major Purefoys souldiers comanded by Corporall Dizon came into his house and violently tooke away the most parte of his household goodes, to the valew of tenne Pounds or upwards; and also tooke away yor petitionr to Compton, where he was unjustly imprisoned by the space of Five or Six Dayes, and nothing being alleadged against him. The Major came to him and used many harsh speeches, & so gave order to the Marshall for to release him, but never examined him of any thinge at all, neither would he give him leave to speake for himselfe to Desire any of his goodes againe . . . His humble request unto Yor Worps is . . . in regard he and his wife are aged, and the sudden fright hath made them both so sickly and weake that they are altogether unable for to get their liveing. . .

The highways were kept under stricter surveillance than ever by Purefoy's men, alert for goods destined, allegedly, for enemy garrisons, which were promptly seized and taken back to Compton: '3 horseloads of Poltry & cheese going to ye enemys garrison', '6 oxen going to Oxford', 'taken from Mr Osburston within 4 mls of Oxford 40 sheep & 10 qr wheate', 'a Pryze of hatts going to ye enemys garrison of Worcester'. Countless such incidents must have been talking-points in cottages and alehouses throughout the region: £3 taken from the constable of Whichford being taken to Banbury; a herd of sheep being driven to Oxford from Mr Palmer's of Compton Scorpion; three loads of salt going towards Oxford, 'a Side of Beafe from a Butcher of Brailes, and who was Carrying of it towards Banbury [which] was disposed of by the Govnor of Compton who had halfe of it and the soldiers the Rest'. At other times the tedium of garrison life was relieved by morale-boosting raids on notorious, or simply defenceless, local royalist sympathizers, many of whom were unceremoniously imprisoned for a time, like Mr Goodyear of Heythrop or Mr Badson of Barton-on-the-Heath. In some cases such acts seemed, no doubt, politically justified, as in that of the family of the unscrupulous local Cavalier, Gerard Croker, already thoroughly unpopular in the district, whose brother was targeted by Purefoy:

> I was Commanded by the Governor of Compton Garrison to fetch into the Garrison fiftie sheepe from Mr Henry Croker of Hooke Norton, wch sheepe were disposed of by the Governor to his owne particular use.

But anyone unfortunate enough to be associated with a known enemy sympathizer was likely to be a victim of such raids, like the curate of Whichford's royalist vicar:

> I had commande from Major Puryfoy to seise upon the person of Doctor Langstons Curatt, and such cattle of the Doctors as I could finde upon his groundes, and to bring the said Curatt and Cattle to Compton Garrison, wch I did . . . To the best of my knowledge the Govnor of Compton had eleaven or twelve pounds for the inlargement of him selfe and the Cowes, of which monies my selfe nor the soldiers had anie parte.

Similarly vindictive reprisals were carried out against former enemy soldiers now disbanded, like Robert Rose and William Bratford returning home to Tysoe hoping to resume their peaceful former existence. Rose was promptly imprisoned by Purefoy, and

even though 'he had his Dyett sent him from his Mother' to the prison quarters at
Compton was retained until £5 ransom was paid.

All in all, the colourful George Purefoy is worth rescuing from oblivion, such was his
undoubted impact on south Warwickshire and far beyond during these troubled years.
The royalist newsletter, *Mercurius Aulicus*, whose objectivity is clearly suspect, alleged
that the Earl of Northampton's local strength cooped up the Parliamentarian at
Compton to such an extent that:

> . . . his cummings abroad are more like a theife than a souldier, creeping sometimes in the darke,
> where he steals contributions to keepe himselfe in heart to pen blustering warrants.

But there is little evidence of this from local sources, and his two-year reign at
Compton, unchallenged apart from one abortive counter-attack from Banbury in
January 1645, perfectly fits Clarendon's description of a garrison commander's 'illimited
tyranny'. His contribution to the war was very different from that of his competent
committeeman relative, Gamaliel Purefoy, at Coventry; his aggressiveness, like that of
his similarly ruthless puritan kinsman, William, was presumably ideologically-inspired.
Before taking up arms he had indulged in charitable works on his Buckinghamshire
manors, while becoming associated with the radical puritan circles of Fenny Drayton,
near William Purefoy's own Caldecote, and the religious extremist, Abiezer Coppe, who
became his chaplain at Compton. The treatment he meted out to those he considered
'base and malignant' was that of a puritan zealot, reminding one once again that this was
a religious war. The Royalists mockingly dubbed him the local Wat Tyler, and certainly
his reign at Compton was notorious, immediately provoking comment in the petition
from local gentry already referred to and attracting criticism in Parliament. To the
delight of the Royalists he later suffered a preposterous riding accident when attending
exercises in a military pageant in Hyde Park in May 1646. His horse ran into a tree and
was killed on the spot, while Purefoy himself lost his diamond-studded hat worth £150
and 'sorely bruised, fell with his horse [and] was carryed halfe dead to a house in the
Parke'. More seriously, he interfered, as we have seen, with elected parish representatives and rigged local elections. Not content with managing for a time to enjoy the huge
profits from the Earl of Northampton's sequestrated estates and the weekly haul of
plunder from near and far, he was not averse to appropriating the schoolmaster of
Combrook's salary, forcing the hapless parson of Butlers Marston, Edward Langley, to
teach the village children without remuneration. If the words *plunder* and *highwayman*
both made their entry into the language during the Civil War, they might almost have
been coined specifically in memory of George Purefoy. He went on to be named Knight
of the Royal Oak at the Restoration, with an estate of £3,000 per annum. He had a good
war.[3]

'A DANCE BEYOND WORCESTER': CROPREDY

Like many of the battles of the Civil War, Cropredy was largely an accident, unplanned and unforeseen by either side until the last minute, when their armies stumbled into each other in the open, rolling country north of Banbury. Only when a confrontation could no longer be avoided, on 29 June 1644, did the King finally turn his army to meet Sir William Waller's which had been shadowing his for the past three weeks. The complicated manoeuvrings which formed the preamble are as fascinating as the actual battle, but as with Edgehill the course of the engagement itself, which has been well charted elsewhere, will only be briefly summarized, in order to focus on the impact of the campaign as a whole on the locality.[4]

Soon after Parliament had ordered the Earl of Essex and Sir William Waller to confront the King at Oxford, in May 1644, it became clear that the scheme was over-optimistic. Charles had no intention of being attacked by the combined parliamentary armies and had escaped in the celebrated episode of the night of 3 June and, marching via Burford, Bourton and Evesham, arrived in Worcester three days later, leaving the two enemy commanders in disarray at Chipping Norton and Stow-on-the-Wold. Shortly after, the parliamentary council of war at Chipping Norton had decided to separate their two armies: the King was left to Waller, while Essex marched to relieve the West Country. It was a decision which astounded the royalist commanders as much as it has done successive generations of historians ever since. As Lord Digby wrote to Rupert on 17 June from Broadway, 'Had Essex and Waller jointly pursued us or attacked Oxford, we had been lost'. Reluctantly accepting this change of strategy, Waller loyally pledged his resolve 'to follow the King wherever an army can march' pursuing the King doggedly in dismally wet weather, capturing the usefully-situated Sudeley Castle on 10 June and continuing through Stow to Evesham. Already, some Warwickshire parishes were being drawn in to the pursuit; Wolford was only one of several instructed to send Waller provisions at Sudeley as he passed northwards to Stourbridge. The district of Salford was particularly heavily quartered by Waller's own regiment of horse for several nights, with even cottagers at Abbots Salford being called upon to provide free board and lodging. Others further north, like Lapworth, were soon enduring similar experiences at the hands of Waller's soldiers 'when they marcht thorow Warwick sheare After his Matie', as also on the return journey south shortly after. Waller's hope was that even without his superior, Essex, a 'universal conjunction' of his own forces with those of Denbigh and Massey would strike a decisive blow to the King's army before it could proceed north to join Rupert's in Lancashire, and thus, 'with Gods blessing, make the work short'. The Earl of Denbigh, however, was fully extended in Staffordshire and, indeed, himself calling up reinforcements from Warwickshire to help assault Dudley and prepare an attack on Banbury, while Massey's help was also largely unforthcoming. The King, however, having reached Bewdley, instead of continuing northwards as expected, suddenly swung south once more and was soon heading for Worcester and Evesham again, breaking down bridges to hinder pursuit. He had soon re-crossed the Cotswolds via Broadway and Burford to Woodstock, leading Parliament what a contemporary journalist wryly described as 'a Dance beyond Worcester'. The King's apparently puzzling strategy was in fact very simple; he had admitted to Rupert, in a celebrated letter from Bewdley on 14 June, that his purpose was 'to spin out time until you come to assist me'. The mid-June English weather was bad: 'even in that season of the year the ways in that vale [of Evesham] were very deep', wrote one Cavalier relishing the thought of the 'ill ways [Waller] must pass . . . far enough behind' if he continued the pursuit. The project of trapping the King at Oxford which had begun so promisingly was in shreds.[5]

After much hesitation and confusion as to the best course of action, Parliament finally decided to approve Waller's expressed willingness to continue following the King, now marching eastwards to Buckingham. Thoroughly alarmed at what they feared might be a threat to East Anglia and perhaps even London itself, Parliament promised Waller substantial Warwickshire reinforcements as well as other contingents from Northampton, Newport Pagnell and elsewhere. At the same time, General Richard Browne, much derided by the Cavaliers as 'woodmonger', 'faggot-monger Browne' 'Sergeant Major of the Wood-yard', or 'the wooden General' since his attempt to supply London with fuel by shipping firewood down the Thames in barges, was to march north from London to assist Waller if need be. Waller consequently gathered his forces together and after a largely fruitless and time-wasting detour through Worcestershire to Gloucester in the hope of gaining help from Massey or, as the delightful royalist jibe put it, 'patching up his rabble', turned north again, re-entered Stow and prepared to march east to challenge the King.

While resting at Buckingham, meanwhile, a delighted Charles wrote to the Queen to congratulate her on the birth of a daughter, at Exeter, and the morale of the royal army was boosted by successful raids in this largely hostile region, 'his troops every day bringing in store of provisions . . . which were passing . . . from London to Coventry and Warwick; all of which were very welcome'. One success was the capture at Brickhill on 22 June, on the day when the King arrived at Buckingham, of '16 Cart-loades of wine, Grocery & Tobacco', the wine including not only '4 Tun of Sacke and Claret' but, according to the mocking royalist report, a vintage collection of 'select extraordinary bottles for certaine particular Brethren of Coventry and Warwicke'.

Equally welcome was the seizure of more consignments of cloth travelling the highways, as Philip Willoughby told his master the absent Earl of Northampton on 24 June:

> If you please to tell his Matie, a Troop of yor Horse tooke some pack-horses neer North[amp]ton, and desyre his Matie to let you dispose of it towards the redeeminge your brother Spencer's Company, & clothing the Troop [with] these 22 packs of cloth & 30 packs of London ware, I will be sure to see the best made of this Prize; and then yr Lopp. may dispose of it as you please & to whom you please.

At the same time, the King's army and Oxford itself continued to receive supplies from a whole network of regular contacts when they could elude the vigilance of Bridges at Warwick and Purefoy at Compton. Some, as already noted, were intercepted: a 'parcel of sheep' from Giles Palmer at Compton Scorpion being driven to an Oxford butcher for slaughter, a consignment of stockings from Evesham, three loads of salt. But many others, it must be assumed, reached Oxford safely, like the supply of 400 bushels of malt which John French of Broughton had ready for collection on 12 June, when

Captain Henry Stevens, the King's wagon-master general, was ordered to 'provide Carts as neere that place as conveinently may bee, and bring the said Mault to this Citty for support of the Garrison, where satisfaccon shalbe given for the same'. On 10 June Stevens, who was not only keeper of the magazine at Oxford but also commissary of victuals, was sent on missions to fetch in large quantities of corn from many places in Oxfordshire, to Alvescot, Burford, Chadlington, Churchill and Witney – some, if not all, from regular contacts. A little later, wheat, meal, bread, malt, cheese and biscuit were ordered, while a further warrant instructed mills on the river above and below Oxford to receive wheat from Stevens's agents and grind it into meal. It was only after the war that the contribution of many of these paid suppliers and informers, usually benefiting from armed protection, emerged to become the subject of sometimes protracted legal wrangling. The case of William Dewes of Coughton is typical. Besides rearing cattle for the royalist garrisons, it was implied that Dewes:

> . . . did hold correspondency and intelligence wth ye late Kinges Garrisons, vizt. Worcr, Easam [Evesham], Tewkesbury, Hartlebury, Banbury, Compton howse and Oxford . . . and did buy much plundred goods and conveighed them and send to ye Garrisons aforesd, for wch he had protections from Prince Maurice and Colonell Knutsford, for wch he gave them somes of money.[6]

The scouring of the countryside for useful enemy equipment left behind was periodically stepped up. On 15 June, for example, the Royalists' headquarters were informed that 'the Rebells in their march through [Oxfordshire] have left Horses, Carts and Harnesse scattering in divers places and Villages', and Captain Stevens was again instructed to make enquiries and bring them to Oxford. Sure enough, shortly after eight teams left behind by the Parliamentarians were collected and immediately redeployed to carry provisions to the King's army assembling near Banbury.

By 20 June Parliament was refining plans to mount a concerted attack on the King, and had ordered the Warwickshire commanders Purefoy, Bridges and Barker 'to march with your regiment of horse to such place or rendezvous as [Waller] shall appoint', and Waller himself, a few days later, to follow the King to Buckingham 'with all expedition'. On 25 June Waller accordingly left Stow, his troops – such was the rudimentary fieldwork of the day – having literally gone round in a circle. The army must have entered Warwickshire near the Four Shires Stone, following not the ancient Fosse Way, as has been supposed, but a more easterly route roughly parallel to it. In the usual way, a substantial part of his forces had gone on ahead, and were already making their presence felt in the south Feldon villages. Waller's forces spent the next two days and nights scattered in a wide circle of villages centred on Shipston-on-Stour, extending from the Wolfords, Burmington, Cherington, Willington, Barcheston and Brailes in the south to Oxhill, Halford, Pillerton, Kineton and Radway in the north. There was thus a distance of some 12 miles at least separating the rearguard at Wolford from the forward contingents not far from Banbury, with groups of officers being 'lodged in town' at Shipston and the common soldiers 'lodged in field', as a contemporary report states. Among many other villages, Kineton was once again full of soldiers, this time Colonel Thompson's cavalry, quartering for three nights. Accompanied by many of his senior officers, Waller himself lodged not at Oxhill, apparently, as might be supposed from the letter he dispatched to the parliamentary authorities in London, but at Purefoyregimented Tysoe, where the wealthy Francis Clarke had little option but to incur the huge losses when 'he quartered Sr William Waller & about 120 of his Comanders & souldiers, some of them quartered their five Dayes'. The period of five days specified suggests that not all these officers continued to Cropredy. After the recent atrocious downpours which had prevented the army from marching at all on some days, the English weather had now turned exceptionally hot, as Waller's increasingly foot-weary and demoralized band halted, awaiting a convoy bringing supplies and pay. Waller had time to write to his superiors a letter yielding interesting detail:

> I onely desire that it may not be expected that I should take long marches and not sometimes rest, this extreame hott weather, especially wth the foote who are very much diminished and would be quickly ruined if I should not spare them as much as I can. I am come to Oxhill, neare Keynton feild [Edgehill], and the foote are at Shepstone; and purpose to march in ye coole of ye Evening. I have recd some spplies of Horse & foote from Gloucester & Warwick & Coventry. I humbly desire yt Major Genall Browne & such forces of ye [Eastern] Association as can be drawne into ye feild may march to Bedford, & I shall by ye meanes of Sr Sam. Luke direct a way how wee may joyne. I humbly beg that a months pay (wch was pmised) may be sent down wth Major Genll Browne, and it will be a meanes to prserve this Army from dissolving. I desire all expediency may bee used in this.

It is clear that although morale among the troops was near breaking point Waller intended to continue his march to Towcester to intercept the King, who had been reported to him between Buckingham and Wellingborough, but who was in fact by now much nearer, at Brackley, approaching Banbury. The collision of the two armies was imminent.[7]

Once again, all the surrounding villages must have been humming with intense activity as they were harassed and impoverished by the unwanted occupying forces – all the more so as Waller, in view of the warm weather and the fragile morale of his troops, had decreed a day's rest for his forces, giving them time to indulge themselves at the expense of the more affluent local gentry. Once again William Sheldon was victimized at Long Compton, his servant Thomas Savage later reporting to a parliamentary committee that an official warrant from Waller had ordered the seizure of 200 of his master's best sheep. Whatever the military timetable of the commanders, the villagers were adamant that the troops quartered on them for at least two or three days, and some of the individual household thefts take on the character of organized crime rather than petty pilfering for basic sustenance. The wealthy Simon Underhill, for example, reported from Idlicote:

> Taken away by Capt. [Joseph] Hawkesworths men at the same tyme [June 1644]: a Beaver hatt, a sword, a payre of silke stockings, 3 gold capps, a new payre of bootes, one fyne Holland table cloath conteyninge 6 els in length; valued at £5.

As noted before, too, not just twos and threes but huge contingents of men and horses were foisted upon some particularly unfortunate villagers, especially those known to be royalist sympathizers like Richard Randall and Lot Keyte at Wolford. Keyte, a garrulous and self-important village constable, is one of those delightful personalities whose detailed testimony is invaluable for reconstructing events inevitably ignored or glossed over in the historian's wider concerns. Having already been implicated in the violent skirmishing in Wolford the previous year in the Hastings Ingram episode, Keyte had very recently suffered from the Earl of Essex's forces when they had arrived near Chipping Norton, and been wounded by some Cavaliers from Banbury or Compton sent to harass them. He had been forced to provide six horses and a cart for transporting supplies 'towards ye West 6 Dayes' and quarter eighteen of Essex's cavalry, losing another horse in the process, necessitating his pursuing 'ye army towards the west 3 dayes' to reclaim his horse, as well as being obliged to maintain at his own expense post-horses to transmit messages to Richard Browne, a postmaster of Moreton-in-Marsh. Hardly had he time to recover from these events than Waller's army arrived, marching in the opposite direction and making new demands:

> About ye 26 of ye sd month [June 1644] I being then a Constable, a warrant came to me to presse 2 Carts for Sr Willm Waller, and by reason that a little before I was wounded in two severall places of my body by the kings souldiers I was not then able to execute the sd Warrant, but did send it to the Tythingmen to execute. But being not executed, one England, a Commissary, came with other souldiers and tooke from me for the sd service 3 horses & 3 paire of geeres worth at the least £9 0 0.

In addition, the unfortunate Keyte had to quarter 'ye rere of ye Army that night' (24 June), estimated at forty men and horses, losing yet more 'in pvision and things taken out of my house by them'. He even had to care for two of Waller's sick soldiers, one of whom 'dide at my house: the charge £1 5 0'. Keyte's neighbour in Little Wolford, Richard Randall – a friend of William Goodman of Winderton and therefore associated with the Earl of Northampton – suffered similar harassment. His losses included the usual provision and quartering and stolen horses, pastures damaged and over-grazed by 'a multitude of horses' of Colonel Prince's regiment under Waller, and almost two hundred sheep 'lost, kild & taken away at that tyme' at an estimated value of £90.

Only a little further north the situation in the villages was if anything even more chaotic. A three-hundred-strong Tower Hamlets regiment, soon to fight 'very honourably and stoutly' at Cropredy, battened on the vicar of tiny Barcheston, Nathaniel Horton, for two days and nights, enlivening the summery Warwickshire lanes with their outlandish Cockney accents. Neighbouring Willington and Burmington suffered particularly: 160 men and 30 horses invaded Thomas Walker's at Willington, with another 140 at Thomas Fletcher's and further troops of 100 each with William Ashby and William Humphreys. Other large detachments were billeted in nearby Burmington, sixty foot soldiers spending two days and nights with Nicholas Hunt, another sixty each with Francis Court and Richard Hall, fifty more with Richard Sammon, forty more each with Giles Thomas and Robert Beale. In all, well over a thousand of Waller's men were quartered, with all the attendant imaginable turmoil, in Willington and Burmington alone in those two long summer days before moving on to disaster across the hills at Cropredy.[8]

Reassembling his widely-scattered forces for a rendezvous near Edgehill, Waller was now strengthened by the arrival of the additional Warwickshire forces already mentioned. That Parliament intended a decisive showdown is made clear by the substantial nature of these reinforcements. The royalist newsletter mockingly enumerated them: Waller had 'gotten assistance from Coventry, Kenelmworth Castle,

HANWELL CASTLE, NEAR BANBURY. The early Tudor mansion of the Copes, the leading puritan family of the district. Probably occupied by Royalists at the battle of Edgehill, and again by Sir William Waller's parliamentarians before the battle of Cropredy, the house itself escaped war damage but witnessed carnage in the nearby fields after the siege of Banbury as Cavaliers pursued Roundheads fleeing towards Warwick. (Photo: Banbury Museum)

Warwicke &, nay, Mr Massey was call'd on, and Tinker Fox was summoned . . .', adding, perhaps plausibly, that Waller induced them to come by promising them that service would be for 'but very few dayes' and would be rewarded by the capture of Banbury, 'which he knew would please them'. In addition, contingents from Browne, marching to Buckingham, Lord Grey of Groby, the Earl of Denbigh and Northampton were alerted. Leaving his comfortable quarters at Tysoe via Radway, Upton, Hornton and Horley, Waller made for Hanwell, lodging 'on the hills at a faire howse', the castellated Tudor mansion of the Copes, who had until recently befriended the puritan scholar-theologians John Dod and Robert Harris. The sheer logistical problems of moving such disparate forces were clearly daunting, and there was evidently little attempt to fuse the various far-flung regiments into a cohesive, unified force for a battle whose very eventuality was uncertain. Once again, therefore, the military historian's neat arrows, with their implications of an orderly, purposeful advance which insulated the civilian population from contact with the troops, bear little relation to the far messier reality. Soldiers were fending for themselves over a very wide area. Well over a hundred of one particular regiment, for example, many with horses, were taking free quarter in Bishops Itchington for two days and nights, some 10 miles north of Waller's quarters at Hanwell, under a Cornet John Osborne, 'saying theire Captaine was sicke at Gloster'. The village constable later obligingly listed the numbers of soldiers billeted on each villager: ten with Richard Hunt, seven with Widow Avery, ten Robert King, eight William Poole, six at the Parsonage, twelve John Tomkins, and so on. Colonel William Purefoy's regiment, on the other hand, was quartered at Warmington, 6 miles away, that of Waller's second-in-command, Sir Arthur Haselrig, with many of the quartermasters, at nearby Mollington, while other units were as far south as Broughton, now evidently back in parliamentary hands. In these conditions, the contribution of some detachments to any engagement, when one eventually occurred, must have been either minimal or, perhaps, actually non-existent.

Provisioning was likewise as chaotic and wide-ranging as ever, supplies filtering in apparently at random from far and wide, from Brailes in the west to Priors Marston far to the north: few villages escaped commitments of one kind or another. For the individual, supplying provisions was far from being a clear-cut, single operation when an entire army was camped in the district for several days. Radway's William Hyarne (Hiorne?), for example, carefully noted his apparently never-ending obligations to Waller's various units, while at the same time pinpointing incidentally the complicated manoeuvrings of the campaign:

> Pvision Carryed to Sr Wm Wallers armie, and to Warr. Regiment: first to Upton. 2. to Horley bridge. 3. to Hanwell, twise. 4. to Drayton elme. 5. to Bourton, thrice. 6. to Croppready. and lastly, to Wardont [Wardington] ash.

Other neighbours did likewise. Thomas Mills sent supplies successively to Broughton, Bourton and even, as Waller moved away into Northamptonshire after the battle, to as far away as Preston Capes. Barrels of beer were mysteriously lost while being transported towards Cropredy. . . .

At Buckingham, the King had learnt of Waller's impending reinforcements and, realizing that confrontation was unavoidable sooner or later, called a council of war on 24 June at which immediate preparations for battle were decided. Supplies of ammunition were to be sent from Oxford and, a few days later when the army resumed its march north towards Daventry, supplies of bread and cheese 'to his Mas Army at or neere Banbury'. The King was continuing from Brackley to Culworth, making for Daventry (and ultimately, it was assumed, York) when news of Waller's proximity forced him finally, in an act similar to that immediately before Edgehill, to accept the challenge. Wheeling about, the royal army marched back towards Banbury via Chacombe or along the ancient Banbury Lane on a dank morning 'to lay hold of a fitt opportunity there to give the Rebells Battell', as the King's secretary, Sir Edward Walker, later put it. There are few details of royalist quartering, apart from the King himself who, *faute de mieux*, lodged successively at 'a yeoman's house' and 'a very poor man's house' at Grimsbury and Williamscot respectively, but there can be little doubt that the picture already drawn of parliamentary quartering west of the Cherwell was repeated by that of the Royalists to the east. But as the rivals engaged in this bleak upland country, the relative security of cottage and barn finally gave way to the open field for Roundhead and Cavalier alike. The pious Parliamentarian Thomas Ellis, in a

CROPREDY, NEAR BANBURY. The battlefield on the banks of the River Cherwell near the bridge which provoked the battle between the King's forces and those of Sir William Waller in June 1644. Several of the nearby river crossings and low-lying meadows saw fierce hand-to-hand fighting and many fatal casualties. (Photo: Banbury Museum)

rare burst of Civil War poetry, dutifully insisted on making the best of it when writing to a friend in London: in spite of 'our lodging having for severall nights been, and still is, on Gods cold earth', they were, he pointed out, 'over-shaddowed with the Canopie of heavens sweet Firmament, and God in much mercy hath afforded us sweet temperate weather. . .'[9] As the converging armies 'marched out of the pasture ground into the corne fields', large-scale disruption to the life of the communities which lay in their path must have occurred; quite apart from the actual fighting, mass quartering, the constant transporting of provisions, over-grazing of pastures, trampling of crops and theft of stores and belongings ranged over many miles, from Broughton in the south to Priors Marston in the north.

The course of the battle itself – as usual, a series of scattered and intermittent engagements rather than a set-piece battle – has been well described and analysed in the eye-witness reports since drawn upon by generations of historians from Clarendon to the present day, and requires only a brief summary here. By the morning of Friday 28 June, with Waller already quartered at Hanwell on the low hills to the north of Banbury, the King's troops had arrived from Northamptonshire and were assembling at a rendezvous on the eastern approaches to the town in mid-morning, somewhere on the hills between Edgcote, Chacombe and Middleton Cheney. The two positions were therefore clearly intervisible, once the morning mists had cleared from the Cherwell valley which lay in between. Neither army was prepared at this stage to attempt the risky river crossing, vulnerable to enemy fire, to attack the other. The opening tactic developed almost immediately into a race for Crouch Hill, commanding Banbury to the south-west, which Waller, slightly nearer than Charles and without the river to negotiate, won and promptly secured, leaving the Royalists in the fields at Grimsbury, immediately east of Banbury. The emotions of the royalist garrison in Banbury Castle, watching proceedings exactly half-way between the rival armies, can only be conjectured. A brief skirmish at Neithrop between small detachments from the two armies, and 'some scowting beyond Banbury', were the first contact between the opposing forces that day before the King retired to lodge 'in a private House neare the Army', traditionally identified with Grimsbury manor house. Early next morning the King decided to resolve the stalemate by attempting to lure Waller from his better position on Crouch Hill by conspicuously marching his army north, as though pursuing his original plan of eventually joining Rupert in Yorkshire, but in reality in order to 'observe Waller's motion, and to expect a fitter opportunity and place to give him Battell'. Observing his enemy 'going with bag and baggage towards Northampton' Waller promptly shadowed the King by following a

CROUCH HILL, BANBURY. Dominating the undulating Banbury countryside, the hill was repeatedly occupied by troops, used as a command post and rallying point and saw much skirmishing. From here Sir William Waller's army marched to defeat at nearby Cropredy in June 1644. (Photo: Centre for Oxfordshire Studies)

parallel northward course along the Cherwell, still keeping the river between them, and established a new, equally strong position on Bourton Hill, commanding uninterrupted views across the undulating countryside to Wardington. The two armies were almost equally matched numerically. Matters were suddenly precipitated by a move by the royalist cavalry to secure the tiny yet strategically-important bridge at Cropredy, in case Waller should attempt a surprise attack on the royalist flank across the river, and by ominous news of the approach of strong parliamentary reinforcements from Daventry towards Hays Bridge, just north of Wardington, which the Royalists' advance guard hurried to intercept. Observing the widening gap between the Royalists ranged beyond Hays Bridge and those in the rearguard, perhaps still not far north of Grimsbury, the tactician Waller seized his chance to cut the enemy's straggling army in two by sending two strong cavalry forces to attack across the Cherwell, the one by capturing the royalist outpost at Cropredy Bridge, the other by storming the ford at Slat Mill, one mile further downstream. Both forces, one commanded by General John Middleton, the other by Waller himself, successfully crossed the river towards Wardington hill at about midday before being counter-attacked by the Royalists who quickly rallied and were joined by their vanguard doubling hurriedly back from Hays Bridge. The Earl of Northampton's regiment repelled the attack at Slat Mill, while the Earl of Cleveland threw the Parliamentarians back across Cropredy Bridge, capturing many of their guns in the process. The fighting lapsed and resumed several times during the afternoon, 'the weather very fair and very warm', with Lord Henry Wilmot of Adderbury being wounded, captured and rescued and the parliamentary Tower Hamlets regiment heroically resisting at Cropredy Bridge, before Waller's forces withdrew to Bourton Hill. Volleys of gunfire continued for some time, the Royalists firing at the positions on Bourton Hill while the King, returning to the field, was himself targeted on Wardington hill, according to the royalist journalist, by Parliamentarians using 'severall perspective glasses'. The evening saw the King's fruitless but characteristic attempt at offering a pardon to his enemies by a trumpeter's message, duly rejected by Waller who protested that he had no political authority from Parliament to negotiate, and as night fell the two armies lapsed into silence and the King retired, fairy-tale-like, to a 'very poor man's house at Williamscot'. The next day, Sunday 30 June, neither army could summon any real enthusiasm to resume hostilities, Waller's army in particular having suffered heavy casualities and many desertions.

The movement of both armies after the battle poses some unanswered questions. The King's morale was high. He had attended an open-air thanksgiving service on 29 June and hanged a spy, and the following day wrote from Williamscot to tell the Queen of his victory and to give advice on 'the christening of my younger and, as they say, prettiest daughter' before deciding on his next move. This, somewhat unexpectedly in view of earlier reports that he intended joining Rupert in Yorkshire, was to march south again. The parliamentary army was in such disarray that a sustained royalist attack could have resulted in a spectacular victory for the King, and it is unlikely that Waller could have prevented Charles moving north via Daventry had he wanted to. But the King was aware of the exhaustion of his troops and the scarcity of basic supplies and decided to call off an engagement which neither side showed any desire to resume. Towards midnight on Sunday 30 June, therefore, as the King's secretary recalled shortly after:

. . . his Matie tooke resolutions answerable to those necessities, & thereupon early upon Monday
morning beeing the First of Julye his Matie drew of his whole Army in very good order, & in full
view of Waller, who did not so much as attempt to fall on oure Reare (no question beeing very well
pleased so to bee ridd of Us . . .

The royalist antiquary Richard Symonds, 'himself being personally present' as a cavalry
officer, waxed almost lyrical in his description:

Munday morning, about four of the clock, his Majestie, with all his army, drums beating, colors
flying and trumpets sounding, marched through Middleton Cheney, from thence to Farmigo
[Fartheringhoe] [and] Aynoe on the hill . . .

The unwelcome news that General Richard Browne was at Buckingham preparing to
march to Waller's assistance forced a royalist change of plan, however, and once again
confounding parliamentary expectations Charles veered west, crossed the Cherwell to
Adderbury, exchanged prisoners with Waller and made for Deddington, where he slept
at the parsonage. The following day the morale of the Cavaliers remained buoyant as
they resumed their march through Great Tew and Chipping Norton, where Captain
Henry Stevens had been ordered to send a large consignment of bread for the troops,
skirting Warwickshire within sight and sound of Long Compton and Barton-on-the-
Heath, and so on to Moreton-in-Marsh, where the King lodged at the White Hart. The
royal progress continued the following day as they approached the relative safe haven of
Evesham, and the royal diarist Symonds was impelled to repeat his lyrical passage of a
few days earlier: 'his Majestie with all his army, drums beating, colors flying and
trumpets sounding, marched over the Cotswold Hills'.

The plight of the severely-mauled parliamentary army, on the other hand, was very
different as Waller attempted to retrieve some semblance of honour and order from a
near-disaster and face the multiple problems: low morale, widespread desertions, guilt
over the 'dishonourable loss of a part of my traine of Artillery', an elusive enemy whose
next move was unknown, and hesitant and conflicting instructions from the remote
London committee. His army was fast disintegrating and there was certainly no orderly
withdrawal to Towcester, where he eventually joined Browne. Many of the parliamentary troops scattered, literally in all directions and for indeterminate periods, with
little discernible attempt at regrouping. Some, for example, including some of Sir
Arthur Haselrig's wounded, were at Priors Marston, while many others are discovered
quartering, apparently at random and for eight days or more, at Wolfhampcote,
Sawbridge and Flecknoe, well to the north. A hint of the confusion in the army ranks,
and perhaps of the exasperation of the villagers, may be gained from incidental
comments, like those of William Clarke at Willoughby, complaining of:

. . . 7 of Sr Willim Warlers [sic] soldirs Coming bee fore the armie, and Coming without order: 2 of
them Coming uppon Sundaie morning, 2 other Coming the same daie, & three more Coming upon
Mondaie night very late . . .

Yet others were reported travelling in opposite directions, however, as though anxious
to distance themselves from the battle area as quickly as possible. On Sunday morning,
30 June, with the King attending an open-air service, the Royalist Symonds reported:

'Sermon ended, we saw part of the body of the enemy march away towards Warwickshire, about xi. of the clock', while the royalist newspaper added that '240 were met towards Warwickshire, labouring to find out a better Master then Sir William'. The parish accounts again confirm such reports: groups are found quartering at Brailes, and as far north as Newbold Pacey and even Milverton, Leamington, where some of Waller's wounded were still recuperating in August and September. Clearly, none of these had any intention of following Waller or, one suspects, resuming their service. The collapse of Waller's army is understandable. Quite apart from the notorious question of pay, one historian has calculated that between 23 May and 31 July, Waller's infantry had marched on thirty-six of the sixty-nine days, staying no more than three nights in any one place. In a summer by turns appallingly wet and scorching hot they had slept in the open without cover on twenty-one of those nights. In his Oxhill letter Waller had warned that his unpaid men, already 'much diminished', were soon likely to be 'ruined'. Some of them had marched well over 300 miles, and had been soundly defeated at Cropredy into the bargain and seen friends slaughtered. No wonder that an unfortunate few were caught running away or inciting mutiny, and were summarily dealt with at courts martial held at Fawsley, Daventry and Abingdon, at which the unbending William Purefoy and Godfrey Bosevile sat in judgement. At Daventry on 12 July two common soldiers were sentenced to be hanged and one, presumably a gentleman, 'shalbe harguebuseerd to death'.

Although precise estimates vary, casualties were substantial, particularly on the parliamentary side, and the burial registers of Wardington, Chipping Warden and Cropredy bear silent witness to a random few whose recorded names must stand for the vast anonymous majority of their fallen comrades. Although only one name is recorded at Wardington, for example, the eye-witness Coe reported that 'in the Church and Churchyard were many Commanders buried who had been slaine in the fight', and it is known that there was heavy slaughter at Cropredy Bridge itself. Many cannon balls and bullets have been found on the site over the years, including some poignant relics, like the small, bugle-shaped silver whistle attached by two chains to a ring, well into this century. Although Cropredy was a relatively minor affair and looms less large in the collective folk memory than Edgehill, Marston Moor and Naseby, it has its equal share of picturesque human vignettes: the King, sleeping not at Williamscot house, where there was an outbreak of smallpox, but in 'a very poor man's house' long since gone, or taking refreshment that fine midsummer's day under the Wardington Ash as battle was about to begin; the parliamentary cavalry quartering in the stables of Prescote's burnt manor house; the smoke rising from distant Banbury after a vengeful royalist attack on supposedly unfriendly households; parliamentary soldiers fleeing over Cropredy Bridge crying 'The field's lost! The field's lost!' or chanting, as Waller himself reported despondently, 'Home! Home!'; the burial mounds, naked corpses and 'many stately horses' strewn across the lane to Wardington; Cropredy's 6 ft high medieval eagle lectern hastily consigned to the Cherwell on the eve of the battle lest it should be destroyed, along with the churchyard cross, and remaining there for the next fifty years; the sporadic night-time volleys and the smoking match hung on the hedges to lure enemy fire; the parliamentary minister preaching in the fields on the Sunday morning. . . As usual, the odd individual anecdote conveys something of the grim heroism and brutality of a war far removed from the quaint costume drama of the popular imagination, like that of a royalist officer, John Gwyn, rescuing a nineteen-year-old youth:

> Just as he came out of the mill, stripped and wounded, a lusty soldier was fetching a desperate blow with the butt-end of his musket to make an end of him; which of a sudden I prevented, and made him prisoner upon the top of the hill by the windmill.

Almost unique, however, are two delightfully incongruous episodes concerning Sir William Waller which lend Cropredy that human dimension which history needs if it is to be more than abstraction. On the Sunday morning, 30 June, while 'in his lodging at Great Bourton to consult about business', the commander narrowly escaped what could have been a fatal accident:

GREAT BOURTON MANOR, BANBURY. Subsequently rebuilt but retaining its original seventeenth-century core, the house is likely to have been Sir William Waller's headquarters at the battle of Cropredy, where the general and his officers fell through rotten floor-boards into the cellar below during a council of war. (Photo: Banbury Museum)

> Being with my officers att a councell of warr, the floore of the roome where I was sunke, and wee all fell into a sellar that was underneath itt. I lay overwhelmed with a great deal of lumber that fell upon me, and yet I bless God I had no hurt att all.

The previous evening at sunset an offer of pardon from the King had been accompanied by a private message for Waller carried by the King's trumpeter:

> . . . which to my great shame and surprise came from the Lady [   ]. In it she besought me to betray my cause; and this she did so wittily and kinde, that I had much ado to be angry. Before this lady's marriage I had been her suitor, and did dearly love her, and she remembered me of this, and of some soft passages. Whether or not she was putt on this by some greater than herself I never knew; but I returned for answer, that as I had never been traitor to my love, so I would not to my cause, . . . and after this I heard no more . . .

Waller was as dejected after the battle as the Royalists were elated, and the King's unexpected tactical skill seems to have thrown the parliamentarian camp into some confusion, as well it might. Conflicting reports emerged of the King's whereabouts, and the disarray evident in the exchange of letters between Waller and his superiors and Waller's own slightly puzzling conduct are faintly comical. Although he confessed to be 'utterly tired out', he summoned his reserves to assure the authorities from Towcester on 3 July of his continued determination to follow the King, instructions, he promised, 'which I will observe as long as I have breath'. Assuming the King was still intent on marching north, he asked for horses to be sent to Warwick, proposing, curiously, to pursue the enemy by 'coasting them by way of Leicester . . . to gain ground of them'. The London committee duly instructed Sir Samuel Luke to comply and send horses to Warwick three days later. At one point, Waller wrote, 'being assured the King was gone towards Buckingham . . . I marched with all speed after him', though there appears little evidence of this move. Understandably, Waller remained confused, petulant and inert. While the London committee was under the impression on 9 July that he was marching from Northamptonshire towards the King in Worcestershire, Waller had in fact simply moved to Daventry where he intended awaiting the promised reinforcements with evidently little intention of moving:

> I continue here at Daventry, in expectation of those horses promised . . . Were I supplied with some foot, in lieu of those who basely ran away from their colours to London, I would march up to [the King in Worcestershire], but till then I suppose I shall do you the best service by temporising . . .

Presumably because Luke's reinforcements never materialized, Waller eventually returned to Towcester, then Buckingham, Bicester and Abingdon, still complaining bitterly of his depleted forces: 'I am like to be left naked if not speedily supplied'. The whole plan to pursue the King was in tatters. Charles had won, at the very least, a tactical victory, and parliamentary morale was at its lowest ebb.

None of these decisions, however, was as important to the local inhabitants as the loss of their carts and teams of horses, once again requisitioned for weeks of unpaid service at the height of summer when the countrymen could least afford them, for open-ended commitments to transport supplies and goods to whatever destination eventually materialized. Many of the inhabitants of tiny Mollington, for example, complained of forced payment 'towards the hire of a Cart wch went wth Sir Willm Wallers Army for 14 dayes when he went from Cropredy'. Similarly, the inhabitants of Priors Hardwick, having already supplied Waller at Bourton on 1 July, were then called upon for a contribution of 5s. each 'for a teeme to goe to Abbington [Abingdon] wth Sr Will. Waller his carriage' and for the wages of the men accompanying it. William Heritage's claim is typical of many:

> Paid to wards the Settinge forth of ateeme to the same armie to Draw a carriage from Bourton to Buckingham, & from thence to Abington.

Neither side had much cause for congratulation at the end of the so-called Oxford campaign. The King's secretary's description of that midsummer as 'His Majesty's happy progress and success' which 'by his conduct and valour' had triumphantly divided the two parliamentary armies and then defeated them both, was that of a loyal and tactful servant rather than of a detached observer. Meanwhile parliamentary morale was in shreds, Waller and Essex having accomplished none of the original objects of the exercise. There seems no obvious reason why the King should not have joined Rupert in the north had he really wished to do so – before or after Marston Moor. For the country-folk in whose fields, barns and cottages the many regiments camped as they trudged across the region there was no change. From Salford Priors and Shipston-on-Stour in the south-west, east to the Northamptonshire borders, village after village had experienced, or in many cases re-experienced, the insecurity, the losses and the harassment of war. And as the sequel to Cropredy, the siege of Banbury, was now about to begin, there was to be little respite for many a long week.

Politically, however, the militarily minor Cropredy campaign coincided with three significant developments. As the royalist newspaper *Mercurius Aulicus* was quick to point out, Parliament could no longer maintain its fiction that its sole enemy was not the King in person but his evil counsellors, for these had remained safely in Oxford while the King himself had come under deliberate selective fire at Cropredy. Waller's often-quoted complaint to his superiors about the quality of the troops in a ludicrously inadequate military organization contributed eventually to the formation of the efficient New Model Army. Finally, Cropredy was followed immediately by an unexpected offer of peace negotiations by the King, on arriving at Evesham on 3 July, which if accepted, could have changed the course of English history (see Appendix C). In view of what he considered his victory at Cropredy, Charles no doubt considered the time opportune; but this is no reason to doubt the genuineness of the King's motives, his profession of despair at 'the grievous sufferings of our poor subjects' or his wish to 'prevent the further effusion of blood'. Shortly after the dispatch of the King's message to Parliament, however, news of the decisive parliamentary victory at Marston Moor began to arrive, and the King's initiative went unanswered.[10]

THE FIRST SIEGE OF BANBURY

Nothing had come of the Earl of Denbigh's reported intention in the spring to attack Banbury Castle, or of a half-hearted attempt on it in May, and even less, as we have seen, of Sir William Waller's rumoured promise of capturing it to entice local forces to join him against the King's army. How the much more sustained – and very nearly successful – campaign against Banbury in the summer of 1644 originated is far from clear. But as with the recent seizure of Compton House, the initiative was probably local rather than national, since there is at first no reference to it in the state papers. Banbury's strategic importance and its very notoriety clearly presented a tempting consolation prize for commanders baulked of their major prey at Cropredy, and with the King's forces quickly vacating the area the moment must have seemed overwhelmingly right to commanders like John Bridges at Warwick and William Purefoy at Coventry to offer their forces for a determined assault which, if successful, would retrieve honour lost at Cropredy. Although Waller's army had largely disintegrated when many had, as he put it, 'basely run away from their colours to London', some of the better paid and therefore more dependable local forces, with their stronger, county allegiance and competent leadership, remained in position in the neighbourhood eager enough, one suspects, to assault the detested 'den of thieves' at Banbury. No record of a formal decision appears, but if there was one it must have been taken locally, perhaps soon after the disgruntled Waller had left Daventry to go south, about 12 July. Only later, when Waller had arrived at Abingdon in late July, did the parliamentary authorities in London, preoccupied with so many other urgent national considerations, accept and encourage the venture. Overall command of the operation devolved to Colonel John Fiennes, who arrived in the district in early July, no doubt in recognition of his family's unique local associations, and it must be significant that his father, Lord Saye, was a prominent and influential signatory of many of the parliamentary committee's directives during this period. Colonel Nathaniel Whetham, the experienced commander of the Northampton parliamentary garrison, acted as second-in-command on his arrival in late August. The other major commanders were Colonel Godfrey Bosevile, the Coventry committeeman and close associate of William Purefoy, the reinstated Colonel Constance Ferrar, recently in command of the Gloucester convoys, and Northampton's Major Lidcot. Neither John Bridges nor William Purefoy was much involved, though many of their companies were in active support under veterans like Captains Joseph Hawkesworth, Thomas Wells, Anthony Otway, Abraham Pont and John Cheshire.

As already seen, there was considerable confusion in the parliamentary ranks after Cropredy, and it is often quite unclear to what extent local commanders complied with frequently tentative or ambiguous decisions taken in London. After Cropredy the Warwickshire and Northamptonshire forces had been instructed to continue with Waller, who at first remained at Daventry smarting from defeat and awaiting new supplies before eventually moving away to Towcester, Buckingham and Abingdon. But Waller was already complaining that these local forces were 'in the main part recalled to do service in their own counties'. While some accompanied him obediently to Abingdon and were then ordered to remain there as late as 23 July, it is clear that others, from Warwickshire and beyond, had not in fact strayed far from Banbury. Captain Purbeck Temple's soldiers, for example, were quartered at Idlicote on 7 July, a whole troop at Drayton on 10 July before moving to Farnborough, while others under Temple were soon receiving provisions from surrounding villages at Broughton, Hanwell and elsewhere. Far from being evacuated after Cropredy, the Banbury district saw a continuous regrouping of forces already there and, indeed, the influx of new ones which had probably not fought at Cropredy. Contingents of Oliver Cromwell's forces preparing to move west, for example, were already quartering at Kineton in June and Radway in July before being reported scattered at Wormleighton, Bodington, Shuckburgh and Farnborough in August and September. Similarly, others under the Earl of Denbigh, in theory earmarked for action at Evesham via Alcester, had evidently been diverted for service at Cropredy and were still quartered at Shipston, Brailes, Idlicote and elsewhere in July, remaining in the district until at least November. Yet others, like the Earl of Manchester's at Brinklow and Lord Grey of Groby's at Cherington in August, in addition to soldiers from Aylesbury and Newport Pagnell, were straggling throughout the district during the summer, without their precise destination or contribution to the war effort ever becoming quite clear. What is quite certain, however, is that for the local population there was no respite, since many of the same units which had taken part at Cropredy and even Compton were redeployed almost immediately for 'the service against Banbury', particularly the local ones. Captain William Sambidge (or Sambach) is no doubt a typical example of a committed local partisan turned parliamentary officer. Of Kineton and Pillerton, he had already contributed money and goods worth £20 to the parliamentary coffers in Warwick Castle at the outset of the war, and given quarter to parliamentarian officers at Edgehill (and the wounded after) and now, more recently, to Waller's quartermasters, presumably *en route* for Cropredy. Having raised a troop under Colonel John Fiennes at some uncertain date, his men quartered at Brailes for the storming of Compton House before proceeding to Cropredy and Banbury, and were at Hanwell in mid-August with Sambidge himself comfortably ensconced at Calthorpe manor-house in Banbury for the siege. Similarly, Captain Thomas Wells's men were at Brailes and Tysoe for the three nights necessary for capturing Compton, and were there again in September in order to escort a mortar gun from Sudeley Castle to Banbury's siege, his troop of eighty men and horse having spent an intervening eight weeks and three days – the parish accounts are fastidiously precise – quartered at Hornton. Again, Captain Abraham Pont's men were quartered in nearby villages at the capture of Compton in early June before inflicting themselves on Hanwell for nine long weeks, arousing bitter complaints from the villagers when invited later to submit their claims for compensation via their constable, Edward Borton:

> Major Pont, Beinge in the Regiment of Colonell Purefoy . . . with his Whole Troope to the Number of forty and two men, With forty and five horses, Quartered Uppon Us for the space of Nine Weeks, And Promisinge to pay for the Quartering of his Troope . . .

In humbly asking the parliamentary authorities 'to Consider this our great Burthen', the inhabitants of Hanwell pointedly emphasized that while taking free quarter of them, Pont was in regular receipt of 'his Constant pay from the townes Adjacent to us'. What is

CALTHORPE HOUSE, BANBURY, c. 1900. The original sixteenth-century house, subsequently much altered, was one of several local manor-houses used as parliamentary military headquarters during the long but unsuccessful siege of Banbury in the summer of 1644. It now stands forlorn, threatened by industrial redevelopment. (Photo: Centre for Oxfordshire Studies)

conspicuously lacking from the published accounts of the siege of Banbury and, indeed, most other military engagements, is any real sense of the enormities of such burdens on poor villagers. The impoverishment of Burton Dassett, when Colonel Edward Whalley's troop of 146 men and horses billeted themselves there for eight days during the siege of Banbury, must have been well-nigh total, without taking into account the usual incidental plunder. Nor was a shorter stay by the troops necessarily more painless, for what they did not consume there and then they would often take with them or order to be sent after them. Thus, Brinklow protested that William Purefoy's soldiers going to besiege Banbury 'had all our pvision & carried it after them to Woolston'.[11]

There was no clearly-defined opening to the operation to besiege Banbury's royalist garrison, but rather a gradual build-up of activity in July once the King's army had left the area. While John Bridges at Warwick was issued with forty more barrels of gunpowder and several tons of match for defending the town and castle on 12 July, parliamentary troops began moving south from Coventry and Warwick to join those already scattered throughout the locality, taking up new positions and awaiting decisions which there was as yet no commander-in-chief to make. In mid-July, 'reducing the Cavaliers in Banbury-castle' was only one of several options being discussed by General Richard Browne at a meeting in Berkshire. Nevertheless, after a rendezvous at Rugby, the two regiments of William Purefoy and Godfrey Bosevile marched through Brinklow and Wolston south along the Fosse Way, while John Fiennes and nine of his officers quartered at Bourton-on-Dunsmore before establishing quarters in the Kineton–Idlicote district in mid-July: 'Colonell Fynes & his Company when they went to beseege Banbury quartered here one night in July 1644'. Nearer Banbury itself strategic points were being occupied on the low hills commanding views of the town: Hanwell Castle and Bourton, both recently vacated by Waller, to the north; Warkworth manor house, home of the Northampton parliamentary committeeman Philip Holman, to the east, with good views over north Oxfordshire and a convenient reception post for the Northampton contingents which were beginning to assemble; and Lord Saye's ancestral Broughton to the south-west, already vacated by the Royalists. The royalist newspaper *Mercurius Aulicus* reported the occupation of Broughton 'and other places thereabouts' on 19 July, pointing out maliciously the coincidence of the rebel activity with the baleful Dog Days, and Dugdale confirmed Fiennes's arrival at Broughton and Holman's 'at his owne house at Warkworth on the other side Banbury'. Little other activity was reported in July, however, and there is no evidence to support the *Victoria County History* assertion that roads around Banbury were being blockaded as such. The castle in fact continued to receive at least some provisions from named suppliers in Banbury and the surrounding villages throughout the siege: Nathaniel Vivers of Banbury, William Gubbin of Middleton Cheney, Thomas Pomfret of Fawcet . . . The troops were still without a commander-in-chief and, fairly clearly, any concerted plan of campaign. Indeed, not until 1 August did the London committee resolve to instruct their Northampton colleagues tentatively to capture Banbury 'if they find an opportunity . . . without breaking [up] their forces' and, two days later, to order General Richard Browne and others to march to Banbury to join the 'expected' Northampton and Warwickshire forces 'for the service against Banbury'.

August saw the parliamentary deployment continuing throughout the entire district. By 8 August, at least some Northampton units, those of Major Leonard Lidcot, were positioned at Williamscot and Wardington, already receiving large consignments of provisions from Burton Dassett, Avon Dassett, Mollington, Wormleighton, Farnborough and even villages as distant as Napton, while other Northampton units were arriving at Shotteswell and nearby, all 'comeinge agt. banbury', as the parish archives put it. The forces under Colonel John Fiennes, meanwhile, were assembling or regrouping in the villages between Hanwell and Kineton, with one detachment occupying the psychologically-important position at Broughton, as though ready to avenge its recent indignities at the hands of the Cavaliers. In support of this massive build-up, the parliamentary committee in London belatedly awoke to its responsibilities and on 8 August ordered its general of ordnance, Sir Walter Erle, to deliver seventy barrels of gunpowder and bullets to Lord Saye's gunner, Thomas Wright, with a further consignment a fortnight later. As a further precaution, detachments of Cromwell's cavalry were in the district keeping guard and awaiting orders; one, under Captain Robert Swallow, was quartered at Bodington throughout August and September. Few villages were without their contingents of unruly soldiers and their various additional obligations. Among Radway's contributions were 'lights' supplied to the Northampton soldiers in the district, peas to Fiennes at Broughton and the reception of some of Waller's men, on 10 August, recently released from prison for some undisclosed crime (mutiny or intended desertion?). Fenny Compton's case is a typical illustration:

The Inhabitants of Fenicompton were chardged wth: 2 quarters of provender to Major Lidcott, pric £2; and for pvision for Capt. Sambidge his Troope, to the valew of £10. 12s; and to Capt. Swallow under the Comand of Lieuetent Generall Cromwell for two qters of Provender, price £1 4 4; and to Capt. Philips, belonginge to Aylesbury, for two qters of Oates, price £1 4 4; and to Capt. Lidcott, belonging to Northton, for Provender, to the Valew of £3 . . .

On 17 August, after much indecision, Parliament officially instructed those Warwickshire forces still accompanying Waller towards Abingdon (probably few) to be released for action at Banbury, and for more arms and ammunition, including three guns, a mortar and a fire-master to work it to be sent from Aylesbury. The Warwickshire men were 'to be employed conjoined with those of Northamptonshire which are there already', and the dependable Purefoy and Bosevile were briefly recalled to London to receive instructions before being charged with escorting this valuable cargo from Aylesbury to Banbury. The build-up was gathering momentum, and on 23 August Parliament ordered Colonel Nathaniel Whetham to take charge of the Northamptonshire forces as the first real skirmishing began to be reported, each side testing the resolve of the other. In one well-reported incident on 22 August a royalist cavalry sortie from the castle drove back a small parliamentary force towards Warkworth before being counter-attacked and losing their officer, Captain Middleton, 'by a carbine shot thorough the braine', and his cornet, 'one Smith, a stout plunderer' — 'whose bodyes', Sir Samuel Luke reported, 'Major Lydcott carryed the same night to his quarters' [at Warkworth] for burial. With parliamentary forces arriving all the time the conflict now rapidly escalated. By late August the Northampton forces were virtually complete, while others belonging to General Browne were reported to have arrived from Aylesbury to join a strong detachment under Fiennes occupying the town. Very early on Sunday 25 August the besiegers signalled their resolve by occupying St Mary's church, well within range of the castle, posting cannons and musketeers on the tower to draw enemy fire, while more troops were busy setting up positions in the town and unloading ammunition. Skirmishing almost immediately swept through nearby streets and gardens, and in and out of houses, until Whetham finally arrived at midday from Northampton with two 'great guns' and more reinforcements and 'made some shott at ye castle', as Dugdale wrote, as the Royalists retreated behind the stout walls. During the following days the besiegers were busy making fortifications for an assault on the castle, coming under frequent fire to such an extent that they were obliged to continue during the night-time. Fiennes, apparently superseding Whetham as commander, signalled his authority by promptly sending a trumpet summons to the besieged under the Earl of Northampton's brother, the nineteen-year-old William Compton. Predictably, given the hatred between the two families since pre-war days, the summons was rejected in the heroic terms beloved of court newspaper and parliamentary broadsheet alike:

. . . they kept the Castle for his Majestie, and as long as one man was left alive in it, [William Compton] willed them not to expect to have it delivered.

During the last days of August William Purefoy and Godfrey Bosevile brought up yet more reinforcements of men and armoury, and as more cannons from Northampton were being positioned there was an intensification of the fighting and serious damage caused in the town. Thirty houses near the castle were reportedly burning furiously for two days, deliberately fired by the Royalists to prevent use by the enemy and force them to retreat 'to a more mannerly distance', breaches were made in the castle walls ('a hole foure or five yards square', by one report) and cart-loads of parliamentary dead were carried away, sixteen in one direction, five in another – inspiring later more than one desperate petition from local widows requesting relief for their families rendered destitute in the state's service, like Hester Whyte, or Margery Browne of Pillerton. The church itself, at the centre of the fighting, suffered serious damage, the tower being destroyed by a fire which each side contemputously claimed the other to have started deliberately, and two years later the town's inhabitants petitioned Parliament for aid to fund repairs to 'part of the Church and Steeple pulled down'.

A new twist came one day late in August when two youths, variously called 'boyes' or, in a vivid description which has the ring of authenticity, 'tatered rogues without hose or shooe put over the castle-wall early in the morning', were caught by the Parliamentarians each carrying half of a message from the castle governor to Prince Rupert:

> . . . a letter in a shred of paper, close-written and cut in the middest, [so] that if but one of them had been taken we had not known what to have made of it . . .

The message entreated Rupert, marching south into Worcestershire after his defeat at Marston Moor, to send a strong detachment to the area to punish the supposedly demoralized besiegers and the depleted Northampton garrison at one swoop. The possibility of an intervention by Rupert at Banbury was sufficiently real to alarm Parliament, and partly explains the otherwise curious decision suddenly, at the beginning of September, to abandon the siege. The order was quickly withdrawn in favour of a recommendation that the decision be taken locally, but this demoralizing episode did little to revive flagging parliamentary spirits further weakened, according to plausible royalist reports, by widespread desertions. The complexion and morale of one company at the time, under the former Coventry physician who had barred the King's entry into his city in 1642, Colonel Robert Phipps, may be glimpsed in the later complaints of many of his men against their captain, Thomas Hobson, an ex-butcher of Coventry. During their service at Banbury for 'about five weeks and odd daies', the men complained that they were unpaid, promised arrears were unforthcoming and no proper accounts were kept, since they had no 'clarke', 'unlesse the Lieutennt [Hobson] executed it himself'. One corporal testified that 'hee had two Souldiers slaine out of his squadron, three ranne away and one died as they came back from thence', while another, Reginald Allen, 'out of some distaste betwixt the said Lieutennt and him was cashiered and turned away without pay'. Hobson inflated company numbers when musters were due, cashiered men arbitrarily and continued to receive his pay for those long since gone or even, like Edward Mannering, dead. An entire catalogue of serious breaches of discipline and 'contempt' for orders was later compiled by the Coventry command against the thoroughly unreliable Hobson, and orders were issued in 1647 'to attach and seize the body of the said Lieutennt Thomas Hobson and him to keep in safe custody'. Although some Warwickshire troops seem to have been relatively well paid, there is no reason to suppose Hobson's company in any way unrepresentative, and this illustration of chronic indiscipline, petty corruption and sheer unprofessionalism makes it all the more surprising that such ragged troops under, probably, a divided command, were able to mount and sustain a reasonably effective campaign for so long.[12]

The Royalists' much-feared intervention from Worcestershire never in fact materialized. Sir Marmaduke Langdale's intention to join with local forces under Colonels Samuel Sandys and Sir William Russell to relieve Banbury was thwarted by another of Colonel Edward Massey's timely initiatives from Gloucester. Marching to Stanway on hearing that Royalists were moving east through Stratford, Massey clearly announced his intention of blocking any such attempt; a parliamentary newspaper reported him on 14 September near Moreton-in-Marsh, 'bending towards Banbury to be a reserve to the besiegers there, if occasion be'. When the Royalists 'made a show as if they intend to relieve Banbury', another report continued, 'they were so closely pursued upon the Reare . . . that they ranne back to Worcester as fast as they could without attempting any thing'. As a further precaution shortly after, Cromwell, whose own forces had been positioned near Banbury awaiting orders for some time, was recalled to London for consultation and then promptly dispatched to Banbury in case Rupert should intervene, whereupon, according to parliamentary sources, those Royalists already near Stratford 'did presently retire'. Banbury remained for the time being unrelieved. Although outwardly confident, neither side seized its chances or even acted coherently at this time. A determined royalist strike might well have routed the ill-organized and demoralized Parliamentarians, planning to remove their artillery to Compton as a prelude to abandoning the siege, as Fiennes himself reported to his superiors in London at the beginning of September that there was little hope of success. But the besieged Royalists were also in an unenviable plight: the intended relief from Worcester, as we have seen, never materialized, nor that from Leicestershire which Cromwell predicted shortly after; and the castle itself was reported to be 'closely begirt' and 'extreamly battered', supplies were desperately needed and plague was reportedly breaking out among the garrison. Above all, Cromwell, after his recent triumph at Marston Moor and with substantial forces ready in the locality, was condemned by quarrelling and indecisive superiors to waste much of September and October in futile marching to and fro on the fringes of the action at Banbury. Nevertheless, intense, if intermittent action continued. The Parliamentarians, attempting to tighten the screw before the King could regain Oxford from the West Country and send a relief force, were still moving up guns at the beginning of September. Some, planted at Neithrop, outside North Gate at the bottom of North Bar, and near the scene of recent skirmishing immediately preceding Cropredy, were firing across the open meadows separating their fortified positions from the castle, provoking fierce counter-attack. In a further ominous development, the dependable Warwick captain Thomas Wells was charged with escorting a heavy mortar from Waller's recently-captured Sudeley, and yet more quartering was required of the intervening villages as it was hauled through the Warwickshire lanes via Tysoe on its way to the siege. With more substantial quantities of gunpowder, match and grenades being issued on 16 September by the parliamentary ordnance, a new tactic was tried in mid-September when, following a second fruitless summons by Fiennes to the garrison to surrender, miners were imported from Bedworth for one of the Civil War's periodic attempts at underground warfare. But while their allies suffered heavy casualties from the enemy walls in draining part of the outer moat, the miners themselves, attempting to tunnel under the castle walls, were in their turn defeated by underground streams flooding their primitive efforts.

Late September saw the one desperate and costly assault on the castle. With its walls now seriously breached (a parliamentary report claimed a gap 'neare 30 yeards in length'), bribes were used to induce volunteers to mount an assault, blocking the partially-drained moat with imported soil and brushwood in carts requisitioned from nearby villages along with scaling ladders:

> About 9 of the clocke that morning [Monday 23 September] they began to fall on. Their foote had beene so banged by continuall sallyes that they were not hardy enough for this service; therefore they hired Troopers to lead them on, 12 out of each company, with their best officers. These were to have £300 (as was confest) for their paines. The number of assaylants was about 1000. They came on with burdens of furrs [furze] on their backes, which they cast into the Mote the better to passe the mud, and so assaulted it in 5 severall places at once. The greatest number were on that side where the breach was; on all other partes they brought ladders, but the courageous defendants never suffered them to reare so much as one ladder, but cut them off with great and small shot, which was sent among them like haile. . .

As usual, neighbouring villages were ransacked for available supplies and implements or received imperious warrants to send them. Shotteswell's contribution was one among many:

> One Loade of Ladders, one Loade of haye, one loade of bushes, Diggers, Cartes to carrye awaye soyle, Labourers to fill them, Carryinge away twoe Loade of maymed souldiers to Coventry, one Loade more to Southam and two more to Warr. [Warwick], with mattockes, shovells and spades, amountinge to the sum £14 08 04.

The constable of Wroxton received the following demands from Fiennes on 20 September:

> These are to charge and command you that upon sight hereof you gather together all the Ladders in your Towne with one Load of Hay bound hard together into Fardles with Thumb-ropes. And one Load of good brushy Faggots. And bring the said things into the Church-yard in Banbury by one of the Clocke this day at the furthest, where there shall be some men appointed to receive them. Hereof faile you not upon paine of Death and forfeiting your whole estate.

The royalist newspaper, no doubt fairly accurately, reported 'so many killed and wounded that they were ready to quit the siedge', followed by a desperate truce and scenes as grisly as Banbury's market place had ever witnessed:

> Towards evening that day they sent a trumpet to desire the bodies of their dead, which was granted upon condition that those which had fallen within pistoll shot of the Castle should be stript by those of the garrison and delivered naked in the Market place; which was done accordingly. All Tuesday last [24 September] they spent in solemnizing the burials of their dead with drumms, trumpets, vollies of shot and now and then a Psalme . . . they were much broken as they expressed at their funeralls, having lost so many of their best officers. Themselves have acknowledged above 300 slaine and wounded . . .

Many of those fortunate enough to survive were in a desperate plight, as is evident from one human document, a letter from a Banbury resident, John Harby, to a Northampton relative member of the town's parliamentary committee, Edward Harby, dated 29 September:

> Sir, I have sent in these twoe Carts all the wounded men of our Regiment att the last storme. I would desire that they may be provided of Quarter in Northampton, and I have sent one of our Chirurions [Surgeons] and the Chest with them, and I hope he wilbe very Carefull to dresse them constantly. But the truth is, here is noe accomodation of bedds to be had for them . . . Sr, I doubt not but their pittifull Condicon is argument sufficient to move the Gentlemen of the Comitteee to take care of them . . .

The request was accepted, but recovery from wounds and the primitive surgery was uncertain, and some, described as 'very much wounded', were still being cared for months after, in late January 1645.

Despite this rebuff the Parliamentarians maintained the siege into October, though with what progress, if any, is not clear from the often biased contemporary reporting. That work on yet more defensive fortifications was planned is clear from parliamentary resolutions dated 30 September for Essex's chief engineer Jacob Kuilenburg to be escorted from Abingdon to Banbury to advise on defences, as he was already doing at Abingdon and Reading, and for large-scale civilian recruitment of labourers:

> It is this Day Ordained by the Lords and Commons, etc. That Colonel Fienns, Colonel Boswell, Colonel Wetham, Lt. Col. Ferrar and Major Lidcutt, now employed in the Siege at Banbury, shall have Power to take, out of all the Towns within Ten Miles of Banbury, proportionably, such Number of Workmen for Pioneers as they shall think fit.

It is equally clear that these instructions were acted upon, even in villages situated at the outer limit of the stipulated 10 miles radius, like Brailes and Tysoe, where villagers later claimed expenses 'for digging at Banbury', and the rigorous enforcement of such edicts may be judged from the case of Richard Woodward at Avon Dassett. Woodward, as a wealthy man, had already been heavily penalized during the Cropredy campaign in June and imposed upon throughout July and August. In an incident which perhaps suggests a personal vendetta he was now summoned by Fiennes to appear at Banbury to dig in person and fined because he was absent from the locality:

> A party of horse, by Warrant under the hand of Coll. John Fienes, required of the sayd Richard Woodward for not appearinge in pson to digg when the seidge began at Banbury 1644 (although he had fower men servants there two dayes, and he himselfe at the tyme of the Summons twenty miles distant from Banbury), and he payd, £0 2 0.[13]

The hopes of the besiegers fluctuated wildly in the contemporary reports. On 1 October some were in 'great expectation that . . . the Castle of Banbury will be surrendred into the Parliament within fifteene dayes', but a more gloomy note was introduced the next day in the admission that 'the besieged are not without hopes of reliefe' and, in a loaded reference to the castle's surrender without a struggle in 1642, a pointed reminder that 'such places which are easily lost are so hard to regaine'. Cromwell had returned to the district and was quartered at Syresham, Northamptonshire, again awaiting orders and planning a rendezvous at Sulgrave to prepare for the still expected royal relief force. When his orders came, they instructed him to march those of his cavalry still 'att or about Banbury' southwards to Reading to counter the mounting threat from the King. Although the surrounding villages were sending as many provisions as ever to the parliamentary quarters encircling Banbury and, indeed, providing for Waller's belated carriages which had still not all reached Abingdon, the Banbury operations were inexplicably being scaled down at a time when the besieged garrison was becoming desperate. Shotteswell reported horses stolen one day by one of Fiennes's quartermasters 'to Drawe the morter peece awaye for the States service', and by 17 October all the Banbury guns had been withdrawn and had reached safety at Northampton. Occasional forays were still reported, however. In one incident, John Fiennes, still receiving regular provisions at Broughton from nearby villages, destroyed royalist cavalry quarters at Kidlington suspected of being part of an intended relief force, pursuing the Cavaliers 'even to the walls of Oxford'. This success proved, ironically, the death-knell for the entire Banbury campaign. Hardly had Fiennes's party returned exhausted to their base at Adderbury, having negotiated severe weather conditions in a flooded countryside, when they were confronted by the large royalist relief force which had been dreaded for so long. The King in Berkshire, hearing that the Banbury garrison was on the point of surrendering, had finally decided to act, and sent three crack cavalry regiments under the Earl of Northampton, Lord Wilmot and the Earl of Brentford from Newbury to join with Colonel Henry Gage's Oxford forces. The Royalists had marched quickly via Witney, met Gage near Woodstock and arrived late at night at Deddington, being impeded by the flooding along the Swere valley, where 'they found the waters so high that they could not without much difficulty get over the Bridges to Adderbury'. Aware that his forces, 'much wet and wearied by reason of their long march', were in no condition to withstand a major cavalry attack from three experienced commanders in charge of a numerically superior force under his arch-rival, Fiennes hastily called a council of war which decided to abandon the flagging siege immediately:

> It was ordered by the Councell of Warre . . . that all the Forces in and about Banbury should march from beleaguering the Castle to Warwick, by 5 of the clock in the morning, the enemy being within 4 miles of the Castle.

Perhaps significantly, in view of later recriminations, the most senior commanders like Whetham and Bosevile seem not to have been consulted; there was probably no time to do so. At daybreak the next morning, Friday 25 October, the Royalists advanced to Bodicote to be confronted, at 7 a.m., by about eight hundred enemy cavalry drawn up on the southern approaches to the town in an attempt to guard what was intended as the phased withdrawal to Warwick. The artillery had already left during the night, and other units had begun to follow, leaving Banbury at 5 a.m. by what a contemporary account refers to as Bull Bar, when the Royalists, as parliamentary officers explained, 'came so suddainly on us that we could be no means avoid an engagement, . . . [and] our horse were forced to fight before we could draw them or our foot into any good posture'. The axle-tree of a large cannon unearthed at Easington in the nineteenth century substantiates the contemporary reports and subsequent local tradition that the first engagement took place here, near Crouch Hill, as it had a few months earlier prior to Cropredy. The withdrawal towards Hanwell turned quickly into what even the Parliamentarians termed a rout, with only isolated pockets of resistance temporarily holding up the Royalists' pursuit across the countryside. The royalist attack appears to have been well conducted, Gage's Oxford cavalry attacking from the commanding Crouch Hill position in the west, Gage himself entering the town to relieve the castle, the Earl of Northampton hurrying directly north to intercept the retreat towards Hanwell and another detachment securing the eastern sector in case the enemy attempted to retreat towards Northampton. Some parliamentarian foot soldiers, 'having lyned the hedges neare Hanwell Warren', attacked the Earl of Northampton for a time before being dispersed: 'left in the Pastures against the Warren, [they] escaped through the enclosures by help of hedges and ditches'. As usual, the defeated scattered in all directions, some eventually towards Northampton but most westwards towards Broughton and Kineton, while others, as an officer's report noted graphically, 'found a way from hedge to hedge to march to Compton house, though the horse were gone to Warwick'. There is no reason to doubt the royalist claims of heavy parliamentary losses in men and equipment as their supply trains were abandoned near Warmington, and the royalist report was quick to point out the curious parallel with the equivalent loss of the Banbury magazine under Lord Brooke two years previously at the same spot. The human toll was substantial: 'from Hanwell to Edge-hill the way was spread with the Rebells dead bodies, whereof many rich cloathed with buffe coates, silver laced . . .'.

Besieged for three months by a large, if ill-conducted, number of parliamentary troops under individually-competent and experienced commanders like Whetham, Bosevile and Ferrar, Banbury was, like Wellington's Waterloo, 'a damned nice thing', as C.V. Wedgwood concludes:

> Twice the enemy had penetrated the shattered walls and twice been driven out again, now ammunition was running low, water was short, all the horses except two had been eaten and the walls, plugged with turf and mud, were becoming indefensible . . .

Nevertheless, for the second time within that short summer of 1644, Parliament had lost a strategically-important battle in the south Midlands, causing widespread impoverishment and disruption in the local community and substantial loss of life. The countless dead included hundreds of anonymous soldiers and, doubtless, recently-recruited civilians and volunteers, as well as a few notable officers, like the much-travelled Ferrer. The defence of the castle by the nineteen-year-old William Compton and his small band under Colonel Anthony Greene was widely hailed, with justice, as heroic. But the parliamentary defeat was caused, as so often, by a combination of factors other than the tenacity of the defenders. The besiegers continued to the end to receive the loyal support of local sympathizers like William Gubbin at Middleton Cheney who was reported to have frequently passed to and fro furnishing arms and provisions and supplying information of enemy movements and:

> . . . assisted in making fires to inform them of coming relief, whereon the castle held out several days more, till the Earl of Northampton came and raised the siege.

But more disastrous still were the missed chances on the Parliament side, the inconsistent direction from the remote London authorities, the under-use of major assets like Browne and Cromwell and, above all, the ineffective local organization compounded, probably, by personality clashes among the various commanders and

lukewarm support for the commander-in-chief. Without subscribing to the contemptuous royalist dismissal of John Fiennes as an incompetent from a family already
militarily discredited by his brother Nathaniel's highly controversial surrender of Bristol
in 1643, Fiennes lacked the experience, strength and sheer personality to inspire and
weld together such a disparate collection of regiments against a determined enemy. If
the extracts from captured letters from Lord Saye to his son are to be believed – widely
and mockingly publicized by the Royalists but claimed as authentic – Fiennes was
diffident and indecisive and his relationship with at least Browne uneasy, and he was
reportedly reduced not only to begging beds for his soldiers from Lady Cope, the
parliamentarian mistress of Hanwell Castle, but pleading for refuge at Compton house
and being refused admission by the arrogant Purefoy. Lord Saye's own involvement in
decision-making at this time is in itself ambiguous. The Royalists, in a possibly
significant phrase, referred to the Banbury siege as being 'so long continued by the Lord
Saye' and made much of the fact that it was the family's regiment which had surrendered
the castle without a fight two years before, when John Fiennes had shed tears at the
disaster. With Broughton once more in parliamentarian hands, Saye would clearly have
taken the closest interest in further redeeming the family honour by capturing Banbury
too. It is significant that when the London committee instructed the dispersal of the
besieging forces and the abandonment of the siege, it was careful to stipulate that a
strong guard should be left at Broughton, and the family letters confirm his interest in
the conduct of the Banbury campaign. But Lord Saye's authority was remote from the
volatile local situation and was likely to have been as ineffectual against experienced
commanders in the field like Whetham and Bosevile as was, perhaps, his son's. What is
certain is that the psychological blow to Parliament was acute, and that recriminations
began immediately after the ending of the siege. On 28 October a demoralized
Warwickshire committee wrote a veritable wail of despair to Sir Samuel Luke at
Newport Pagnell:

> We are unhappy in the last disaster at Banbury, and are like to be worse, the King's party increasing
> there. Yesterday the Earl of Northampton summoned Compton house, and we hear since that he has
> sat down before it. The Northampton forces are going home and we are unable to deal with the
> enemy. We know not where his Excellency [the Earl of Essex] or the Earl of Manchester are . . .

John Bridges at Warwick was more specific in his criticism to Luke in early November:

> Our horse are now marched towards Chipping Norton, to attend some opportunity to regain their
> honour which was woefully lost [at Banbury] for want of conduct and order. Never so brave an
> opportunity so lost by ill management . . .

Luke himself, who had contributed a contingent to the Banbury siege, shrank from
giving details of 'this unfortunate turn at Banbury' to a correspondent: 'the particulars I
cannot relate you, fearing them to be so bad that the enemy could not desire them
worse . . .', while reporting to Essex bluntly that 'many of my countrymen resolve never
to go to Banbury again'. The House of Commons passed a resolution 'to examine the
Business concerning the Miscarriages of the Forces at Banbury' and ordered an enquiry
into 'such as were defective in their duty, whether Commanders of Horse or Foot'.
Although the court newspaper, in a show of mock sympathy, was unable to resist

pointing out that chief among the parliamentary 'miscarriages' was the commander John Fiennes himself, many of the defeated commanders must have come under suspicion. One who certainly did so was Captain Purbeck Temple, a Newport Pagnell officer on detachment under Fiennes, against whom specific charges were laid shortly after. Quartered at Bloxham the night the Royalists had so suddenly arrived, Temple had, it was alleged, panicked and inexcusably:

> . . . brought Col. Fiennis . . . a false allarum, affirming yt ye enemy was in his Qtrs, & yt he had turned all his owne best rideing horses loose, and was necessitated to hide himselfe in a woodpile, [and] that diverse of his men were taken Prisoners . . .

The result was that Fiennes had ordered an immediate withdrawal of troops guarding the strategically-vital Adderbury Bridge, so allowing the Royalists unimpeded access into Banbury. Moreover, it was claimed, Temple had disobeyed orders by instructing a charge instead of the withdrawal towards Warwick which had been ordered, and had then left the field. Clearly such accusations are one-sided, and must be treated with caution, but the insight they offer into the confusion of midnight alarms is revealing. Fiennes himself came under suspicion, and shortly after a group of well-intentioned officers under Colonel Mark Forbington, wishing to 'bring the truth to light, which hath been universally stifled by false reports', compiled a detailed, though confused, account of the events in an attempt to exonerate Fiennes from blame for the Banbury disaster.

The effects of the siege at Banbury on the local community have already been touched on; the material and psychological fall-out, though difficult to quantify, evidently covered a wide area, and the dislocation to ordinary life must have been severe. In Banbury itself there had been much destruction of property, including serious damage to the church and a probably significant increase in the incidence of plague. The castle garrison had for a long time used a system of brutal extortion and imprisonment of known enemies in the district, and this had financed the garrison but effectively polarized opinion. Sir Anthony Morgan, Augustine Harriotts of Blakesley and Nathaniel Vivers of Banbury are only some of the many local royalist sympathizers reported to have constantly informed against neighbours and 'violently carried away several men from their dwellings and took them to the garrison and kept them there under restraint until they paid several sums unjustly demanded'. Even the laconic entries in the Banbury burial register contain a hint of the anarchy unleashed by the siege, as in 'A soldiar slaine pulling downe Humphry Robbins house buried 8th day' [August]. The intensity of local feuding may be glimpsed in the case of the controversial George Raleigh of Farnborough. Raleigh, who did not deny his royalism, bitterly complained that Captain Joseph Hawkesworth's men had stolen 'about 60 Casements wth windowes, Barres, bolts & other Irons' from his manor house, and during the siege itself '40 ashen Trees and other Woods, wth sheepe rackes That was Carried to Banbury' and much else, besides the usual provisions to Fiennes, Cromwell, Aylesbury and Northampton contingents in August, September and October. A different slant is given by post-war petitions by local residents, however, who claimed that Raleigh, as a royalist captain, had burned their homes and estates and imprisoned them. The prominent Aynho Parliamentarian John Cartwright, in particular, fell foul of Raleigh and presented an emotional case in 1647. He and his mother Mary had been indicted of high treason at Oxford on Raleigh's instance, plundered and dispossessed by the Royalists who had commandeered Aynho house and demolished his mother's house at Astrop. His mother, already over seventy years old, was 'cruelly used, being burnt with matches put between her fingers and a sword run through her gown, narrowly missing her body'. Aynho house was eventually burnt down by the Banbury garrison, leading Cartwright to claim £10,000 after the war from the Earl of Northampton as compensation. As for Raleigh's defence in 1646, he claimed that he had acted as a soldier at that time, and was not now answerable to civil law. . . .

This particular siege at Banbury was over, and not only the commanders but others, who had themselves played insignificant roles there before soon becoming major national figures, had left the district: the kindly and humane Richard Baxter, chaplain to the Coventry regiment; the combative radical John Lilburne, the future Leveller, among the Earl of Manchester's force; and above all Cromwell himself, the rising star, soon to become Lord Protector, whose experience at Banbury must have convinced him more than ever of the need of a professional army. But once again it must be stressed that the formal close of a campaign meant little difference to the long-suffering local community. Royalist soldiers were still quartered about Adderbury, Aynho and Brackley in November, but parliamentary troops were scattered in even greater numbers throughout the district, awaiting redeployment but lingering for weeks in little hurry to go anywhere. Many filtered slowly back towards Warwick and Coventry, retracing routes taken in July or earlier. Bourton-on-Dunsmore, having billeted John Fiennes and his officers 'going to besiege Banbury', also carefully noted quartering them again 'att theyre returne when the siege was removed'. Bourton's crossroad situation near the Fosse Way, equidistant from Warwick and Coventry, made it a particularly busy transit point for north–south parliamentary troops, and many of the Earl of Denbigh's men were particularly in evidence there in November, returning from either Banbury or Evesham:

> One Troope of ye Honoble ye Earle of Denbigh his Regimt, consisting to ye number of Threescore horse whereof Captayne Cotton was Major tooke free qter within our p[ar]ish & therein continued two Dayes & two nightes . . .
> Thirteene shillings Foure pence [stolen] by two or three souldiers of Captayne Cotton his troope wth [sic] then qrtered at widow Warens howse, & there and thence eate and carryed away the same . . .

Others of Denbigh's companies too, like Colonel Archer's, were continuously in the neighbourhood. At Kineton, Radway, Idlicote, Halford and Tysoe throughout September and October, they are also reported quartering in Brailes vicarage for a week, attending a rendezvous at Matthew West's house there, stealing in Lower Shuckburgh about 20 November, at Milverton for another week, at Brinklow in November and even December. Little, in fact, had changed for the villagers, and Major George Purefoy's warrants continued to rain down upon Kineton and other villages as he subjected royalist sympathizers to physical ordeal. One eminent victim was the seventy-two-year-old scholar and rector of Alkerton, Thomas Lydiat, who wrote on 10 December to Sir William Compton, recently knighted for his gallantry at Banbury, that he had been continually pillaged by parliamentary troops from Compton, physically ill-treated and imprisoned. Another Purefoy victim among so many others had been William Calloway in Tysoe. As the siege at Banbury ended with royalist troops pursuing the fleeing Parliamentarians westwards, an imminent siege of Compton house seemed inevitable. The prompt and characteristic response of Purefoy was to imprison his wealthy neighbour until Calloway had restocked his garrison with a large quantity of butter and cheese, worth £22, against a siege which did not, in fact, immediately materialize. As for the Royalists, they immediately set about resupplying Banbury Castle through renewed pillaging expeditions, digging a new moat and repairing the battered fortifications as aggressive sorties from the castle were resumed:

> The Enemie hath brought in very large victuall and supplie into Banbury Castle, which they have robd and pillaged the countrey people thereabouts of and undone them, Plundering many to the very walles, especially some honest people in Banbury.

One raid, impudently, went as far as entering parliamentary Warwick, daring the garrison to an encounter and taking many prisoners, 'beside one hundred and twenty yards of red Cloth . . . to cloath [the] Souldiers'. Returning to Banbury, the Royalists 'calld on some Factious creatures that were at Tatchbrook', provoked another skirmish and reportedly captured many 'Buffe Coats and other warlike apparell'. The long siege had achieved nothing for the Parliamentarians at Banbury, but ironically, had produced a more positive result elsewhere. In another illustration of the way one campaign could affect another the King's army, weakened by the dispatch of a major force to relieve beleaguered Banbury, had been defeated at Newbury. The pendulum had swung again.[14]

Chapter Ten

'The Purple Testament of Bleeding War'

SIEGE AND COUNTER-SIEGE

The prolonged siege at Banbury had concentrated the minds of many of the major commanders for several months but had not, of course, suspended operations elsewhere in the region. Tension remained particularly high in the west, along the Warwickshire–Worcestershire borders, provoked initially by the passage of both armies towards Stourbridge and back, and by the Earl of Denbigh's siege of Dudley, and after Cropredy detachments from both sides – whether taking part at Cropredy and Banbury or not – remained scattered throughout the region long after the two armies had moved away and Denbigh been recalled to London. In mid-July the King marched for the West Country, but left two brigades behind, 'one neere Warwicke, the other about Shudeley'. Sudeley itself was still garrisoned by Waller's soldiers, and Bridges, as ever, remained alert at Warwick. Other parliamentary troops were quartered at Alcester and Studley, and included detachments of Northampton and Aylesbury regiments. Evesham, on the other hand, was a strong royalist centre, and the Earl of Northampton's troops were reported plundering and kidnapping in south-west Warwickshire. The activities of many of the smaller units remain obscure and were, no doubt, purposeless, but their presence was real enough. In August some of Waller's soldiers under Captain James Hopton quartered at Barton-on-the-Heath, Denbigh's were still at Shipston-on-Stour receiving provisions from nearby Willington and Halford, while the Royalists were fortifying the manor house at Lark Stoke, near Ilmington, and had even established a small garrison in Pebworth church by December. The picture is a confused one of units adrift, scattered throughout the countryside awaiting orders from superiors unable to devise a coherent strategy. The parliamentary authorities occasionally recognized the burdens such troops placed on villages by attempting to deploy them in areas which had so far, supposedly, escaped the worst of the war; thus some of Denbigh's cavalry were quartered just outside the Warwickshire borders, near Bromsgrove, specifically, it was claimed, 'to ease the county'.

Once the King had finally moved away south Parliament adopted a more aggressive policy in this district. Warwick's governor, John Bridges, was one in particular who was anxious, after the failure at Banbury, that his men be given an opportunity to retrieve their lost honour. There was skirmishing at the end of July between Royalists under Sir Gilbert Gerard and a combined Earl of Denbigh–Warwick force, when Parliament ordered Evesham itself to be captured and temporarily garrisoned by Captain Thomas Archer until Colonel Edward Massey could send reinforcements from Gloucester to secure it as a permanent base. Alcester and its district suffered heavy quartering as it was used as Archer's advance base on 24 July for the assault on Evesham. Archer routed the Royalists, who fled back towards Worcester, and took many prisoners, the rest 'escapinge with much difficultie through dangerous waters'. After a night in Evesham, however, hearing of the approach of strong royalist reinforcements, Archer returned to Alcester where, evidently alarmed, he reported to Denbigh on 27 July, 'at present we are barrocatting the townes end'. In early August Archer briefly occupied Chipping Campden, dutifully notifying Denbigh on 11 August, 'At this instant we are quartered in Campden, from whence we imploy parties out every day to gett contribution money in . . .'. He requested Massey to send whatever help could be spared for the planned new garrison at Evesham, pointing out his own company's weakness for the purpose, 'I am unwilling . . . to goe nakedly with a few foote into the towne . . .'. But once again disunity and lack of resources hampered plans: Massey at Gloucester and Bridges at Warwick both found plausible reasons for declining to send help, while Colonel 'Tinker' Fox at Edgbaston sent only sixty men, unarmed and so unserviceable that Archer sent them back. Everywhere the unpaid troops were mutinous and the Earl of Denbigh's own Staffordshire forces were themselves only saved from wholesale disintegration by the intervention of Major Frazer and other officers at Warwick, who pawned their horses and very clothes to pay the rebellious soldiers. The disconsolate Archer could only return to Alcester, about 15 August, but continued his tireless activities throughout the autumn, seemingly everywhere, quartering, 'himselfe and the greatest partt of his regimentt' at Edstone one moment, shoeing their horses at the Hatton blacksmith's, John Rutter, the next.[1]

Confused and partisan reporting makes it unusually difficult to gain a clear picture of events in this district during this autumn of 1644, but it is evident that the region was highly militarized. In once incident admitting of widely varying interpretations, Captain John Cheshire, cordially despised by the royalist journalists as an upstart Alcester chandler to whom the war had given a power well above his lowly station and whose speciality was sheep-stealing, was reported to have attempted to fortify Alcester church as a garrison. Accounts suggest that Cheshire was loitering at his father's in his home town when he was simply caught unawares by a surprise incursion into the town by scavenging Royalists under Sandys and Knotsford and took refuge in the church used, perhaps, as a military assembly post. The parliamentarian version reports that an unnamed captain was rescued from the church by a relief force under Archer. The royalist version of events, dated 8 October, is considerably more racy and circumstantial and may, for that reason, be nearer the truth. After a virulent attack on Parliamentarians as 'High-way Commanders who have cast aside their Aprons and made Robbery their Trade', the royalist journalist continues:

One of these is Captaine Chandler, Governour (forsooth!) of Alcester Church in Warwick-shire . . . This Chandler had for 10 weekes last past made the Parish Church a Garrison for his horses and (which is worse) for himselfe and foot-Rebells, out of which Church (now if ever a Den of theeves) he still sallied to steale sheepe from the Country. Whereof Sir Gilbert Gerard taking notice, sent out a strong party of horse . . . who advanced to Alcester to the Chandler and his sheep-stealers, and on Tuesday night last encompassed the Towne round, drawing out a certaine number to assault the Garrison in the Church. The Chandler at that time was in bed with a woman in the Towne, and upon the Alarme fled in his shirt to the Church; but that place which they had so much abused before protected them not an houre. For the valiant assailants . . . forced their entrance into the Church; whereupon the Rebells fled all into the Steeple. But the Colonell fired some wet Straw and so smoaked them downe, which forced them all to submit themselves to mercy, Captaine Chandler himselfe leading the way; who with his Officers, 38 Souldiers, 50 Muskets, 30 horse, good store of Pistols and Carbines, all their Powder and Baggage (except the Chandlers Bedfellow) were brought safe to Worcester.

With Campden now back in royalist hands after Archer's brief occupation in August, parliamentarian news-sheets described the harassment to which the inhabitants of Broadway and Alcester were subjected by marauding Cavaliers. In October, it was claimed, parties of 200 at a time plundered these towns, the reporter concluding dolefully:

Thus every weeke they range about, committing but mischief . . . But untill Banbury Castle be taken, we have left us but little hopes. It is every day expected that the Castle will be delivered up, and certainly without relief they cannot long subsist.

Parliamentarian fortunes sank lower as one of their able commanders, Major Abraham Pont, was killed near Pershore in November and as confirmation came that the Royalists were consolidating at Lark Stoke and Campden under a succession of governors, beginning with Rupert's firelock William Duggan, at Campden at Christmas 1644. Although Duggan was confident that the lush Cotswold country would provide rich pickings, he was disappointed that 'the howse noe wayes answers my expectations, beinge in my opinion neither of it selfe nor of any thinge I see about it tenable'. He promised Rupert nevertheless to obey instructions and 'labour in it [fortify it]' to the best of his ability. At the beginning of the New Year the King appointed Prince Maurice as general of Worcestershire, Herefordshire and Shropshire, and one of his first acts was to strengthen the royalist presence in the north Cotswolds and appoint Prince Rupert's colourful and unscrupulous protégé, Colonel Henry Bard, to the governorship of the strategically-placed Campden House. Bard immediately set about further reinforcing the garrison, advising Rupert elatedly in January:

I thought good to signify to you that I am here at Campden House with my forces, which I conceive will be very advantageous to the strengthening of this association for your Highnesse, as we are taking great pains with spades, shovels and mattocks . . .

The parliamentary authorities in London were seriously alarmed, writing urgently to Massey on 15 January:

We are informed by some letters intercepted that the Kings forces are about to fortify Campden. If they should perfect that work it will be of very ill consequence in many respects, and especially to cut off all intercourse between you and Warwick. We therefore think it necessary that the enemy be removed from thence by all means, and so recommend it to you to be done with all possible speed.

The Committee duly ordered reinforcements for Massey's Gloucester forces from Worcestershire, Warwick, Northampton and Fox at Edgbaston in order to attempt this. But once again the respective parliamentary regiments were too widely scattered, ill-prepared and depleted by dispersal and, indeed, desertion to act decisively. Massey replied, courteously but firmly on 22 January, that he was quite unable to mount an effective assault on Campden, or garrison it once captured. The Royalists throughout the district continued their destructive pillaging, from Banbury, Oxford, Campden and Evesham, though without any coherent strategy. One of Banbury's own first exploits of the new year, on 9 January, was to attack Kilsby, notorious to them not only as 'the busie Rebellious Towne', which had attempted to obstruct the Royalists at the outset of the war but one which had always been reluctant to pay contributions and, allegedly, to have long 'maintained Scouts and Parties to seize all honest Passengers and carry them to Northampton'. As a final provocation, Kilsby Parliamentarians had recently mounted a successful armed attack on some Banbury cavalrymen, using the safety of their church and the town's stone walls as effective barricades. Sir William Compton sent a determined punitive expedition which:

> Marcht thether with 400 Horse and, disposing a good party to prevent their running to Northampton, set a guard upon the Church. The Rebellious Townesmen were soon Alarm'd and zealously cryed out 'Arme! Arme!'. Some made towards Northampton and were taken by the Party, others with Muskets made to the Church and were seized in the Church-yard. Thus being all Masterd, Sir William brought 24 of them to Banbury, togeather with 200 head of Cattle and 60 Horses (some worth £20 a Horse), good store of Muskets and other Armes, with a great deale of very good booty.

The inhabitants of the town had been plundered, it was alleged, 'to their very shirts'. Not for the first time the village womenfolk took matters into their own hands. In a picturesque sequel, having roundly cursed the soldiers in distinctly unscriptural language, to the delight of the royalist reporter, the women sent a deputation to Banbury three days later to demand their cattle, horses and menfolk which all 'belonged to them'. The Banbury governor agreed, on condition that the valuable horses were exempted from the bargain, that arrears of taxes were paid and that the prisoners once released would never bear arms again. The 'sisterhood', as the royalist reporter mockingly describes the women, lectured their sullen menfolk into submission, and 'men, women and cattell returned to the place whence they came'.

At the same time as the Kilsby incident, another parliamentarian newsletter reported a further royalist outrage, this time at Culham, near Abingdon, where 'the enemy . . . plundered most miserably, stripping from women of rank all their clothes, [and] took from Lady Carey, an ancient Lady sick in her bed, her rings from her fingers, her watch and whatsoever they could carry away'. This incident may have been one of the vindictive lateral operations of the abortive royalist attempt to take Abingdon, repulsed by the alert General Browne. Yet another destructive royalist sortie was also jeeringly reported:

> A great party of the Cavaliers came into Chipping Norton, where they quartered, and at their going thence, to show their impartially (though there was but one Roundhead in the town), they plundered every house therein of whatsoever was of value, and took two hundred sheep and above forty pounds from one man . . .[2]

The Royalists at Banbury had, meanwhile, devised plans for a more spectacular operation than those involving elderly ladies in beds, plundering villages or igniting straw in church towers, namely the recapture of Compton House from the detested Major George Purefoy, dubbed by the royalist journalists the local Wat Tyler. The Royalists left Banbury by moonlight at about midnight on 29/30 January 1645, and evidently took the sleeping garrison completely by surprise. The graphic account, written by Purefoy himself at 9 p.m. the same evening, is among the most detailed and dramatic of all local actions in the war, and is worth quoting in full:

This night, about two of the clock, about a 1,000 or 1,200 Horse and Foot fell upon me at Compton, storm'd my outworks, gain'd the stables and cut down my great Draw-bridge and possest themselves of all my Troop horses, and took about 30 of my foot Souldiers in their beds who lay over the stables, almost before a man could think what to do. We received that alarm as we had good cause, and presently made good the new Sconce before the stone Bridge & beat them out of the great Court, there being about 200 entred and ready to storm the Sconce. But we gave them so hot a sallie that we forced them to retreat backe to the stables, Barns and Brew-house, where from the windowes they played very hot upon us. I then commanded Lieutenant Purefoy & my quarter-master (having no other Officers of quality at home, the rest being abroad with about 30 of my best Troopers) to sally out upon the enemy with a partie of some 40, & to attempt the regaining of the Brew-house and the roomes above, which they did with gallant resolution and courage. Sergeant Bird was one who came not short in bravery of any. This party fought with the enemy and came to push of Pike, nay, to swords point, and did lay about so bravely that they forced the enemy to retreat from chamber to

COMPTON WYNYATES, WARWICKSHIRE. The home of the earls of Northampton, the great Tudor mansion saw little activity until it was captured by Parliament in June 1644. The new military governor, the notorious George Purefoy, fortified it and terrorized the entire neighbourhood into supplying his garrison for the next two years. Although much damaged by occupation and a fierce royalist attempt to recapture it, the house survived the war, although the nearby church was completely destroyed. (Photo: Centre for Oxfordshire Studies)

chamber. I then sent out my youngest brother the Ensign with my three corporalls of horse and about 40 more men to relieve the first partie; and I will assure you, the young boy will fight: he led on his men bravely, and relieved his brother, by which meanes all the upper roomes were gained. And the enemy kept onely the stables and barns, stoutly, [but] my resolute soldiers did then thunder their horses and reserves of foot that stood within pistol shot, that Sir William and Sir Charles Compton began to give ground, which my souldiers easily perceiving, some leapt out at the windowe and so into the out-works, by which means I recovered my out-works againe, and made good a sally port, by which the enemy endeavoured to retreat at; but finding they were frustrated of their hopes, and that my Musketeers did play so hot upon the great Draw-bridge that they could not be relieved; & withall having beaten the enemy out of that worke, which we stormd when you took the house, I had time to recover the great Draw-bridge and presently got new ropes and new lockes, and drew it up againe in spight of them all. Now these whose names you have here inclosed were all in Cobbs pound, having no meanes in the world to retreat. Whereupon they fought desperately for the space of 3 hours, & the valiant Comptons perceiving their extreame losse attempted three severall times to storm and to regain my outworkes, but all three times were beaten off with as much resolution and gallantry as could be. The enemy within set fire on the hay, straw and all combustible stuffe, to smother my men out of the upper rooms, which did indeed much annoy them; and the Enemy without threw at least 100 hand Granadoes upon the houses that they set them on fire in divers places. Sir Charles and Sir William Compton then thinking all was their own sent a Trumpeter to parlie, but I commanded that none should parlie, nor would I permit the Trumpeter to speak at all, though faine he would have said something to my souldiers, but commanded him upon his life to be gone and return no more at his perill. We continued in fight still, and the fire did so encrease that I thought it fit to offer quarter to all those in the stable, for their lives onely; but they would not hear me. Upon which I drew all my men together and fell violently in upon them, wherein were slain and taken prisoners all whose names are in the ensuing list. This did so dishearten the Comptons and all their forces that they did draw presently off all their foot, and onely faced me with their horse, and sent another Trumpeter to parley. But I commanded to give fire upon him, so that he returned with no other answer but what a Musket could speake. Sir, this is as true and as short a Narration as I can give you. I am, as we all are,

Your obliged servants & kinsmen

George Purefoy
William Purefoy

After listing the prisoners taken, Purefoy adds a summary: 'The fight began about two of the clock in the morning and continued till about nine, in which they stormed us foure severall times, and were beaten off', and that in the process stables, barns and brew-houses were all burnt. Further accounts of the siege, including one by John Bridges, give similar details, with interesting minor variations. One speaks of the governor 'making good the Draw-bridge, for the House is moated about', and specifies that the royalist assault party was finally 'inclosed in betweene the Hils and the House'. Several report that the prisoners taken outnumbered the garrison to the extent that Major Joseph Hawkesworth was called out from Warwick to help escort them away, while one concludes with a self-congratulatory flourish:

The enemy carried away with them eight Cart-loades of dead and wounded into Banbury, and it is believed will hereafter have but little stomacke to make an onset upon Compton house.

Shortly after, an official communiqué from the Coventry authorities congratulated Purefoy on his success in repulsing the royalist onslaught. The unfortunate Cavaliers, for their part, had barely regained their quarters at Banbury and Kings Sutton when they were set upon by a strong cavalry force from Northampton, losing a few prisoners and many horses, sold the following day at Northampton, while the Royalists fled for safety inside the church and the local manor house.

After the successive restorations of many years, the precise extent of the damage to the house is impossible to estimate, but it was probably no more severe than that already caused by the parliamentary garrison in residence. At some point the Comptons' alabaster effigies in the church nearby were vandalized and the church itself wrecked, to await rebuilding at the Restoration. The moat was later filled in following a precautionary goverment decree. Centuries later Henry James described its opulent setting:

> . . . its air of solitude and delicate decay – of having been dropped into its grassy hollow as an ancient jewel is deposited upon a cushion, and being shut in from the world and back into the past by its circling woods.

It is difficult today to imagine the murderous activity on these green slopes of that moonlit winter's night of 1645.

A week after the siege at Compton John Bridges at Warwick, not to be outdone, determined to act against Colonel Henry Bard's strongholds at Campden and Lark Stoke, the fortified home of the wealthy Richard Brent, connected to the Sheldons. Bard, a colourful war-scarred veteran who, although not more than thirty years old, had already lost an arm at Cheriton and who was later accused at Leicester of inciting his men to follow his example in raping local women, had soon become notorious throughout the entire district for his ruthlessness. Described by a contemporary as 'a compact body of vanity and ambition', his ability to match Purefoy's insolence at Compton in terrorizing a district is well caught in one of his later surviving 'warrants' to the constables of Twyning, near Tewkesbury, warning them sharply that as 'I finde in you no compliance':

> Know therefore, that unlesse you bring into me to Worcester . . . the monethly Contributions of six moneths past on Thursday next . . . You are to expect an unsanctified troop of horse among you, from whom if you hide your selves (As I believe each of you hath his hole), they shall fire your houses without mercy, hang up your bodies wherever they find them, and scare your Ghosts into your drabbling garrison.

Stoke was well situated on an eminence at the northern end of the Cotswolds, commanding extensive views over the Vale of Evesham to the south and to Warwick and beyond to the north, and Bridges must have been only too conscious of its potential to the enemy as an observation post threatening his own security. Aware of the danger in delay in allowing Bard to continue strengthening his garrison, and being 'affected with the sad complaints of the Country', Bridges sent two or three companies from Warwick as decoys to scour the countryside collecting contributions, a routine practice which would arouse no suspicion of ulterior motive, but with orders not to return. He then collected a force of eighty horse and seventy foot and set out himself for the rendezvous, as he explained in his account dated 8 February:

> I marched all that night, and being come to [Stoke] I began to storm it, and the next day fell upon the House and stables by break of day, both at once. The House was of stone, very strong; they within it had made up the windowes and doores with brick and stone, and defended the House very

stoutly for about an houre and a half. But at length wee entred by force . . . notwithstanding that in
all that time wee were without shelter, and the bullets and stones flew thick about our eares.

Aware that nearby Campden and Evesham Royalists would instantly mobilize a strong
counter-attack and stressing, with the bigotry so characteristic of the times, that the
entire garrison was composed of detested Catholics, the pious Bridges concluded that 'to
prevent the building of any more such Rookes nests, I fired the House'. It was, as a
parliamentarian colleague wrote admiringly, a typically 'brave peice of service performed
by Major Bridges'. The Warwick men hastily returned to base, some refreshing
themselves at Loxley, exactly half-way to Warwick. Among the prisoners taken back to
the castle and promptly ransomed were, allegedly, captains from the major landowning
families of the district, the Brents of Stoke, the Keytes of Wolford and the Cannings of
Foxcote Manor, near Ilmington. Controversy immediately erupted in parliamentary
circles over this policy, one correspondent issuing a severe warning:

> The prisoners that were taken at Stoake House, the House of Mr Brent, a convicted Papist, by Major
> Bridges . . . are all set at libertie againe, for Money; who before they were gone out of Warwicke,
> threatned to make the Countrey repay their ransome. This is not the way to make an end of the warre;
> but it is a way to make some men rich, and to beggar the whole Kingdome.

Confirmation soon came that these were more than idle fears. By the end of April
informants in Stratford, in another revealing insight into Bard's character, reported:

> . . . that Captain Brunt, the great Papist of Stoak-house who, with a silver key which (as it is
> thought) cost 50 pound, got out of Warwick-castle, is now for certaine at Campden . . . and was one
> of the chiefe in setting on the enemy to plunder Winchcombe, and hath been the cause of taking
> many thousand pounds out of some hundreds in Gloucestershire, . . . so that the well-affected in
> Worcestershire and Warwickshire have payd above twenty times the value of Stoake-house. This
> Papist gave intelligence of a Constable at Qurniton [Quinton?] and enforced him to bring his
> collection money to Colonell Bard, Governour of Campden. The poore Constable brought as much as
> he could get, and certified the Governour (then in bed) thereof. The Governour demanded if it were
> all. The Constable answered, 'He could not bring all, for the plague was in some houses'. The
> Governour replied, 'That if the Plague were in one, and the Pox in the other, he would have all the
> money, and would talke with him further when he was up'. After he rose, he commanded the
> Constable to be throwne into a pond to swim for his life, where he had been drowned had he not
> beene helpt out by one of the souldiers . . . They are now fortifying of Cambden stronger than ever.

Such events as these at Stoke, insignificant on a national scale, yet traumatic for the
district and similar to so many taking place throughout the land, continued to arouse
bitter local passions long after the war. Cases of alleged 'malignancy', or active, armed
delinquency, became the subject of often protracted legal action as the parliamentary
authorities tried conscientiously to sift hundreds of controversial cases using local
testimonies. That of Richard Canning of Foxcote throws an interesting light on such
issues. To John Bridges and his troopers the case was clear-cut. Canning was an odious
papist captain, already deservedly punished by having been plundered by Essex's troops
before Edgehill and now again, when he lost seventeen more sheep as the troops passed
by Foxcote. There were even worse charges, of stocking the manor at Stoke, governed by
his brother Thomas, a Catholic priest, with goods and provisions extorted under threat
from the nearby villages, on gaining permission from Bard, the local tyrant, to convert

it into a garrison. Worst of all, this 'notorious and pestiferous Papist' had, it was alleged, secretly plotted the betrayal of some of the Compton Parliamentarians into royalist hands. The Stoke garrison, a 'swarme of Hornets' under his reign, had become instantly notorious, one of their recent exploits being the plunder of 'poore Salmon of Campden of 24 pounds worth of goods, and other Carriers of their Sacke and Strong waters'. When charged with active royalism in January 1647, however, Canning submitted an impressive defence. Although he had indeed been taken prisoner inside the garrison by Bridges, it was:

> . . . provd by wytnesses that the dwelling house of the sd Rd Canninge stands wthin halfe a mile of Stoke house and that he was then under the Power of that Garrison and [had] Remayned at his house during all the late warres untill the night before the sayd Guarrison was taken. Not wth standing, he went thether, as is aleadged being sent for, to get the parish to be Freed from Sondery men to digge at Stoke house for Fortifying it . . .

The sequestration order on his estate was accordingly lifted, the parliamentary authorities being always surprisingly ready to concede extenuating circumstances of this kind, where the accused lived within the orbit of an enemy garrison and dared not do other than cooperate with it. Three years later, however, the case was reviewed in the light of further charges brought by Ilmington residents. It was claimed that Canning had ordered some neighbours, John Lidsey and Richard and George Archer, to work on fortifying Stoke for five days, had often been seen 'riding in and out of the house with officers' and, according to one witness, 'with a stringe about his necke wch he conceives was a Spanner, [*Note*: possibly for winding up a wheel-lock pistol, and thus incriminating] & also with a sword by his side'. Finally, putting all this into a damning perspective of inveterate recusancy, Canning had not attended his parish church at Ilmington for either service or sermon in twenty years. This time the weight of such evidence was considered 'such proof of delinquency . . . as yt wee have thought it our Duty to secure his Estate'. Little emerges on Canning's subsequent fortunes, nor on the no doubt serious repercussions they had on the livelihood of his tenants, but the family, unbowed, later produced a prime minister. As for the Royalists' other garrison at Campden, it was left, for the moment, to continue its predatory and destructive raids unchecked. But Bard's reign of terror there was nearing its end.[3]

WANDERING FIRES

It is amid such inconclusive, confused activity that there emerged an astonishing series of events which comprises one of the most dismal chapters in English history: a renewed spate of wanton destruction of a handful of midland England's finest country seats. Unlike the great medieval bastions of Warwick and Kenilworth, the manor house had been vulnerable from the outset. As a visible and permanent reminder of the power of the mighty, often economically and socially dominating the country for miles around, it was as natural a rallying point for the friendly as it was an irresistible target for the enemy. The degree to which these mansions were strengthened as the war set in remains obscure, but it is likely that most – even the seats of political leaders, like Compton and Broughton – were not fortified to any extent and many, like Coughton, Charlecote, Aynho, Wormleighton and Packington, were almost certainly not strengthened at all. The outbreak of hostilities had, after all, taken many by surprise, and there were few Midland landowners prepared to equal in energy and foresight Lord Brooke's systematic fortification at Warwick. All, therefore, were clearly vulnerable in an increasingly personalized, acrimonious conflict and were pillaged, some more than once, by enemy troops acting often, as we have seen, on direct orders. Where it was thought profitable by the commanders in constant search for comfortable quarters, some had become relatively unimportant temporary garrisons, like Rousham, Shuckburgh, Warkworth and Baddesley Clinton, while a few, like Coughton and Maxstoke, had become occasionally useful outposts of the major garrisons – though rarely more than a minor irritant to the enemy. But very early in the war in the Midlands, in August 1642, Prince Rupert himself had set a deplorable example in storming an enemy's home as a deliberate vindictive measure when he had attacked William Purefoy's Caldecote, near Nuneaton. Never one for half measures, Rupert had then gone from bad to worse in adopting arson as a deliberate military policy, most notoriously at the 'miserable destruction of Burningham (Birmingham) by fire' in April 1643, bitterly mocked by parliamentary pamphleteers as evidence of 'Prince Rupert's burning love for England'. Soon such assaults became common practice on both sides on the pretext of rendering property useless to the enemy. One must be careful to avoid exaggeration since, surprisingly, many great houses survived the war relatively unscathed – some, like Charlecote and Wroxall, presumably protected by parliamentary connections, and some, like Compton and Broughton, almost miraculously in spite of everything – while others, curiously perhaps, appear to have played no part whatsoever in the war and are almost totally absent from the archives, like Wroxton, Clopton, Billesley and Grove Park. But increasingly, as the war dragged on, a few major houses succumbed to the momentum of violence, and although documentation on them is often patchy it is with these that we are concerned here.

The manor-house was regarded as being particularly expendable, and one which had already disappeared, literally overnight, was Beoley, near Redditch, one of the ancestral homes of the great catholic landowner William Sheldon, of Weston, Long Compton. Weston itself had, as already noted, been plundered more than once, but the lesser seat at Beoley escaped notice until December 1643. Probably unfortified to any extent, despite parliamentarian claims of its being 'a place of great strength' yielding 'many prisoners, much armes and ammunition', its primary offence was to belong to Sheldon and, no doubt, to have frequently entertained his co-religionists. It could therefore be plausibly represented by Puritans like William Purefoy as a dangerously subversive papist cell. Little documentation of events survives, but the initial seizure, in early December, on specific written instructions from John Bridges at Warwick, of fifty or sixty 'Fatt beasts' belonging to a catholic neighbour, Jerome Luckett, 'yt were in a certen great meadowe neare Beoley Parke', taken together with a further theft of cattle and horses from the estate of another of Sheldon's intimates, Thomas Savage, near Inkberrow, hints at a concerted campaign against this notoriously catholic district.

Captain Fulke Estopp drove the Beoley herd to the nearest parliamentary garrison at Coughton, where a few were promptly killed before Bridges himself appeared the next day to examine them and ordered the remainder to be driven back to Warwick Castle. Luckett's incensed wife journeyed to both Coughton and Warwick – a round trip of some 30 miles from Beoley along wintry roads – to demand the cattle, and half of the then remaining beasts were released a week later and wearily trudged back to their pastures driven by an Alcester butcher, Thomas Round. But Royalists were now assembling in large numbers to attempt to prevent the Gloucester relief convoy crossing the Cotswolds, and Bridges suddenly ordered the abandonment of his exposed Coughton outpost. This was promptly done, the Parliamentarians transporting back to Warwick whatever of the mansion's contents had not already been pillaged in earlier expeditions, comprising in the event a booty of '5 Cart loads of bedding, Hangings, Carpets, Stooles, Chaires, brasse, pewter & other houshold stuffe of Mr Throckmortons'.

Shortly after, using many of the same forces used recently in the attack on Sir Thomas Holt's brand-new Aston Hall, near Birmingham, an assault on Beoley House was ordered, and an unnecessarily large force commanded by Bridges' able colleagues Major Joseph Hawkesworth and Colonel Godfrey Bosevile and including some 'great guns' converged on Beoley from Coventry, Warwick and Coughton, quartering at Henley, Tanworth, Studley and Wootton Wawen. Some reports speak of a 'siege' in which a royalist major and several captains were taken prisoner, but little resistance can have been offered by the occupants against such a force and the house must have been quickly overrun and stripped of its contents. Two highly unpleasant events followed, freely admitted in one parliamentary account: the soldiers 'put all the Irish therein to the sword' before the house was 'burnt to the ground', in the unambiguous declaration of Sheldon himself. The soldiers, mission completed, were once again quartering in similar villages by 1 January as they returned to their bases eastwards, demanding more provisions and stealing again in Rowington, Knowle and Henley, which was particularly heavily invaded. At Tanworth, some celebrated with a seasonal New Year feast of 6s. worth of geese at Henry Hunt's expense. At Henley, one of the most unfortunate victims was John Milward; already pillaged very early in the war, in early August 1642, the soldiers now took from him £30 worth of bedding, brassware, pewter, food and household goods. He would be revisted, with similar results, on several occasions in 1645. Among the alleged 'great store of wealth' taken back to Warwick and Coventry from Beoley were 'three Carts laden wth goods & other things' and one incalculable loss to the historian, a large quantity of the great landowner's legal and estate documents. The cannons were returned to the magazine at Coventry drawn by carriages provided by the active Warwick Parliamentarian Anthony Stoughton. Among the regular officers involved were some whose names were becoming all too familiar to the villagers: Captains Vincent Potter, Thomas Wells, William Colmore and James Castle, all sharing the spoils. Castle received a sorrel mare for his pains, to add to the '2 Little peeces of plate weyinge betweene 6 or 7 ozes' and 'one Buffe Coate taken from a prisoner' from Aston Hall and the grey gelding he would shortly acquire when Compton House was captured. The thorough plundering of nearby Redditch by Warwick soldiers mentioned in the parish accounts, but undated, probably also took place about this time. The wanton incendiarism and slaughter of the Catholics under Hawkesworth, and the repeated insistence on the numbers of offending 'papists' occupying the manor-house, bear all the hallmarks of a religious purge. The puritan zealot Hawkesworth, intimate of William Purefoy, was clearly only too eager to anticipate the later parliamentary ordinance, of 24 October 1644, that no quarter was to be given to any Irish or papist born in Ireland, who were to be instantly put to death. Beoley was indeed an ugly precedent. Yet in deploring it one unusually sober parliamentarian report refers only to the arson, not the slaughter:

> We heare since that [Beely house] is burnt down also, whether because a Papists house, or an house Fortified, we know not; but foresee sad dayes to come in England if we fall to burning . . . [The Royalists] burnt at Bromisham [Birmingham] and divers other places, and in that went before us. It were to be wished we had never taken so bad an example to go by.[4]

Atrocities of this kind by both sides were becoming more common. A similar incident took place at exactly the same time, on Christmas Day 1643, when Lord Byron massacred twenty Parliamentarians at Barthomley, Cheshire, boasting, 'I put them all to the sword, which I find the best way to proceed with these kind of people'. The Midlands culmination of such barbarity was the notorious New Model Army killing of the royalist women camp followers after Naseby. As for the arson itself, this was to become almost commonplace, even without the pretext of offending papist garrisons. Less than a year after the destruction of Beoley, in December 1644, the district witnessed a renewed cycle of devastation, beginning with an even more spectacular event.

The addition of further enemy garrisons at Lark Stoke and Campden, in the strategic north Cotswolds in the autumn of 1644, had alarmed Parliament into supposing that the Royalists were planning a concerted campaign to extend their sphere of influence northwards into Warwickshire and, perhaps, to threaten the nerve centres of Warwick and Coventry themselves. Instead of attacking Campden itself before it could be fortified the Coventry authorities decided to pre-empt matters in December by seizing or neutralizing further potential enemy garrisons, and for reasons which are not otherwise entirely clear the Earl of Middlesex's great Tudor mansion at Milcote, south of Stratford, was selected for immediate action, even though neither it nor its elderly owner who had long abandoned it had played any aggressive role whatsoever in the war. An order dated 4 December and signed by six members of the Coventry committee headed by William Purefoy instructed Major Joseph Hawkesworth:

> . . . with three barrels of Powder to blow up the roofe of Milcote House, thereby to unfitt the said house for the use of the Enemy, and so to disappoint their design of garrisoning it.

Hawkesworth lost no time in acting, nor in interpreting his orders as he thought fit. A unique account of the next day's events at Milcote has survived, due to the conscientiousness of the loyal steward, Robert Fawdon, and is worth quoting at length for the clear, stark light it throws on the nature of this war and its sheer human interest:

> On Thursday the 5th of this Month about 12 of the clocke their came to Melcott house as neare as I can guesse about 200 of horsse of Collonell Purefoy Regiment, comannded in cheife by Major Hauckesworth, with dyvers Captaines & other officers, as Captaine Welles, Capt. Potter & others. After they had sumoned the house [wth 5 or 6 Trumpetts] (when God knowes their was no men in it but my person, [beinge much amazed wth their suddaine approach]), Captaine Welles told me then

they weer comed [sic] to putt a Garrison in the house, by order from the Committee, & called the Major, who Comaunded mee to show them the house; which I did, everie part, within doore & without. [And after they had seene what they desired, the Major wth the Rest of the Commanders went to Consultacon in private, but in the Intrim the House was full of their unruly souldiers, notwithstanding the Majors comand to the contrary, who many of them tooke what they liked] . . . The Major then told me they must either pull down the house or fyre it, for they had certaine Intelligence that the enemie was verie neere & coming to Garrison the house, wch would undoe the Cuntry and Indanger their safetie. To which I answered And desired That they would consider me as a servant, [as alsoe, what such a greate Fabricke as that would cost in buildinge, wch would all be consumed and many Good Moveables therin & benefitt to noe body], and to give me some short time time to send to yor honr; for I was confident the Kings Armie had noe such intention, for their had been such false reports above this twelve monthes, yet never any, either officer or other soldier, ever came to survey the house or ever any of that side was in the house since the warres began . . . save onely Prince Rupert, sixteene monthes agoe, when the Queen lay two nights att Stratford, who then brought with him a Coachfull of Ladies to looke for Fruit. I further desired, if they would not grant me time to send to yor honr, to give me [some litle tyme to pull it downe]; but that would not be granted neither. Then my request was to have Libertie untill the next morning to take away the goods that were in the house, wch would otherwise be Lost; but all the favor I could obtaine was to goe about presently the takeing out of the Goods. The Major told me he would give what time he could, & was sorry to doe what he must, being Comaunded by the Comittee att Coventry to pull it downe or fyre it, and now time would not give him Leave to pull it downe, and he must obey their Comaunds. [For they would grant noe certaine tyme, but spare it as Long as they could and wished me make Hast, when God knowes I had litle help, it beinge Market Day. Neither durst the Neighbours help, for feare of giveinge offence unto them, assuringe themselves such a Horrid thinge would not been [sic] committed wthout some great fault committed by Yor Honnr. Thus helpless & mercilesse I was left, and not above two Houres Libertie to gett what I could of Yor Honnrs Goodes into the open feilds, where the most part Lay that night; and betwixt souldiers & other badd people, a greate deale thereof was lost . . . And many good moveables were burnt in the House for want of a Litle tyme to save it]. And as I understand since, they sent to the Comittee (for indeed I was putt in hope they would not fyre untill midnight), yett stayed nott the retourne; but within two houres after [before foure of the clocke] the house was sett on fyre [in 3 or 4 severall places, and ready to fall upon our Heades while wee were gettinge out the Goodes], saying the enemie was att [Chipping] Cambden, [and yet, God knowes, noe Enemy neerer for ought I could ever yet learne then their Garrisons at Banbury & Worcester} . . . Those who made readie the Fyre & sett it on Burning was one Thomas Bovie a Trumpetter to the Major and dyvers other of their soldiers comaunded by the Major & his officers, who himselfe & other of his Captaines stayed within night to see it unquenchable before they went away, haveing taken the benefitt of the wind to helpe the fire, [protestinge their owne sorrow in this their mercilesse Act, wch is yet the Lamentacon of the whole country]. Ther came Also after their consultation Colonell Archer with his Regiment, whose men began to take what they could; but upon complaint he comaunded them away and did not stay himselfe [to be an Actor in that fearefull desolacon], and for ought I can understand he had no part in the Fyreing. And thus without mercie [to the greife of all Good men, did they in a short tyme destroy this great & goodly buildinge wth many Good moveables, wch want of tyme would not give me leave to prserve} . . . And this is the Truth of that mischeifeous Act, soe farr as I know, which to my continued Sorrow I was a wittnesse of and sufferer in; which with my bounden dutie I most humbly prsent to yor honr.

The Earl of Middlesex, friend of John Donne and Inigo Jones in happier times, was by all accounts a hard, unpopular landlord, and there is more than a suspicion that his tenants' reluctance to help with the salvage operations was more than diplomatic. But the sick old man had done little to deserve this, other than to have accumulated wealth and power as former treasurer to James I, counted the court poet–gallant Sir John Suckling among his near relatives, been a close friend of the royalist Bishop Goodman of Gloucester and held strong views on silencing Puritans 'that will not conform themselves'. He had tried to steer a neutral course, and paid the penalty by being financially harassed by both sides before and after this final catastrophe. Peremptory demands continued to come from both the Coventry authorities and the Chipping Campden Royalists after the house had been reduced to embers. His distraught steward pleaded for estate arrears to be waived in view of the destruction of the house since, he thought, 'they could not for shame, I was confident, have demaunded these'. But he misjudged William Purefoy, for the puritan colonel was unyielding, and Fawdon had no doubt that 'this sudden calling for of all those monies certainly comes from the Colonells orders'.

The third, more ambiguous figure of the puritan trio implicated in the destruction of Milcote was, probably, the Stratford schoolmaster and intellectual John Trapp, mentioned by Fawdon as an intimate of Hawkesworth. As minister of the earl's adjacent living of Welford, the disaffected Trapp had already been the victim of royalist harassment, most recently in an incident in September which stresses once again the religious tensions underlying the conflict, apparent in the indignation of the parliamentarian account:

> It is no Wonder that the godly people in those parts do so much desire his Lordships [the Earl of Denbigh] speedy dispatch [i.e. return from London], for the Cavaliers thereabouts do threaten to suppresse all the godly Protestant Ministers thereabouts, and have already been at Welford in Warwickshire, whither a party from Worcester came in to the Church; and as Master Trap, an honest godly man, was going into the pulpit to preach, they pulled him down, and dragged him as if he had been a malefactor, abused him and called him Roundhead Rogue, Puritan and Parliament dog, and carried him away to Worcester, leaving the poore people without a Teacher.

Trapp's failure to warn Fawdon of the impending assault on Milcote, of which the steward was sure he must have known, may well have been deliberate. As news of the destruction of the house spread, Parliamentarians attempted to claim the act as one of royalist vandalism, but the court newspaper lost no time in pointing the finger at 'the Brethren at Warwick'. Already terminally ill, the seventy-year-old Middlesex soon succumbed to this final blow to his declining fortunes and died in London in August 1645. As for his great old mansion in the meadows sloping down to the Avon which had echoed to the sound of choristers and virginals, where Suckling had delighted in the pipe and tabor in the great hall and where Prince Rupert had ambled with his ladies through parlours and gardens only the year before, it vanished as though it had never been.[5]

The Elizabethan manor-houses at Beoley and Stoke and the great mansion at Milcote had already disappeared, literally in the fires of war. More were to follow throughout the country, as the habit spread as quickly as the flames themselves: Lydney House, in the Forest of Dean, stoically burnt and its woods devastated by their owner, Sir John Winter, to prevent the enemy using them; Lypiatt Park House, Stroud, of Gunpowder Plot fame, burnt by Sir Jacob Astley on New Year's Day 1645; and now, in the spring of 1645, a new batch as the King, with a new-found determination to end the war by acting decisively, left Oxford on 7 May on his third and final, fatal march through the Midlands. The King's immediate objective was to relieve Chester, besieged by Sir William Brereton, and to secure the north before turning his attention towards London and the south. A desperate new ruthlessness seemed to characterize this phase as Charles, who had earlier implicitly rebuked Rupert after the devastation of Birmingham, was now silent as incendiarism was adopted as a deliberate policy. Wallington reported on 17 May that:

> . . . the King's forces have burnt down divers houses between Oxford and Bristol, fearing we would make garrisons of them . . . and caused other men to pull down their houses, which otherwise they would have fired.

The King's army marched north into Worcestershire and Warwickshire through Stow-on-the-Wold towards Evesham and Bromsgrove, as usual scattering its respective regiments liberally over many miles to the east and west of the main path. Prince Rupert diverged to go via Broadway, Bretforton, Alcester and Wootton Wawen, where he lodged with the former Commissioner of Array, Sir Charles Smith, and Prince Maurice's regiment was similarly reported on 13 May to have crossed the Avon at Bidford on the way north. Each of these villages, and doubtless many more, would have suffered heavy quartering from the Royalists on this occasion, but the parish officers, instructed to prepare accounts for eventual parliamentarian compensation, saw no point in detailing this. As it passed, the King's army supplemented numbers by drawing out men from nearby garrisons and abandoning others deemed to have outlived their usefulness.

One of these was (ironically, given its effectiveness as a major nuisance to the Parliamentarians) Campden, where Bard was ordered – according to both Sir Henry Slingsby, who was present, and the King's secretary, Sir Edward Walker, by Rupert himself – to deliver his garrison, destroy the house and join the main army on its march north:

> The King's Army . . . marched to Evesham. By the way, the Garrison in Campden House was drawn out, and the House (which cost above £30,000 the building) most unnecessarily burnt by Prince Rupert's Command.

The burning of Campden, on 9 May 1645, outraged even Royalists. The antiquary Symonds added to Walker's evident regret a note of his own, '300 foot taken out of our Garrison of Camden; the howse (which was so faire) burnt'; while Clarendon's own disgust, heightened by his gentlemanly distaste for the unprincipled Bard, has often been quoted:

> . . . [the governor] took his leave of it in wantonly burning the whole structure where he had too long inhabited, and which not many years before had cost above thirty thousand pounds the building.

Several parliamentarian accounts repeat these obituaries of 'a stately building of stone erected by Sir Baptist Hicks' from the Elizabethan wool trade, and suggest that the act was accompanied by widespread plundering and destruction throughout the neighbourhood: 'divers houses in poor Auster [Alcester] they have again plundered, and carry away all the provision they can'. One adds further incidental detail:

> The enemy in the garrison at Cambden house, where . . . Brant [Brent] and divers other Papists nestled themselves, being lately called thence to joyn with His Majesties Army, a night or two before their departure turned their horses into the cornefields and committed many outrages to the Inhabitants, and when they had made such a devastation that nothing was left for them to destroy

and spoyle they set fire of Cambden house it selfe, and burnt and consumed all the wainscots and other furniture of that brave house . . .

True to the end, two of Bard's very last acts had been to plunder Winchcombe to the extent that its inhabitants 'had not a Sunday-shift of cloathes left them', and to dispatch a particularly vicious order to the High Constable of Tredington:

> By vertue of an Order sent to me from his Highnesse Prince Maurice, I command you that you immediately send for the Pettie Constables . . . and give order for the present impressing of 23 able Souldiers for his Majesties Service, to kill and slay all [Parliamentarian] Committee men without exceptions; which men are to be delivered to Lieutenant-Colonell Bellingham in Evesham for his Highnesse use. And this shall be a sufficient warrant for you and your Brethren. Fail not, as you will answer the carrying of Muskets your selves, and be made [to] fight against your Consciences.

This particular warrant was overtaken by events, however. Bard obediently joined Rupert who was then able, according to one jeering parliamentarian report, to march over Broadway hills by the light of the conflagration from Campden House. Another report, with superb Olympian disdain, produced one of the tersest communiqués of the war: 'Campden House is quit and fired'.

The wanton burning of Campden, justifiably, was rounded condemned. But the past is a foreign country, with priorities vastly different from our own relatively modern environmental ones, and war, as our own times have proved time and again, creates its own urgent imperatives overriding civilized values. Our own century has destroyed many a 'faire howse', even without the excuse of war. The destruction of Campden must have seemed a trivial matter in the desperate logic of war, as the royal armies were attacked on this march north. Several assaults were launched by the Parliamentarians, Cromwell's Ironsides attacking the royalist rearguard as it passed through Burford on 8 May and Major George Purefoy sending out several successful expeditions from Compton. In one of these, on 7 May, Purefoy's men took several valuable prisoners in a skirmish near Stow, including Rupert's gun-smith, four of his life guard, and Prince Maurice's surgeon, head cook and farrier. Another followed two days later, when Purefoy's soldiers arrived at Campden to find the house ablaze. Purefoy's own graphic account captures well the immediacy of these small-scale but intense skirmishes, besides illustrating again the brutality to which small towns throughout the region were frequently subjected:

> I sent out another party [on Friday 9 May] to cudgell them up in their Reare, and . . . marched straight to Cambden and found the Garrison set on fire. But the party entred the Town, and found 200 [Royalist] foot in the streets, and about 100 horse in the stables there; which unexpected sight increased my mens courage and resolution, and they feeling themselves ingaged, charged quite through them all, and through the whole Town, where they discovered the Kings forces within half a mile of the Town at their rendevouz, charged therefore through them again, killed 14 of them upon the ground, besides many more wounded, put them all to run, and quit the Town. And my men came off without any losse, and brought 3 good horses with them.[6]

A few days after the destruction of Campden it was the turn of more houses to be burnt, as the King progressed northwards via Inkberrow. Charles left Droitwich on 14 May and the royalist headquarters were established at Bromsgrove, with Prince Rupert deviating slightly east to neutralize a small but uncomfortably close enemy garrison at Hawkesley Hall, Kings Norton. One of the homes of the catholic Middlemore family, the moated Hawkesley had been seized by Colonel Fox early in 1645 and converted into a small parliamentary garrison. It seems to have played only a minor role in local conflicts, though its soldiers are frequently reported taking free quarter in nearby villages – Tanworth, Packwood, Lapworth – on minor, unrecorded missions, besides resorting to the usual obnoxious tactics of property blackmail: some inhabitants of Studley reported 'Colonell Foxes men deceitfully caused us to give unto them to save our house from Plunderinge 11s.'. Hawkesley's small garrison of sixty was in no state to withstand Rupert's imperious summons to surrender and it did so, without a fight, on the afternoon of 14 May, just as the King himself arrived to take control. A month's supply of food and ammunition was discovered in the house, which was promptly plundered, its moat drained, and all the garrison taken prisoner before it too was set ablaze. The Middlemores' other mansion at Edgbaston had a narrow escape at the same time, Colonel Fox's garrison there being besieged, according to some accounts. Charles spent the night at nearby Cofton Hall, dining without doubt in the great medieval hall under its majestic hammerbeam vault, little dreaming that the melancholy duty of his loyal host that night, Thomas Jolliffe, would in a few short years be to attend him on the scaffold at Whitehall. At Cofton the King was joined by a large influx of reinforcements under the respective governors of the other regional garrisons of Hereford, Ludlow and Dudley. On leaving the district the next day, Prince Rupert also ordered the burning of the 'very fair brick house' at Frankley, the chief seat of the Lyttletons of Hagley, another moated Tudor manor-house, before moving into Staffordshire, though the details of this further arson have remained obscure.

The Midland incendiarism was still not complete. In the bitter royalist aftermath of Naseby a few months later there was a fiery epilogue which it is worth interrupting the chronological sequence of events to record at this point. In what appears to be an act of pure vindictive reprisal against the Fiennes family by Cavaliers aware, in the summer of 1645, that the enemy was gaining ground throughout the land, the ancestral home and its nearby subsidiary manor were targeted at the beginning of September:

> The hellish crew of Banbury have lately burnt the Lord Sayes house at Braughton [Broughton Castle], a Prince-like House all of Stone, which they filled with straw and fired it within. Also, they have burnt and pul'd downe Master James Fiennes his house at Newton [North Newington], but a mile from Broughton. Let fire from Heaven consume the destroyers!

No further account of these events survives, and the reporter may indeed be confusing Broughton with Aynho. Whether true or not, however, the report confirms the deliberate campaign of incendiarism throughout the district, for if Broughton survived, Aynho itself was less fortunate. John Cartwright's great house had always been exceptionally vulnerable in view of its conspicuously parliamentarian owner who had long fled the district, the proximity of the notorious royalist headquarters at Banbury and the frequency of skirmishing in the district, yet it had so far escaped all but minor damage, looting and the indignities of half-hearted royalist attempts to fortify it, like that reported in February 1645:

> There are twoe troopes of [royalist] horse quartered at Ano, consisting of about threescore, under the command of Major Compton; and they have made a drawbridge at the gate goeing into

Mr Cartwright's howse where they forme themselves all the night, but in the day-tyme lye drinking in the towne and may easily be surprised . . .

By early September, however, the Royalists' desperation was mounting, and in obscure circumstances the 'fair goodly building' was reduced to a smouldering ruin:

The Kings forces at Banbury did lately carry loads of straw into the house of Mr Cartwright at Ayneho on the hill in Northamptonshire . . . and set the straw on fire and burnt down not only his dwelling house (being a very faire goodly building, wherein the King himselfe lodged after the battell of Edgehill) but also burnt all the barnes, stables and outhouses thereto belonging, least it should be made a garrison by the Parliament; having heretofore plundered him of 940 sheepe and great store of rich house-hold stuffe and other goods and rents to the value of above eight thousand pounds.

Shortly after, in an ever-worsening situation for the Royalists, amid rumours that the Parliamentarians were planning to establish new garrisons throughout the district, it was the turn of one last majestic house, the battlemented Tudor mansion of the Spencers at Wormleighton, likely to have been comparable to Compton Wynyates. The account of its destruction is unique in that although, unlike Milcote, no record of the actual event survives, the precise circumstances leading to its almost total destruction by the Banbury Royalists were recorded by the commander-in-chief himself, Sir William Compton:

Neere upon halfe a yeere sinse I had notise the rebbels did intend to put garrisons into some strong howses, where upon I sent to advertise Mr Secretary [Sir Edward Walker] of it; and my brother Charles brawght me answer that such places that were advantagious to the rebbels if they should poses them selves of them . . . I showld disaible those plaises. At this time, amoungst the rumour of other howses Wormeleighton was nominated for one. Upon which I sent for Mr Barret, the Lady [Dorothy] Spensers steuard, and demaunded of him if he heard that the enemie had any such intention; to which he answered 'Noe', and further towld me he was confident he showld ease such meanes to giet timely advertisement and to give me notise. Whereupon I did nothing to the plase at that time, but thawght it had beene sufitient Warning to him . . . I telling him that I must nescesarily fire the howse if by the enemie theire were any such intention. Never till this present did I heere more of the plase; [when] I received it from soe good a hand that I durst no longer forbeare it that if I did not burne it within three daies the enemie would have forses in it. Upon this inteligense I agwainted the feeld offisers, whose opinion was to fire it; and there upon Capt. Moore was comanded out with his troope and some twenty horse more: the whole number did not exseede 80 horse. I gave him comand that if there were any goods, he should not suffer his souldiers to stur anithing. The sowldiers he comanded to set the howse on fire, and in running into the chambers they tooke some things of which Mr Barret gave notise. Whereupon he dreu his men up before he came away, and all that could be found was restored. But of his whole number he protests to me at that time he did not miss eight men; and how it is posible soe greate a los should be I leave to any one to judge.

What is doubly interesting in this patently honest account by the Banbury governor is that although, to his credit, he was clearly reluctant to commit the act unless absolutely unavoidable, when a decision was made the destruction itself provoked less interest than the question of the plundered contents. Today, only the imposing gatehouse added in 1613 and a tantalizingly small fragment of one of the ranges in mellow brick facing tranquil meadows survive to evoke the house's former splendour. It vanished almost as completely as the medieval village lying under the pastures nearby.

The destructive momentum of war can never be stemmed overnight, and the

WORMLEIGHTON HOUSE, WARWICKSHIRE. The magnificent early Tudor mansion of the Spencer family was a conspicuous Civil War casualty. Prince Rupert passed under its imposing gateway, added in 1613, to establish his headquarters here before Edgehill. Despite playing little or no subsequent part in the fighting, the house was deliberately destroyed by fire in the closing stages of the war to prevent enemy occupation, leaving only the fragments shown. (Photo: Banbury Museum)

'slighting' of fortified buildings became a standard precautionary and vengeful measure after the ending of hostilities. Although strictly outside the time-scale imposed on the present work, it is worth recalling the fate of two irreplaceable buildings which, ironically, survived the war only to fall victim to the fragile peace. Banbury's sufferings had been as great as any, and the town's plight at the end of the war was graphically lamented by the influential Banbury clergyman Joshua Sprigge as 'once a great and faire Market-towne . . . but now having scarce the one halfe standing to gaze on the ruines of the other'. At its centre stood the castle which, 'though old through time, yet was recovered and revived by art and industry unto an incredible strength much beyond many places of greater name and reputation'. In 1648, on a petition presented by apprehensive inhabitants who regarded it with the same feelings as later Parisians the Bastille, an earlier decision to destroy only its earthworks was reversed: the castle was bought for £2,000 and virtually completely demolished, its materials being used to repair the town. But perhaps the most spectacular example of all the wanton post-war destruction was at Kenilworth. Here the town itself had, throughout the war, suffered the usual quartering and plundering from the parliamentary garrison which occupied the great medieval bastion looming on the nearby meadows, under a succession of autocratic and ruthless governors, from Hastings Ingram to John Needham. During these years the town was expected to furnish a constant supply of goods, food and drink, and particularly bedding, from rich and poor alike. Widow Sarah Newby, for example, 'delivered to Capten Ingram and his souldiers one barrell of alle, one fether bedd and other beding and two fowling Gunnes, three pikes and one suite of armour', while items of non-military value could always be sold for profit. Old John Lane, to whom a clergyman, Daniel Bourne, had confided a set of 150 valued books, had the chagrin of losing them to Needham's unruly soldiers. As at Warwick and elsewhere, men were constantly forced into labouring on defensive constructions, both 'in their parsons [sic] and with their teames in Carring Wood, turfe and other things', and as soon as Ingram was promoted to governor from his previous position as merely keeper of the stables, the castle's sumptuous apartments began to be stripped of bedding, furniture such as chairs and stools, even embroidered furnishings and the contents of wardrobes – to the anger of the housekeeper, Gilbert Howe, and his wife, who later submitted a detailed list of compensation claims. Over the period of four years' occupation Howe had lost, besides household plunder, over £60 in salary, the profits from orchards, gardens and woods, valuable turf and timber for fortifications, to say nothing of endless damage caused by countless herds of cattle, sheep and horses, tramping soldiers and teams of carts trudging through his property. The resources of the great lake, on which a floating island 'bright blazing with Torches' and silken-clad goddesses and nymphs had greeted Queen Elizabeth in 1575, were impoverished by over-fishing and:

> . . . a great fishing Nette was torne in peeces with fishing by Captaine Ingrams and Capten Hunts souldiers and the Boate spoyled . . . with Caring wood, turfe and with fishing . . .

One of the castle's former bailiffs, William Phipps, adds to this tale of woe the systematic inroads made in the surrounding woods and chase, vestige of Shakespeare's once-proud Forest of Arden, detailing the depletion, one by one, of Strawberry Coppice, Little Knowle Hill, Harpers Coppice, Butlers Coppice and 'the Kings woods lying

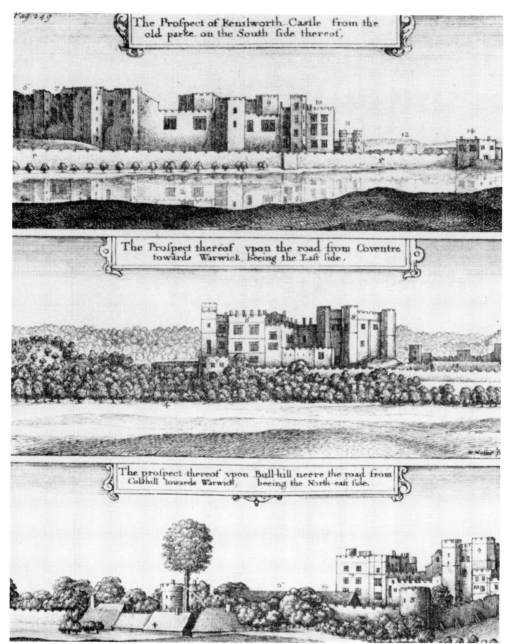

KENILWORTH CASTLE. One of the most spectacular casualties of the Civil War. Although a parliamentary garrison for most of the war it saw little fighting and survived relatively unscathed, only to fall victim to the fragile peace when in July 1649 the parliamentary authorities instructed Colonel Joseph Hawkesworth to make it 'untenable'. The Warwickshire antiquary Sir William Dugdale commissioned this Prospect after visiting the castle on 6 September 1649, shortly before demolition began.

between Kenellworth and Stonly', continuing well into 1645 during Cromwell's visit 'a little before Nasby fight' when more oaks were being felled to make a new mill. Part of the wood went to construct bulwarks against a royalist attack which never came, some was stocked indoors 'to be kept for tyme of danger', but much was simply destined for the governor's vast fireplaces. Phipps concludes with measured grimness:

> The Wood and treese for fier wood fallne and Cleft upon the Chace and parke, which was by the Appointment of Captaine Needham for his owne use and other famallies in the Castle . . . the Quantitie and vallue I cannot Judg, but if there must be an inquirey made the Cleavers and Cariers can best give an amount thereof. But I think it to bee worth at least £300.

The surrounding chase, which had echoed to the pageantry of 'rare Shows and Sports' for morris dancing, fell prey to more mundane preoccupations. Unruly soldiers ran riot, plundering whatever remained once the governor's official exactions were met, breaking one inhabitant's windows, even taking a hive of bees from someone's yard. The church suffered, John Lane being paid 5s. 'for making the church fayre after generall Cromwells soldiers were here', and some of its windows were damaged, Needham allocating £2 as a gesture 'to the Churchwardens of Kenilworth for mendinge Glasse broke by Soldiers'. As at Warwick, Tysoe, Banbury and elsewhere the overall picture is yet another confirmation of the impact of a local garrison on the community. For the castle itself, however, the final indignity was yet to come, when after the war the parliamentary authorities ordered the new governor, Joseph Hawkesworth, to render it useless to a potential enemy. The Great Pool was drained, the remaining woods destroyed, the land divided into farms for worthy Parliamentarians, the majestic towers gutted and the curtain walls breached. Dugdale's *Prospect* (see illustration 221), commissioned on 6 September 1949 shortly before demolition began, records the proud castle for the last time before it became the gaunt romantic ruin which was to catch Scott's imagination almost two centuries later. Curiously, the John of Gaunt whom Shakespeare had only a short while ago imagined predicting England's shameful conquest of itself in an earlier civil war, had been lord of Kenilworth. It was as though the dramatist had recalled this later, in virtual retirement at Stratford, as he looked northwards one day across Arden to the Kenilworth whose unforgettable Elizabethan pageant he is likely to have seen as a boy, before voicing his final poignant prophecy. Like the gorgeous palaces of Wormleighton and Milcote, Kenilworth's cloud-capped towers simply dissolved into the thin post-war air.[7]

CHAPTER ELEVEN

THE DISINTEGRATING CHURCH

ECCLESIASTICAL ANARCHY

Much has already been noted, albeit incidentally, of the religious basis of the Civil War, and how belief and practice reinforced and sometimes initiated political and military action. As the conflict developed and the pace of reform quickened, what has been termed 'ecclesiastical anarchy' replaced the previous uneasy status quo; doctrinal differences became entrenched, religious as well as political views polarized and major changes transformed the old Church. Within a few short years the unpopular and autocratic Laud had been impeached, imprisoned and executed, episcopacy abolished, traditional Church festivities castigated, the Solemn League and Covenant to abolish prelacy adopted, the sequestration of religious offenders pursued, the conservative Book of Common Prayer replaced by the Directory of Public Worship, and a presbyterian form of Church government for every parish set in motion. Although the stages of reform were not as smooth or as continuous as this résumé implies, in retrospect the war years did see what has been described as 'the piecemeal dismantling of the old church'.

But the war had certainly not created the religious conflict. As already noted in Chapter Two, religious tensions were mounting long before, the printing presses had been disgorging a veritable cascade of pious militancy for many years, and a journalist could note in 1640 how 'all the pulpits do now ring of the disorders of the clergy, both in doctrine and discipline'. Existing passions were simply inflamed and given a new and murderous edge by the outbreak of war, and when it finally erupted the conflict was over issues which, it could be argued, were religious more than anything else. The King's repeated assurances, given in his speech at Southam and again, more recently, in his Evesham peace-feeler of July 1644, that he proposed no change in the established 'reformed' Church, impressed few, since most of even those who believed him wanted change in one direction or another from the vacillating, unsatisfactory compromise that existed. Everyone was aware of the deficiencies and abuses of the old system, with

The Religious War
1640 - 60

SOUTH WARWICKSHIRE
NORTH OXFORDSHIRE

⚱ Major catholic gentry or community

☐ Royalist incumbent sequestered/ejected

△ Royalist incumbent severely harassed

☆ Incumbent abandons parish to enlist

■ Leading puritan centre of influence

■ Major puritan gentry or influence

▲ Puritan clergy harassed

● Active puritan ministry

◉ Incipient Quakerism

PT

pluralist and often discredited incumbents frequently either absent, incompetent or corrupt. Wanting to move in one direction were not only the radical reformers and 'lecturing preachers' but the ordinary Puritan, with his fear of Gunpowder Plot popery liable to resurface in endless papist scares and his mistrust of the established Church, suspected of blocking reform, wanting to reinstate Roman services and stifling the individual spirit. On the other hand many Anglicans also shared the fear of Rome while being equally apprehensive about the radicals' attack on civil government by the King and Church government by the bishops, and fearful of the directions in which subversive reforms might lead, possibly to anarchy. In between were those dwindling few adhering to a seemingly lost cause, that of tolerance, gentleness and compromise – and criticized by extremists on both sides for so doing. It was indeed the best of times, and the worst of times.

The story of the impact of the Civil War on the Church in the south Midlands, and how this in turn affected the community, has yet to be told. When it is, it seems certain to confirm the impression of a community, already far from united spiritually before the war, in which the tensions and passions were dramatically exacerbated by the anarchy and the sheer opportunism of war. As already noted, the district had always been one of extreme religious diversity, from papist Worcestershire to puritan Northamptonshire. Dissent in this region is often associated with catholicism in particular. This was indeed recusant country *par excellence*, where small catholic squires in old manor-houses ruled over self-contained independent households – the Middlemores at Edgbaston and Kings Norton, the Cannings at Foxcote, the Bishops at Brailes – and where whole parishes had important catholic minorities: Coughton, Idlicote, Lapworth, Ilmington, Wootton Wawen, Rowington, Beoley. The religious complexion seemed unchanged since 1596, when the bishop of Worcester, whose diocese included most of south Warwickshire as well as Worcestershire, described it to an outsider as being:

> . . . as dangerous as any place that I know. In that small circuit there are nine score recusants of note, besides retainers, wanderers and secret lurkers, dispersed in forty several parishes, . . . many of them not only of good wealth but of great alliance, . . . able to prevail much with the simpler sort. Besides, Warwick and the parts thereabout are freighted with a number of men precisely conceited against her Majesty's government ecclesiastical . . .

Recently, papist scares had implicated some leading families and revived memories of the Gunpowder Plot and the role Midland families had played in that: the Cloptons, Throckmortons, Digbys and Catesbys. When war broke out, many wealthy Catholics immediately declared themselves for the King, and not surprisingly, Parliamentarians repeatedly publicized (and no doubt exaggerated) the numbers of Catholics enlisting in the King's forces, often with ill-concealed horror:

> It is informed out of Worcester-shire and Oxford-shire that the Papists which are in his Majesties Army do openly set up Masse, and that some of the Cathedrall men of Worcester have bin Agents therein; and at Oxford it is reported there is dayly Masse (although not so openly as at Worcester).

It is certainly true that many of the great catholic families of the neighbourhood, the Sheldons, Savages, Morgans, Smiths, provided in their younger members an officer nucleus for many a royalist regiment, even if their contribution to the war effort remains impossible to evaluate, and equally, that Catholics were prominent among those taken prisoner when fortified manor-houses like Beoley and Stoke were stormed by parliamentary troops.[1]

Catholic dissent is, however, only one aspect of the disunity in the area, for under the blanket Anglicanism lay seed-beds of progressive non-conformity which had long ago created the Marprelate controversy and an early attempt at forming a presbyterian structure at Coventry, as well as districts of entrenched puritanism, as at Banbury. Some of the major landowning families were themselves split in religion and politics: the Lucys, Throckmortons and Underhills had puritan as well as conservative branches. Many parishes must clearly have been deeply divided spiritually long before the war, as conflicts such as that already described at Banbury, where John Howes was denounced by puritan parishioners for wickedness, or Lapworth, where John Doughty's flock condemned him for being 'a common resorter to the houses of Popish recusants . . . and a scoffer of goodness and good men', could not have erupted overnight.

Puritan ministers themselves had in their turn been disciplined on doctrinal grounds by the Laudian authorities at Frankton, Honiley, Hanwell and Knowle. Yet others had been periodically disciplined for scandalous conduct. But puritanism itself was splintering. To quote only the most obvious example, the young George Fox was beginning his itinerant ministry in Warwickshire, later recalling the 'brave meetings' when 'ye truth sprange upp first in Warwicksheere in 1645'. Barely ten years later, Quaker meetings at Warwick and Ettington would be forerunners of the regular monthly meetings of the 1670s, attracting large congregations from Long Compton, Brailes, Radway and Ettington. Warwickshire and Worcestershire were both major areas of quakerism in the 1650s, and there were many pockets elsewhere. Evesham, a royalist garrison for much of the war in largely papist Worcestershire, was soon to become a chief centre for quakerism and a focus of persecution. The persecution itself had its roots in age-old controversies and was now fuelled by new fears of social subversion. Lord Saye later spoke of Quakers as the devil's emissaries and had them evicted from cottages in Broughton and imprisoned. One of the most populous parishes in the district, Brailes, might serve as a fairly typical case-study of this spiritual diversity. One of the many Sheldon manors, it was also home to another influential catholic family, the Bishops, who had figured so prominently in recusancy lists over the years, and with a vicar suspected of royalism and friendly with the Crofts of Shipston, themselves allied to the Sheldons. It was William Bishop who later denounced several of his Quaker neighbours, George Wyatt, Edward and John Corbet, seized when harvesting in the fields and thrown into a dungeon at Warwick Castle 'twenty steps under Ground'. The ostensible reason for this persecution was non-payment of tithes to Bishop, a typical Quaker gesture, but as Wyatt had been the village constable during the war, with authority to collect contributions and, perhaps, help implement sequestration proceedings against Bishop, one may suspect the culmination of a bitter personal, as well as a religious, grudge. A similar case involving a Quaker constable occurred at the adjacent village of Sutton-under-Brailes, where the family of Edward Billing, described as 'a noted Quaker', was active in denouncing their rector, Henry Watkins, as an active Royalist. Again, personal malice evidently underscored political grievance, since a brother, Thomas Billing, was in turn accused by the parson of maladministration of taxes collected as constable, on whose destination the royalist rector may well have held very different views. Quakers were subversive trouble-makers, and their independent spirit, along with that of other radical sects emerging in the war years, was feared by Royalists and Puritans alike.[2]

The puritan camp was therefore far from united in matters religious. The new opportunities for free-thinking, social mobility, the dissemination of radical ideas by preaching and printing press and the ever-present fear of Rome encouraged radical splinter movements inside the puritan tradition which worried many thinkers: Samuel Clarke at Alcester bewailed the influence of 'sectaries' among the godly faithful, and John Trapp at Stratford wrote fearfully of radical sectarian activity in the county. The internal dissension among what the Royalists tauntingly referred to as 'the Brethren' occasionally surfaces at parish level. In one revealing incident a suitably horrified royalist journalist reported an open-air conventicle in November 1643 in Humbridge quarry outside Warwick, in which large congregations, including many women, were addressed by a grocer-turned-soldier, Nicholas Hawes, and Lord Brooke's former miller, Adam Dadin. The bailiff of Warwick, John Yardley, was alerted and took action to disrupt this subversive meeting, and:

> . . . with a Guard of such men as he thought misliked the worke, came into the field, seiz'd upon the Two Preachers with their severall Congregations, and brought them before Master [Richard] Vennour [Vicar of St Mary's, Warwick], an honest grave Divine; who asking the men and women 'Why they were not at Church?' the women replyed, 'They knew of no Church we had'. Whereupon Master Yardley committed the Two Preachers.

The following day, however, the two offending preachers were released by the all-powerful military commanders, Joseph Hawkesworth and Godfrey Bosevile. Soon after, Hawes was reported captured by the Royalists at Coughton, so that the 'afflicted Grocer', or 'Nicholas Hawes, the Parson of Stone-pit', as the Royalists jeered, 'hath left the Stone-pit unprovided of a Curate'. At least one pious Parliamentarian was not prepared to leave matters there, however, waspishly pointing out that:

> . . . there may be honester doings sometimes in a stone-pit than in Brasen-nose [sic] Colledge, and that Miller dare grinde Arguments with any Doctor in Oxford; and I am confident he is a man of a whiter conversation than any Prelate you have.

The incident hinged upon personal rivalry between Bosevile and Yardley over local politics, but it also hints at the fear of social subversion by separatist groups, the role of women, the artisan basis of many self-appointed preachers and their dissatisfaction with any 'established' church.

As the war progressed and puritanism slowly triumphed, so its separatist tendencies were strengthened to the extent that a presbyterian minister, Thomas Edwards, could publish in 1646 a bitter, three-volume analysis of the sectarian 'gangrene' which he saw at the heart of the new puritanism, detailing outrages from all parts of the country. Throughout the Midlands, he reported:

> . . . the Sectaries do all manner of wayes, by word and deed, abuse the Ministers by all kind of reproachfull railing speeches, wicked Pamphlets, . . . invading their Pulpits by force, keeping and pulling them out of their pulpits, driving them by violence from their houses and habitations, assaulting them in the way and their houses, putting upon them souldiers . . .

The late Lord Brooke was implicitly criticized, for allowing his coachman to become 'an early Preacher', a precedent now producing unfortunate consequences, like the Coventry shoemaker who had become 'a famous Preacher' and was reportedly going 'up and down Glostershire, Warwickeshire, Wostershire, preaching and venting erroneous Antinomianisme, Anabaptisme, preaching against Tythes, Baptisme of children . . . .'. Inevitably, the disease had spread among the common soldiers. Thus, not only was Cromwell's regiment 'affronting' ministers when preaching in Northamptonshire, but a captain quartering with his troop at Alcester was himself preaching, sometimes twice on the sabbath in the parish church, while regrettably, 'the Minister, though an honest man, is glad to stand by'. Worse still, at Leamington Hastings a company of unruly parliamentarian troops had arrived from causing disturbances in Northamptonshire and, encouraged by their captain preaching sedition, had violated the property of Sir Thomas Trevor, the lord of the manor and a parliamentarian judge. The officer had insulted godly ministers by calling them 'priests' and dissuaded people from attending church, saying that sermons were useless. The damage caused to the estate was such that the steward, John Matthews, concluded that 'he had rather have Prince Rupert and his Company to quarter there then that Troop of Captain P'. A final, particularly disquieting example of separatist subversion in Warwickshire by unqualified soldiers was reported by Edwards in October 1645:

> Two souldiers did preach at Rugby on the 25 of October, and there said that no Minister was a true one except he was rebaptized; and that our Ordinances were false Ordinances; and that the Printers have cozened us in printing the Scriptures . . .; and on the 26 day of October they baptized six women in a Mill-dam, about eleven of the clock in the day, which was strange to us in these parts . . .

It had been in a region already deeply divided in religious matters, aggravated by recent contentious Laudian innovations then being reversed, where what contemporaries termed 'Altar-Priests' officiated here and 'Schismatical Lecturing Preachers' there and where austere lectureships were beginning, in many places, to provide an alternative devotional experience to traditional churchgoing, that Lord Brooke had placed zealous preachers before the war in positions where they could deliberately fuel the religious debate. As already noted in Chapter Two, when war broke out, some of these puritan divines immediately joined the army, either as itinerant padres of regiments on the march or as garrison chaplains. With their encouragement the simple, uncomplicated piety of such as Nehemiah Wharton had made little distinction between psalm-singing as they eagerly marched miles to hear a 'heavenly sermon', destroying church ornaments and victimizing 'base priests' as they took the crusade to the streets and countryside. The war itself had amply proved, month after month, the lengths to which religious extremism could go. But as the threat of catholicism receded so independent sectarian movements grew, fostered by the very success of puritanism and the undreamt-of opportunities of war for social anarchy. Independency was now a cause, and seen by many orthodox presbyterians as almost as dangerously subversive as popery itself. Religious toleration was still in the future. Cromwell was not yet in a position to say 'I meddle not with any man's conscience', Quakers were yet to be persecuted, and John Bunyan, still a common soldier at Newport Pagnell, was yet to suffer long imprisonment. But the genie of free thought, the habit of questioning authority, was out of the bottle.[3]

THE DISORDERLY PARISH CHURCH

For the ordinary villager it was round his parish church that the major controversies naturally revolved. It had often, of course, been the scene of isolated disturbances even before the war; though not necessarily (although probably nearly always) over religious matters. There had been repeated dissension at Wardington, where Thomas Gubbins had slandered ministers, calling them 'drunkards and whoremasters', and attacked the vicar, John Parry, for propagating false doctrine and lying in the pulpit, and where the whole parish had refused to pay to repair the church seats. At Rowington, the vicar, Robert Caddyman, called his clerk and churchwarden 'hellhounds' during divine service in 1640, at Napton-on-the-Hill, the vicar, John Bowyer, assaulted parishioners in the chancel in 1642, while another fractious parson, Thomas Lever, already charged a few years previously with assaulting one of his flock in church on the sabbath, led a brawl in Napton church, and at Stratford, the vicar was suspended for a time because of his habit of keeping his pigs and poultry in the chancel. When the war broke out the village church became an automatic focus of contention and actual violence, symbolizing unmistakably the sources of the conflict in massive, tangible form in the centre of the community. Although precise evidence is sparse at parish level and no uniform picture emerges, most churchgoers were soon having to adapt to new services, new furniture arrangements and, shortly, in many places, new parsons, as their old one, sometimes an absent pluralist or having fled or enlisted, was 'examined', denounced and eventually replaced by an often unpopular, but politically more amenable, substitute. To what extent reforms were being implemented within the Church itself is unclear from the scanty records, but in many places altars and altar-rails were being removed, allegedly idolatrous objects and glass destroyed, seating arrangements altered (causing endless feuds) and the actual scriptural texts contested – as in the violent incident at Adderbury already reported (p. 16).

Even when congregations and parson remained relatively peaceable among themselves, they could seldom have been left to continue their churchgoing uninterruptedly as the war visited their parish in one form or another, for the Church, never treated as reverently as in more recent times, was liable to be damaged, misused or attacked. Prince Rupert used Cirencester church as a prison for captured Parliamentarians in 1642, and the stained glass windows were broken by their relatives bringing food to them. In Worcestershire a stauch royalist high constable incarcerated reluctant recruits in local churches at the beginning of the war before they were forcibly released by John Bridges, the governor at Warwick. As already seen, churches themselves were far from immune from attack, for local skirmishes had a habit, in fact, of reaching a climax at the village church, the only impregnable building in the locality, as at Kilsby, Weedon and Kings Sutton, or at Canons Ashby, Alcester and Chadshunt, where they were set on fire for harbouring enemy soldiers. The method was simple and effective, as described at Westbury, in the Forest of Dean: 'the men got stooles and ladders to the windowes . . ., cast in granadoes and fired them out of the church'. Churches could be severely damaged by a siege in the town, as at Warwick and Banbury, or, if need be, actually demolished as a precaution. At Boarstall, near Oxford, when the church was thought to compromise the security of the adjacent royalist garrison, the King simply gave orders for it to be 'pulled downe'. Misuse was common, the empty spaces of many churches offering tempting accommodation. Horses were reportedly stabled in the churches at Alcester and Burton Dassett, Pebworth was turned into a temporary garrison, and Leamington used as an overnight transit camp for recruits for Sir Thomas Fairfax's fledgling New Model Army.

The visible scars of this mistreatment sometimes remain today to remind the visitor of the violence: the rebuilt chancel at Islip, the countless defaced effigies, the reproachful colourless windows or replaced medieval fragments, as at Cherington, where some early fourteenth-century pieces are thought to have come from the destroyed chapel at Compton Wynyates, or at Adderbury, whose superb stained glass was also probably destroyed in the war. Church doors are pitted with bullet holes at Tredington and Fenny Compton, the towers at Marton, Barford and Offchurch bear shot marks, the recently-uncovered wall painting at Burton Dassett has been peppered with gunshot, parish registers taken away, as at Hanwell and Hampton Lucy, the bells at Southam broken, Deddington's melted down for shot. . . Few local churches are without their stories of Civil War damage, impossible now to authenticate after successive restorations, but entirely plausible, like Thomas Ward's report in 1834 that Kineton's tower was damaged by cannon.

At a time when it seems to have been assumed that apart from 'Edgehill' the region was left largely undisturbed by the Civil War, such stories might have been dismissed as probable fabrications. Now, in the light of the wealth of contemporary detail uncovered in the parish archives, it is no longer possible to do so. Similarly for the suspiciously long list of local churches needing repairs shortly after the war. It is probably not by chance that many, like Alcester, Burmington, Kineton, Shipston and Whichford are in villages known to have suffered heavy quartering or been the scene of actual violence. Even tiny communities were vulnerable to revenge attacks if there were adverse political factors, although precise details have usually not survived. Shawell, conspicuously placed near the Watling Street thoroughfare on the Leicestershire–Warwickshire border, had a notable puritan parson, Richard Clayton, an associate of the even more notorious radical James Nalton of Rugby, while being at the same time home to Edward Leigh, another puritan divine. It is unlikely to be a coincidence that it was reported by some inhabitants of Rugby to have been devastated by fire by Prince Rupert's men 'at severall times', to an estimated total damage of £235, or that the present church is mainly Victorian. At least two churches, Edgbaston and Banbury, were so severely damaged that they never recovered and had eventually to be rebuilt. At Edgbaston, a royalist report that the Parliamentarians 'pulled down the church to make their fortification [and] disposed of the Bells to their fellows in Birmingham' was confirmed shortly after by the parishioners themselves in their claim for £500 to cover 'sustayned losses & damages by the destroying of our Church . . . by those who were under the government of Collonell Fox'. Dugdale himself repeated the account some years later, reporting the church, together with the sumptuous heraldic monuments of the Middlemore family, to be 'utterly demolisht by the Parliament forces in the late wars', and ten years after the war, when the roofless church was still lying derelict, the minister and his parishioners petitioned Parliament for urgent help with rebuilding costs, now estimated at £800, far beyond their means: 'Our parish church, a handsome structure, was partly burnt in the

ST MARY'S CHURCH, BANBURY. Already stripped of many ornaments by local puritans before the war, the church never recovered from damage suffered during the first siege of Banbury in 1644 and was eventually demolished over a century later.

late wars and partly pulled down by Col. Fox . . . and the materials employed for the garrison [of Edgbaston House]'. Banbury's own magnificent medieval church, likened to a cathedral superior even to those at Adderbury, Bloxham and Kings Sutton, had already been stripped of many ornaments before the war by Puritans, who later recalled their own part in the proceedings in response to a preacher's sermon which had stressed that 'it is the duty of every Christian to put his hand to the pulling down of Idolatry'. During the war it suffered substantial damage during the first siege, as already noted: a writer of 1712 claimed the tower to have been originally of three, rather than the two storeys then remaining and illustrated in eighteenth-century views. Only a dozen or so of the sixty heraldic shields in the windows survived the war, Anthony Wood lamenting the church's 'much broken and defaced state' on a visit in 1659. The major devastation at Lichfield and Worcester cathedrals and the Beauchamp Chapel at Warwick has already been mentioned, while one church, that at Compton Wynyates, was completely destroyed.

The foregoing could be considered the accidental damage of war, but the Puritans pursued a course of church damage as official policy, following their ordinance of 26 August 1643 for the 'utter demolishing, removing and taking away of all Monuments of superstition or Idolatry'. The text of the ordinance is comprehensive, and specifies as legitimate targets altars, rails, communion tables, candles, candlesticks, crucifixes, paintings and inscriptions. The extent of the irretrievable loss to posterity caused by this ordinance is impossible to calculate, since the records are virtually silent on the subject, but it must have been substantial, even though the purging of 'papist' trappings was probably not pursued in many parishes by the villagers themselves, largely hostile or, at best, lukewarm on the subject. Occasionally, there are indeed hints of inaction on the part of parishioners. Even at Alcester, where Samuel Clarke prided himself on the beneficial effects of his cleansing ministry in a benighted papist district and where his friend, the influential Richard Baxter, occasionally preached, Major Bridges was still having to insist that 'the Rood loft and all superstitious paints . . . be demolished and defaced' as late as 1657. All in all, however, there is no doubt of the terrible impact of the 'puritan revolution' on the fabric of the parish church – witness the frequency of Dugdale's simple refrain, when later listing the ornaments, windows and monuments in the Warwickshire churches, 'These are gone'.[4]

While it is impossible to determine the precise extent to which political pressures affected the local ministry, the parish church was clearly central to the ideological struggle, and neither side underestimated the political, as well as religious authority the clergy wielded. As already pointed out, Clarendon complained of the perversion of scripture to political ends, and there must have been parishes where the pulpit played a vital opinion-forming role. The opinions of the parson, still very much the community's leader, could have been no secret to his relatively unsophisticated congregation, and sermon, liturgy and the management of parochial affairs were all susceptible to political slant. Religion and politics were in effect indistinguishable. In August 1643 the House of Commons instructed 'godly ministers' to 'go into divers counties . . . to possess the people with the truth and justice of the Parliament's cause in taking up of defensive arms', while shortly after a royalist report claimed that the parliamentary authorities in London had ordered that:

> . . . every Parish from whence the Regiment is drawne shall speedily prepare a large Table, to be fixed within the respective Churches, wherein shall be inscribed the names of all such Souldiers that shall voluntarily in person expresse their alacrity and courage in so commendable a service . . . as a perpetuall memoriall.

Once politicized to this extent, a parish was liable to be subjected to ideological controversy almost permanently as the puritan authorities continued to push through often highly contested measures, and breaches of the peace must have become a regular, or at least periodic feature of parish life and far more frequent than the odd comments in the archives might suggest. For one thing the 'intruding' minister was often highly unpopular, not only with the apolitical traditionalist majority but the puritan separatist minority. In 1649 the official sequestrators were instructed to provide ministers for the vacant cure at Whitchurch, but one nominee named Winter was physically opposed by a local gentleman, Thomas Marriett, and other inhabitants, causing a breach of the peace. The separatist radicals caused endless bickering and, occasionally, violence, long after the war. Although outside the scope of the present work, the Warwickshire *Testimony* of March 1648, for example, signed by many orthodox puritan clergy hostile to the 'errors and schisms' of the radical tendencies, provided further proof of the continuing divisions within puritanism itself. Occasional glimpses are caught of embattled clergy and unruly parishioners throughout the period. There was trouble at Monks Kirby, near Coventry, in the late 1640s, when radical baptist weavers challenged their minister, Richard

Martin, calling ministers 'unlawful and anti-Christian', and the church doors were violently broken open. At Henley-in-Arden in the 1650s orthodox clergy like Thomas Hall were confronted by aggressive lay preachers, including a baker, a nailer, a ploughwright and a weaver, and later attacked by parishioners, prominent among whom were women, and the chapel door was kept locked to bar intruding official preachers.

In such circumstances it is not surprising that the turnover of clergy was high, and it is not always easy to make sense of the comings and goings of incumbents during these turbulent years, for sources are incomplete, sometimes conflict and are usually, of course, silent on such crucial things as motive and explanation. But even the bare facts hint at the confusion which many parishes must have experienced. Some parishes seem indeed to have suffered almost continuous disruption. At Leamington Hastings, for example, the vicar Thomas Lever was, as already noted above, charged with riotous behaviour before the war. He seemed absent in 1643, however, when a Mr Busby was named for the sequestrated vicarage, but it was Lever himself who was sequestrated for malignancy before 1645, when it was ordered that Edward Archer, 'a godly and orthodox divine, shall presently officiate the Cure'. A little later the parish was further disrupted by the violent disturbances already reported and by 1646 Archer had apparently disappeared and John Lee was named as successor. But Lee himself was also duly sequestrated three years later for drunkenness, swearing and malignancy, compounding matters by refusing to relinquish his income in favour of the replacement, Gilbert Warden, who succeeded, allegedly 'by request of the people', but was himself charged later with a whole catalogue of serious offences against which the parish organized a petition. Perhaps Leamington Hastings was, for some reason not immediately obvious, exceptional; it was certainly peculiarly unfortunate. One suspects, rather, that it is simply the random survival of archive material which allows one to highlight this case rather than another, and that further local research would uncover many similar sagas. The absence of recorded controversy certainly cannot be interpreted as proof of parochial harmony, and the list of 'incumbents of this parish' proudly displayed in many a church aisle conceals often, under its reassuring air of serene continuity, a far different reality for this period.[5]

THE EMBATTLED CLERGY

The response of the harassed clergy to the unprecedented pressures of the times naturally varied from parish to parish. Some remained clear-sighted and non-partisan, like Daniel Whitby at Arrow:

> I beleeve that the Parliament tooke up armes for Religion, Lawes and Priviledges, to maintain them, and I beleeve the King doth the same, and I must not drive out one nayle with another.

Many had already taken up strong positions long ago, however – though this was not necessarily a guarantee of consistency of outlook over the period, such were the confusion of the times and the complexities of the issues. The rector of Whitchurch, Thomas Warmstry, originally an associate of the Puritans Thomas Dugard and Samuel Clarke, had condemned Laudian trappings in a lengthy, conscientious and closely-reasoned speech before the war, arguing that images, altars and crosses brought the church 'into suspition of inclination to Popery, [which] is the poyson of the Church'. He later fled to the Royalists, however, and was duly ejected by the parliamentary authorities. In the most clear-cut cases the parson voluntarily deserted his cure to enlist – in some cases, no doubt, after considerable heart-searching, in others willingly and in a spirit of adventure. Henry Twitchet at Stratford lost little time, and fled to take up arms for the Royalists when Lord Brooke occupied the town in February 1643:

> . . . at ye beginning of theise warres in Armes at such Tyme as Capt. Needham came to disarme Stratford, [he] did leave his usuall place of abode and cure & betook himselfe to ye Enemyes Quarters & Garrisons.

John Philpot, rector of Lighthorne, also joined the King at some stage and was later taken prisoner in Compton garrison when the house fell to parliamentary troops in June 1644. Warmington likewise was abandoned when its disreputable vicar Richard Wootton, having from the outset been more active in military than devotional matters, supplying not only horses but swords, pikes and muskets to Parliament, left his parish to captain a parliamentary troop at Warwick and roam the countryside. His colourful career, were it possible to reconstruct it from the fragments surviving in the archives, would read as an adventure in itself. Accused of raping a lady's maid, he fell into disgrace, was relieved of his commission and eventually expelled from Warmington (where he seems to have spent little time) in 1656 – though not before he had enjoyed part of the substantial profits from Sir Thomas Pope's sequestrated estates. Benjamin Lovell, similarly, left his sometimes riotous parishioners at Preston Bagot to become a cavalry captain, soon acquiring a reputation as a horse thief, and was present at the siege of Gloucester under William Purefoy. On the other hand, it was not until 22 May 1646, when the royalist cause was collapsing, that Robert Kenrick finally decided to abandon Burton Dassett to join the King's cavalry at beleaguered Oxford. In few of such cases can provision have been made for a clerical substitute without lengthy delay; the cases of Burton Dassett, where Parliament sent a puritan replacement for Kenrick within weeks, and Easington, Banbury, where Thomas Darrell (or Dayrell), when fleeing to join the King at Oxford, bothered to supply a substitute, must be the exception rather than the rule. In most cases it is to be assumed that the congregation, the parish as a whole and, where applicable, the parson's pupils, must all have suffered. Almost equally extreme were those clerics who, not prepared to brook outside interference with their ministry, were outspoken and provocative, or who were denounced to the authorities by a group of parishioners. The case of Thomas Merriott at Swalcliffe has already been cited, but that of John Doughty, vicar of Beaudesert and a staunch divine-right Royalist, is equally interesting. Doughty is reported to have preached a particularly uncompromising sermon at Lapworth church, in which he asserted that:

> . . . it was not necessary for the Minister to prove his doctrine by Scripture, but the people ought to believe it on his authority; . . . and that there is now a generation of men sprung up that will believe nothing but what is proved by Scripture, insisting that turning and tossing over the leaves of the

Bible is a disturbance to the congregation, with other words to that effect. The said John Doughty, speaking of the new Canons, said there was nothing in them to be disliked, and further that he did verily believe in his conscience that if St. Paul had been there and made them, the Parliament would have condemned them.

Doughty's living was duly sequestrated and he was ejected. As 'a common resorter to the houses of Popish recusants . . . and a scoffer of goodness and good men' [i.e. Puritans] he could expect no less from the parliamentary authorities. The parson-adventurer Benjamin Lovell, already referred to above, somehow managed to enjoy the profits of Doughty's sequestrated living, and a later petition of Doughty's needy wife claimed that Lovell had withheld the pension of one-fifth of the benefice legally payable to the family of an evicted incumbent, causing her great hardship. The similar case of another vehement Royalist, Walwyn Clarke, vicar of Oxhill, who roundly abused Parliament on every occasion, has already been noted. Such energetic and clamorous partisans were clearly notorious in the district and, as soon as military activities began, attracted automatic reprisals from enemy troops well informed, one suspects, by locals with personal grudges and only too eager to settle old scores. Among such were Dr William Smith, vicar of Tredington, targeted by the Warwick garrison, Dr Thomas King at Ilmington, an associate of the Catholic Cannings, Dr Richard Langston, rector of Whichford, deliberately plundered by troops from Compton Wynyates and ruinously quartered upon, and the elderly conservative scholar Francis Holyoak at Southam, who was alleged to have pressurized his congregation in church into joining the Commission of Array and offered them arms in his house to do so. As a strong advocate of 'Obedience, especially unto Authority Ecclesiastical' and with a son Thomas already a captain of foot in the King's garrison at Oxford, Holyoak, already seventy-five years old, was one of the first 'malignants' in the district to be pillaged mercilessly.

What plunged many parishes into bitter and often prolonged controversy was Parliament's deliberate policy of encouraging local informers to denounce their parson's alleged misdeeds, already seen operating to some effect at Banbury, Lapworth and Swalcliffe. Parliament recognized that many of their ordinances relating to sequestration were meaningless without the help of paid informers, and therefore authorized local committees to examine informants on oath, the reward being 12d. for every £1 which accrued to the government. Any local historian can often catch the authentic voice of the simple villagers in the resulting testimonies, as at Stoke Talmage, where the rector Nathaniel Barker, it was claimed, 'frequently enterteyned lewd roguish fellowes from Wallingford Garrison and held private consultations with them in the twylight, and alsoe he, his wife and daughter meeting them at Alehouses'; or, equally, the indignant rebuttals of the accused: 'the Phanatical People would pay him no Tythes' (John Stubbings, vicar of Ambrosden); 'by usurped Authority these many years wrested wrongfully out of my livinge' (John Wiseman, vicar of Rowington); 'the Kinge himselfe is a Papist . . . as bad as the Pope' (John Lee, vicar of Leamington Hastings); and the occasional plea for compassion, such as 'I am growen unweldie and very unfitt for travell' (Ambrose Sacheverell, rector of Tadmarton). Although this system became a permanent feature of parliamentary policy, Ian Green, in his detailed analysis of persecuted clergy, was nevertheless impressed by the relatively small numbers of witnesses prepared to come forward and the relatively high proportion of those who had a grudge against the accused clergyman. Clearly many parishioners found informing distasteful, and the parliamentary authorities had occasionally to stress that this was a civic duty:

> Because it is found by sad experience that parishioners are not forward to complain of their ministers, although they be very scandalous, but having this price and power in their hands, yet want hearts to make use thereof . . . You are therefore required to call unto you some well-affected men within every Hundred . . . to further the public reformation . . . and encouraged by you to inquire after the doctrines, lives and conversations of all ministers and schoolmasters, and to give you information both what can be deposed, and who can depose the same.

Such a system was notoriously open to abuse by unscrupulous parishioners intent on a personal vendetta against their parson, and where the incumbent was prepared to contest the charges proceedings could continue intermittently over many long years, as at Sutton-under-Brailes. Here, although the bulk of clerical ejections began in 1646, the controversy over Dr Henry Watkins began in 1643 and dragged on for many years of protracted litigation involving named parishioners, allegations of personal malice and cross-examination of witnesses in court, before culminating in personal tragedy for the rector. The elderly Watkins finally had both estate and parsonage sequestrated and his money, plate and rents seized, besides being, he alleged, put to great expense and danger by many hazardous journeys to present his defence. No wonder that he complained to Parliament of his harsh treatment. Many accused clergy probably never attempted to defend themselves, either because they had a weak case, lacked the stamina, had fled or refused to recognize the jurisdiction of the new courts. In some cases the ejected clergyman risked imprisonment by refusing to comply with parliamentary orders not to interfere with the new minister or attempt to regain his forfeited tithes. This happened at Welford-on-Avon, already the scene of violence when the outspoken Puritan John Trapp had been assaulted by Worcestershire Royalists when preaching, but the tables were now turned when a later complaint claimed that the sequestrated rector, Dr Jenkin Bowen:

> . . . doth in contempt of the said sequestracon interrupt and disturb Mr Trapp in his receiving of the tythes of the said Rectory, and endeavoreth to gaine them himselfe.

Such intruding puritan nominees were frequently unpopular in the parish, and could aggravate rather than appease local passions or even cause riots, but few details of incidents survive. As for the effect of such events on the individual minister, this must have been traumatic. For many, actual ejection came as the climax to a long and painful history of increasing insecurity, harassment or, as in the case of Thomas Lydiat at Alkerton or John Stubbings at Ambrosden, actual imprisonment by lawless garrison commanders. Many were financially ruined and their wives and children left penniless when, as so often, the fifth part of the profits of the living reserved for them went unpaid. Tredington's William Smith died an embittered man, stipulating in his will in 1658 that he wanted no extravagant funeral, 'suiting neither with my depressed condition nor the present times'. John Arnway, the archdeacon of Coventry, died in exile in 1653, having suffered long imprisonment; he wrote with restrained eloquence that his captors:

. . . granted me not a Bible of my library to comfort me, nor a sheaf of my meanes to nourish me, nor a suit of my clothes to cover me, nor use of common air to refresh me.

Perhaps the most notorious local case is that of the vicar of Adderbury, Dr William Oldys, murdered outside his home in a well-laid trap following a tip-off from a mischievous neighbour. The story, as told by John Walker in his great catalogue of *Sufferings of the Clergy*, is a moving commentary on the times. Oldys' outspoken royalism, in a dangerous area centred on the Adderbury church which had already been the scene of at least one violent incident, had prompted him to endure temporary separation from his family by taking refuge in the royalist garrison at Banbury. Wishing to accompany his son to begin his education at either Winchester or Oxford, however, Oldys met his family at a prearranged spot, only to discover soldiers patrolling the neighbourhood:

He, perceiving that there were Soldiers there and finding himself in Danger, sent his Wife and Son before, telling his Wife that if they were of the King's Party, she should Hold up her Hand, and he would come on; if not, she should pass on without any further Notice. She going on without Holding up her Hand, he knew they were Parliamentarians, and therefore Rid back as fast as he could . . . When his Horse came to his House, he could not by all the means he could use get his Horse forward; which gave them time to Overtake him; which as soon as they had done, one of them discharged a Pistol at him, and Shot him dead. Some of the Parish have since affirmed that the Person who had given notice to the Party of the Doctor's Journey fell down dead upon that very spot of Ground where the Doctor fell when he was shot. I have heard that he [Oldys] scattered his Money along the Highway, and by that Artifice delayed all of them but one, who thirsted more for Blood than Plunder. And 'tis said the Villain had been Supported formerly by the Doctor's Charity; and that his very Comrades abhorred the Baseness of this Action.

The homely, incidental detail of this narrative – the wife and son riding off into the distance, the unwilling horse, the desperate scattering of coins – suggests total authenticity. Oldys left a wife and eleven children; a tablet commemorates him today in Adderbury church, together with a stark entry in the burial register: 'Murdered by the Rebells in Adderbury'.

Perhaps the most dramatic manifestation of the civil conflict at parish level was, therefore, the increasing harassment, amounting to actual 'persecution' at times, of the Anglican clergy, and although clergy had been under fire for a variety of reasons for many years in a widely-recognized need to improve the quality of the ministry, and although one must avoid giving the impression of universally pious, inoffensive and conscientious parsons expelled overnight by barbarous Puritans, the cases already cited do constitute only a representative few from a very considerable body. Slow at first, political pressures built up as the war progressed and Parliament asserted its authority. Puritan-dominated Coventry was clearly an ideological, as well as military capital, and ensured that harsh measures were implemented against politically unreliable clergy over a wide area. The result was, in retrospect, dramatic. By 1646–7, most of the parish clergy in the south Midlands had been interfered with in one way or another at some stage. Many were fairly clear-cut cases of actual or suspected 'delinquency' on ideological grounds, involving a cycle which soon became familiar: parochial and legal wrangling, bullying by unruly troops, interrogation, eventual sequestration and ejection, a vacant living, an intruded newcomer. If to this list are then added the names of parliamentarian clergy who in turn were victimized by royalist soldiers and other apolitical incumbents ejected for pastoral rather than ideological inadequacy, as in scandalous cases at Bidford, Halford, Long Compton and Wolvey, where the parson might well, under less stringent scrutiny, have escaped sanctions, the scale of the disruption in the parishes begins to become apparent. However justified or not the charges – and it must be remembered that 'malignancy' often meant no more than a failure to speak out clearly enough for Parliament and that punishable acts of 'popery' included such simple gestures as bowing at the name of Jesus – tenure was never more insecure nor parochial unity more shattered than now. Nor should it be supposed that only the outspoken or the conspicuously incompetent suffered, although these were clearly most at risk. Moderates who tried to steer a middle course or adopt a low profile were no more safe from interference. In his analysis, Ian Green has pointed out that the less committed 'neutrals' unfortunate enough to serve in contentious areas like Worcestershire and the south Midlands were liable to harassment from both sides. Although evidence is lacking, one suspects that Nathaniel Horton at Barcheston was ruinously quartered upon by parliamentary troops not because of any political stance – for none is recorded – but because it was a 'Sheldon' parish in which Horton had shown the customary deference to the great landowner and needed teaching a lesson, and a similar situation may have contributed to the heavy quartering experienced by other Sheldon, Earl of Northampton or Worcester diocese manors, like Wolford, Shipston and Tysoe, where the incumbents seem to have kept a low profile throughout the war. It is, of course, always difficult to decide to what extent local controversies during the war were caused by purely political differences. How far was John Williams' drunkenness and depravity at Halford indirectly ideological? How far was his profanation of the sabbath with sports a political gesture and how far the mere irresponsibilty of a lovable rogue? Some parsons, clearly incorrigible, moved from one sequestration to another. William Morris, a rector in Kent guilty of swearing and drunkenness, was further accused of drinking Prince Rupert's health in an alehouse with malignants on a fast day and kissing the mistress of the house. Duly sequestrated in 1644 he reappeared as vicar of Kenilworth in 1646 to be sequestrated again there the following year. It is perhaps debatable which was worse for the parish: to endure a reactionary, inadequate or alcoholic parson or not to have one at all. The effect of the war was often to replace the former situation, at least temporarily, by the latter.

Similarly with the vexed question of tithes, one of the most contentious issues of all at local level, as in the tortuous cases at Ilmington, Kingham, Sutton-under-Brailes and Welford-on-Avon. Tithes were not in themselves a political issue, but just as many estate-owners were worried that their tenants were unable to pay rents so many incumbents were worried that their financially-overburdened parishioners simply could not pay their tithes. The war focused such issues more sharply than ever, and they cannot be excluded from any consideration of the impact of the war on the parishes.

As already stressed, the ecclesiastical chaos was far from being confined to the few war years under discussion. Many of the often bold reforming initiatives took many years to unfold, and their repercussions and the passions which their new directions aroused were unending. Some of the most interesting, and most provocative, measures envisaged the redistribution of wealth on ideological grounds, as when the proceeds from sequestrated estates like that of William Bishop at Brailes went to establish a lectureship in the supposedly spiritually-undernourished and populous parish of St Mary's, Coventry.

Similarly, such revenues often augmented poorly endowed livings, as at Alcester, Baddesley Ensor, Claverdon and Haseley, or when delinquents' estates at Burton Dassett, Fenny Compton and Tysoe assisted 'Trinity in Coventry'. Here too the impact of the war on the parishes was complex and difficult to evaluate, but was nonetheless profound and long-lasting. On a personal level too the turmoil was often protracted. Some of the displaced clergy left the district for good, but others remained nearby, nursing bitter grudges against the intruder for many years and awaiting an opportunity to settle scores. One such was Henry Beesley, ejected from Swerford for profanity after the war, but reappearing to cause trouble a dozen years later in an incident reported to the House of Lords:

> One Beesley and other insolent Persons came into the Church of Chipping-Norton . . . and when Mr Stephen Ford . . . was going to exercise the Duty of his Place by Prayer and Preaching, they fell violently upon him, pulled him by the Neck and Throat and by the Hair of the Head, and wounded him and pulled him out of the Church, calling him 'Rogue and Rascal' and other opprobrious and odious Words without any Cause or Provocation of the said Mr Ford, and afterwards proudly and insolently said: 'Let the Justices of the Peace relieve him, or do any Thing herein for him at their Peril'.

The conclusion is inescapable: the well-intentioned reforming zeal of the puritan authorities culminated in one of the most chaotic periods in the chequered history of the Church in England as the war brought so many things to a head, as bewildered parishioners saw bigotry, contention and politicking replace the traditional ministry, and as their parson, not necessarily young and resilient, was harried, plundered, perhaps physically assaulted by oafish troops or unruly villagers, often evicted and eventually replaced by an unwelcome, possibly short-lived intruder. And shortly after, at the Restoration, when the recently-appointed newcomers were called upon to subscribe in person to an oath of loyalty to the new regime and many promptly resigned rather than face ignominious dismissal or only grudgingly 'conformed', the hard-won puritan achievements were put into reverse.[6]

ENDGAME: 1645

THE WAITING GAME

Although it did not necessarily appear so to the combatants, early 1645 appears in retrospect a period of waiting for both sides. In some quarters, even at Oxford, there was talk of a negotiated peace, but with the King's various armies as strong as ever, the King himself intransigent following the execution of Archbishop Laud and buoyed up by victories in Scotland, and Parliament, frustrated by recent failures and internal dissension, beginning to pin fresh hopes on the formation of a vastly superior 'new model' army, there was little hope of averting further violence. Public executions of captured soldiers by both sides at Abingdon and Shrewsbury in January and February were not a good omen for peace. But although early 1645 saw no major campaigns in the region under discussion, this meant no lessening of military activity. Military stalemate in the English Civil War never implies inaction at local level or respite to the war-weary local community, and during this period, as we have seen, the northern Cotswolds royalist garrisons were being consolidated and attacked, small towns everywhere were liable to be violated, as at Kilsby, Chipping Norton, Chipping Campden and Culham, Bridges at Warwick and Purefoy at Compton continued their usually highly successful raiding, the Campden and Banbury Royalists were as aggressive as ever, and Compton was stormed once and was, it was rumoured, likely to be so again. Even the temporary absence of troops on duty elsewhere could attract opportunistic strikes from others. For instance, when Warwick garrison's cavalry left to assist Brereton in the north in February, they had got no farther than Stafford when Worcestershire Royalists promptly looted the tiny hamlet of Loxley and another party from Banbury the very outskirts of Warwick itself.

Perhaps more than anywhere else in the region Banbury continued to be the focus of violence throughout a wide radius. Its battered castle, a section of whose walls had collapsed 'towards the Markett place', was being repaired by artisans using 'great stoare of Ladders [from] all ye Country round'. Inside, life was gruesome for plague was rife,

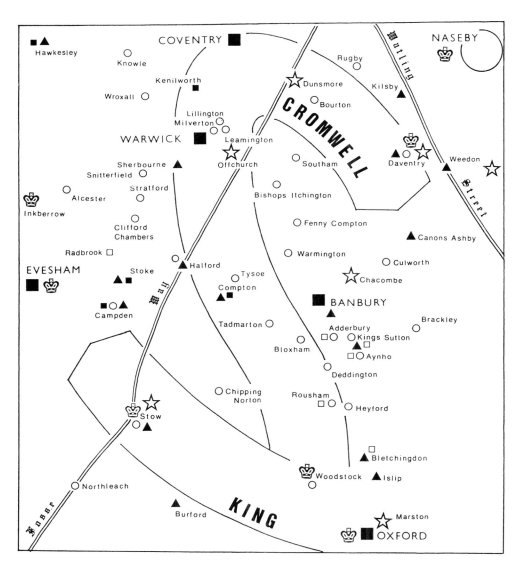

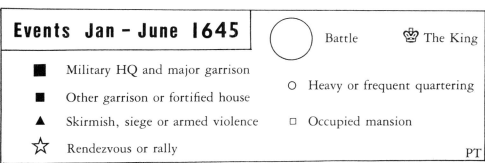

Events Jan – June 1645

◯ Battle   ♕ The King

■ Military HQ and major garrison

■ Other garrison or fortified house

▲ Skirmish, siege or armed violence

☆ Rendezvous or rally

○ Heavy or frequent quartering

□ Occupied mansion

PT

with three or four soldiers dying daily according to parliamentarian spies, with officers too being buried. Notwithstanding the sickness groups of wretched prisoners were herded together 'confined to a close chamber . . . and soe wanting ayre', while others had escaped, the marshal responsible being promptly arrested and facing hanging in Oxford. The governor himself, Colonel Anthony Greene, had recently died and been replaced by Sir William Compton. The unfortunate town itself was being further vandalized:

> They are pulling downe the Markett place and other howses neere the Castle, and are dayly at worke in making trenches and bulwarks and repaireing the breaches wch were about it.

To remedy the chronic lack of gunpowder saltpetre was being dug in Banbury and Astrop and a gunpowder manufactory hastily built nearby. Throughout the district troops were everywhere. To the north, in constant communication with Warwick and Northampton, parliamentary units still not dispersed since their abortive siege of Banbury the previous autumn lingered in many villages – Cromwell's alone were scattered at Southam, Fenny Compton, Tysoe, Warmington – with the able Colonel Lidcot keeping watch at Daventry, while royalist units dominated the southern approaches to the town. Besides those in Banbury itself under Sir William Compton and Sir William Farmer, more were posted at Aynho and Kings Sutton in January, the Earl of Northampton with his regiment at Lord Wilmot's manor in Adderbury in February and again at Adderbury, Bodicote, Aynho and Deddington in March. Large troop movements were frequent. 'Thousands' of Royalists were reported leaving Deddington in late February by a parliamentarian observer. As though this were not enough, relative newcomers were also moving into the district. One such was the Royalist Colonel Richard Palmer, who transferred his quarters from Bletchingdon to Sir Robert Dormer's splendid new house at Rousham in the New Year. Palmer's detachment trudged north along the Banbury road carrying all their bedding, covering their redeployment by the now familiar expedient of destroying bridges along the Cherwell and making fords impassable, and coming under attack by roving Parliamentarians who beat up their quarters on one occasion. By early February the move was completed, an enemy scout reporting that sixty royalist cavalry 'secure themselves every night in a gentlemans house in the town', described as 'a very strong [i.e. fortified] house of Sir Robert Dormer's'. The shooting holes bored into the oak doorway of the Great Hall that are still visible today are no doubt a reminder of this occupation. The build-up also included parliamentarian newcomers to the district, like Captains Ennis, Goodman and Abercrombie, sent by Sir Samuel Luke to the Aynho district on 5 February, and (perhaps connected) instructions sent to Colonel Nathaniel Whetham at Northampton in March for the establishment of a rival garrison somewhere near Banbury.

The whole district was militarized to the extent that the movement of any group of soldiers in a given direction was likely to attract a counter-attack from an enemy patrol collecting 'contributions' and generally looking for trouble: the Northampton committee complained to Sir Samuel Luke at Newport Pagnell on 25 February that 'those of Banbury watch all opportunities to do us mischief'. A typical skirmish was the one at Kilsby at the end of January already reported, but there were many others. On 2 February, for example, units of the Adderbury and Kings Sutton Royalists were sent to Aynho to fortify the great house when their colleagues at Kings Sutton were attacked by Parliamentarians from Northampton. For a time the royalist cavalry loitered at Aynho, improvising a drawbridge, barricading themselves in the Cartwright home by night, drinking in nearby taverns by day and hurriedly retreating to Nell and Twyford Bridges whenever a substantial threat from the enemy seemed likely. Although much of the reporting is partisan it is often circumstantial enough to appear trustworthy:

> At Kings Sutton there lye about 50 Dutch men of the Kings souldiers comanded by the Lord Comptons Major, — they dig Salt peeter. They ly in Mr [Richard] Kenricke's house & their horses in the kitchin. Some of the rescells are at Astrup.

Shortly after the Aynho company was reported to have withdrawn back towards Bloxham, breaking Nell Bridge on the way. Many other royalist sorties were reported towards Rugby and Daventry, a major rendezvous took place at Chacombe, there was violent skirmishing near Weedon and a particularly hard-fought encounter at Kingsthorpe on 18 March from which the four Compton brothers were reported by the court newspaper, *Mercurius Aulicus*, to have been lucky to emerge alive. William Compton's horse was shot from under him, Spencer was at one moment surrounded by eight of the enemy, Charles narrowly missed death when an enemy pistol failed to fire and the earl himself had his head-piece beaten off. All four brothers eventually escaped, but not before they had 'charged and rescued one another so often, that if any of the foure had beene absent, one of them might have fallen'. A minor battle took place near Daventry when Sir Marmaduke Langdale left Banbury to relieve Pontefract and was attacked. According to a royalist source the Comptons sallied to the rescue, routed the Parliamentarians on Borough Hill outside Daventry and chased them to Weedon. At times the Banbury Cavaliers struck west as well as east, on one occasion seizing the consignment of cloth in the dramatic encounter at Halford already reported. Most of the manor houses in the district were occupied by soldiers at one time or another: besides Aynho and Rousham, Richard Kenrick's at Kings Sutton and William Cobb's and Lord Wilmot's, both at Adderbury, were all mentioned in scouts' reports. There was such a congregation of Royalists in the Banbury and Chipping Norton districts that a nervous Coventry committee was alarmed at the prospect of a renewed attack on Compton Wynyates in late February and appealed to Luke at Newport Pagnell for help for 'our friends now in danger', while the expected arrival of Rupert at Stratford and then, perhaps, Banbury, announced by Luke on 6 March, did little to calm fears. But neither threat, surprisingly, materialized. Thus the general picture for the first months of 1645 is one of sporadic skirmishing, of a futile expenditure of energy and resources with no overall strategy, and of militarily unproductive alarms and excursions. The New Model Army was not yet ready and the King, although reportedly preparing to take to the field, was as yet stationary in Oxford. Circumstantial evidence occasionally offers a revealing insight into the amateur and haphazard nature of military logistics still common even at this relatively late stage of the war. A letter from Northampton written by an anonymous parliamentarian soldier whose company was travelling from some undisclosed point in the south-east to Massey at distant Gloucester, for example, blames his unit's slow progress over such vast distances not on wasteful use of resources or fundamentally flawed organization but, touchingly, simply on an English April:

ADDERBURY EAST MANOR-HOUSE, NEAR BANBURY. The much-altered home of the staunch Royalist, Lord Henry Wilmot, must have been almost continuously occupied by the Cavaliers throughout the war. The district was dominated by the royalist garrison at Banbury, and witnessed repeated fighting and military occupation, in some of which Wilmot was prominent. (Photo: Banbury Museum)

> My Colonell & all of us came safe and well to Northampton this Thursday. We would have got to Warwick in all likelihood, had wee not been yesterday in the after-noone so sorely weather-beaten by a storme of haile, snow, wind and raine, and all in our faces, without so much as a hedge-shelter, that we were glad to make Bedford Towne our Haven till this morning. I hope wee may come as well to Glocester by Saturday night or Sunday morning, if God permit.

Although the Northampton to Warwick road was reported safe, protected by the parliamentary detachments referred to above, Bard's notorious Campden garrison gives him pause for thought for the final stage as he concludes, with English understatement, 'I feare the way is something dangerous from Warwick to Glocester'.

With Cromwell and Fairfax still far to the south, one of their prickliest colleagues, the Scots veteran Major-General Lawrence Crawford was ordered to go from Aylesbury to protect the east Midlands, and soon decided to take matters into his own hands and 'have a bout' with the Earl of Northampton. From Northampton Crawford quartered at Rugby on 31 March (*Note*: not Cromwell, as is sometimes claimed) and arranged a rendezvous on Dunsmore Heath in order to 'fall on them', inviting Colonel Lidcot's and

Sir Robert Pye's troops to join him 'at some place betwixt this [Rugby] and Adderbury or Aynho'. As so often, however, there was no unanimity and precious time was lost when Lidcot proposed an equally attractive variant. With a rendezvous at Brackley and Helmdon ingeniously arranged to coincide with Banbury market-day (still flourishing, apparently, in spite of everything!) they could, he argued, 'happily have a blow for ye Castle' [Banbury] with 'some small Petarrs & Granadoes'. In the event, plans petered out when they were discovered by 'a boy from Daventry'. Aided by detachments from Colonels Sheffield, Dalbier and Behr, Crawford crossed the Cherwell at Cropredy on 1 April, but learning that they had lost the initiative the soldiers fell to plundering the Adderbury and Middleton Cheney districts instead of assaulting Banbury. Crawford quartered at Culworth before eventually withdrawing towards Stony Stratford a few days later, receiving complaints about his troops' behaviour as he did so. More successful, as usual, was the energetic John Bridges at Warwick, who although only recently having to admit, with perhaps a shade of disappointment, that 'these parts are very barren of news', was now able to relate to a friend in London a dramatic exploit at Sherbourne, outside Warwick, on 18 April. His dispatch of a large consignment of gunpowder and match to his colleague Massey at Gloucester had provoked Prince Maurice, the newly-appointed commander of Worcestershire and adjoining counties, into assembling a strong force to seize the convoy. Frustrated at arriving too late at Quinton, the convoy having already passed 'some houres before', and aware that most of the Warwick cavalry were well out of range escorting the now distant carts, the Royalists decided to compensate for their disappointment by pillaging the defenceless countryside. Extorting £100 from Stratford and emptying the fields of all available cattle *en passant*, they reached Longbridge, within sight of the enemy battlements, and 'drew up and faced Warwick upon an hill about a mile distant from the Towne', unaware that the depleted Warwick garrison was temporary home to passing Worcestershire and Newport Pagnell Parliamentarians destined to reinforce Massey at Gloucester. The combined allies under Bridges and his able colleague Hawkesworth routed the Royalists in a vicious running battle lasting four hours through the springtime lanes about Sherbourne, with much close combat graphically described, as when 'Captain Halford . . . expressed much courage, and . . . strucke off [Major Pilkington's] head-peece and perriwigge with the first blow, and with the next gave him a wound [to] his head . . .'. Many Cavaliers were killed, others fled towards Campden and Evesham, 'many without Hats, others without Horses, and few with swords . . .'. The spoils included fifty prisoners, over a hundred horses, the herd of frightened cattle, and 'one cart load of broad cloath'.

All told, however, this was a frustrating period for both sides, with no clear advantage to either. At the end of March the long-expected departure of the King from Oxford had still not materialized, sufficient numbers of carts not having been collected, and the Earl of Northampton's regiment, later to accompany the King, was still stationed near Banbury awaiting orders. Finally, a hint of imminent action came in mid-April when Northampton ordered his regiment to abandon quarters to the east of the Cherwell and regroup on the west, ready to join the King. But although the Parliamentarians had as yet made no headway against the royalist domination of the entire Banbury district, at least one unusually percipient journalist was confident that royalist supremacy was nearing its end:

They are very busie in Fortification at Banbury, as if they meant to make it impregnable. It is their wisest course; for if Oxford miscarry (as it may) then nothing remains for them but Banbury to hold life and soule together in the heart of the kingdome.

Unbeknown to the author and to anyone in that ravaged countryside the prelude to Naseby was about to begin, and justify his optimism. For both sides, the waiting was almost over.[1]

'A RUMBLING IN THE AIR': THE PRELUDE TO NASEBY

What some far-sighted contemporaries themselves suspected was to be the ultimately-decisive campaign of the first Civil War began on 7 May 1645, when the King left Oxford for the last time on the journey which was eventually to lead to Naseby. He was buoyed up by the prediction of the court astrologer of a splendid royal victory and imminent retribution for the rebellious city of London, though a rival parliamentarian astrologer saw a very different picture in the heavens:

God is on our side. The constellations of heaven after a while will totally appear for the Parliament, and cast terror, horrour, amazement and frights on all those damne-blades now in armes against us.

Charles travelled directly north-west via Woodstock, Stow, Evesham and Bromsgrove intent on relieving Chester, being besieged by the tenacious Sir William Brereton, though not until a month later, when the situation had changed dramatically, was the new parliamentary army under Sir Thomas Fairfax to march north, into Northamptonshire. Taking Oxford as the point of departure, therefore, each of the main armies acted in a manner that seemed likely to spare the central Midlands further disruption. But that would be to ignore many of the characteristic factors of campaigning already amply illustrated in the foregoing chapters: the incessant demands for supplies from far as well as near; the likely involvement of far-flung garrisons; the necessity of calling upon distant reinforcements; the hasty regrouping of available regional units which time had dispersed; the precautionary alerts in anticipation of an enemy change of strategy; the effects of rumour or disinformation; the very eagerness of regional commanders to join the fray. Above all, a distant event – the abandonment by Brereton of his attempt on Chester – was to alter the entire strategy of both camps. Although at the outset, therefore, neither main army moved towards the south Midlands, but rather away from it, the entire region was unable to remain untouched by events as they unfolded.

Long before the King left Oxford, indeed, the intended departure began to have repercussions on even quite distant parts as rumour began to do its work. In mid-March carts were being requisitioned from Souldern and Fritwell and, no doubt, countless other places, when 'it is generally reported . . . that [the Royalists] intend to besiege Newport [Pagnell] & Northampton both together'. It was common knowledge in

March that 'great preparation' was being made for the King's departure, though his ultimate objective remained unclear: 'Tis generally said the King in person with Prince Rupert is resolved to the field with a Horse Army into the North', admitted one correspondent before concluding, 'but [it] is rather beleived they will attempt to breake into the Associated Counties' [East Anglia]. The uncertainty of the King's plans filled the parliamentary authorities with near-panic. In one measure among many others large reinforcements were ordered urgently on 10 April from Aylesbury, Newport and Northampton to march towards Warwick to be at Massey's disposal there, while some of Massey's own units began moving towards Stratford. Already arrived at nearby Snitterfield was Sir Robert Pye's regiment, enjoying free quarter at the expense of the vicar Edward Nicholls, putting two thousand horses to graze the clergymen's 'mowing groundes', drinking six barrels of beer and taking whatever provisions they needed. 'All this', the vicar carefully stressed, 'I will affirme uppon Oath'. Meanwhile, as we have seen above, the build-up of forces in the Banbury district in the early months of 1645 had already meant sporadic and at times vicious skirmishing in eastern parts.

The King's immediate intentions soon became clear. On 3 April parts of Worcestershire were sent detailed instructions by Prince Maurice, his deputy, to prepare for the privilege of receiving the royal army, 'who are to make their rendezvous in this Country very speedily'. The warrant reminded the High Constable that:

> . . . whereas the time is now approaching for his Majesties Army to draw into the field, and his Majesty having given commands that there be great store of biscuit bread speedily provided out this County,

'bushels of good, sweet, sound and marketable wheat' as well as 'shovels, spades, pick axes and such like Instruments' were instantly required. The following day, to avoid any possibility of uncertainty, 3,000 bushels of wheat, 500 implements, and huge quantities of hay, straw, oats and beans were specified, all to be 'laid in at the Cross Inn [Worcester], His Majesties Horse quarters for his own Retinue'. Furthermore, 'a great number of teams for the necessary carriage of the Army' was required. Accordingly, '28 sufficient and serviceable Teams of horses, with 5 able Horses at the least, a strong and able Cart and two Carters with each Team', including a three-day supply of food for themselves and their horses, were to be brought to College Green in the city on Friday 11 April. Nor did the matter end there, for attempts were promptly made by Parliament to nullify the royal command by threatening the hapless constables with imprisonment if they complied with the Royalists, and as the King's progress began there is evidence of further harassment and impressment of villagers, as in the Tredington warrant already quoted. The whole series of warrants and counter-warrants to these unfortunate Worcestershire constables offers a clear picture of the local disruption caused by the mere approach of an army through a locality, without taking into consideration the depredations of that army once it arrived.

News of the King's long-expected departure from Oxford galvanized Parliament into an attempt to devise something approaching a concerted strategy based on the fledgling New Model Army, though the King's ultimate objective was still unknown and plans had to remain flexible enough for several different eventualities. The basic plan was to mobilize the Midlands to prevent the King's return south, while besieging the supposedly-weakened Oxford, using Parliament's two ablest commanders, Fairfax and Cromwell, but supported by other dependable veterans like Browne. Regional garrison commanders like Massey at Gloucester, Bridges at Warwick, Luke at Newport Pagnell and Whetham at Northampton could be counted upon to lend whole-hearted support, while other officers like Whalley, Fiennes, Lidcot, Pye and Crawford were permanently in the field eager for action. None of this is to imply a formal council of war to finalize such a strategy, and even if there had been one the dispersion of forces, the ever-present difficulties of communicating rapidly over long distances, the unreliability of some units, poor intelligence and, not least, conflicting counsels and the need to keep options open would have largely invalidated it. Improvisation and sheer chance gained many a day in the Civil War, as the incident near Warwick related above amply illustrates. When Luke, already beset by severe discipline problems among his long-unpaid troops, had been instructed to send 200 horse from Newport to join Massey's destined for Warwick, the mutinous soldiers flatly refused to march. Forty-one of them banded together and presented a strongly-worded petition to their governor, protesting that they had no clothes, ammunition or supplies for their horses, and that if they continued to live on free quarter, 'the people may rise and cut our throats'. Disaster was only averted by the chance arrival of their pay at the last minute. They had eventually arrived at Warwick only to find that their Aylesbury and Northampton colleagues, instead of awaiting them at Warwick, had already gone on to join Massey. Bridges was able to mollify the disgruntled Newport men by using them successfully in the minor but satisfying victory at Sherbourne. Only weeks later, nevertheless, the Newport governor was admitting 'the falling away of 300 foot from the garrison' and anticipating further desertions at harvest time for 'want of husbandmen'.

Cromwell, who had been cooperating with Fairfax in the south, had already been ordered by the London committee on 20 April to march north to interpose his forces and those of Fiennes between Oxford and the Royalists under Prince Rupert on the Hereford–Worcester borders to prevent the King supplying them with ordnance, and had carried out such a successful harrying campaign about Oxford throughout April and early May as to open up the possibility of bottling up the King at Oxford, an elated Massey boasting that Cromwell had 'almost frightened them out of their wits at Oxford'. In the event, however, neither his capture of Bletchingdon, nor the serious clashes at Islip, Bampton, Faringdon and Burford, had prevented the King leaving Oxford on 7 May, holding a council of war at Stow on 8 May and progressing into Worcestershire. Cromwell duly informed his superiors on 9 May that he was 'resolved to follow them', but by the time the King had reached Evesham the parliamentary committee had decided instead, with perhaps some foresight on this occasion, to order Cromwell north into Warwickshire. Torn between conflicting options and with the New Model Army fully occupied in the south, however, Parliament's committee waited another ten days before recalling the recently-appointed supreme commander, Sir Thomas Fairfax, from the south-west to besiege Oxford. With General Richard Browne ordered to garrison Bletchingdon, and with Massey preparing to storm north from Gloucester to capture Evesham and then reported by Luke to be marching from Burford to join Fairfax, things seemed in place for a spectacular showdown.

Ironically, as Parliament struggled to maximize its resources, so the Royalists perversely frittered theirs away. Their councils of war were still too often hampered by personal jealousies between rival commanders, whereas Parliament increasingly made strenuous efforts to remedy the obvious defects in their own cumbersome organization. Recently two major, far-reaching steps had been taken towards Parliament's ultimate victory, namely, the passing of the celebrated Self-Denying Ordinance to remove aristocratic generals from the army and replace them by trained professionals, and the creation of the New Model Army, properly administered and financed. Meanwhile, at a council of war at Stow-on-the Wold on 8 May where, curiously, almost exactly a year ago Waller and Essex had made the fatal decision to separate their forces, the Royalists decided that Goring should march to the south-west, leaving the King and Rupert to go north to relieve Chester and deal with the Scots. As they marched north they seriously weakened their local strongholds by withdrawing most of their forces from their garrisons to augment the main army, and one immediate result was that the redoubtable Massey, recently promoted general of the parliamentary western forces, promptly seized Evesham on 26 May, little more than a fortnight after the King had vacated it. The loss of Evesham, cutting the vital royalist link between Wales, Worcester and Oxford, was considered by Clarendon as 'an ill omen to the succeeding summer', and such indeed it was soon to prove. The King's march northwards along the Worcestershire–Warwickshire borders was accompanied by the usual plundering and by the destruction by fire of the string of stately homes that has already been described. As the King and Prince Rupert moved past Birmingham into Staffordshire and Shropshire parliamentary commanders waited anxiously for news of their latest moves, in particular Sir William Brereton in Cheshire, increasingly apprehensive about the approaching royalist tide. On 14 May he told Cromwell that he was expecting the King's arrival 'daily', and was counting on the 'uniting of our forces', if possible reinforced still further by Fairfax: 'It were to be wished that Sr. Tho. Farefax his Army were hastned after you'. But these hopes were not to be realized.[2]

As noted above, the parliamentary committee in London had instructed Cromwell on 10 May to abandon pursuing the King directly into Worcestershire and instead to march 'toward Warwick'. He lost no time in obeying, and accompanied by General Richard Browne left Woodstock on 11 May, was joined by reinforcements from Hertfordshire and Buckinghamshire and was soon reported to be 'upon his march after the enemy towards Warwickshire'. Although they allowed him some freedom of action, Cromwell's specific instructions were not to engage the enemy 'unless you see apparent advantage', but rather to concentrate on a potential royalist threat to East Anglia and, eventually, a junction with the Scots in the north. Given the complexities and uncertainties of the situation, these instructions were perfectly sensible. The King's army had a good start, and although not large included the regiments of Prince Maurice and the formidable Rupert. It must be remembered that the King's ultimate intentions were unknown, and that although the consensus was that his 'design' was for the north of England, several alternative contingencies had to be catered for. It was entirely feasible that Charles should either double back to Oxford, as he had done the previous year before Cropredy, or alternatively strike suddenly east into the heart of parliamentarian country, threatening Warwick and Coventry or even East Anglia. The impression is sometimes given that the King marched directly north to Market Drayton keeping well to the west, but as usual his army was far from compact and dispersed across a wide area, and by the time he had reached Birmingham on 14 May some of his forces were beginning to stray considerably to the east, being reported by Cromwell himself to be not only near Wolverhampton and Stourbridge but at Sutton Coldfield, Coleshill and Lichfield. To send Cromwell to shadow the King to the east and 'observe his motions' was a natural precaution until the New Model Army could be fully assembled, and if Fairfax could meanwhile capture Oxford and advance to join Cromwell in Warwickshire and the Scots be persuaded to move south, the King could be trapped between Brereton in the north and the newly-deployed Midland forces, and a spectacular transformation of Parliament's fortunes might result. Such, crudely, must have been the thinking at the outset, as Cromwell moved obediently north from Woodstock.

As for Brereton, he saw the King's march north as a tactical error which played into their own hands, and was convinced that ultimate victory was perhaps at long last in sight. He tried hard to convince the distant committeemen in London with sound reasoning:

> In my judgmt this resolution of his Mties [to march to Chester] gives much advantage to your service, and the finall periode of these unnaturall Warres, if this oportunyty might bee made use of. Doubtlesse [if] the Scottish and Northerne Armies and Lieut. Collonell Cromwells Forces did hasten this way, the King and his Army beeing drawne into this Angle of the Kingdome might bee surprised before they grow too numerous.

It seemed to many, indeed, a time for optimism about the approaching climax. Lord Digby, one of the King's most sanguine advisers, confidently predicted 'the last blow in the business'. At the heart of it all Major John Bridges, recently promoted governor of the town of Warwick as well as of the castle, watched the parliamentary troops converging on Warwick for the showdown and saw a sky pregnant with meaning: 'there is a rumbling in the air as if it were great; yet I cannot tell where it is . . .'. The commanders in the field sensed what was less obvious to the committeemen: that the countdown to Naseby had begun.[3]

CROMWELL IN WARWICKSHIRE

The whole episode of Cromwell's fruitless expedition into Warwickshire before Naseby has provoked surprisingly little comment, and most historians and biographers have simply ignored it or managed to convey the impression that Cromwell marched directly to Naseby from Oxfordshire. The fact is that although it produced no 'battle', the episode offers fascinating insights into the complexities and ironies of the war, as well as adding more strands to the rich fabric of fact and speculation in the folk memory of a district once again subjected to the depredations of marching soldiers. Leaving Woodstock on 11 May, Cromwell and Browne reached north Oxfordshire the next day, Browne pausing for some unknown reason at the Heyfords (awaiting reinforcements?), Cromwell quartering at Tadmarton, west of Banbury. At this stage, with the Earl of Northampton absent accompanying the royal army, the general parliamentarian build-up in the district further intensified by a new influx of Northampton troops 'now abroad toward Banbury . . . this 3 or 4 days' and, not least, the brisk arrival of Cromwell, there was a real prospect of a renewed onslaught on the war-torn Banbury Castle, full of sick and feuding Royalists. On 15 May Sir Samuel Luke spoke of the possibility of 'a new siedge before Banbury', and there were rumours of a secret plan which Cromwell had devised. Perhaps surprisingly, however, the assault never came. As for the apparently curious choice of two insignificant villages for billets, speculation is rarely profitable, as quarter was usually determined by simple, on-the-spot convenience. But Tadmarton was conveniently close to Broughton and offered Cromwell, perhaps, the choice of the Fiennes's ancestral home or, alternatively, of commandeering Tadmarton rectory, by far the largest house in the village and long abandoned by the eighty-two-year-old parson, Ambrose Sacheverell, an absentee Royalist awaiting the inevitable sequestration. Coincidence or not, both the Heyfords too presented a similar case of easily-requisitioned comfortable rectories with royalist parsons, Thomas Cole and John Hungerford, facing ejection, while for good measure, the district boasted a collection of tithe barns of cathedral-like proportions, at Adderbury, Swalcliffe, Tadmarton and Upper Heyford, potentially useful as troop dormitories. One of Lord Saye's local spies, a scout named Parris, 'well acquainted about Banbury side', had, moreover, been active the previous week on some mysterious mission.

Either marching together or keeping in such close contact as to inspire one parliamentary journalist to compare them, with fulsome piety, to David and Jonathan, Cromwell and Browne crossed into Warwickshire and continued through Warmington, a favourite hill-top position already used as a look-out post by both sides and the scene of skirmishing earlier in the war and, more recently, as quarters for soldiers taking part in the siege of Banbury. The usual food and provender were being supplied by nearby villages, Avon Dassett and Fenny Compton being merely two among others contributing to Cromwell and Browne, 'when they marched by with there Armie'. As usual too, neither plunder nor free quarter was limited to the wealthy. Although Richard Woodward at Avon Dassett contributed, so too did the Warmington carpenter and constable, Simon Davies, when Cromwell's Colonel Charles Fleetwood passed through on 13 May. The army was now in parliamentarian territory, and as it progressed north it was protected by numerous encampments and 'guards' being manned in nearby villages, at Ratley, Northend in Burton Dassett, Combrook, Shuckburgh and Ufton, where the parish scribe recorded his small community's contribution in a report evidently more painfully transcribed than usual: 'Payed by waye of Levie to wards ye Vittuling of a partie of Colonall Crumwells solldurs yt kept Coarte of Guard at the end of our Towne'. At Shuckburgh, twelve of Colonel Fleetwood's men were keeping guard comfortably ensconced in Sir Richard Shuckburgh's mansion, while the proximity of the ever-active George Purefoy at Compton and John Bridges at Warwick was additionally reassuring. Some reports speak of a rendezvous 'at Edgehill', and even a lightning meeting between Cromwell and Massey 'upon Broad-way Hills' at which Massey promised Cromwell all the help he could, before Cromwell and Browne passed through Southam, while a detachment under Major Anthony Buller separated to quarter at Stratford. Uncertain of the Royalists' intentions the parliamentary tactics were clearly to provide for every eventuality:

Our Armies lye on this side Coventry and on this side Warwicke, about Southam, Keington and Chadshunt; and some in Coventry, and as farre as Staffordshire . . .

Cromwell and Browne finally arrived at Warwick on 14 May to find it once again the hub of frenzied activity. The town and nearby villages were being swollen by the arrival of troops from seemingly everywhere, in anticipation of a decisive encounter with the King, who was himself now at Droitwich, within a day or so's march, but with reports that some of his troops were much nearer. An excited Warwick town newspaper reported the arrivals with undisguised pleasure:

There came a gallant army of horse and foot the 13th of this instant May into our quarters neare this towne, much encreased by additionall forces from Northampton, Newport Pagnell and Aylesbury. We understand that they are to follow the King; and it is yet uncertaine wch way the King will take . . . This army is able to give the King battell in our parts betweene Warwick and Coventry because we are all ready . . .

John Bridges was proud to entertain his two celebrated superiors, presumably in the great hall, on what must have been a sumptuous occasion heightened by a throng of commanders tensed for the expected battle: 'they were pleased with divers other of their officers to honor mee soe farr as to dine with mee yesterday [14 May]'. Whereas not so long ago John Bridges had complained to his regular confidant Sir Samuel Luke at Newport Pagnell that Warwick was unusually quiet, it was now Luke's turn to envy his colleague his centre-stage role in the coming drama:

I hope you will not expect newes from hence, when you are at the Fountaine, neere 2 armies the conjuncture whereof is expected hourely.[4]

As so often, however, the momentum that had built up was now lost in delays and confusion caused by Parliament's continuing uncertainty over the most effective strategy to counter the conflicting signals emerging from the royalist camp and their own divided counsels. The King's forces loitered apparently aimlessly nearby, and when Sir Robert Pye went from Warwick on a foraging expedition to provoke an encounter with them he returned intact none the wiser. Cromwell, Browne and Bridges were still expecting the arrival of their supreme commander, Fairfax, to precipitate matters: 'there will be no fighting until Sir Thomas Fairfax comes up, which is expected to be very suddenly', Bridges advised Luke on 15 May, while Sir Edward Nicholas at Oxford relayed the same information to Rupert. While Fairfax was still considerably south of Oxford, however, and the situation near Warwick unchanged, the parliamentary committee in London decided, for reasons which are not entirely clear, to reverse previous instructions. Whereas on 10 May John Fiennes had been told to remain near Oxford, he was now instructed, on 15 May, to join Colonels Vermuyden, Sidney and Pye and to march north towards the Scots, while Cromwell, although still allowed discretionary powers to act differently if new developments occurred, was ordered to return to garrison Bletchingdon and prepare for the siege of Oxford with Fairfax. These instructions were repeated with some urgency, when Cromwell was ordered to 'hasten' the dispatch of the northern-bound forces, and although there was a slight delay they were soon complied with, and Vermuyden, Fiennes, Pye, Sidney and Okey, with a combined force of about three thousand, quartered with Cromwell at Coventry on 18 May before moving off north via Coleshill. Cromwell's uncharacteristic delay in obeying these instructions seems to have been due in part to a commander's natural distaste at depleting his forces at such a critical time, to a reluctance to disappoint his colleague Brereton and, perhaps, to other, more obscure reasons. The orders to return to Oxford had still not, apparently, reached him on 18 May, when he wrote to Brereton from Coventry that he was still counting on Fairfax's arrival for the approaching climax:

> Wee lye here attending ye Kings motions, with Comands to dispose of ourselves according to ye direcons wch wee have received from ye Committee of both kingdomes with relacon to the mocons of ye enemy, as they shall be either ye one way or ye other. Sir Tho. Farefax is not yet come up, but wee have sent to him upon yor l[ett]re to hasten to us.

He urged Brereton to be patient, and to trust that the end of the war was in sight: 'God has sett ye way and tyme of putteing a period to ye miseries of this distressed kingdome. It is good for us to waite upon God . . .'. Brereton himself, meanwhile, who had 'long expected' Cromwell, was alarmed: '[I] wonder at the Cause of theire delay'. The new instructions eventually caught up with Cromwell, now at Kenilworth, on 19 May, when he wrote apologetically to Brereton:

> No man is more troubled (that I cannot advance to the assistance of friends) than myself. I must obey Comands, and truely, Sir, I am just now by orders wch I received this day to returne backe upon Important Service.

He assured his colleague, however, that large reserves of troops were stationed 'not farr from Rugby, and will be marching on Northwards towards ye Scottish Army' and 'to attend ye motions of the Kings Army'. The next day, a bitterly disappointed Brereton had no option but to accept 'yor being called backe by Order of Parliamt, wch wee must submitt unto'. Reluctantly, Cromwell abandoned hopes of forcing the King to a decisive encounter, and with his depleted force turned south once again. But in exactly one month he would be back at Warwick again, this time with Fairfax in the triumphant aftermath of Naseby.

Cromwell's actions during this somewhat tortuous episode have never been satisfactorily established. Luke implied that he had deliberately stalled on the new instructions, 'pretending himself to be too weak to deal with his Majesty', and added a further tantalizing twist to the mystery: 'As I hear, he has some further design thereabouts'. At the same time, it is clear that Cromwell, far from banqueting at Warwick for these two or three days, must have been almost continually in the saddle, visiting Warwick, Coventry and Kenilworth for urgent consultations while quartering, probably, at Southam in the meantime. The utterly reliable Bridges wrote on 15 May that Cromwell and Browne had 'layne neare Warwicke these 2 dayes', not at Warwick itself, and Browne at least was certainly at Southam for several days, receiving much provision there from Priors Hardwick and Wolfhampcote on 14 and 15 May, and writing to Luke from there on 16 May. Sir Edward Nicholas informed Rupert on 16 May that Cromwell 'marched yesterday from five miles beyond Banbury towards Coventry', which might suggest Warmington rather than Southam, though he told Rupert a few days later that 'Cromwell, with about seven thousand horse and foot, hath lain long about Southam, expecting Sir Thomas Fairfax; but on Sunday last [19th] . . . quartered at Killingworth [Kenilworth]'. A parliamentarian newspaper further adds that on Saturday 18 May, Cromwell and Browne were both:

> . . . at Southam; there was their head-quarters, their body quartering all thereabouts, within 10 miles of Coventrey, most part of them quartering in the enemies quarters neere Banbury.

Whatever the mystery surrounding Cromwell's precise movements, the effect of the presence of his army on the locality is not in doubt. No less than ten thousand soldiers, perhaps many more, given those already there before Cromwell's seven or eight thousand arrived, were scattered throughout the entire district, with the usual voracious demands on free quarter, food, drink and provender, the usual incidence of theft, and with teams of horses and oxen being seized whenever they could be found. Whitnash was simply one village among others where Cromwell's wagon-master arrived to requisition four teams for some undisclosed task lasting five days and nights, with two further teams demanded a little later for carrying ammunition for Fairfax for another four days. Evidence of the effect on individuals is supplied on every page of the parish accounts: when Leamington was invaded by large numbers of Browne's men for these three or four days Nicholas Sharples' experience was doubtless typical: he was forced not only to provide free quarter for them but suffered materially when 'they put threscore and five horses in my Close of mowing grasse 2 dayes & nights'. Troops were everywhere, many evidently under instructions to halt while their commanders consulted over the next move, enjoying the pause from the desperate marching, while others continued to converge on the district from afar. Some of Massey's Gloucestershire men continued east after capturing Evesham, and were promptly reported looting in Stratford and elsewhere. In tiny hamlets like Marton, where Captain Thomas Berry's men filled 'Mr John Walters groundes', virtually every inhabitant is often named as having quartered groups of soldiers. A troop of fifty men and horses was billeted at Long Itchington, and at Kineton:

> . . . there was a Guard kept in the Towne when Major generall Browne lay at Southam by severall Troopes of Lieutenant generall Cromwells and Col. Fynes Regts, for 5 nights from the 20th of May 1645.

Cromwell's cousin, Colonel Edward Whalley and his troop of horse, lingered at Bishops Itchington, recorded in a delightfully pointed comment, for 'Fowre nights and nine meales' by one inhabitant. At Bourton-on-Dunsmore and Draycote, the parish representative, clearly a fastidious and conscientious man, reported the burdens placed on his neighbours with unusual clarity:

> Captayne Pakers troope of horse under ye Comand of Corronell [sic] Cromwell, consisting to the number of Fourscore horse, had free qrtr in our p[ar]ish & theyre continued two Dayes & two nightes. The charges whereof (accounting as formerlie sixteene pence for everie horse & man for eyther nighte & day) ariseth unto in the whole Tenn powndes thirteene shillinges & Foure pence, pportionablie to bee divided amongst the Inhabitants as aforesayd.

As usual, units were often dispersed at considerable distances from their commanders. Many were north of Warwick: some of Luke's Newport troops had already reached

Stoneleigh by 19 May and it was perhaps one of these who stole a horse from John Fetherston's at Packwood. Nearby, practically every inhabitant of secluded Wroxall quartered soldiers during these days, typical instances being the 26 with their horses camped in Thomas Wright's field and the 120 horses over-grazing Theophilus Weall's meadow. Others of Cromwell's were farther off, at Meriden, Solihull and Knowle, where some quartered for sixteen days 'att William Ingaram's howse' or others, under Captains Wallington and Badger, for a very precise twenty-six days. Kenilworth too, already well used to unruly soldiers from the castle's parliamentary garrison, suffered a further influx as Cromwell himself arrived. The surrounding woods of the once mighty Forest of Arden, already depleted to help construct Warwick's defences, were continuing to shrink as one by one its great oaks were hacked down on the orders of the governor, Captain John Needham, for more fortifications, fuel for the castle's capacious fireplaces, private profit and the making of a new mill:

> About midsumer a little before Nasby fight weare fallne in the Chace by Sergeant England and others by the appoyntment of Captaine Needham to make a millne for the Castell two oakes, the tops and barkes sould by Serjeant England . . .

But it was seemingly at Cromwell's headquarters at Southam that the troop concentration was felt most by the unfortunate villagers, from the repeatedly-victimized royalist rector, Francis Holyoak, who complained of having to supply food, hay and straw to 100 cavalrymen on his own property, as well as to other soldiers elsewhere in town, to Widow Lyndon, who had to tolerate another 80, 'besides country teemes that came in to draw the Carriages'. One officer, Lieutenant Mercer, was accompanied by his wife for three days at John Hanslop's, and there is occasionally a touch of humour in the sombre litany of claims: one Southam inhabitant insisted on recording the theft from him of 'one Fleebitten gelding by Major Okey's souldiers who quartred att Napton on the hill', valued notwithstanding at £6. Southam's crossroads situation had already frequently attracted military activity to the area, and the unpopularity of the troops may be imagined from one single, undated report of an incident provoked by the arrival one day there of the Alcester parliamentary captain, John Cheshire:

> Paid to Leifft. Chesheere of Warr. [Warwick] uppon a demand which he Laid upon the towne when a quarrell [was] made by his souldiers with some of the townes men, att which tyme they wounded a townesman that he dyed prsently after . . .

Cheshire had demanded £5, and he now raised it to a punitive £13. 6s. in consequence of the obstructive villagers. These were indeed eventful days for the neighbourhood, yet they find little or no place in the standard histories. However, the villagers could not forget, and Cromwell's passage imprinted itself permanently on many a local place-name. At Frankton alone, 'Cromwell's House and Yard' and 'Oliver's Lane' perpetuated his memory until recent times, and today there are roads, lanes and streets named after him in Leamington, Kenilworth, Coventry, Rugby and, no doubt, countless other places in an area not traditionally associated with him.

Once having received his instructions to return to Oxford, at Kenilworth on 19 May, Cromwell lost no time in moving off. One rendezvous took place at Offchurch, soon to be reoccupied to saturation point shortly after Naseby, and another, presumably the main one, on Dunsmore Heath the following day, when Dunchurch alone reported 475 foot soldiers quartered in town, suggesting something of the secrecy and desperate urgency of these nocturnal journeys 'when they marched from beyond Coventry towards Daventry in the nighte'. Once at long-suffering Daventry, to be reoccupied and plundered by the King's own army only a fortnight later, Cromwell wrote briskly to Luke on 20 May to ensure that his soldiers' pay be sent to Brackley, where he would be 'tomorrow night'. Pay was apparently as problematical as ever. As one wise Parliamentarian commented blandly: 'some say the Foot are apt to run away when they receive much together; better they were paid weekly . . .'. Cromwell dutifully joined the recently-arrived Fairfax at Marston, outside Oxford, on 22 May. The same day, the King at Market Drayton learnt that Brereton had abandoned the siege of Chester, the action that triggered the *dénouement* of the first Civil War.[5]

'THE LAST BLOW': THE PATH TO NASEBY

Cromwell and Fairfax remained almost a week near Oxford, collaborating with Browne and Skippon on defensive measures and strategy for the projected siege of the city, during which dramatic news came of the King's sudden change of plan. With Chester no longer a priority and Oxford now under serious threat, Charles yielded to those arguing, like Rupert, that the best strategy now was to strangle the much-despised 'New Noddle Army' at birth by luring Fairfax from Oxford by threatening Parliament's lush north Midland and East Anglian counties. Recalling both Goring and Charles Gerard from the west to a rendezvous at Market Harborough, Charles accordingly struck swiftly east via Stone, Uttoxeter, Ashby and Loughborough. Thoroughly alarmed, Parliament ordered Massey, already at Evesham, to Burford and then to continue towards Fairfax, while Cromwell, on 26 May, was to march at once to protect East Anglia and remain at Ely, 'in case the King's forces should march that way'. Two days later these instructions were reinforced when it was learned that the King's advance was continuing, while forces from Coventry and Warwick were 'to send such forces [to Massey] as they can spare'. Fairfax for his part was to be ready to march at a moment's notice. Rupert's simple plan for luring him away from Oxford was beginning to work.

Relieved of Cromwell's threatening presence the King's eastwards march was not interrupted by any serious attempt from parliamentary forces deployed in theory for just that eventuality, before veering abruptly south to storm Leicester on 31 May. The brutality of the sacking of Leicester sent waves of horror through the entire parliamentary camp, and even more so the local community. Although Parliamentarians had a vested interest in alarmist propaganda, a letter from Northampton dated from the moment the Royalists arrived before Leicester's walls on 30 May paints a graphic picture of a terrified population transporting livestock and belongings to the supposedly safe haven of Coventry:

> Wee heard yesterday from Lutterworth that the country people about Lutterworth, Rugbie and the adjacent parts drive their horses and other cattell in great abundance, and carrie in other things to keepe from the Cavaliers plunder, in great abundance into Coventrey . . .

Fears were expressed that Northampton would be the next to fall, Bedford 'quickly destroyed' and Coventry itself in serious danger. The parliamentarian sheriff of Warwickshire, 'conceiving it not secure to live in any part [of the county] but in the City of Coventry', had already petitioned the House of Commons shortly before, to bring the desperate plight of its inhabitants to the attention of the politicians. A disgruntled Fairfax wrote despondently to his father about his enforced idleness at Oxford:

> I am very sorry we should speend our time unproffitably before a Towne whilst the King hath time to strengthen him selfe. It is the earnest desire of this army to folow the King; but the endeavours of others to prevent it hath so much prevailed.

Gorged with plunder and their appetite whetted for more, the triumphant Royalists moved at leisurely pace south from stricken Leicester towards Rugby, immediately subjected to a heavy tax, with the worst fears of the country people seemingly confirmed by news from far and near of renewed looting. Although usually undated, reports from Rugby of Prince Rupert's plunder and destruction, his burning of Shawell on the Leicestershire border to an estimated £235, and thefts from Hillmorton and beyond, all probably relate to this period. Typical was the experience of the tiny community of Flecknoe, one of the few parishes thinking it worth while to detail claims against the Royalists as well as the Parliamentarians. Having already recently contributed its share of carts and provisions for Browne and Fiennes at Southam and Shuckburgh on 15 May, while continuing to pay Banbury's Royalists well over £5 per week contribution, it now fell victim to renewed plundering by 'the King's party'. The merchant John Goode and his son Henry, for example, recorded losses of 21 yards of woollen cloth, pairs of sheets, jewels, 2 pairs of 'Holland drawers', 1 flaxen board cloth, 3 table napkins, clothes, linen and money, all 'taken away by violence', besides having to supply free board and lodging. A few months later, Flecknoe would be revisited, this time by Colonel John Desborough's Parliamentarians for another fortnight's free quarter, in October.

The King, meanwhile, settled comfortably at the Wheatsheaf, Daventry, on 7 June, arranging a hunting party at Fawsley Park while remaining, in Clarendon's genteel expression, 'in a quiet posture the space of five days'. The King's good humour was further boosted by the news that Fairfax had, as expected, abandoned the siege of Oxford and, as he told the Queen, that serious dissension had broken out in the parliamentarian camp, 'Fairfax and Browne having been at Cudgels, and his men and Cromwell's likewise at blowes together, where a Captaine was slaine'. On 8 June he wrote blithely to the Queen, 'My affairs were never in so fair and hopefull a way', and again, banteringly, to Sir Edward Nicholas the following day, 'If we Peripate-tiques get no more mischances then you Oxfordians ar lyke to have this Somer, we may all expect probably a merry Winter'. The feelings of this local community, only recently relieved of their occupation by hordes of Parliamentarians and now reinvaded by increasingly indisciplined Royalists, can only be imagined. One journalist described recent events:

[The Royalists] leave none of the fattest soyles, for they come by . . . [Market] Harborough, Rugby, and so dispersing themselves in Northamptonshire, take up their Head quarters at Deintry [Daventry], in the Road to Coventry . . . They spoil and destroy both Corn and Hay, saying they will make our Garrison seek further off for their provision, and boast how many fat Cattle they have made stop of . . .

Another told of widespread kidnapping for ransom. The Royalists:

. . . had made an utter desolation in most of the Towns between [Daventry] and Leicester, carrying and driving away not only many thousands of sheep and other Cattle, but even the Countrymen themselves, and those of the best ability, inforcing them to purchase their liberty at very deare rates, not permitting them to goe away without paying large summes of money.

From Daventry the entire country was once more being scoured, as far as Banbury in one direction and Northampton in the other: 'all on that side of the county [Banbury] was summoned to send in provisions to Daventry by 8 of the clock', reported Luke on 7 June, and two days later, 'The enemy continues still at Daventry, pillaging and plundering the country round, and this day came within half a mile of Northampton and drove away an herd of beasts'. It was further reported that the King 'indeavours to intrench himself about Daventry hils . . . and to that end have summoned the County to bring in Shovels and Pike-Axes'. One Parliamentarian summed up the situation quite simply: 'I am confident the counties of Stafford, Warwick, Leicester and Northampton have suffered more within six weeks than would pay our new army in six months'.[6]

DAVENTRY AND BOROUGH HILL. Situated near the busy Watling Street – Coventry route, Daventry saw much military activity throughout the war, quartering large numbers of soldiers and being repeatedly plundered in the process. In early June 1645 the King's forces 'possessed themselves of the hill neere Daintry and planted some of His Ordnance there', before withdrawing into Warwickshire and then towards Naseby, where they were annihilated. The engraving shows a view unchanged some 70 years later (see pp. 257–61).

The sack of Leicester concentrated parliamentarian minds, and 'many discourses were raised . . . [so] great was the discouragement'. Even moderates like Sir Simonds D'Ewes had been stung by the recent bungling of the London committee to condemn the appalling waste of Cromwell, forced into idleness at the critical moment, 'Wee are sure that the first Error was the calling back [from Warwickshire] or Colonel Cromwell'. D'Ewes was not alone in his criticism. In the first week of June a bluntly-worded petition from the Lord Mayor and Corporation of the City of London catalogued the mismanagement: 'The not compleating of Sir Thomas Fairfaxes Army . . . The calling back of Lieutenant Generall Cromwell and Major Generall Brown when they were pursuing the Enemy, The not advancing of our Brethren of Scotland into these Southern parts . . .'. Belatedly, Parliament sprang into action. On 2 June Fairfax was instructed to 'rise immediately from before Oxford' and then, crucially, allowed freedom as commander-in-chief to act as military judgement alone decided. On 5 June a relieved Fairfax moved purposefully into action to confront the King. Marching through the rain via Great Brickhill and Stony Stratford into Northamptonshire he sent to Cromwell at Ely to tell him of Parliament's acceptance of his own proposal that Cromwell be appointed commander of cavalry and second-in-command of the New Model Army, to warn him of the coming engagement and order him to rejoin the main army without delay. The governors of Coventry, Warwick and Northampton were also instructed to send whatever reinforcements were available. Continuing due north, Fairfax's scouts discovered the royal army amateurishly scattered on Borough Hill outside Daventry, with the King absent hunting, horses at pasture and the soldiers 'in no order, . . . having not the least knowledge of our advance'. Marching through the night via Bedford, Cromwell joined Fairfax at Kislingbury at a council of war at 5 a.m. on 13 June, being greeted by the soldiers with 'a mighty shout for joy of his comming'. Immediate preparations for an attack were made: what Lord Digby had accurately predicted as 'a battle of all, for all,' the battle that was to end the Civil War, was imminent.[7]

The course of the momentous battle near Naseby lies outside the thematic and geographical scope of the present work; the campaign and actual battle have often been subjected to detailed comment and analysis, from the descriptive contemporary tracts to the most recent scholarly study, that by Maurice Ashley. One little-explored aspect, however, merits comment, namely the confusion, uncertainty and initial reluctance to fight in the royalist camp, for which several explanations have been suggested. Not only was the King still awaiting the expected reinforcements from Goring and Gerard in the west (which never materialized) and the return of the detachment escorting the supplies to beleaguered Oxford, but, as Clarendon was the first to stress, the royal army was depleted by recent losses at Leicester, by the need to leave behind forces to garrison it and by major desertions among the plunder-laden Cavaliers. Clarendon's conclusion was that the royal army before Naseby was 'not a body sufficient to fight a battle for a crown'. Moreover, the King's camp was still (perhaps more than ever) deeply divided. Some were anxious to regain their comfortable quarters at Oxford, others were counselling a strike into the parliamentary heartland of the Eastern Association, while yet others were eager to march north, in accordance with the earlier plans – particularly in view of new, disturbing reports that the Scots were advancing on Nottingham. According to one parliamentarian report the Scots were the determining factor for the King, who accordingly 'threw downe his workes at Daintry . . . [and] marched away towards Coventry'. Moreover, the long-smouldering Banbury feud in the Earl of Northampton's family, already referred to in Chapter Six, was resurfacing with renewed intensity and now implicating leading royalist figures like Prince Rupert himself, the King's Oxford secretary, Sir Edward Nicholas, and Sir Christopher Hatton, the Comptroller of the King's Household, and prompting charges not simply of insubordination but treachery. At one point an exasperated Northampton had been about to take drastic measures: 'if itt had not bin settled, my Lord would have clapt up his brothers [in prison] att Banbury'; while even more serious, lurid accusations were made by one family retainer, Philip Willoughby, that at Daventry Hatton 'used forcible perswasions to the Earle to have wthdrawne him from ye Kings service' and collaborated with the detested parliamentary garrison at Northampton. Prince Rupert was evidently called upon to intervene and he responded, characteristically, by ordering his Oxford intimate, Colonel William Legge, to pacify one of the outraged brothers with a gift, rather like an attempt to pacify a sulky child by means of some expensive toy:

> Let Sir William Compton have one of the twelve field-pieces I left at Oxford. He deserves encouragement, for his brother and he are fallen out . . .

Meanwhile, a veritable anthology of insults was traded, from 'false rascally knave' and 'craftye close fellow' to 'hairebraind simple foole' and 'lyeinge jugling knave'. The King himself was described, with possibly unsuspected accuracy, as 'a most irresolute man, & soe false yt he was not to be trusted, [and] advised by none but knaves and fooles'. It is tempting indeed to see the acrimony of this Northampton–Hatton correspondence as part of the collapsing royalist morale on the eve of Naseby, as news of Fairfax's astonishing proximity reached the Royalists camped on Borough Hill, and it may well have been a contributory factor to the defeat at Naseby which remains puzzling to this day. For surprisingly, as Fairfax advanced north to meet the King, the royal army, instead of attacking before Fairfax could be rejoined by Cromwell, abandoned its dominant and carefully-entrenched position outside Daventry and split. Part of it at least, including many gun carriages, began a curious evasive action westwards into Warwickshire, retreating at least as far as Shuckburgh, and not initially (as almost invariably reported) moving directly north-east towards Market Harborough. Even on-the-spot parliamentarian commentators were puzzled at '. . . for what reason we know not . . . the Royal armies leaving their advantages and marching towards Southam'. Once Cromwell had joined Fairfax the Royalists again abruptly changed direction: 'we resolved to follow the enemy, who left the way to Warwicke, which was Woodland (for what reason likewise we know not), and wheeled to [Market] Harborough'. There is no doubt about this manoeuvre, several independent Parliamentarians reporting it, sometimes with incidental detail reflecting the royalist confusion. One for example, after reporting Fairfax's arrival at Kislingbury 'so privately that the Royall Army had little intelligence of him', describes how the Cavaliers marched away

> . . . through Daventry towards Southam, the road to Warwick, 3,000 Horse facing us on each side the Rivolet the next day. It was thought by their march they would divide, and go part into the North . . .',

before the King wheeled his entire army about towards Market Harborough on 'Friday in the afternoon.

No one could have been more relieved than the long-suffering inhabitants of the Daventry region – of Flecknoe, already looted by the Royalists, as already reported, of Willoughby, where the King's guards had been stationed, of Flore and Heyford, where the royalist horse-guard was billeted under Colonel Carey, of Staverton, home to more cavalry – to see the King's army veer away abruptly north-east towards Lubenham. The likelihood that Southam would stage the ultimate, as well as the initial, battle of the Civil War was that day a real one. As it was, the Royalists marked their departure by leaving a trail of havoc as far as Upper Shuckburgh, only recently vacated by John Fiennes's Roundheads, as faithfully recorded the following year by William Masters and the churchwardens in an account whose repetitiveness is an indication of how much such experiences rankled when added to the already exorbitant burdens of taxation:

> The Towne hath paid the £400,000 Subsedie and other paymts more then our abilities. But the acquittances being lost, for the Officers in whose handes they were beinge plundered by the Kinges Armie when his Mats Armie quartered in theise pts the Last Somer, and soe was the whole Towne then plundered and all our Acquittances beinge by the said Souldiers carryed away and torne to peeces, soe that wee doe not remember what wee did pay . . . And therefore wee cannot tell what to set downe. And for our Taxes, wee sett downe Lesse then wee have paid, and farr lesse for free quarter then it would amount unto if wee should have sett down any thinge neere the worth thereof.

One fascinating and little-known contemporaneous explanation of the strange indecisiveness in the royal army which, until so recently, had been supremely confident of annihilating the New Model Army, lies in the story related by a cavalryman from Newark of the King's receiving a supernatural warning. Charles had been awoken one night in great distress by an apparition resembling the executed Lord Strafford who warned him 'by no means to fight the Parliament army that was at that time quartered at Naseby, for in it was one whome the king should never conquer by arms'. Prince Rupert and others persuaded the King to dismiss this advice, and a resolution was taken to confront Fairfax. The spectre reappeared, however, to warn the King in the sternest terms that 'that would be the last advice he should be permitted to give him; but that if he kept his resolution of fighting, he was undone'. Fairfax's speed of pursuit had finally forced the reluctant King to fight, and what has been justly termed the royalist 'suicide' followed. It is easy to dismiss such a story as a wild farrago, and it certainly has the hallmarks of a wise-after-the-event concoction by, perhaps, a reader of Shakespeare's history plays. There is, however, nothing inherently implausible in that the King, whose father had burnt witches, kept astrologers and had himself sent his experts to investigate the Edgehill apparitions, should at moments of stress have had bad dreams to which he attached importance, particularly if they should feature the reproachful figure of Strafford (or, for that matter, the newly-executed Laud). Nor would royal dreams lack pliable court commentators willing to interpret them to the volatile and impressionable monarch. Given the formidable composition of the royal army with Rupert and a host of experienced veterans at its head, and its entrenched and virtually impregnable position at Daventry, the monumental ineptitude of the Royalists' pre-Naseby behaviour is indeed puzzling. The medieval dramatist would have ascribed the catastrophe quite simply to *hubris*.[8]

Epilogue: The Path from Naseby

T he importance of Naseby as a decisive turning-point was instantly recognized, being, as one contemporary journalist wrote, 'an afternoon for a Kingdome'. But such a grandiose national perspective meant little to either the soldiers surviving the slaughter or the long-suffering local community through whose impoverished villages they passed. Many royalist prisoners were promptly locked in Market Harborough church the same night, before being conducted to London, where some five hundred 'lodged under the blew Canopy of Heaven in Tuthill-fields, in the Artillery-Garden', but remnants of the King's army were still able to plunder Rugby again as they careered north towards Leicester once more, as reported by a shopkeeper, Edward Holden:

> When prince Robert [Rupert] went by to wards Leister the [sic] tooke wares out of my shope & other things out of the house, & Banbury men toke my wives money out of her purse at our towne.

Defeat improves no one's temper, and even with the Roundheads in hot pursuit time was still somehow found to settle scores, as Rugby's John Jones found:

> I were plundered by prince Rupert his forces, by my Lord of Northampt Regement & imprisoned by them, being but newly Relesed from my imprisonment at Nasby fight, being in the hands of the cavallers nine or tene dayes, which did prededuce me £20.

No sooner had the Royalists left Rugby than the pursuing Roundheads arrived for more free quarter and provision, under Major Temple, Captain Abbott and others, with nearby villages forced, as usual, to send ahead more food and drink: Long Lawford was one village sending beer to Leicester for Fairfax's men. Recapturing Leicester from the dispirited Royalists, Fairfax had to decide quickly how best to capitalize on his triumph at Naseby: whether to pursue the King, moving rapidly west through Ashby, Lichfield and Wolverhampton into Worcestershire, or to go south to deal with Hopton and Gerard. He opted for a cautious compromise allowing for both eventualities:

> The army marched toward Warwick, solicitous in nothing so much as which way they might best serve the Publike . . . being very doubtfull whether it were better to follow the King and hinder his recruiting, or go down to the West, to relieve the other part of our Army . . . But not willing to lose any time we marched on to Marlborough with a disposition either to go over at Gloucester toward the King in Herefordshire, or to move Westward and joyn with Col. Massey.

Fairfax's long and purposeful march south-west from Leicester after Naseby, averaging an impressive 20–30 miles a day, is usually dismissed in an admiring sentence or two as though its rapidity somehow insulated the country through which he passed from further damage. Far from that being so, however, one parish after another in a broad band on either side of the Fosse Way felt the full impact of yet one more marching army, from Lutterworth to Chipping Campden and beyond. Fairfax and Cromwell may themselves have maintained a brisk pace, but their soldiers were evidently less eager to do so, and as usual individual soldiers and units were constantly being relayed by others, so that villagers invariably experienced harassment before the commanders arrived and often long after they had left the district altogether. Villages at the northern end of the route were particularly unfortunate, as so often they were the same as those which had been occupied in the pre-Naseby weeks. Willey, for example, on the county border near Lutterworth, had indeed felt the impact of Fairfax's march before Naseby, when his life guard had quartered there on the eve of the battle, well in advance of Fairfax himself who was then at Guilsborough in Northamptonshire. Although many of the parish accounts are undated, making it impossible to reconstruct events precisely, Willey recorded 13 June very precisely among its entries relating to Fairfax, and unless it is an error, makes it clear that the village's occupation extended over several weeks both before and after Naseby. Typical was the case of John Beale, who billeted 'six gentlemen wth there men [servants] belonging unto his Exelencie Sr Thomas Fayrefax his life gard in June 1645, wth 19 horses, for diet, hay and provender'. Robert Steane likewise quartered another nine, William Wright a further eight, and so on. The situation at Churchover was similar, while nearly every inhabitant of Polesworth, well to the north, received groups of more soldiers, suggesting that precautions were taken to prevent a royalist escape northwards. Brinklow was particularly overrun as 'his Excellencie Sr Thomas Fairfax marcht through our Towne wth his maine bodie, and they had our pvision & tooke awaie all our Poultrey wth other things . . .'. John and Richard Mason lost linen, George Sedgley 'garden stuffe', Robert Sedgley the moletaker linen, woollens and clothes. The army's forward planning meant that Philip Hartley lost his entire team of horses:

> My Teame was taken at Rugbie, and enforced to Carrie Beare to Lillington for Sr Thomas Fairfax his head quarters, and 5 horses in my Teame were so tyred I could not recover them all Somer after.

The usual disturbances broke out, as another inhabitant recorded:

> Paid for victualls for Captaine Flowers Troope, by Capt. Flowers enforcement, besides mowinge grasse eate upp and trodden downe in our feild by them, & [they] would not quit, though ye Constable demaunded it.

Shortly after it was the turn of Wolston and Marston to endure similar experiences 'when Sir Thomas Fairfax Army came through our towne', while Coventry's contribution was considered generous enough to receive official recognition through a resolution passed in the House of Commons thanking its people for the help afforded Fairfax 'in his March by that Place'.

Following the broad corridor along the Fosse Way the New Model Army under Fairfax and Cromwell moved directly south-west towards Warwick, Fairfax establishing his headquarters at Lillington, and with all the nearby villages crowded with sometimes large detachments from the various regiments. Few of the villages were new to the experience of lodging soldiers. Most in the district, indeed, seem to have been almost continuously occupied since at least Cromwell's northward march in May. Bishops Itchington, for example, which now quartered Colonel Butler's men 'after Nasby Fight, two days and nights', had already received Whalley's cavalry the previous month. Wappenbury, besides sending provisions to Fairfax's 'own regiment' at Southam, also recorded Captain Gladman's troop of 100 horse and 85 more under Captain Berry, though since these entries are undated it is unclear whether these were before or after Naseby, or both. There is no doubt that troops continued to pass through the district long after the dust of Naseby had settled, irrespective of the precise whereabouts of Fairfax and Cromwell themselves. While Fairfax was still at Lutterworth on 20 June Colonel Nathaniel Rich was already well ahead, at Kineton, far to the south, where he quartered for three nights. Some unfortunate villages were selected by the respective quartermasters to receive particularly large numbers of soldiers. Milverton was occupied by Colonel Pickering's regiment of foot, comprising 700–800 men at the beginning of July, coming, evidently unhurriedly, from Naseby (fought on 14 June), by which time Fairfax himself was already in Dorset or Somerset. The parish officer carefully noted: 'The souldiers genally paid for their quarters. But some of the horsemen & Officers did not pay'. In addition, Henry Ireton, soon to become Cromwell's son-in-law, was also at Milverton:

> Quartermr genall Ireton (sithence Comissary genall to Lievetennt genall Cromwell) his troope, consistinge of about 120 men & 120 horse, about the moneth of June 1645, three dayes & nights.

At adjacent Leamington, Colonel Montague's eighty men quartered for two days and nights, and the church was used as a temporary dormitory and recruitment centre, many villagers noting, 'Pvision sent to a foot company that lay in our Church one night, wch marched unto Sr Tho. Fairfax'. One company lost no time in finding quarter at a Leamington alehouse, quantities of malt being specified by the owner, William Handcorne, as well as 'Beere which 60 of his exelencies foot dranke at there first coming to their quarters'. A typical experience was that of John Olney, who claimed for twenty-three horses put into his meadows, 'ready to mow', their owners stealing his sheep into the bargain. Sir Robert Pye's soldiers, no strangers to the district, quartered at Whitnash, and the village had also to provide two more teams for carrying ammunition for four days, while Wasperton was chosen for the unenviable distinction of holding one of the frequent rendezvous. This, near John Greene's house, cost him and his neighbours much food and drink and there was, inevitably, much theft. Robert Bradshaw lost a pint flagon, cheese, butter and bread, and his new pair of shoes, Thomas Handy complained that the soldiers 'cut my Geares, and tooke away Leathern haulters . . .'.

Continuing steadily south Fairfax's army approached Stratford. Fairfax himself stayed at Clifford Chambers on 23 June, reportedly with 'his whole army', though it is clear that units were scattered over a wide area, at Binton, Bishopton, Lighthorne and Moreton Morrell for example, with Charlecote billeting large numbers of his rearguard and a court of guard established in Shottery. It is not immediately obvious why Fairfax should choose to quarter at Clifford Chambers rather than take advantage of the resources of prosperous Stratford like many of his officers, unless the comfortable late medieval manor-house of the Rainsfords or the company of puritan ministers in the district were the attraction. As with Cromwell at Tadmarton the previous month, such decisions are likely to have been taken *ad hoc*, in the light of volatile local circumstances now often difficult to discover, but local mansions belonging to royalist sympathizers were still – perhaps more than ever – being requisitioned. One such, Radbrook, at nearby Quinton, was taken over at precisely this time when the Parliamentarian Captain Roberts was instructed to 'enter and garrison' the vacant home of the active Royalist Colonel Roger Lingen and to 'keepe and maintain in and about the same for the Defence of the country forty foote Souldiers and a Troope of three score Horse at the least' in July 1645. This was a district rich in detested catholic 'delinquents' whose estates were already sequestrated and whose wealth could conveniently be appropriated to support such garrisons. In Radbrook's case this involved redirecting the tithes of Ilmington and Quinton belonging to Francis Hodgkins and Edward Savage respectively, and the income of the Brents of Lark Stoke, Rainsfords of Clifford and, particularly satisfying, the King's favourite, Sir Endymion Porter, at Aston-sub-Edge and Mickleton. At Clifford Chambers, Henry Rainsford's manor-house stood temptingly vacant, its master having fled to join the King, and the parson, William Albright, was an uncompromising Puritan.

Meanwhile, Stratford itself was reoccupied by groups of Fairfax's and Cromwell's officers and their men 'when Sr Tho. Fearfaxe past by' or 'when Generall Fearfaxe went to the West'. Colonel Buller's company had already been stationed in the town on and off for some time, and there was now a new influx with the arrival for three or four days of the New Model's dragoons under Colonel John Okey, variously said to have been until recently a stoker in an Islington brew-house, a drayman and a tallow-chandler, and so exemplifying the new, democratic military thinking. The usual chorus of complaints arose as groups of up to twenty or so soldiers at a time with their horses installed themselves for board, lodging and grazing around the town centre in most of the more prosperous households. Most, like William Lindon in High Street, 'lost in grasse' in over-grazed closes, but some lost household goods too; a few, like Richard Smart in Wood Street, specified the 'drawing of Beere to Clifford for Genall Fearfaxe army', and everyone listed 'charges' of one sort or another. Elizabeth Wheeler's was one more house to be converted into a temporary guard post, while William Greene in Wood Street even complained that he had 'lost a Mare, shott by Sr Tho. Fearfaxe soldiers'. The Hathaways, Priscilla in Bridge Street and John at Shottery, once again recorded losses. Once more, however, it was Shakespeare's grandson-in-law Thomas Nash at the poet's New Place who was one of the most conspicuous victims, with little option but to be host to one of Fairfax's leading commanders:

> Colonell Oakey, from Saterday to tewday [sic], himselfe with servants & 6 horses at house . . . . a meadow of Grasse eaten upp at the same time, . . . which in part of satisfacion be paid me £5, soe yt I was dampnified more then he paid me . . .

Straw was taken from Nash's barns for litter and makeshift beds for the soldiers, and he even insisted on recording 'a dunckart broken & burnt & a gate, when the generalls Army was there'.[9]

While at Clifford Chambers Fairfax held a council of war, on Monday 23 June, at which, according to Sir Edward Nicholas, he decided to make for Bristol. Attracted by the King's presence at Hereford, the focus of military activity swung westwards again as parliamentarian detachments began to converge on the Cotswolds. There was talk of a general rendezvous at Worcester, and a large contingent from Luke at Newport Pagnell was already on the way to Chipping Norton. The Royalists, although dismembered, were not yet powerless. The King, disregarding sombre counsels from his advisers, was busy recruiting for a fresh army, while surviving remnants from Naseby were still able to mount small but effective counter-attacks whenever the opportunity arose. Sir Samuel Luke reported a 'hard misfortune' on 22 June when one of his troops marching to join Massey was destroyed at Church Honeybourne in the Vale of Evesham by the Earl of Northampton who, having loyally accompanied the King west after Naseby, was now returning to base at Banbury. Luke gave news of renewed royalist activity around Oxford, a rendezvous near Bicester, and further royalist atrocities. Northampton was, he predicted, about to 'fall upon his old sport of plundring . . . they take away every man along wth them that is able to pay any money, and leave not a horse wheresoever they come'. Fairfax himself, however, resisted any temptation to deviate from the major task he had set, and continued his brisk march. Continuing to spend only one overnight stay each time, he quickly moved from Clifford to Chipping Campden, still receiving provisions and beer from Stratford. Detachments of the New Model Army were meanwhile still scattered throughout south Warwickshire, with Colonel Charles Fleetwood returned from Naseby to make his headquarters at long-suffering Southam again, while heavy concentrations of troops were reported from villages like Halford and Ilmington, on or near the Fosse Way. It must have been recalling a period such as this, as yet another seemingly endless procession of unwelcome soldiers streamed through village after village taking free quarter and whatever else suited them, that a tiny community like Stretton-on-Fosse gave up trying to count the cost: 'we have bene charged so often wth so many [soldiers] that we cannott make any certeyntie thereof, but yett we conceyve the same will amount to above thirty pounds for our village'. The soldiers finally moved away from the district, to Northleach and beyond, to further spectacular successes in the west.

Fairfax would not return to the Midlands for almost a year, but for the local population Naseby, and the New Model's absence, had changed nothing. As the summer of 1645 wore on, other parliamentarian forces were approaching to capitalize on their recent triumph and counter more royalist threats. The Scots under Leven were at last preparing to march south from Nottingham for Hereford, and in early July Prince Maurice, in a precautionary measure at Worcester, ordered all able-bodied males between sixteen and sixty to report for large-scale work on the city's fortifications, on pain of death. With Evesham now in parliamentary hands, but much of the countryside still under royalist command, an increasingly outraged local community was abused equally by both sides, to the point where apportioning blame to one or the other was no longer possible or relevant to the exasperated people. One lengthy document, undated but reflecting conditions throughout Worcestershire during this summer, provides a veritable catalogue of complaints, ending with a thinly-veiled threat of insurrection:

That the Country is fallen into such want and extremity through the number and oppression of the Horse lying upon free quarter that the people are necessitated (their Hay being spent) to feed their Horses with corn, whilst their Children are ready to starve for want of Bread.

Their exacting of free quarter and extorting sums of money for the time of their absence from their quarters, mingled with threats of firing their Houses, their persons with death, and their goods with pillaging.

Their barbarous seizing men's persons and compelling them to ransom themselves with very great sums of money to their undoing . . . and that, without any order or warrant . . .

Their daily robberies of all Market people, killing and wounding men who resist and stand on their own defence, their contempt of all discipline to all orders, Quartering where they please and how . . .

Their opprobrious and base language [against] the Commissioners, intermingled with scorns and threats . . .

That all the country lying between Severn and Teme . . . and also all the parishes adjacent within 4 miles of the City [of Worcester] are by free quarter of the Horse eaten up, undone and destroyed, together with the country lying about Kidderminster and Bewdley, with their several Armies passing to and fro . . .

That the Insolencies, oppressions and Cruelties have already so disaffected and disheartened the people, that they are grown so desperate and are already upon the point of rising everywhere . . .

If these charges, all too familiar, were levelled at the Royalists, threats to at least one Worcestershire parish, dated 14 October 1645, came certainly from the new Evesham parliamentary authority, urging the constable and tithingmen of Elmley Lovett to produce arrears of taxes immediately, 'at your perils of pillaging and plundering, and your houses fired and your persons imprisoned'. It is, moreover, against such a picture, of a civilian community pushed almost beyond endurance, that the further havoc wreaked by the Scots themselves must be set. Crossing Warwickshire diagonally from Tamworth to Alcester, Pershore and Droitwich and back again shortly after, across a countryside so impoverished and sullen that their commander wrote of his men's starvation level, they left such an unprecedented trail of pillage and destruction that local bitterness reached a new pitch and many parishes listed their 'charges by the Scots' separately from the rest, as a kind of crowning outrage suffered at the hands of these new barbarian hordes. This episode, with all the makings of a minor folk epic, would alone merit separate and extended treatment. After the Scots came others, allowing little or no respite, under Poyntz, Brereton, Whalley and others, with John Bridges at Warwick still as active as ever, countering royalist threats in December by constantly manoeuvring between Warwick, Stratford, Shipston, Banbury and Coventry, breaking bridges along the Avon, including Stratford's, and dragooning 500 Warwick citizens into guard duty at the castle during his men's absence.

Militarily, however, Naseby had dealt a mortal blow to royalist fortunes, and as Wormleighton and Aynho disappeared pointlessly in the flames, one by one their garrisons capitulated and within a year, in quick succession, the second, eleven-week siege of Banbury, the battle of Stow and the final twin sieges of Oxford and Worcester made Naseby irreversible. Each of these events, excluded from the present work purely by the time-scale imposed, exacted their further toll of misery on ordinary people; each, again, is reflected in the fractured mirror of the parish books, and each, too, fuelled the growing trend in many parts to the active neutralism of the Clubmen. Long after Naseby, nevertheless, raucous and unruly soldiers continued as a virtually permanent presence in village and market town. Mutinous rabbles were still rampaging through Warwickshire as late as April 1649, after the execution of the King, when the London authorities, justifiably anxious about the 'pressure upon the people, both by the charge of free quarter, and yet more by the insufferable insolencies and incivilities of many unruly soldiers', gave strict orders to one commander in Warwickshire:

Take special care that quarter may be paid, and that in a time of so great dearth, the men be content with moderate provision and abstain from insolence and incivility, which is the greatest difficulty for free people to bear . . .

The war and its aftermath would continue to be felt for many a weary month yet in this English heartland. In an undated post-war petition to Parliament, Warwickshire underlined the degree of suffering the people of a small and unprosperous county had endured, as yet unrecognized by the authorities, concluding pointedly that 'as this county was one of the first in the Parliament's service, so it is like to be one of the last to suffer in the same'. Yet so widespread were the disruption and hardship that few indeed of the Midland counties could not have made a similar claim, with almost equal justice.[10]

CONCLUSION

This work has, first and foremost, tried to discover what actually happened in the south Midlands for a short three-year period of the Civil War, to enquire into the impact of events on ordinary people and to examine the claim that 'the Civil War from below remains hidden'. At least one modern Warwickshire specialist, in a nevertheless valuable pioneering study, has concluded that, apart from Catholics, 'in the Civil War the bulk of the population appeared to be relatively unaffected by the traumatic experience of warfare'. Yet that Midlands eye-witness Richard Baxter described bloodshed in virtually every parish, and wrote of 'a War in every county', while the clergyman Joshua Sprigge bewailed his native Banbury at the end of the war as having suffered a blitz, 'having scarce the one halfe standing to gaze on the ruines of the other'. The parish books would alone suggest the real extent of the war's impact. As the surviving testimony of ordinary people, mostly illiterate and without the modern habit of recording experience, these accounts allow often, as we have seen, a detailed and at times graphic running commentary on conditions of living already bleak enough without the arrival of unruly soldiers, and they suggest that disruption and hardship were endless and extensive. Despite their fragmentary nature they come close to providing that image of the war 'from below' that is supposedly missing. Nor should the soldiers themselves be ignored. They also were ordinary people, and, as pointed out, their lot was often as pitiful as that of their village neighbours left behind, and sometimes worse, and their numbers were not inconsiderable. It has been variously estimated that one in ten, or even perhaps one in four or five, of all adult males bore arms at some point in the war. Of these, many were killed outright, died through inadequate care or were permanently maimed, while others trudged back to village life unable to re-adapt and to become a permanent drain on the meagre parish resources. Moreover, only intermittent reference has been made to one central issue, that of the financial burden on the people as one tax after another rained down on rich and poor alike. The parish accounts invariably give financial estimates for both taxes and losses, both individually and communally, and although no comprehensive study of these has yet been attempted – perhaps understandably, given the methodological problems – the consensus among historians is that that burden was crippling. For the ordinary individual, as well as the landed gentry, the effects of the war could not be avoided. Professor Everitt's reservations on the scale of the war's impact provincially, quoted at the outset of this book, do not prevent his conceding that 'there is no need to minimise the impact . . . [which was] obviously far-reaching'. The parish accounts and the contemporary journalism which have formed much of the source material for this enquiry amply illustrate this, and their value lies not only in the sheer bulk of information they supply, great though that is, but in the vivid, authentic record of the speaking voice of the past. And that voice is our own, overheard years gone by, telling of Shakespeare's 'testament of bleeding war', of 'old, unhappy, far-off things, and battles long ago', but as though it were yesterday.

SIR WILLIAM DUGDALE'S ANALYSIS OF THE LOYALTIES OF LEADING WARWICKSHIRE MEN AT THE OUTBREAK OF THE CIVIL WAR, SUMMER 1642

Note: Apart from the obvious exception of the 1645 parliamentary commissioners in part 2, Dugdale's list was probably substantially compiled in the summer of 1642, and is written in his own hand. It is given complete, but for convenience is rearranged alphabetically in three sections instead of the original's somewhat confusing seven. Notes within curved brackets are Dugdale's own (with minor omissions), those in square brackets the author's. Spelling has been modernized where practicable. Dugdale's analysis unaccountably contains many important omissions, and raises many complex questions, not least in the 'neutrals' section. *Source*: Northamptonshire Record Office, Finch-Hatton 4284.

1. ROYALISTS

*Active as Commissioners of Array in August 1642

*Adderley, Sir Charles [of Nether Whitacre]
*Arden, Robert [of Park Hall, Coleshill]
Beaufoy, Henry, of Emscote
Betham, Walliston, of Rowington
Bird, Thomas, of Coventry
*Boughton, Sir William [of Little Lawford]
Bracy, Henry, of Eastcote
Bromley, William, of Baginton
Burnell, [Thomas?], of Exhall
Calcott [Caldecote?] − of Long Itchington
*Chamberlaine, Richard (Sen.), [of Temple House, Chilvers Coton]
Clarke, John, of Coventry (alderman)
Clarke, Matthew, of Oxhill
*Clarke, Sir Simon, [of Bidford]
Clarke, William, of Oxhill
Clopton, [Thomas], of Clopton (captain)
Cokayne, Aston, of Pooley
Comberford, William, of Tamworth
Corbin, Thomas, of Hall End [Polesworth]
Dawkins [Dakins], John, of Maxstoke
*Devereux, Sir George [of Sheldon]
Digby, Lord [Robert], of Coleshill
Dighton, Thomas, of Stratford[-on-Avon]
Dilke, Fisher, of Shustoke
Dormer, Anthony, of Grove Park [Warwick]

Dugdale, William of Blyth Hall

*Dunsmore, Lord Francis [Leigh], [of Kings Newnham]

*Feilding, Sir Roger [of Newnham Paddox]

*Fisher, Sir Robert [of Great Packington]

Fortescue, William, [of Weethley]

Gibbons, William, of Coventry

Gramer, Francis, of Kenilworth

Green, Edward, of Little Alne

Green, Richard, of Wyken

Griffin, Edward, of Bickmarsh

Grosvenor, Fulke, of Sutton [Coldfield]

Halford, [William], of Halford

Hanslap, Richard, of Southam

Hickman, William of Radbourne

Hinton, Dr Samuel, of Coventry

Holbech, Ambrose, of Mollington

Holbech, Thomas, of Meriden

Hopkins, Samson, of Stockton

Kempson, William, of Ardens Grafton

Kempson, William, of Hillborough

Knight, Nicholas, of Ullenhall

Knight, William, of Rowington

Knotsford, Fulke, of Studley

Lapworth, Edward, of Sowe

*Lee, Robert, [of Billesley]

*Leigh, Sir Thomas, [of Stoneleigh]

Loggins, William, of Butlers Marston

*Lucy, Spencer, [of Charlecote]

Middlemore, [Richard], of Edgbaston

Mordaunt, Sir Charles, of Walton Mauduit

Morgan, Thomas, of Weston [under Wetherley]

*Northampton, Earl of, Spencer [Compton, of Compton Wynyates]

Norton, Simon, of Coventry

Pearce, Thomas, of Alveston

Rainsford, Henry, of Clifford [Chambers]

Raleigh, George, of Farnborough

Randolph, Ferrers, of Wood Bevington

Repington, Sir John, of Amington

Ridgley, William, of Dunton

Sacheverell, Valence, of Newhall, Sutton [Coldfield]

Sheldon, Brace, of Temple Grafton

Sheldon, William, of Temple Grafton

Sheldon, William, of Weston [Long Compton]

Shuckburgh, Thomas, of Birdingbury

Skinner, [William], of Kinwarton

Smith, Sir Charles, of Wootton Wawen

Spencer, Thomas, of Harbury

Stainford, John, of Salford

Throckmorton, Sir Robert, of Coughton

Underhill, Thomas, of Loxley

Wagstaff, Edward of Harbury

Walsingham, [Maurice], of Exhall

Waring, Maurice, of Oversley

Warner, George, of Wolston

Westley, William, of Eathorpe

Whitwick, John (Sgt at Law), [of Coventry?]

Wise, Richard, of Gilson, [Coleshill]

Worcester, Thomas, of Draycote

2. PARLIAMENTARIANS

*Active organizers of the Militia Ordinance in August 1642

*Abbott, George, [of Tamworth]

Abraham, William, of Butlers Marston (captain)

Acock, William, of Sheldon

*Barker, John, of Coventry

Bentley, Charles, of Little Kineton

*Bosevile, Godfrey, [of Wroxall]
Boughton, Thomas, of Bilton
  (committee)
Bourne, Abraham, of Coundon
*Brooke, Lord Robert [Greville], of
  Warwick Castle
Brown, George, of Radford
*Burgoyne, Peter, of Coventry
Colmore, William, of Birmingham
  (captain)
Combe, William, of Stratford-on-Avon
Cookes, [Henry], of Snitterfield
Dering, Thomas, of Baddesley Ensor
Eglionby, Richard, of Knowle
Fetherston, John, of Packwood
Fullwood, Thomas, of Little Alne
Greville, Francis, of Shotteswell
*Hales, John, of Coventry
Nash, Thomas, of Stratford-on-Avon
  (captain)

Odett, –, of Mollington
Perkins, William, of Marston Jabet
  [Bulkington]
*Peto, Sir Edward, of Chesterton
Purefoy, Gamaliel, of Wolvershill
*Purefoy, William, of Caldecote
St Nicholas, [John], of Knowle
Sambidge [Sandbach], [William], of
  Pillerton (captain; since came over to
  the King) [Note: Dugdale error?]
*Stoughton, Anthony, [of St John's,
  Warwick]
Stratford, Edward, of Nuneaton
Temple, John, of Frankton
Throckmorton, Clement, of Haseley
*Wentworth, Sir Peter [of Wolston]
Wilcox, Richard, of Brandon
Willington, Waldive, of Hurley
  (captain)
Willis, [George], of Fenny Compton

*Others who withheld horses and men from the
King's Commission of Array*

Astley, Sir Isaac, of Hillmorton (sheriff)
Burdett, Sir Thomas, of Bramcote
Burgoyne, [John), of Wroxall
Conway, Lord [Edward, of Ragley]
Craven, Lord [William, of Combe
  Fields]
Denbigh, Lord [Basil Feilding, of
  Newnham Paddox]
Devereux, Sir Walter, of Castle
  Bromwich
Middlesex, Lord [Lionel Cranfield, of
  Milcote]
Monmouth, Earl of [Henry Carey, of
  Kenilworth]
Newdigate, Richard, of Arbury
Shirley, Sir Charles, of Ettington
Somerville, [Edward], of Edstone
Spencer, Lord [Thomas], of
  Wormleighton
Temple, Sir Peter, of Burton
  Dassett

*Parliamentary Commissioners at Warwick
Assizes, held July 1645*

Note: Some of these later additions to
  Dugdale's original list had only minor
  interests in Warwickshire

Bolingbroke, Oliver St. John, Earl of
Bosevile, Godfrey [of Wroxall]
Bridges, John [Governor of Warwick
  Castle]
Browne, Samuel [of Cestover?]
Colmore, William [of Birmingham]
Denbigh, Basil [Feilding] Earl of [of
  Newnham Paddox]
Devereux, Leicester [of Castle Bromwich]
Devereux, Sir Walter [of Castle
  Bromwich]
Dryden, Sir John [of Canons Ashby,
  Northants.]
Essex, Robert [Devereux], Earl of
Hales, John [of Coventry]
Kent, Henry, Earl of [of Leics.]
Lucy, Richard [of Charlecote]

Parliamentary Commissioners at Warwick
Assizes, held July 1645

Mackworth, Humphrey [of Shropshire]
Newdigate, Richard [of Arbury]
Palmer, Sir William [of Ladbroke]
Prideaux, Edward
Purefoy, Gamaliel [of Wolvershill]
Purefoy, William [of Caldecote]
Skeffington, Sir Richard [of Staffs.]
Temple, Sir Peter [of Burton Dassett]
Wentworth, Sir Peter [of Wolston]
Wilde, John (Sgt at Law) [of Worcs.]
Willington, Waldive [of Hurley]
Willoughby, Thomas [of Sutton
    Coldfield]
Yelverton, Sir Christopher [of
    Bulkington]

3. NEUTRAL

Note: Later allegiance indicated where reasonably clear

Archer, Sir Simon, of Tanworth
    [Parliament]
Astley, Thomas, of Wolvey
Booth, Richard, of Warwick
Boughton, Henry, of Cawston
Broome, William, of Woodlow
Burnaby, Eustace, of Coventry
Burnaby, [John?], of Rugby
Chamberlaine, Edward, of Princethorpe
    [Parliament]
Combe, Thomas, of Welcombe
Dalby, Richard, of Brockhampton
Danvers, John, of Upton [King]
Dixwell, [William], of Coton
Draper, [Edward], of Bubbenhall
Enyon, Sir James, of Bishops Itchington
    (since came in to the King at
    Nottingham) [King]

Ferrers, Edward, of Baddesley Clinton
Gibbs, Sir Henry, of Honington [King]
Glover, Thomas, of Baxterley
Hales, [Stephen], of Snitterfield (under
    age)
Harvey, –, of Moreton Morrell (under
    age)
Hill, Edward, of Charterhouse, Coventry
Hill, John, of Grandborough
Hobday, John, of Ettington
Holte, Sir Thomas, of Aston [Hall]
    [King]
Huband, John, of Ipsley [King]
Ingram, Hastings, of Little Wolford
    [Parliament]
Kinnersley, John, of Ward End
    [Birmingham]
Knightley, Robert, of Offchurch [King]

Lisle, John, of Moxhull
Lytton, Sir Robert, of Berkswell
Maine, John, of Elmdon
Matthew, Henry, of Murcote Hall [Berkswell] [Parliament]
Middlemore, Robert, of Edgbaston [King]
Nethersole, Sir Francis, of Polesworth [Parliament]
Newsam, Edward, of Chadshunt
Noell, William, of Langdon Hall
Overbury, [Nicholas], of Barton-on-the-Heath (under age)
Pawlett, William, of Maxstoke
Porter, Richard, of Ettington
Prescote, James, of Warwick [Parliament]
Pudsey, George, of Langley [King]
Roper, Samuel, of Monks Kirby (since a captain of horse with the Rebels) [Parliament]
Scarning, [Ezechias], of Wolvey
Shuckburgh, Richard, of Shuckburgh (since knighted) [King]
Shuttleworth, William, of Fillongley
Spencer, Sir William, of Claverdon
Townsend, [Richard], of Warwick [Parliament]
Underhill, George, of Oxhill
Underhill, Sir Hercules, of Idlicote [King]
Verney, Greville, of Compton Murdak [Compton Verney]
Ward, Rowley, (Sgt. at Law) [of Barford], [Parliament]
Waring, Charles, of Solihull [King]
Willoughby, Sir Francis, of Middleton, [Parliament]
Woodward, Richard, of Avon Dassett

APPENDIX B

THE KING'S SPEECH TO HIS TROOPS SHORTLY BEFORE THE BATTLE OF EDGEHILL, AT SOUTHAM, 21 OCTOBER 1642

Note: This is a transcript of the manuscript version, Bodleian Library, Ashmole 830/277–278, by some unknown hand (not the King's). A printed version with minor variations, printed in London, 27 October 1642, is in the Thomason collection in the British Library: E. 124(19).

Gentlemen,

I know you are not insensable of the many fayre letters of Treaty which have issued from us to both our howses of Parliament, and the slight effect they have produced (notwithstandeinge they have bin seconded with many vowes and Reall protestations, in which God and men are called for wittnesses, wherein wee have ingaged the temporall and eternall happines of us and all our Royall posterity, that our determinacon tendeth to noe other end then the whole kingedomes happines, establishinge the same flourisheinge Religion professed in the tranquile Dayes of Queene Elizabeth, and Confirmed by our Royall Father; likewise to maintayne the Law and Liberty of the subiect, with the iust priviledge of Parliament which in all theire petitions hath beene required, and by us gratiously heard, granted, and not beleived, but most unreasonably suspected). What actions or action of ours from the begininge of our Raigne till this present howre shall urge the cause of soe inhumain and most impious a misbeleife we are yet to learne, since in all this tyme of trouble wee could not bee informed it may bee feared wee can now bee instructed. The strainge and disloyall causes which have forced us from our Throne of peace and, as we thought, security, to appeare in hostile manner in the bowells of oure owne kingedome, a man of Common Reason cannot censure to bee ours, and since hee must conclude that whosoever hath the victory wee are sure to bee the looser. Ambition (which fills the veynes of great ones to bee greater) must needes bee free from us, since wee are greatest; Envy or Malice are as farre, since wee have noe Competitor. Wee have protested in the word of a kinge, and called the searcher of all harts to record, that wee intend not the alteracon of the true professed & established protestant Religion, the lawes of the Kingedome, and the knowne liberty of the subiect, the right and iust preveledge of Parliament, and all this Confirmed with such imprecations as may urge beleife in Common men one towards another although strangers and at the first sight. If this bee granted, wee would knowe for what other cause then the safety of our endaingered person and the protection of our subiects wee have raysed (with the love and free will of our people) this necessary guard about us, onely putting our selfe in a posture of defence against most eminent and active violence, and not (as ill pretences would instigate our good subiects) to wage warre against our parliament, whoe had theire beeinge from our prerogative (without which they had not beene, or at least not had a warrant for continuance). Moreover, for the cleer understanding of our resolucion to maintayne peace, we may have the confidence and happines to referre (against all malignity whatsoever) to our former sixteene yeares Raigne (too longe to dissemble our nature) if in all this tyme we have ever caused the effusion of one drop of blood. It must needes bee thought that in our Riper iudgement of government wee should never open such yssues as might drown us and our posterity in them; but wee are sure to have no Enemies but in defence of the true protestant Profession, the right of the established Lawes, and for the preservation of peace, and certainely all theise must bee all yours, as well as our enemyes.

And to the end that this present posture wherein wee are should not disturbe you with the distempers of the tymes (the example of the two howses haveinge made us prepare for a guard to us and our Childrens persons), we wish you to looke into the Composicon and constitucon of it, and you will find soe farre from the face or feare of warre that it serveth to secure you as well as us from it, since you know our choyce is of the prime gentrye. And wee further assure you, wee never intended to usse forraigners or disaffected in Religion. And that you may fully afford your selves of our sole dependency upon the love and service of our people to live and dy with them, wee have armed you our subiects, which had been most irrationall if wee had ever intended to have used straingers. And further, you may perceive that wee receive non but those that stand cleere in loyalty and Religion, for which reason you see wee have caused the oathes of Allegiance and Supremacy to bee given them. And for the prevention of any innovated power over you, you shall have us with you to govern you and protect you in peace, and to releive you against all oppressions (for that, as wee have formerly tould you, might arise from some greate violacon, which wee hope God will prevent), and not from this Forward preparacon of our subiects. Therefore let none of you bee discouraged with vayne fears if such a warre must follow: it will follow the authors home to theire owne doores (and such, by the Confidence of our person with you, wee assure ourselfe you are not).

The discontented people whose lives are but a Continuall rumor and faction have endeavoured to make us and our Army odious, by castinge many aspersions and Calumnyes upon them, as (I have received notice by Assured intelligence) that you should sally out of your severall quarters to plunder and pillage the howses of knowne protestants. Wee hope it is not soe, and am the rather confident in that the relacon sprounge from these whoe have taken liberty to vent most unbecoming language against our owne person. Notwithstandeinge, we hould it most necessary to advertise you (since your hostility is in a righteous and Religious cause) that you use noe sinister action. Good causes never produce unrighteous effects, nor canne truth be fortifyed with falsehood. Theirefore we will and Commande you to march peaceably and quietly as a defendinge party, not a provokeinge. Dispoyle noe mans goods, not in the least degree. Abuse not theire wives or servants or cattell, or what else shall appertaine to them, least you make a breach in the Lawe and Liberty of the Subiect, the cause you stande to defende. Defraude noe man, wheresoever you are quartered, but give satisfaccon for what you have, that you may not ware a vizard before trueth but seem like that trueth you serve under. Doe not plunder or pillage, under the pretence of Papists howses, till notice bee given, that they bee legally, not riotously, examined or detected. Avoyde vayne and rash swearing, excessive drinkeinge and effemenacy (by some esteemed the property of a souldier, but the shame & Corruption of a good Christian). Be sure you cast an eye upon your cause, which invites you to a more sanctifyed rule. A voide all inward quarrells and selfe destroyeinge mutanye. Let the feare of God, the preservacon of a good Conscience, the Contemplacon and exercise of trueth & true Religion bee alwayes acceptable and received by you, that you may not feare the Change of your mortallity (since you have lesse assurance to preserve your lives now then ever you had).

Officers, and you that have Command: it shall beecome your Charge, soe farre as in you lyes, to see theise observations mainteyned, and bee your selves the examples. And wee doubte not but in tyme, just God will direct and protect us in all oure actions, and bringe our weary labours to a good Conclusion, when all our sadnesse shallbee tourned into joy, the subiect possesse his fee liberty uncontrolled, and the kingedome Continue in firme peace for ever.

THE KING'S LETTER TO PARLIAMENT FROM EVESHAM, 4 JULY 1644, SHORTLY AFTER THE BATTLE OF CROPREDY BRIDGE

We, being deeply sensible of the Miseries and Calamities of this our Kingdom, and of the grievous Sufferings of our poor Subjects, doe most earnestly desire that some Expedient may be found out, which by the blessing of God, may prevent the further effusion of Blood, and restore the Nation to Peace: From the earnest and constant endeavouring of which, as no discouragement given us on the contrary Part shall make us cease, so no success on ours shall ever divert us. For the effecting whereof, we are most ready and willing to condescend to all that shall be for the good of us and our People, whether by way of Confirmation of what we have already granted, or of such further Concession as shall be requisite to the giving a full Assurance of the Performance of all our most real Professions concerning the maintenance of the true Reformed Religion established in this Kingdom, with due regard to the Ease of tender Consciences, the just Privileges of Parliament, and the Liberty and Property of the Subject, according to the Laws of the Land; as also the granting of a General Pardon without or with Exceptions, as shall be thought fit. In order to which blessed Peace, we do desire and propound to the Lords and Commons of Parliament assembled at Westminster that they appoint such and so many Persons as they shall think fit, sufficiently authorized by them, to attend us at our Army, upon safe Conduct to come and return (which we do hereby grant) and conclude with us how the Premises, and all other Things in question between us and them, may be fully settled; whereby all unhappy mistaking betwixt us and our People being removed, there may be a present Cessation of Arms, and as soon as may be a total disbanding of all our Armies, the Subject have his Due, and we be restored to all our Rights. Wherein if this our Offer shall be accepted, there shall be nothing wanting on our Part which may make our People secure and happy.

Given at our Court at Evesham, the Fourth Day of July, 1644.

J. Rushworth, *Historical Collections*, London, 1721, Vol. V, p. 687.

NOTES AND REFERENCES

ABBREVIATIONS

Abbott	Abbott W.C., *The Writings and Speeches of Oliver Cromwell*, Cambridge, Mass., Harvard Univ. Press, 1937–41
App.	Appendix
Beesley	Beesley A., *The History of Banbury*, Nichols & Son, 1841
BL	British Library
Bloxam	Bloxam M.H., *Warwickshire during the Civil Wars of the 17th Century*, Warwick, Robert Spennell, 1880
Bund	Bund J.W.W., *The Civil War in Worcestershire*, Birmingham, Cornish Bros., 1905
CAM	*Calendar of the Proceedings of the Committee for the Advancement of Money, 1642–1656*, ed. M.A.E. Green, HMSO, 1888
CCC	*Calendar of the Proceedings of the Committee for Compounding, 1643–1660*, ed. M.A.E. Green, HMSO, 1890
CJ	*Journal of the House of Commons*
Clarendon	Clarendon, Edward, Earl of, *The History of the Rebellion and Civil Wars in England*, ed. W.D. Macray, Oxford, Clarendon Press, 1888
Corbet	Corbet J., 'An Historical Relation of the Military Government of Gloucester, 1645', in Washbourn, q.v.
CSPD	*Calendar of State Papers, Domestic Series*, HMSO, 1887–1939
CSPV	*Calendar of State Papers, Venetian Series*, HMSO, 1864–1947
DNB	*Dictionary of National Biography*
Dugdale	Dugdale W., *The Antiquities of Warwickshire*, ed. W. Thomas, Osborn & Longman, 1730 (*see also* Hamper)
E	British Library reference of Tracts collected by George Thomason
Firth	Firth C.H. (ed.), 'The Journal of Prince Rupert's Marches' in *English Historical Review*, vol. 13, 1898
Fletcher	Fletcher A., *The Outbreak of the English Civil War*, Arnold, 1985
Hamper	Hamper W., *The Life, Diary and Correspondence of Sir William Dugdale*, 1827
HMC	Record series published by the Historical Monuments Commission
Hughes	Hughes A.L., *Politics, Society and Civil War in Warwickshire*, Cambridge, 1987
Hutton	Hutton R., *The Royalist War Effort, 1642–1646*, Harlow, Longman, 1982
LJ	*Journal of the House of Lords*
Luke	Philip I.G. (ed.), *The Journal of Sir Samuel Luke*, Oxford Record Society, 1947–53
Matthews	Matthews A.G., *Walker Revised*, Oxford, Clarendon Press, 1948
Merc. Aul.	*Mercurius Aulicus* (regular court newspaper printed in Oxford, collected by Thomason: *see E above*)
Morrill	Morrill J.S. (ed.), *Reactions to the English Civil War, 1642–1649*, Macmillan, 1982
PRO	Public Record Office
QS	Ratcliff S.C. and Johnson H.C. (eds.), *Warwick County Records, Quarter Sessions Order Books*, Warwick, L. Edgar Stephens, Shire Hall, 1935–53
RO	Record Office
SP	Collection of State Papers, Public Record Office
Spencer	Spencer T., 'The Genealogie, Life and Death of the Right Hon. Robert, Lord Brooke', ed. P. Styles in *Dugdale Society Miscellany*, I, OUP, 1977
Strider	Strider R.E.L., *Robert Greville, Lord Brooke*, Cambridge, Mass., Harvard Univ. Press, 1958
TBAS	*Transactions of the Birmingham Archaeological Society*

Tibbutt   Tibbutt H.G., *The Letter Books of Sir Samuel Luke, 1644–1645*, Bedfordshire Historical
                Society/HMC, 1963
Toynbee   Toynbee M. and Young P., *Cropredy Bridge*, Roundwood Press, Kineton, 1970
 and Young
Warburton   Warburton E., *Memoirs of Prince Rupert and the Cavaliers*, Bentley, 1849
Washbourn   Washbourn J. (ed.), *Bibliotheca Gloucestrensis, A Collection of Scarce and Curious Tracts relating
                to the County & City of Gloucester*, 1825
Wedgwood   Wedgwood C.V., *The King's War, 1641–1647*, Collins, 1978
Wharton   Wharton N., 'Letters from a subaltern', ed. H. Ellis in *Archaelogia*, vol. 35, 1853
Whetham   Whetham C.D. and W.C.D., *A History of the Life of Col. Nathaniel Whetham*, Harlow,
                Longman Green, 1907
VCH   *Victoria County History of England*
Vicars   Vicars J., *Magnalia dei Anglicana*, Rothwell & Underhill, 1646
Young   Young P., *Edgehill 1642*, Roundwood Press, Kineton, 1967

PREFACE

1. *Victoria County History*: see Ch. 1, note 1 below; one notable exception to the silence is Philip Styles's
   excellent article on the war in Stratford-upon-Avon in vol. III. The more recent volumes attempt to
   remedy this defect. A. Everitt, 'The Local Community and the Great Rebellion', Historical Assoc.
   Pamphlet G. 70 (1969), p. 24. Marston Moor: repeated M. Ashley, *England in the 17th c.*, Penguin,
   1952, p. 79; P. Young, *The English Civil War, A Military History*, Eyre Methuen, 1974, p. 53, etc., but
   rejected as apocryphal by I. Roy in Bond and Roy (eds.), *War and Society*, 1975, p. 31 and R. Hutton in
   Morrill, p. 51. Dugdale and Tysoe: Dugdale I, p. 309; W.H. Hutton, *Highways and Byways in
   Shakespeare's Country*, Macmillan, 1926, p. 29.
2. Thomason Tracts, BL, 'E' refs; useful, though far from comprehensive index, by G.K. Fortescue, 1908.
   PRO: State Papers SP. 28 series (unindexed, mostly uncalendared and often unnumbered). J.F.C.
   Harrison, *The Common People, A History from the Norman Conquest to the Present*, Fontana, 1984, p. 203.
   T.S. Eliot, *Four Quartets*, 'Little Gidding', 1942; the 'broken King' Charles I visited the religious
   community of Little Gidding, Huntingdon, in May 1646, alone, shortly before being captured.
   Anecdotes: see text. W.G. Hoskins, *The Making of the English Landscape*, Hodder, 1955, p. 233.
   R. Baxter, *Reliquiae Baxterianae*, ed. M. Sylvester, 1696, p. 44.

1. INTRODUCTION: THE BACKGROUND TO WAR

1. Petition: *CSPD 1645–47*, p. 289. The extent of Warwickshire's involvement has only recently been
   acknowledged, by modern historians like Hutton and Fletcher. The earlier *VCH* volumes scarcely
   mention the war, though vol. II contains a brief résumé of some events affecting the county. Still
   useful are the much older Beesley, Bloxam and Bund. Most useful for detailed study are two recent
   academic theses: D.F. Mosler, 'A Social and Religious History of the English Civil War in
   Warwickshire', Stanford, 1975 (unpublished), and, covering much the same ground but more
   detailed, Hughes (well researched, if indigestible). A. Woolrych, 'The Civil Wars', in B. Worden,
   Stuart England, Phaidon, 1986, contains a useful summary of the Wks. beginnings of the war,
   pp. 100–1. Ultimatum: E.112(44). Standard: E.114(10). Warwick E.114(10), E.239(7). Meriden:
   Firth, p. 731. Hutton, p. 19.
2. John Ogilby, *Britannia*, 1675 (facsimile edn, J.B. Harley, Amsterdam, 1970, p. 41). J. Taylor,
   The Carriers Cosmographie, 1637, repr. A. Lang, *Social England Illustrated*, 1903. Whetham, p. 75.
   SP.28/185, Stretton-on-Fosse. I. Roy, *The Royalist Ordnance Papers, 1642–46*, Oxfords. Rec. Soc.,
   vols. 43, 49 (1964, 1975); some of this section is based on his excellent introduction. Hutton,
   p. 76. Warburton III, App. I. Bund, Introdn., and quoting Worcs. Sessions Records I,
   p. ccxxiv. E. of Worcs: 27 *HMC* XIIth Rpt. App. IX, p. 60. *CSPD 1645–7*, p. 289. Hughes,
   pp. 265–6.

3.   Fletcher, p. 45; contested by Hughes, who argues that Wks. lacked both a unified economy and a
recognized capital, and that many parts of the county had more economic ties with adjacent counties
than other parts of Wks. Digby to Rupert, Oxford, 2 Apr 1645, in BL Add 18982/44–45; cf.
Clarendon, pp. 37–8. Corbet I, p. 63. Whetham: E.8(9). Glos.: Godfrey Goodman, Bishop of Glos.,
declared the relief of the city 'the turning of the wheel, for ever after the parliament forces prevailed':
VCH Glos. IV, p. 92. SP.28/184–5, Brailes, Tysoe, Wolford; SP.28/201, Ashow, Sherbourne.
4.   Hutton, pp. 12–13. 'Horrible Newes from Warwickshire', 1642. E.109(3). BL 669/6(50, 58).
Brooke: LJ IV, p. 625 (actual nomination 11 Feb: CJ II, p. 426). Strider. DNB. W.B. Compton, A
History of the Comptons, Bodley Head, 1930. Hughes, pp. 21–5, 119–25; interesting résumé of
Brooke's polemical writings. W. Dugdale, A Short View of the Late Troubles in England, Oxford, 1681,
p. 117. Warburton I, p. 322; II, pp. 137–8. Clarendon II, pp. 477–8. Spencer, p. 178. DNB.
Hughes, p. 126. Young passim. Dormer: HMC Vth Rpt., p. 191 and Wedgwood passim. Dugdale,
op.cit., p. 110. The Broughton meetings were first reported in the royalist pamphlet Persecutio
Undecima, 1648, pp. 10, 55–6, and later repeated almost verbatim by A. Wood, Athenae Oxonienses,
ed. P. Bliss, 1817, III, p. 546. G. Grenville, Lord Nugent, Some Memorials of John Hampden, Murray,
1832, I, p. 327. Beesley, p. 295. W. Potts, A History of Banbury, Gulliver, 1978, p. 182.
5.   Saye: DNB: LJ VIII passim; A. Wood, The Life and Times of Anthony Wood, ed. A. Clark, Oxford, 1892,
I, p. 61 etc. Young, p. 247, says Saye transferred his regiment to the Scots veteran Meldrum before
Edgehill. Hughes, passim. Militia Ord., 30 May 1642: CJ II, p. 595. Warwick siege: HMC XIIth
Rpt. App. II, p. 320.
6.   Loyalties: Hughes, passim, esp. 221ff. W. Molesworth (ed.), The English Works of Thomas Hobbes, Bohn,
1839–45, VI, p. 166. M.W. Farr, 'The Fetherstons of Packwood in the Seventeenth Century',
Dug.Soc.Occ.Pubs., OUP, XVIII, 1968, pp. 6–7. SP.28/136/8, Kenilworth. HMC Vth Rpt. p. 28;
cf. Cal. of HL for 11 Jun 1642. C. Thompson (ed.), Walter Yonge's Diary of HC. 1642–45, Orchard
Press, 1986, I, p. 8. CAM, p. 1155.
7.   Ingram: Hughes, pp. 109, 163n, 181, 190, 224; HMC IVth Rpt. p. 270 (19 Aug 1644). Hamper,
p. 47. SP28/139/3, Accts. of R. Wilson. SP.28/37/126. Combe: CSPD 1641–3, p. 343. M. Eccles,
Shakespeare in Warwickshire, Wisconsin, 1963, pp. 119–21. Hughes, p. 164. Dugdale: Northampton
RO, Finch-Hatton 4284: see comments by P. Styles, 'Dugdale and the Civil War', TBAS 86, 1974,
p. 132–3, and esp. Hughes, passim. Clarendon II, p. 469.

2. THE DRIFT TO WAR

1.   W.H. Coates (ed.), The Journal of Sir Simonds D'Ewes, Yale, 1942, pp. 144n, 146, 172; cf. Fletcher,
p. 139. CSPD 1641–3, p. 166. QS II, Int. xxiv. H. Stocks (ed.), Records of the Borough of Leics.,
Cambridge, 1923, p. 313. Fletcher, pp. 139, 215–6. L. Fox, The Borough Town of Stratford-upon-Avon,
Stratford 1953, p. 23. VCH Wks. III, p. 235. Spencer, p. 175n. VCH Wks. VIII, p. 459. For a good
account of the petitioning process, see Fletcher Ch. 6, on which some of this résumé is based; cf. LJ
IV, p. 579; E.135(27), 'The Two Petitions of Warwick and Coventry'. J.L. Malcolm, Caesar's Due,
Royal Hist. Soc., 1983, pp. 21–3, quoting CJ II, pp. 629, 650, 681; Hughes, pp. 131–2, 135–6.
Compton MSS, Castle Ashby 1083/1. BL Add 14827/144, A Book of Parliament, 9 Jul 1642. Several
recent historians have expressed reservations on Fletcher's view, e.g. R. Ashton, The English Civil War,
Weidenfeld, 1978, pp. 148–9, Hughes, pp. 135–6, 229–30, etc. Brooke: BL 669/5/55 (similar
version reproduced in QS II, App. I, xxii–xxiii). LJ V, pp. 195–6. Fiennes: Fletcher, quoting BL Harl
162/377, 480(127).
2.   Banbury: Beesley, pp. 454–62 etc.; Potts, op.cit., pp. 133–4. Fletcher, Chs 6 and 9. Oxford: 77
HMC De l'Isle & Dudley, VI, p. 364 (letter to Earl of Leics. Jan 1641). D.F. Mosler, 'Warwickshire
Catholics in the Civil War', Recusant History 15, 1981; Hughes, pp. 133–6. 37 HMC XIVth Rpt.
App. VIII, p. 203 (King from York to Worcs., 16 Aug 1642). S. Clarke, A Generall Martyrologie,
1651. VCH Oxon IX, pp. 114–19. DNB. Beesley, 283ff.
3.   P. Styles, 'Thomas Pilkington of Claverdon', TBAS 65, 1949 (described by Styles as 'somewhat of a
Vicar of Bray', p. 114). Holyoak: DNB; E.114(25); Matthews, p. 363. Harvey: DNB; Fletcher,
p. 291; Hughes, p. 325. HMC Vth Rpt. p. 15. Kenrick etc., Matthews. Wootton: SP.28/182,
Hughes, p. 205. Merriott; DNB & CJ II, p. 692. Clarke: CAM III, p. 1412. Jones, Williams:

Matthews. Howes: 45 *HMC* Buccleugh III, pp. 398–9; Beesley, pp. 296–7; *VCH* Oxon X, p. 98; *LJ* IV, pp. 108–9. For Banbury and religion, résumé in *VCH* II, pp. 46–8.

4. Clarke, Hall: Hughes, pp. 63, 314 etc. Brailes: A.J. Tennant, 'Brailes, A Feldon Community', Univ. of Leics. 1977 (unpublished; copy at Warwick RO). SP.23/84, pp. 259, 261 etc. Cropredy: *VCH* Oxon X, p. 162. Hanwell: ib. IX, pp. 114–19. Adderbury: E.81(19). Matthews, p. 299. Sutton: ib. 366. Temple: E. Sussex RO, Dunn 51/54. Fletcher, p. 108. Hughes, p. 131.

5. Hughes, p. 73 and *passim*, on which part of this section is based; the key work on chaplains is A. Lawrence, *Parliamentary Army Chaplains 1642–51*, RHS/Boydell, 1990; *DNB*. Hutton, p. 13. Clarendon II, pp. 320–2. Warwick: *HMC* IVth Rpt. p. 264, letter of 17 Mar 1644. Dugdale, op.cit., pp. 117, 95. E.114(15). BL Add 11045/144, Scudamore MSS, V, Nov. 1640. R. Baxter, *A Holy Commonwealth*, 1659, p. 457, and *Reliquiae Baxterianae*, ed. M. Sylvester, 1696, pp. 40–1, 44; *DNB*. Worcester: E.118(27), A True Character of Worster's late Hurly-Burly, 22 Sep 1642. Fletcher, pp. 417–18.

6. L.G. Schwoerer, *No Standing Armies*, Hopkins, 1974, p. 34 and Ch. III. Wedgwood, pp. 71–5; A. Woolrych in Worden, op.cit. p. 97. Selden: Wedgwood, p. 101. Wks. Commission of Array: Hutton, pp. 5–6. For some reason the King delayed until 10 July the order to the Earl of North. 'to put the Commission of Array into execution': Castle Ashby 1083/2. York: *LJ* V, p. 115. E.109(3). Offchurch: Wks RO N4/18/177–8. Alveston: SP.19/146/17; cf. Coleshill's warrant, SP.23/170/143; the commissioner omitted is Sir George Devereux of Sheldon.

7. Alcester: E.109(3). BL 669/6/50, 58. Bribes: *CSPD* 1641–3, 361; E.109(3). R. Bulstrode, *Memoirs and Reflections*, 1721, p. 72. E.110(8). Colours: BL Add 11364/15; SP.23/170/115–240, Coleshill. Southam: SP.19/146/19. Brooke: Hughes, p. 140; 23 *HMC* XIIth Rpt. II, p. 318. Lee: E.202(26); Hughes, pp. 140–1. *LJ* V, pp. 241–2, 256. SP.28/136, Accounts of John Needham.

8. Many unsolved mysteries remain concerning the musters, not least the delay in the Royalists', which may have been due to local hostility: cf. Hughes, p. 139n. Brooke's Southam rally may likewise have been abandoned as unsafe: Hughes 110. Northampton's Coleshill one was planned for Sat 30 Jul, but seems to have been postponed, apart from some 'exercises', until the following Monday, because of the Banbury magazine affair: see next chapter. Neither Northampton nor Dunsmore attended Coleshill 30 Jul nor, probably, 1 Aug either, but the details are unclear and testimonies inconsistent: SP.23/170/115 sqq., Coleshill, Kittermaster case. Shakespeare, 2 Hen IV, III (ii). Worcs.: *HMC* Portland I, p. 52 (12 Aug 1642), quoted Fletcher, p. 359; E.239(8). BL 669/6/50. Corbet. Saye: Clark, *The Life and Times of Anthony Wood*, op.cit., I, pp. 64–5 (Saye even imprisoned some). W.C. Abbott, *The Writings and Speeches of O. Cromwell*, Camb., Mass., 1937–47, I, p. 204. *CSPD* 1644, p. 301. Bulstrode, op.cit., quoted Young, pp. 264–74; numbers estimate by Young, p. 206; cf. Mosler, op.cit. pp. 103–4. Boughton: Sp.19/146/7–20. Tibbott: *CAM*, p. 1109. Hutton, pp. 22–3. BL 669/6/58; 669/6/50. *LJ* V, pp. 187–8. Nether Whitacre: Warwick RO, DRB 27/9, which itemizes attendance at musters of both camps, and on the King at Stoneleigh and Packington also.

9. R. Gough, *The History of Myddle*, ed. W.G. Hoskins, Centaur, 1968, p. 67. Winderton: Birmingham Ref. Lib. 167904 and SP.19/21/253, calendared *CAM* 13 Jul 1649. Interestingly, Hutton, p. 28 points out that the Myddle Civil War casualty rate was higher than that of the 1914–18 war. E.108(26); E.111(11); E.109(3); E.239(6). M.W. Farr, 'The Fetherstons of Packwood', op.cit. Bible: Matt. 5, 9. BL 669/6/58; E.113(14). Brooke: *CSPD* 25 Jul 1642; BL 669/6/50.

10. York: *LJ* V, p. 115. Commissions of Array: see Hutton, 5–7 for the whole process; *CSPD* 1641–3, pp. 343; full text of Wks. commission reprod. in J. Rushworth, *Historical Collections* 1721, IV, pp. 674–5. Coventry: *LJ* V, pp. 163–6, including letter of J. Barker to Brooke. BL Add 14827/144, 'A Book of Parliament'. Hughes, p. 139. Hutton, p. 19. E.202 [9, 12); E.92(18); *CJ* 27 Jun 1642.

11. E.109(3); BL 669/6/50; 669/5/55; Add 11364/14–15. Cannons: *CJ*, pp. 678, 690; E.202(21, 25); E.111(11) says 6 guns; dates confused, but before 18 Jul: BL Add 14827/163. Stoneleigh: SP.16/491/89, calendared *CSPD* 1641–3, p. 361; SP.19/21/246; it is likely, but not certain, that the Warwick armourer was the same Thomas Tibbott of Rowington who recruited men. Brooke: QS II App. I reproduces the full text of the Certificate of the Dep.Lts.; cf. E.202(15); E.112(42); BL 669/5/55; E.154(43). Reeve. Fletcher, p. 366. BL Add 14827/144; Hughes, pp. 140–1.

12. E.154(8), full text in Rushworth, op.cit. Castle Ashby 1083/2, 10 Jul 1642. Hastings: 78 *HMC* Hast. II, p. 86; E.202(15). Royalist musters: see Ch. 2, note 8 above; several parliamentarian news-sheets refer to the planned musters but say they had not yet taken place (eg. E.202(15), 9 Jul,

E.154(43), 12 Jul, etc.); Vicars, p. 99, claimed Northampton 'durst not appeare . . .'. Recruitment: E.110(8). Petre: SP.19/143/24 and *CAM*, p. 1256. Warwick: E.202(21, 25: 'some designe was in hand against Warwicke Castle').

13. E.111(11), 'The Proceedings at Banbury'. Earle: SP.19/157/142 and *CAM*, p. 1413. E.112(12); E.109(19, 35); BL 669/6/58; E.109(35); E.116(32); 78 *HMC* Hast. II, p. 86.

14. Dugdale, dated 4 Aug 1642 and reprod in QS II, App. II. Leics: *Records*, ed. Stocks, op.cit., pp. 313–4 (dated York, 5 Aug); Castle Ashby 1083/3. E.112(21); E.111(11). Stuart: E.53(10), reprod. Young, p. 294. Allies: 78 *HMC* Hast. II, p. 86; *LJ* V, pp. 286–7; *CSPD* 1641–3, p. 367. Rumours: E.111(11); E.112(12, 21); E.110(8); E.239(8). Kilsby: E.53(10), reprod. Young, p. 294. Clergy: E.111(11); E.112(21). Dunsmore: SP.28/186, Rugby. *CSPD* 1641–3, p. 368; SP.16/491/105; E.112(12, 21); Hughes, pp. 143–4; Beesley, pp. 298–303; E.202(35).

3. THE OUTBREAK OF WAR

1. E.112(3). Warburton II, p. 383. Spencer. E.239(7). 23 *HMC* XIIth Rpt. App. II, p. 320, Letter from Edw. Reed to Sir J. Coke, 14 Aug 1642, implying local inertia: 'as yet the country stirreth not . . .'. Fortifications: SP.28/4, Bridges' accounts, Aug–Sep 1642; E.109(3). M.W. Farr in *VCH* Wks. VII, p. 459, quoting Wk. RO CR 1866, Castle accounts. Hughes, p. 137. *VCH* Oxon I, p. 450. T. Cave & R.A. Wilson (eds.) *The Parliamentary Survey of Worcester, 1649–50*, Worcester, 1924. SP.28/25B. SP.28/183–6 and 201, Warwick, Ufton, etc. Hughes, p. 145. E.109(3). SP.28/4/71–93. Bulstrode, op.cit., reprod. Young, pp. 264–74. P. Styles, 'Sir Simon Archer', *Dug. Soc. Occ. Papers*, VI, pp. 35–40.

2. Dugdale illustrates Old St Mary's Church (destroyed in the great fire of Warwick, 1694, and replaced by the present one). E.109(3). E.239(7); Spencer; E.112(3). 23 *HMC* XIIth Rpt. App. II. p. 320. Bulstrode, op.cit., p. 73, reprod. Young, p. 265. E.113(1); E.239(10). Swan: SP.28/253B/10. W. Dugdale, *History of St. Paul's*, Int., p. xiv; P. Styles, 'Dugdale and the Civil War', *TBAS* 86 (1974); Hamper; G. Taggart, 'Dugdale and the Civil War', *North Arden History*, Coleshill, no. 11, 1988. QS Int. pp. xxx–xxxi. Banbury: E.112(21). Waller to Sir R. Hopton, 16 Jul 1643: cf. Wedgwood, pp. 226, 651 n. 92.

3. SP.28/184; E.239(7); E.113(1); E.110(8); E.114(3): BL 669/6/58. Hamper, pp. 15–17. Bulstrode, in Young. *CJ* II, pp. 682, 690, 693. *CSPD* 1641–3, p. 361. 23 *HMC* XIIth Rpt. App. II, p. 320. Mosler, op.cit., pp. 17–23; Hughes, pp. 234–7; résumé in *VCH* Wks., p. 459. E.239(8). Hutton, p. 19 comments: 'In the process they brought about the appearance of a new animal upon the scene, the regular soldier, caring nothing for a local community in which he had no place, acting only at the will of his paymaster'. Tanworth: SP.16/539/347. E.239(10); E.113(1); E.239(7). Spencer, pp. 180–1.

4. E.112(15, 29); E.114(25). Bucks: *Merc. Rusticus* for 10 Jun 1643, and G. Lipscomb, *The History and Antiquities of the County of Buck.*, 1847, III, p. 47; Sir Peter Temple of Stowe, a parliamentary colonel whose family had estates at Burton Dassett in Wks., is also named as culprit. Oxon: *LJ* V, pp. 286–7. E.114(3). R. Spalding (ed.), *Diary of Bulstrode Whitelocke*, OUP, 1990, pp. 134–5; B. Whitelocke, *Memorials of the English Affairs*, Oxford, 1853, p. 59.

5. *LJ* V, pp. 286–7. Wood: Clark, op,cit., pp. 52–7. E.111(11). 29 *HMC* XIIIth Rpt. p. 52, Sir W. Brereton to Sir Ralph Ashton/Assheton, 13 Aug 1642. 17 *HMC* Vth Rpt., p. 43. 53 *HMC* Montague 157. J.W.W. Bund (ed.), *Diary of Henry Townshend*, Worcester, 1920, II, 72ff. E.111(11); E.114(10); E.113(14). Bund, op.cit., II, p. 74 (appended note dated 15 Aug). E.239(10). *HMC* XIIth Rpt. App. II, p. 320 (14 Aug). King's ultimatum: E.112(44); cf. Strider, pp. 53–6; Young, p. 75.

6. E.113(14). Bloxam, p. 4. Bund, op.cit., II, p. 79. QS xxxi; Dugdale was involved in the Royalists' retreat from Kenilworth shortly after, and the skirmish at Curdworth. A.C. Wood, *Nottingham in the Civil War*, Oxford, 1937, Ch. 3, esp. pp. 19–20. Wedgwood, pp. 117–18. E.114(1, 10). Castle Ashby 1083/5, 22 Aug. P. Styles, 'Dugdale in the Civil War', *TBAS* 86 (1974), p. 133. Coventry: E.114(1, 10, 15, 23). Clarendon II, pp. 288–9. BL Add 11364/14–15. Bloxam, p. 7. Dugdale II, p. 931. E.114(36); E.115(4, 21). Wharton, pp. 315–27. E.115(2); SP.28/253B. Spencer. SP.28/184. Henley. Castle Ashby 1083/4. SP.28/185, Hillmorton. E.114(1, 34); E.115(2, 4). Clarendon II, p. 289. E.114(34).

7. SP.28/186, Whitnash. Southam: E.114(23, 25, 27); E.115(2); E.240(15). *LJ* V, p. 321. Clarendon,

p. 289. J. Vicars, op.cit., I, pp. 141–3; N. Wharton, op.cit., pp. 315–16 (reprod. *CSPD* 1641–3, pp. 380–94). Holyoak: *DNB*; E.114(25); Hughes, pp. 67–9. B. Townsend, *Southam through the Centuries*, Wks. Co. Lib., 1981, pp. 6–11. Prisoners: BL Add 11364/15. Marton: J.T. Burgess, *Historic Warwickshire*, Midland Educ. Co., 1893, p. 161; E.114(25, 36).

8.   B. Townsend, op.cit., p. 11. Spencer, p. 181; E.114(27); Young, pp. 15–16 gives other examples of accidents due to lack of training. E.240(15). Firth. Many villages date the levies for Brooke's horse from 20 Jul. SP.28/184, Long Itchington; SP.28/183, Dunchurch, Southam, Aston Cantlow; Wharton, pp. 317–25. E.114(25, 36). SP.28/183, 184. Frankton: Hughes, pp. 154–5. Holyoak: SP.28/183, Southam; E.115(2). SP.28/182, Packington. C. Thompson (ed.), *Walter Yonge's Diary of Proceedings in the House of Commons*, 1642–5, Orchard Press, 1986, I, p. 31; Fetherstone-Dilke MSS, Wks. RO.

4. THE EDGEHILL CAMPAIGN

1.   V.F. Snow, *Essex the Rebel*, Nebraska, 1970, pp. 324–5; S.R. Gardiner, *History of the Great Civil War*, Longmans, 1901, I, pp. 23, 26–8; Wedgwood, p. 120; *CSPV* 1642–3, p. 165. E.200(59, 60). Wharton, op.cit., p. 324. SP. 28/184, 186, Rugby, Wolfhampcote. Rupert: Warburton, pp. 408–9. Wilcox: SP.28/182 Brandon and Bretford; De Boyes was later dismissed for incompetence: Young, pp. 69, 103, 156, 306. E.124(26). Wharton, op.cit., p. 325; for 'backbiters', cf. Shakespeare's punning reference, 2 Hen IV, (v). SP.28/184, 186, 201, Leamington Priors, Whitnash, Ashow. Clarke: cf. Hughes, pp. 63, 67, 82, 314–15.

2.   SP.28/183, Charlecote, and A. Fairfax-Lucy, *Charlecote and the Lucys*, OUP, 1958, p. 143. SP.28/210, Edstone; SP.28/186/, Binton. Coughton: E.240(23). *CSPD* 1641–3, pp. 372–3. Alcester: SP.28/201. SP.28/183, Butlers Marston. Worcs. and Powick: E.118 (17, 22, 43). E.119 (2, 5, 6, 8, 9, 11, 21), E.126 (38–9), E.240 (16, 20, 21–3). Clarendon VI, pp. 44–6. Wharton, pp. 325–6. Rupert: Warburton I, pp. 400–1. E.119(9). Essex: Wharton, p. 330 mocks 'those famous lawes'; they were often reprinted, e.g. E.75(34), E.77(25), etc. Wedgwood, p. 123.

3.   Wharton, p. 330 claimed Essex himself ordered Russell's house to be plundered. Cathedral: Letter of A. Trevor to Marqu. of Ormonde, Dec 1642, in T. Carte (ed.), *A Collection of Original Letters and Papers*, 1739, I, p. 15; Wedgwood, pp. 123–4. Lichfield: Dugdale, *Short View*, op.cit. pp. 559–60. E.124(18). Gardiner, op.cit., I, p. 39. *LJ* V, p. 412. *HMC* Xth Rpt. VI, p. 88. Firth, p. 731. Bund, pp. 10–13, quoting county sessions records for 1633; cf. Worcestershire Co. Rec., *Quarter Sessions Rolls*, 1899, ed. Bund, I, pp. 511, 593. Alvechurch: R.E. Sherwood, *Civil Strife in the Midlands, 1642–51*, Phillimore, 1974, p. 33. Roads: *HMC* Vth Rpt. p. 211; W. Marshall, *The Rural Economy of the Midland Counties*, I, pp. 70–1; J. Ogilby, op.cit., *passim*; C. Morris (ed.), *The Journal of Celia Fiennes*, 1947, *passim*; J. Taylor, The 'Pennylesse Pilgrimage', in *All the Works of John Taylor*, 1630, facs., Scolar, 1973, p. 124.

4.   Clarendon II, p. 536, Spencer, p. 182.; cf. E.124(26) (incompetence of De Boyes). V.F. Snow, op.cit., p. 334; Snow is unfair in claiming that Essex 'allowed his artillery unit to lag behind'; Young, pp. 72–7. Lord Wilmot to Rupert, 1 Dec 1642, quoted Warburton II, p. 74. Wharton, p. 327; Essex's orders are reproduced in full in G. Grenville, *Some Memorials to John Hampden*, Murray, 1832, II, pp. 257–61. SP.28/184–6, Temple Grafton, Ilmington, Studley. Lark Stoke: Vicars, op.cit., IV, pp. 107–8. Stratford: E.124(27); SP.28/136, 183, 201; BL Add 28565.

5.   W.H. Hutton, *Highways and Byways in Shakespeare's Country*, Macmillan, 1926, pp. 28–9. SP.28/182–6; Willoughby presents a puzzle, since Brailes is the only parish to mention him (and not his men); Whitelocke says he joined the battle late, but another source that he fought 'bravely' (BL 1104.a.22, 'A True Relation . . .'); according to Peacock (*Army Lists*, 1874, p. 48) he arrived too late. With due respect to Clarendon (II, p. 356: 'neither army knew where the other was'), it is difficult to accept that neither army was aware of the proximity of the other, since Essex had sent his petition to the King at Packington, who was then known to have moved to Kenilworth, with 4,000 men reported near Warwick, where the ever-alert Bridges, Lord Brooke's trusty commander, would certainly assess matters. Reports of the King's march were sent to Westminster several times after he left Shrewsbury (e.g. E.124/4, 15, 16 etc.), some quite accurate: the King 'marched to Meriden . . . and intends to march towards Banbury'; 'Upon Friday last his Majesty marched by Coventry, & . . . came that night

to Southam and . . . from thence to Banbury . . .'. Bridges' capture of the royal carriages near Warwick also proves that the parliamentary information service was reasonably efficient. I. Roy, op.cit., p. 153; Firth. SP.28/185, Leek Wootton; Bloxam, p. 11. B. Townsend, op.cit., p. 11; T. Carte, op.cit., I, p. 9, A Relation of Edgehill Fight. Clarendon II, pp. 358–9, 364.

6. Bodleian Lib. MS Ashmole 830, copy at Wk. RO Z112/SM; cf. E.124(19). Firth. SP.28/186, Rugby. Young, *passim.* Banbury: E.124(27). Warwick booty: SP.28/253B. Offchurch: Wk RO N4/18/177–8. *CSPD* 1645–7, pp. 240, 522, etc. *LJ* VI, p. 196. SP.16/57/1–11; SP.16/511/106ff.; SP.28/36/143/ 365–6; SP.28/253A,B,255–6; Hughes, pp. 215–6; E.124(27). Beesley, p. 312. *VCH* Oxon X, p. 198. Edgehill speech reprod. Somers, op.cit., IV, p. 479. Cf. Young, Plate 6, The Recruiting Areas; *CSPD* 1641–3, pp. 439, 453, 467. There are many contemporary references to the Welsh at Edgehill, and cf. F.G. Stephens (ed.), *Catalogue of Political and Personal Satires*, British Museum, 1870–1954, I, pp. 1320–1689, nos. 312ff. Myddle: R. Gough, *The History of Myddle*, ed. D. Hey, New York, 1986, pp. 71–2. Kingsmill: W.H. Hutton, op.cit. p. 30; A. Fairfax-Lucy, op.cit., pp. 142n, 154n, 156.

7. Social mobility, urban development, time and the vagaries of modern cartographers all threaten old place-names, but most of these are still current, though Prince Rupert's Tent, marked on Beighton's 1725 map, seems a casualty. Beacons: E.124(27); the nearest were at Shuckburgh, recently replaced by a new one (QS II, p. 53), and Burton Dassett (ib., III, pp. 76–7). There is a mystery about the beacons: Grenville's *Memoirs of Hampden*, op.cit., pp. 311–12, says Essex had received orders to signal to Parliament when he overtook the King by firing the nearest beacon, and that this was done at Burton Dassett, so relaying the news to Ivinghoe, Bucks., Harrow and London. There is no reference to the beacons in the parish accounts, however, and F. Kitchen, *Fire over England*, Brighton, 1988, says 'the beacons played no part in the Civil War'.

8. R. Baxter, *Reliquiae Baxterianae*, London, 1696, ed. Sylvester, I, 43; Baxter was deputizing for Samuel Clarke, Lord Brooke's protégé. Bloxam, p. 14. B. Smith, *The Village of Oxhill*, 1989, p. 14. E.124(33). C.V. Wedgwood, *The Common Man*, Leics., 1957, 9. T. Carte, op.cit., p. 13. SP.28/182, Kineton; Rupert was alleged to have massacred many parliamentary wounded: E.126(4). C.H. Firth, *The Memoirs of Edward Ludlow*, Oxford, 1894, I, p. 46, reprod. Young, p. 314. N. Wallington, *Historical Notices of the Reign of Charles I*, Bentley, 1869, II, pp. 115–6. Hester Whyte: SP.16/539/358, calendared *CSPD* Add. 1625–49, p. 693. G. Miller, *Rambles round the Edge Hills*, Banbury, 1896, p. 70. Dugdale, *Short View*, op.cit., p. 109. Warmington: Wk RO, parish reg.

9. Edgehill topography: cf. contemporary accounts in Young, pp. 93, 94, 111, 114, 119, 262, 267, etc. Danvers: SP.19/144/12–24. Spencer, pp. 182–3; Young, p. 130. Clarendon, pp. 375–6. Wedgwood, *The Common Man*, op.cit., p. 14, quoting H. Ellis (ed.), *Original Letters*, 3rd series, 1846, IV, p. 216. SP.28/184, Tysoe. Clarendon, pp. 364, 373. Wounded: SP.28/253B. *CJ* III, 187. Offchurch Wk RO N4/18/177–8. Hughes, p. 256. SP.28/136/19, Barker's Accounts, Coventry. SP.28/182, Bishops Tachbrook. Throckmorton: SP.28//253B; Hughes, p. 228. Sir Philip Warwick's Memoires of 1702, reprod. Young, pp. 282–3. SP.28/182–5, Kenilworth, Warwick, Snitterfield, Wappenbury, Willoughby. F. White, *Historical Gazeteer and Directory of Wks.*, Sheffield, 1850, p. 680, and *VCH* VI, p. 262. Sheldon: SP.16/511/106, Examination of Thomas Savage. Temple: C. Thompson, *Yonge*, op.cit., p. 82. James II's account of Edgehill, reprod. Young, p. 279; SP.28/248. Hutton, p. 35. Clarendon II, p. 364. BL Add 35098, The Book of Sequestrations, 1646.

10. Dugdale, *Short View*, p. 110 (Burton Dassett is not mentioned, but is the traditional identification). Welsh: Bulstrode, *Memoirs*, reprod. Young, pp. 272–3. Essex: C. Thompson, *Yonge*; C.H. Firth (ed.), *Ludlow*, op.cit., I, p. 45. Harvey: A. Clarke (ed.), *John Aubrey, Brief Lives*, Oxford, 1898, I, p. 297. Prince Charles: Young, Plate 39, Arlescote House. Astley: Young, p. 115. E.127(47), Strange News from Warwicke. Somers *Tracts*, p. 305. Royalist gallantry medals were minted, for the first time, another indication of the national importance attributed to Edgehill: Young, pp. 30, 147, 271 and Plate 43. Stoneleigh: E.75(28, 29). Ghosts: E.M. Symonds, 'The Diary of John Greene, 1635–1657', *Eng. Hist. Rev.* 43 (1928); E.85(41); E.86(23), abstracted in Young, pp. 162–6. Brailes: E.A.B. Barnard, 'Old Days in and around Evesham', *The Evesham Journal* no. 907, Feb 1941; the name Traitors Ford pre-dates the Civil War and probably relates, in any case, not to a person but, less romantically, to the treacherous nature of this low-lying area still liable to flooding. Poem 'After Edgehill' by Gladys Mary Coles, from *Leafburners: New and Selected Poems*, Duckworth, 1986.

11. QS xxv, pp. 125–6. Fletcher, p. 336, and 'The Coming of the War', in Morrill, pp. 30–1. Poem:

E.669/6/87 (punctuated and abridged); cf. H.E. Rollins, *Cavalier and Puritan*, New York, 1923,who stresses the great influence of the street poets as opinion-formers (an aspect often neglected by historians of the Civil War).

5. WINTER TRIALS

1. There were many royalist desertions; cf. Hutton, p. 35; Clarendon adds (II, p. 373) that many either had no arms, or had lost them at Edgehill. Pardon: BL 669/5/88, from 'Our Court at Edgehill', 24 Oct 1642, and Aynho, 27 Oct; full text reprod. in J.F. Larkin (ed.), *Stuart Royal Proclamations*, Oxford, 1983, II, p. 803. Declaration: Rushworth, op.cit., V, pp. 39–41 (and parliamentary reply, pp. 41–9). Beesley, p. 326. N. Cooper, *Aynho, a Northamptonshire Village*, Banbury Hist. Soc. 20 (1984) pp. 80–1; and N. Wallington, *Historical Notices of the Reign of Ch. I.*, Bentley, 1869, II, p. 272. Potts, op.cit, pp. 184–5.

2. Bulstrode, in Young, pp. 264–74. J. Sprigge, *Anglia Rediviva*, 1647, facs. ed. H.T. Moore, Florida, 1960, pp. 251–2. Whetham: E.8(9), A Full Relation of the Siege of Banbury; Clarendon II, p. 374; the King's advisers could not know it was only weakly defended. Broughton: T. Carte, op.cit., pp. 13–14. Grenville, op.cit., II, p. 314. Whitelocke, op.cit., I, p. 188. Beesley, p. 326n: H.G. Slade, 'Broughton Castle, *The Archeol. Journal* 135 (1978); Saye: E.127(6); *LJ* VIII, p. 39; it is unclear whether Broughton was captured before or after Banbury: Clarendon says before, Rupert's Journal after, others the same day.

3. 'Prince Rupert's Diary', Wilts, RO, reprod. Young, pp. 285–6; E.127(18), 'Prince Roberts Disguises; or a perfect true relation of the several shapes he has taken since the Lord Generall went forth first from London', 16 Nov. 1642. E.126(12). C.H. Firth (ed.), *The Memoirs of Edw. Ludlow*, Oxford, 1894, I, 46, reprod. Young, p. 314. Whitelock, op.cit., I, p. 188 (cf. Warburton II, p. 39, n.3). Beesley, pp. 326–9. Clarendon II, pp. 373–5. E.126(23). Young, p. 264. Letter to Greville Verney of Compton Verney, 20(24?) Dec 1642, reprod. Beesley, p. 330. Banbury Castle: SP.16/492/43, repeated in Thompson's *Yonge*, op.cit. pp. 99–100, and calendared *CSPD* 1641–3, pp. 402–3. E.126(24) reprod. Rushworth, op.cit., V, pp. 33–5, and Young, p. 264.

4. Castle Ashby 1083/9a–20, reprod. in A. Compton, 'Notes on the Civil War' *Trans. Arch. Soc. Northants.*, Oxford, 1854, pp. 26–32. Aynho: Cooper, op.cit. p. 81. SP.28/185, 186, Hillmorton and Rugby. Whetham: E.8(9). W.B. Compton, *History of the Comptons of Compton Wynyates*, Bodley, 1930, p. 83. King's appeal: E.83(470. Dyve: Warburton II, p. 85 (31 Dec 1642), BL Add 18980/5 (21 Sep, Abingdon). Deddington: BL Harl 6851/107; F. Sharpe, *The Church Bells of Oxfordshire*, Oxford Rec. Soc. I, 1949, p. 116; *Archeol. Journal* VI (1849), p. 179; J. Skelton, *Engraved Illusts. of the Antiqs. of Oxfordshire*, Oxford, 1823, Wootton Hundred, p. 7; *VCH* Oxon XI, p. 115.

5. J. Sprigge, op.cit., p. 253. Castle Ashby 1083/12–16. Warburton II, p. 84 (Northampton to Rupert, 27 Dec 1624), 91 (King to Northampton, 2 Jan). Warburton II, p. 79. Bristol: SP.28/253B/2. J. Larkin (ed.), op.cit., II, pp. 826–7. E.129(7). Warburton II, pp. 84 & I, App., Abstract of Letters. BL Add 18980/12. *VCH* Oxon X, p. 9. Sailors: E.86(3, 22). Firth, pp. 31–2. *HMC* IXth Rpt. App. p. 434. Castle Ashby 1314/4 (Northampton to Rupert, 4 Jan). Beesley, pp. 331–2, 'Exact & Full Relation of all the Proceedings at Banbury', 29 Dec 1642. Wallington, op.cit, II, p. 138. Thompson's *Yonge*, op.cit., p. 267. Daventry: E.86(3, 5), E.245(21). 78 *HMC* Hastings II.

6. Ghosts: E.86(3). Stratford: BL Add 28565; SP.28/136/51. Twitchet: Matthews, p. 366; BL Add 35098/36. Trapp: Laurence, op.cit., p. 180; Eccles, op.cit., p. 114. Stratford confrontation: E.86(22); Sherwood, op.cit., pp. 225–6, quoting SP.24/75, Sharpe v. Green (cf. *CAM* for other cases); Hughes, pp. 151, 207, 303. Spencer, pp. 184–5.

7. Stratford: E.86(22, 41); SP.28/136/51; BL Add 28565. Nash: J.O. Halliwell-Phillips, *An Historical Account of the New Place*, Stratford-upon-Avon, 1864, pp. 114–15. Shakespeare: Halliwell-Phillips, op.cit., E.K. Chambers, *William Shakespeare*, Oxford, 1930; E.I. Fripp, *Shakespeare's Stratford*, Oxford, 1928; S. Schoenbaum, *William Shakespeare, A Compact Documentary Life*, Oxford, 1987. Both Fripp and Chambers consider it likely that Shakespeare was born in the eastern part of the Henley St property (Fripp, p. 19, Chambers II, p. 33).

8. Castle Ashby 1083/15. 78. *HMC* Hastings II, p. 94–5 (Nicholas to Hastings, 25 Feb 1643). SP.28/201. Stratford skirmish: E.91(5, 19): E.246(37); *VCH* III, p. 235. The otherwise obscure

mention of 'when the fight was by Snitterfield' (SP.28/184, Snitterfield) probably refers. Market house: Spencer, pp. 184–5, and esp. E.A. Barnard, 'The Building of the Old Market House at Stratford', *Evesham Journal*, 4 and 11 Feb 1928, quoting PRO Chancery C2/P78/34 & P91/27. SP.28/136/1. Cooke: Schoenbaum, op.cit., pp. 291–2; Eccles, op.cit., p. 114. Verney: Halliwell-Phillips, op.cit., p. 117. SP.28/185, Kenilworth. Banbury: E.247(13).

6. THE GRIP OF WAR: SPRING 1643

1. SP.28/184, Warwick. Warburton I, App: Abstract of Corresp. BL Add 18980/23, 28. Wedgwood, p. 180. Death of Brooke: E.94(11); E.246(39). Windsor: BL Add 18980 26. Warwick Castle: E.94(14, 18); E.96(12); E.102(6). Warburton II, p. 116, Dugdale, p. 47. Hughes, p. 181. Parliament reported 'proof' of Northampton's catholicism in the crucifix found on him: E.94(15, 29); Denbigh: *CJ* III, p. 121; Hughes, 221ff.; death of Northampton: E.99(18), letter of 22 Mar 1643. Wedgwood, p. 181.
2. Hughes, p. 181. Rupert: Firth, pp. 732–3; 15 *HMC* Xth Rpt. VI, p. 95; *HMC* IXth Rpt. App.; Warburton II, App; Shipston: E.96(2). Henley: QS III, pp. 271–2. Luke, p. 56 (6 Apr 1643). E.100(8). P. Rupert's Burning Love for England. E.99(25). Weather: Wedgwood, p. 187. Alcester: E.99(21); E.99(15); E.105(10). Ilmington: E.105(17).
3. Warwick fortifications: SP.28/136/13; SP.28/184; Hughes, p. 234; SP.28/183; cf. the excellent article by D. Pennington, 'The War and the People', in Morrill. Worcs.: SP.28/253B/13. Tysoe: SP.28/184; Studley: SP.28/185; Pierce: E.247(26); Pierce (or Peers) was listed as a prominent Royalist by Dugdale. *CSPD* 1644–5, p. 562, etc.; *HMC* IVth Rpt., p. 265 (Coventry, 6 Apr 1644, Denbigh to Committee for Both Kingdoms). Warwick: E.105(12); Castle Ashby 1083/23, 24, Coventry, 10 Jun 1643. Bridges: *LJ* VIII, p. 47 and *HMC* VIth Rpt. App., p. 88.
4. Castle Ashby 1083/18, 20, 21, 25; BL Harl. 6851/70, 105–106, 120, 135; BL Add.18980/58; resistance was also reported from Bucks: BL Add. 18980/66, 68; cf. Hutton in Morrill, pp. 55, 60; for Worcs. resistance: J.L. Malcolm, *Ceasar's Due: Loyalty and King Charles, 1642–1646*, Royal Hist. Soc., 1983, pp. 210–11. Warburton I, p. 506, BL Harl. 6852/7. 78 *HMC* Hastings II, p. 103. Hutton, pp. 92–3. E.105(17). Hunks: Young, p. 231. Warburton I, p. 507. Middleton Cheney: E.249(2, 4, 5, 6); Beesley, pp. 345–7; *Merc. Aul.* 6 and 9 May 1643; 78 *HMC* Hastings II, p. 101; Middleton Cheney burial register, 7 May 1643; Warburton II, p. 186. Northampton dispute: BL Add. 29570 (Hatton correspondence).

7. SUMMER PASSAGES

1. Tredington: J.W.W. Bund (ed.), *The Diary of Henry Townshend*, Wcs.Hist.Soc., 1920, II, pp. 102–5; BL Harl 6804/78–9. Fiennes: Tibbutt, p. 76; Hutton, pp. 98–9; cf. D. Pennington in Morrill, pp. 118–20; *HMC* IVth Rpt. p. 308; Cherington: SP.28/184; Cox: SP.28/136/32; SP.28/184, Tysoe (cf. Hughes, pp. 197, 257, Lovell); SP.28/182, Bretford.
2. Queen's letters: Comte de Baillon, *Henriette-Marie de France, Reine d'Angleterre*, Paris, 1877, pp. 481–99 (some translated in M.A.E. Green (ed.), *Letters of Queen Henrietta Maria*, 1857). Queen's journey: Clarendon III, p. 19; *CSPV* 1642–3, pp. 258–8; W.A. Day (ed.), *The Pythouse Papers*, 1879, pp. 48–9, H. Percy to Rupert, 29 Apr 1643; gossip: Wedgwood, p. 231; Warburton II, pp. 229–30; *HMC* VIIth Rpt. App. p. 244; J. Kenyon, *The Civil Wars of England*, Weidenfeld, 1988, p. 78.
3. Luke, pp. 113–14. Wks: E.60(17); E.62(2, 3). SP.28(182, 185), Kenilworth, Churchover. Castle Ashby 1083/23, 24. Purefoy: E.62(13); E.56(11); Hughes, p. 175 and *passim*. H.T.Cooke, *Notices of the Church of St Mary and the Beauchamp Chapel*, Warwick, 1845, p. 63. Dugdale, I, p. 445, and *The Restoration of the Beauchamp Chapel, 1674–1742*, Oxford, 1956, pp. 17–18 (accounts of 4 Oct 1682). Cromwell: C.H. Firth, *Cromwell*, Putnam, 1935, pp. 94–5; Abbott, op.cit., I, p. 235–6; *HMC* VIIth Rpt. App., pp. 551–2. Essex: E.71(7), A Remonstrance . . ., 17 Aug 1643. Convoy: Warburton II, p. 189, Nicholas to Rupert, 11 May 1643, 223ff. Hamper, p. 50–1. Beesley, pp. 347–8. 78 *HMC* Hast. II, pp. 99–100. Luke, p. 105 (26 Jun 1643).
4. Warburton II, pp. 224–7; Firth, pp. 733–4. Baillon, op.cit., pp. 489–9. Hawkesley: *VCH* Worcs.

III, p. 184. *CSPD* 1644–5, p. 393; Clarendon IV, p. 38. SP.28/183, Edgbaston. Warwick: SP.28/253B; SP.28/136/13. Tradition: Sir Hugh Clopton to Lewis Theobald, 1733. Plays: Chambers, op.cit., II, pp. 352–3; F.E. Halliday, *A Shakespeare Companion, 1550–1950*, Duckworth, 1952, p. 114. Baillon, op.cit., pp. 198–9. Wallington, op.cit., II, p. 169; Stratford borough records quoted by Halliwell-Phillips, op.cit., p. 115.

5. M. Prestwich, *Cranfield: Politics and Profits under the Early Stuarts*, Oxford, 1966, p. 571. Charlecote: Fairfax-Lucy, op.cit. Luke, pp. 113, 117. Kineton meeting: E.61(11); E.62(3); Beesley, p. 348; Bloxam, pp. 22, 29. Pope: Sherwood, op.cit., p. 103; Beesley, p. 618. Bonfires: Luke, p. 117. Royalist quarters: Firth, Luke, pp. 114, 117, 118, 121, etc.

6. Relief of Gloucester: E.67(13); E.69(15); E.70(10), reprod. in Washbourn (including 'Historical Introduction'); Dugdale, *Short View*, op.cit., p. 187; for importance of Glos., cf. Clarendon III, p. 129, Wedgwood, p. 243, etc.

7. Essex: *HMC* IVth Rpt. p. 263; Clarendon III, p. 170; Waller: J. Adair, *Roundhead General, A Military Biography of Sir W. Waller*, Macdonald, 1969, pp. 96–7; *CSPV* 1643–7, p. 1; E.61(22, 25); Bridges: Washbourn, op.cit., Hist. Int., p. clxvii (Warwick, 28 Aug); Luke, p. 142; Vicars III, p. 404; march: E.69(15), E.70(10) (in Washbourn, op.cit.); Snow op.cit., pp. 368, 383; Clarendon III, p. 170; Luke, pp. 121, 135–6, etc.; E.67 (13,30); Essex at Tewkesbury, 10 Sep: *LJ* VI, p. 218; *Merc. Aul.*, 2 Sep 1643; E.71(7), A Remonstrance to Vindicate Essex, 17 Aug 1643. Quarters: regrettably, virtually none of the Civil War parish accounts for north Oxfordshire villages survive, including Hook Norton, Deddington, Adderbury.

8. SP.28/182, Willington, Wolford; SP.28183, Milverton, Bilton, Ascot and Whichford; SP.28184, Brailes; Sheldon: SP.19/146/71 (calendared *CAM* 1289). Ingram: *HMC* IVth Rpt. (Denbigh), p. 270 (19 Aug 1644); Banbury: Beesley, pp. 353–4; Parliamentary march: Washbourn, op.cit., pp. 235–71; E.67(30), *Merc. Civ.*, 14–21 Sep 1643; Essex: *The Parliamentary or Constitutional History of England*, London, 1772, XII, p. 470. E.68(3); E.70(7). Vicars III, p. 49. E.77(22, 23). SP.28/185, Studley. Hampton: Dugdale, p. 957; A.E. Everitt, 'Hampton-in-Arden', *TBAS* 8 (1882), p. 8. Dugdale, p. 56 (though *Merc. Aul.* of 20 Nov reports a successful royalist attack on Coughton).

9. SP.28/184, Tysoe. Wells: Letter to inhabitants of Weston-on-Avon, Oct 1643, quoted Hughes, p. 189; Parlt.: *LJ* VI, p. 218–19 (10 and 16 Sep 1643); *CJ* III, p. 277 (16 Oct 1643, pp. 284, 294–5, 305); Ferrer (or Farrar): *CSPD* 1641–2, p. 491 (11 Oct 1643); Gerard: Warburton I, p. 500; Northants & Towcester: E.67(22); E.69(25); E.74(1, 4, 21,); E.76(3); Luke, p. 159; Whetham; G. Baker, *The History and Antiqs. of Northampton*, 1822–30, II, pp. 175–6, 322–3 etc.; G. Lipscomb, *The History and Antiqs. of Bucks.*, 1847, IV, pp. 272–3, 281–2; Beesley, pp. 352–3; E.74(1,4); SP.19/22/288–9 (*CAM* 1399); Firth.

10. Warburton, p. 503; SP.28/185, Hillmorton; SP.28/184, Wolfhampcote; Grafton: *CSPD* 1641–3, pp. 507–9; *Merc. Civ.* A True Relation of the Taking of Grafton House, 29 Dec 1643; Baker, op.cit., II, pp. 175–6; Essex: *CSPD* 1641–3, pp. 510 (31 Dec 1643). *HMC* VIth Rpt. App., p. 11; *LJ* VI, p. 535. Massey: Corbet lxxxv-v, quoting *Merc. Verid.* of 17–24 Jan 1644; *CJ* III, p. 392. SP.28/182, Warmington. Gardiner, op.cit., I, p. 275. Warburton I, p. 495, Biron to Rupert. Coventry: *HMC* IVth Rpt. App., p. 264. BL Add 11364/16 (undated 1644). Warburton I, p. 500, Gerard to Rupert. Convoy: Luke, p. 254; one journalist states categorically in Jan 1644 that the convoy 'is now gone from Northampton to Leicester' (E.81/23). Hamper, p. 61; *CSPD* 1644, pp. 28–9. D.R. Guttery, *The Great Civil War in Midland Parishes*, Birmingham, 1951, pp. 63–5.

11. *CSPD* 1644, *passim*; BL Eg. 785 (Luke's Letter books), 5, 7; Luke, p. 261; Hamper, p. 62; Warburton I, p. 497; *HMC* IXth Rpt. App., p. 434; BL Add. 18981/45, 76, Vavasour to Rupert, 17 Feb, 1 Mar 1644; *CSPD* 1644, pp. 29–30; Cromwell: *CSPD* 1644, pp. 33–4; E.252(23). For once, Beesley, p. 355, is careless in accepting the false report of Cromwell at Banbury, corrected in E.252(14, 24). *Merc. Aul.*, 8 Jan 1644. Hilsden: H. Roundell, 'The Garrison of Newport Pagnell during the Civil Wars', *Records of Bucks.*, II, pp. 231–3; *HMC* IVth Rpt., App., p. 271.

12. E.34(21); E.252(18, 26); *HMC* IVth Rpt.App., p. 264, Massey to Bridges, 28 Feb (Massey repeated similar royalist dispositions to Essex on 11 Mar: BL Eg 785/7 and to Luke, ib., p. 271, undated; Tibbutt, p. 331. E.35(23); E.37(16, 21). Vicars, op.cit., p. 182. Luke, p. 266; *CSPD* 1644, pp. 55. 57, 63. Wasperton: Wk.RO CR 2017/C9/67. Warburton I, 498. E.252(17). W.A. Day (ed.), *The Pythouse Papers*, 1879 (D. O'Neille to Rupert, n.d.). E.252(27). For Denbigh controversies, see

Hughes, p. 227 and *passim*. Essex: *LJ* VI, p. 505; Ferrer: *CJ* III, p. 476; E.46(9); *CSPD* 1644, p. 30: Denbigh to Committee of Both Kingdoms, 29 Feb.

13. E.37(24). Parish accounts, SP.28/182–186. Denbigh: *CSPD* 1644, pp. 67–8, 91, 97. Chipping Campden: E.252(17,25). Cromwell: *CSPD* 1644, pp. 33–4; *HMC* VIIth Rpt. App., p. 446, Sir R. Burgoyne to Sir R. Verney, 7 Mar 1644; *CSPD* 1642, p. 562; Abbott I, p. 276; Perf. Occs., 1–9 Mar; E.37(7, 27). *Northants Notes and Queries*, I, 1866, p. 36, Sir G. Dudley to Rupert, Newark, 4 Mar 1644, says many Royalists left Banbury via Daventry, incl. Sir Wm Compton, 23 Feb. Chadshunt: E252(23); E.36(6); E.37(21); Tibbutt, p. 628; Beesley, pp. 354–5; Hawkesworth: E. Carey-Hill, 'The Hawkesworth Papers, 1601–1660'. *TBAS* LIV, pp. 1929–30.

14. Newsam: the family loyalties were ambiguous; see Hughes, pp. 97, 239, 248; Canons Ashby: E.45(1, 6, 10); E.252(31); Beesley, 335–6; Hamper, pp. 64, 67; Castle Ashby CA 1083/29, King to W. Compton, 18 Apr 1644.

8. THE PITY OF WAR

1. Marq. of Worcs: see above, Ch. 1/1. For whole subject, see C. Clay, 'Landlords and Estate Management in England: the Civil War and Interregnum', in J. Thirsk (ed.), *The Agrarian History of England and Wales*, Cambridge, 1985, V(2), Ch. 14. E. of Northampton: Castle Ashby 1083/40, 41; *CCC* 1247–8. Saye: see above, Ch. 5/1. Pope: *CCC*, pp. 934–5. Milcote: Prestwich, op.cit., pp. 571–2, quoting Sackville MSS, Maidstone (cf. detailed summary of Cranfield's problems in Hughes, pp. 262–7). Hardwicke, Glos.: Clay, op.cit., p. 127. Broughton: E.61(11) (Beesley, p. 349); E.77(22). E. of Leics: 77 *HMC* VI, p. 554, 558. Sheldons: E.A. Barnard, *The Sheldons*, Cambridge, 1936, pp. 49–50; *CAM* 1953; SP.23/116 *passim* (e.g. pp. 1085–1103). *CSPD* 1645–6, p. 456. Warner and Warde: *HMC* IVth Rpt. App., pp. 264–6; SP.46/83–5. Raleigh: SP.28/182, Farnborough. Shenington: I am grateful to Mrs Nan Clifton for this information.

2. Rupert: Luke, p. xiii. Denbigh: *CSPD* 1644, p. 97 (6 Apr 1644). SP.28/184, Brailes; Hearth Tax: E.179/259/9,10. Poor: A.L. Beier, 'Poor Relief in Wks. 1630–60', *Past & Present* 35 (1966). QS II, III, IV (see detailed index). E.M. Leonard, *English Poor Relief*, Cambridge, 1900, p. 268.

3. SP.28/185, Leek Wootton. Brailes: Huntingdon Liby., Cal., USA, Stowe MSS, St. 1444; PRO E.179/395/23 (22 Oct 1641). Castle Ashby 1083/33; cf. Hearth Tax exemptions, E.179/194/334; E.179/347. QS, *passim*. Mills: SP.28/248. *CSPD* 1625–49 Add. 692. Exhall: SP.28/136/32. Wounded: SP.28/248. Vagrancy: cf. Beier, op.cit.

4. Almshouses: Leonard, op.cit., p. 269, quoting BL 669/10/26; E.G. Tibbits, 'The Hospital of Robert, Earl of Leics.', in Warwick', *TBAS* 60 (1936), dated 10 May 1644; Wk RO CR 1600/LH51/7. SP.28/136/13. Stoneleigh: E.75(28); E.53(5). Rugby: W.H.D. Rouse, *A History of Rugby School*, Duckworth, 1898, p. 67 (enquiry of 1653). Hereford: E.264(16).

5. Schools: A.F. Leach (invaluable if occasionally unreliable) articles in *VCH* Wks. II, Oxon I, Glos. II, Wcs. *passim*; excellent recent work by P.K. Orpen, 'Recruitment patterns of the schoolmaster in the 17th c. – a study of Wks. schools', *Wks.History*, IV, vol. 3 (1979); A. Smith, 'Endowed schools in the Dioc. of Lichfield & Coventry, 1660–1699', *History of Education*, IV/2 (1975), and 'Private schools and schoolmasters in the Dioc. of Lichf. & Cov. in the 17th c.', *Hist. of Ed.* V/2 (1976); R. O'Day, *Education and Society 1500–1800*, Longman, 1982. Grimston, Norf.: *CSPD* 1655–6, pp. 387–8; Dugard and Trappe, Hughes, pp. 71–80.

6. Rugby: Rouse, op.cit., pp. 67–8; Cromwell: G.H. Bettinson, *Rugby School*, Birmingham, 1929, p. 19; M.H. Bloxam, *Rugby, the School and Neighbourhood* (ed.), W.H. Payne Smith, London, 1889, p. 143 (quoting letter dated 31 Mar 1645). Wharton, p. 324. SP.28/186, Rugby (Pearce's claims). Brailes: Leach, op.cit., *VCH* II; Wase Collection, Bodleian CC 390/2/203, and Worcs. RO., St Helens, Churchwds. Pres. Hampton Lucy: W.A.L. Vincent, *The Grammar Schools, 1660–1714*, Murray, 1969, p. 81. Alcester: Dugdale, p. 774; BL Add 35098/118 (Oct 1648); *CCC* 2217 (10 Dec 1650). Thame: *VCH* Oxon VI, p. 166. Banbury: *Oxf. Rec. Soc.*II, 'Parochial Colls.' (1920), 21. Compton Wynyates: PRO E.134/39 Eliz. Easter 1597. Shipston: Wase, op.cit., Henley: SP.28/184; Matthews, p. 363. Combrook: SP.28/201, *VCH* II, p. 369. Swalcliffe: *VCH* Oxon X, p. 250, Matthews, p. 298; SP.28/43/V/652.

7. Bridges: QS II–IV, *passim* (see Index); Worcs. Co. Recs., Quarter Sess. Rolls, ed. Bund, op.cit., I,

p. 593; Bidford: *CSPD* 1644, p. 247. Stratford: QS II, pp. 26, 46, 63, 116–17, 159; *CSPD* 1645–7, p. 241. Halford: BL Add 18981/76 (Vavasour to Rupert, 1 Mar 1644). *CSPD* 1644, pp. 29–30, 29 Feb. Beesley, pp. 397–8. Tredington: Wk RO DR 279.

8. M.W. Farr, 'The Fetherstons of Packwood', *Dug. Soc. Occ. Pap.* 18 (1968). J. Ogilby, op.cit. Travel: J. Parkes, *Travel in England in the 17th c.*, OUP, 1925. SP.28/136/19 (Barker). Milcote: Kent RO, Maidstone, Cranfield MSS, Fawdon to Cranfield, 17 Dec 1644. Danvers: SP:19/144/12. Adderbury: N. Cooper, op.cit., p. 84. Alcester: E.13(18). SP.28/185, Hillmorton. Stratford: Wallington, op.cit., II, p. 163 (18 Apr 1643). Stow: Hughes, p. 257, quoting Cranfield MSS Kent RO. Evesham: Hutton, p. 99. Trade: cf. excellent M. James, *Social Problems and Policy during the Puritan Revolution*, Routledge, 1930. (e.g. p. 40). Hughes, p. 257. *CJ* III, p. 510. I. Roy, 'England turned Germany?', *Trans. R. Hist. Soc.* 1978, specifically analyses the impact on the Severn Valley. F. Madan (ed.), *Oxford Books*, II, p.299. Rushworth, op.cit., II, pp. 365–7; BL 669/7/52; *CSPD* 1645–7, p. 258. Dudley: Sherwood, op.cit., p. 101. *HMC* IVth Rpt. App., p. 67. Lucy: document on display at Charlecote, Nat. Trust (with imperfect transcript); Sir W. Compton pass: Tibbutt, p. 493, reprod. Beesley pp. 402–4. Wellesbourne: Hamper, p. 67. Halford: Beesley, pp. 398–400; E.274(2). Tibbutt, p. 205. Corbet I, pp. 137–8; Wallington I, p. 256. E. of Northampton: *CSPD* 1652–3, pp. 385–6, and *CSPD* 1653–4, p. 62. M. Toynbee (ed.) *Papers of Capt. Henry Stevens*, Oxf. Rec. Soc. 42 (1962), p. 16. Worcs.clothiers: *LJ* IV, p. 237; E.53(11). Northampton: A.E. Everitt, 'The Local Community & the Gt.Rebellion', *Hist.Assoc.Pamphlet* G.70 (1969), p. 14. Butchers: Wk.RO CR 2017/C10/77; R.B. Wood-Jones, *Traditional domestic architecture of the Banbury region*, MUP, 1963, pp. 11–12, 99, 107. James, op.cit., p. 40.

9. E.47(27). Petition: E.7(17, 20); *HMC* VIth Rpt. App., pp. 27–9. Note: it is clear that the county committee's reply is a response to a fuller version of the gentry's petition than that abstracted in E.7(20); Hughes, 170ff., pp. 233–8.

10. Barton: QS IV, p. 178; Cubbington: *HMC* IVth Rpt. App., p. 272 and *HMC* VIIth Rpt. App., pp. 565–6; Rowington: J. Woodall, *From Hroca to Anne*, Shirley (Wks.), 1974, pp. 56–7, 114; *HMC* IVth Rpt. App., p. 272; Alcester: *HMC* IVth Rpt. App., p. 266, 3 May 1644; Lillington: Bloxam, pp. 26–7; D. Underdown, *Revel, Riot and Rebellion; Popular Politics and Culture in England, 1603–1660*, Oxford, 1987, pp. 148–9.

9. THE HEIGHT OF THE WAR: SUMMER 1644

1. Campden: Clarendon IV, p. 378 (small garrisons were absurdly costly to maintain, quite disproportionate to their supposed usefulness: see Sherwood, p. 117), Coventry: *HMC* IVth Rpt. App., p. 267; Rousham: Tibbutt, p. 663; Compton: BL Harl 6804/101–102; SP.28/43, Pts.IV, V; SP.28/136,184, Major Purefoy's Accounts; Burford: E.47(7). Capture of Compton: E.50(35); E.51(2,10,14); BL Eg. 785/29. (Sir Samuel Luke's Letter Books). Vicars; Dugdale; BL Add 29570/102 (Northampton correspondence). Weather: J. Kenyon, *The Civil Wars of England*, Weidenfeld, 1988, p. 97.

2. SP.28/184, Brailes. Constables: SP.28/182–186, various; cf. Hughes, p. 278. Compton inventory: SP.16/539/Pt.2, f.207; Goodman: PRO PROB 11/216, 8 May 1651; SP.23/88, ff.717–27; SP.23/121/ff.201–11, etc.; SP.28/253B; SP.28/184, Tysoe.

3. SP.28/184, Tysoe. Alkerton: A. Wood, *Athenae Ox.*, 1813, III, p. 187; Beesley, p. 397. North Oxon parishes: SP.28/43/Pt IV; SP.28/136/37, 44 & SP.28/184, Accounts of Maj. Purefoy and Lt. H. Smith; Moorcroft: SP.28/43/IV, f.589, and Matthews, p. 298; Epwell: SP.28/184, Tysoe (an Oxon stray); *Merc. Aul.*, 4 Mar 1645; Purefoy: T.J. Pickvance, 'George Fox and the Purefoys', *Friends Hist. Soc.*, 1970; A. Lawrence, *Parliamentary Army Chaplains, 1642–1651*, RHS/Boydell, 1990, p. 186. Accident: E.337(28), Scottish Dove, 13–20 May 1646; Hughes, pp. 248, 333; BL Add 35098, f.3 SP.28/201, Combrook; Wedgwood, pp. 532–3.

4. Cropredy is well covered in contemporary accounts, much used since in: Clarendon III, pp. 353–65; J. Adair, op.cit., ch. XIII; Toynbee and Young; R.E. Sherwood, *Civil Strife in the Midlands, 1642–1651*, Phillimore, 1974, ch. XIII; brief résumé by A. Woolrych in B. Worden (ed.), *Stuart England*, Phaidon, 1986, pp. 108–9; the four celebrated contemporary accounts, by Coe, Symonds, Ellis and Walker are all substantially reproduced in Toynbee and Young. The most lucid short account

is in P. Young and R. Holmes, *The English Civil War*, Eyre Methuen, 1974, pp. 185–9. 'Dance': E.284(5).

5. Digby: Warburton II, pp. 418–19; the jealousy between Waller and Essex was notorious, and Essex has often been blamed for the armies' separation; but see Snow's defence, op.cit., p. 432; *CSPD* 1644, p. 293. Sudeley: ibid., p. 219. SP.28/182, Wolford; Wk.RO CR 2017/C9/119A (*HMC* IVth Rpt. App., p. 267); Dudley: *Merc. Aul.*, 13 June 1644. Massey: according to Clarendon III, p. 365, Massey refused, 'being a creature of Essex's' (other reports claim Massey sent some reinforcements); weather: Clarendon III, p. 359.

6. *CSPD* 1644, pp. 250, 272, 220, 253–4; Browne: *Merc. Aul.*, 16 June 1644; Wedgwood, p. 404; Clarendon III, p. 363; *Merc. Aul.*, 26–9 June 1644; Willougby: BL Add 29570/80. M. Toynbee, op.cit., pp. 17, 27, 56. Dewes: SP.19/158, calendared *CAM*, p. 1423.

7. Toynbee, op.cit., pp. 27,29; *CSPD* 1644, pp. 254ff.; E.2(20), R. Coe, An Exact Dyarie of the Progresse of Sir W. Waller's Army, 24 June 1644; Toynbee and Young, op.cit., p. 68, conjecture understandably that Waller followed the Fosse Way to Shipston, but there is no clear evidence of this; the parish accounts prove that perhaps the bulk of Waller's forces diverged well to the east, some as far as Brailes, 5 miles away; Oxhill itself is $3\frac{1}{2}$ miles to the east of the Fosse Way; Oxhill: SP.21/16 f.74, 26 June 1644, calendared *CSPD*, p. 279.

8. Sheldon: SP.16/511/106, Examination of Thos. Savage, 6 Feb 1646; SP.28/182,183,185, Idlicote, Wolford; Tower Hamlets: Thomas Ellis's account, E.53(18), reprod. in Toynbee and Young, pp. 128–31; SP.28/182, Barcheston, Willington, Burmington.

9. E.2(6), *Merc. Aul.* 29 Jun 1644; Hanwell: R. Symonds, *Diary of the Marches of the Royal Army*, ed. C.E. Long, *Camden Soc.*, LXXIV (1859); SP.28/186, Bishops Itchington; SP.28/182, Mollington, Radway, Maj. Castle's Accounts; King: M. Toynbee, op.cit., p. 28; Beesley, p. 358; Sir Ed. Walker, *His Majesties Happy Progresse*, Christ Ch., Oxford, MS 164, reprod. Toynbee and Young, p. 73; Iter Carolinum, in Somers *Tracts* V; Wharton, op.cit.

10. Cf. Coe, Symonds, Walker and Ellis, all reprod. Toynbee and Young. Beesley, pp. 357–66. H.A. Evans, op.cit., p. 96; *CSPD* 1644, *passim*. J. Adair, 'The Court Martial Papers of Sir W. Waller's Army, 1644', *Journal of Soc. for Army Hist. Research 44* (1966), p. 216. VCH Oxon X, p. 173. Waller: E.252(51), and 'Recollections by General Sir William Waller', in *The Poetry of Anna Matilda*, London, 1788, pp. 107–8. *HMC* VIIIth Rpt., 3. Villages: SP.28/182–6 *passim*. Waller's army: C. Carlton, 'The Impact of the Fighting', in J. Morrill (ed.), *The Impact of the English Civil War*, Collins & Brown, 1991, p. 21. Evesham peace: Rushworth, op.cit., V. p. 687 and C. Petrie (ed.), *Letters. Speeches & Proclamations of K. Charles I*, Cassell, 1935, pp. 145–6.

11. Waller: *CSPD* 1644, *passim*. Pay: Hughes, pp. 198–9. Quarters: SP.28/43/V, 653, Hornton, and SP.28/182–6. Hanwell: SP.16/539/338, calendared *CSPD* 1625–49 Add 689. Warwick: *CJ* III, p. 559.

12. Browne: E.2(16), *Merc. Civ.*, 11–17 Jul 1644; Banbury: Beesley reproduces lengthy extracts from many contemporary reports, e.g. E.2(6, 20), pp. 336–84, though no parish accounts and largely ignoring the build-up and effects on the local population; SP.28/182, Bourton and Draycote, Kineton, Brinklow, etc.; Hamper, pp. 71–2; VCH Oxon X, p. 10; suppliers: *CAM*, pp. 996–7, 1127, 1359, etc; Tibbutt, p. 23; church: *LJ* VIII, p. 434; *HMC* VIIth Rpt. App., p. 448, Sir A. Denton to Sir R. Verney, 5 Sep 1644; Phipps and Hobson: SP.28/201, 248, 253B & Hughes, p. 148 etc.

13. Langdale: E.256(3, 8, 9), Perf. Diurn., etc.; Cromwell: Abbott I, pp. 293–4; *CSPD* 1625–49, Add. 693; QS II, pp. 179, 231, 256; contemporary news-sheets reprod. in Beesley; SP.28/186, Shotteswell; Wroxton: E.17(10), *Merc. Aul.*, 25 Oct. 1644; wounded: SP.28/255; *CSPD* 1644, p. 546; *LJ* VII, p. 4; Woodward: SP.28/182, Avon Dassett.

14. Cromwell: *CSPD* 1644, *passim* and Abbott, Vol. I. Banbury: E.170(10); E.256(30); E. Walker, *Historical Discourses*, 1705, p. 109. Tibbutt, *passim*. Wedgwood, p. 378. Gubbin: *CAM*, p. 1359. Saye: E.17(10) and *CSPD* 1644, pp. 467–8. *CJ* III, p. 690. Temple: Col. Rich. Cockayne's charges detailed in H. Roundell, 'The Garrison of Newport Pagnell during the Civil Wars', *Records of Bucks.*, II, pp. 364–5. Forbingon: E.256(35). Morgan etc.: *CAM*, pp. 893, 1406, 1127. Raleigh: SP.28/182, Farnborough. *HMC* VIth Rpt. App., pp. 122, 175, 213. *LJ* VIII, p. 377. *CJ* V, p. 170 etc. Beesley, pp. 384–5. Tibbutt, p. 676–7. Bourton: SP.28/182–6. Lydiat: *DNB*; Beesley, p. 386. Purefoy: SP.28/184, Tysoe, Maj. Purefoy's Accounts; E. 256(33). Tachbrook: *Merc. Aul.* 19 Nov 1644.

10. 'THE PURPLE TESTAMENT OF BLEEDING WAR'

1. Quarters: E.2(16); SP.28/201, Alcester, Studley, Northampton: E.2(19). Hopton: SP.28/43/V/642. Archer: *HMC* IVth Rpt. App., pp. 269–70; Wk. RO CR 2017/C10/25; Fraser: Sherwood 151. SP.28/201, Hatton, Edstone.

2. Cheshire: E.16(3). Plunder: E.13(18). Campden: Rupert correspondence, Duggan to Rupert, 23 Dec 1644, BL Add 18981/338; Perf. Occs. 23 Jan 1645. *CSPD* 1644–5, pp. 253, 255, 267. Kilsby: *Merc. Aul.*, 18 and 26 Jan 1645 (reprod. Beesley, pp. 389–90). Culham: Wallington II, p. 247; Chipping Norton: ib. p. 246.

3. Purefoy: *Merc. Aul.*, 4 Mar 1645. Compton: E.238(12) (reprod. Beesley, pp. 390–3). E.268(1), Bridges' account; E.268(9, 13) and E.269(3); H. James, *English Hours*, 'In Warwickshire', 1905. Bard: *DNB*; GEC *Complete Peerage*; E.238(37) ('Bard gave command to ravish all . . . and brag'd he had done it the same day, severall times'). Wood, *Athenae Ox.*, op.cit., Fasti, p. 66; Bund, p. 151. Stoke: E.266(24), Bard to Twyning, 1 Nov 1645. Vicars IV, pp. 106–8. SP.28/182, Loxley. Ransome: E.274(17); E.282(7). Canning: BL Add 35098/82, The Book of Sequests,. 1646. SP.19/145/53–8, calendared *CAM*, p. 1278. E.269(21). E. 270(9).

4. Atrocities: cf. C. Carlton, 'The Impact of the Fighting', in J. Morrill (ed.), *The Impact of the English Civil War*, Collins & Brown, 1991. There exists no general work on the destruction of the country house in the war. Birmingham: E.100(8). Beoley: SP28/253B, Andrew Yarranton's Testimony. E.81(6, 23, 30). SP.28/182, Jas. Castle's Accounts. SP.28/182–6, Tanworth etc. Stoughton: SP.28/184, Warwick. There seems no evidence to validate claims reported in *VCH* Worcs. IV, p. 14 that Beoley may have been fired by the Royalists, and Sheldon's own testimony seems conclusive. Parl. ordinance: *HMC* IVth Rpt. p. 271.

5. Milcote: E. Carey-Hill, 'The Hawkesworth Papers 1601–1660', *TBAS* 54, 1929–30, p. 28; Kent RO, Maidstone, Cranfield MSS U..269/1, R. Fawdon to Earl of Middx. The quotation conflates two of Fawdon's accounts, 17 Dec & (in square brackets) 18 Jan; cf. the detailed biography of Middlesex by M. Prestwich, Cranfield: *Politics and Profits under the Early Stuarts*, Oxford, 1966. Welford: E.256(15) and *Merc. Aul.* 30 Dec 1644.

6. Lydney: Corbet, op.cit., I, p. 147. Lypiatt: *VCH* Glos. XI, p. 103; *CSPD* 1644–45, pp. 237–8. Campden: E. Walker, *Historical Collections*, 1707, p. 126; Symonds, p. 166; Wallington II, p. 259; Clarendon IV, pp. 37–8; E.284(2, 5, 7). Tredington: E.262(2). R.N. Dore, *The Letter Books of Sir Wm. Brereton*, Rec. Soc. of Lancs. and Cheshire, 123 (1984), p. 394. E.284(7). Vicars IV, p. 147. SP.28/184, Tanworth etc. Bund, p. 158. Symonds, p. 167.

7. Hawkesley, Cofton, Frankley: *VCH* Worcs. III, pp. 56–7, 120, 184. Edgbaston: Dore, op.cit., pp. 431, 446. Aynho: J.T. Page, 'The Great Civil War in Northants.', *Northants. Nat. Hist. Soc.*, 28 (1936–7), p. 127; E.264(18) (reprod. Wallington II, p. 272). Wormleighton: BL Add 29570/54 (undated, but Dugdale dates burning 7 Jan 1646: op.cit., p. 83). Banbury: Sprigge, p. 251; *LJ* VIII, p. 551; *CJ* V, pp, 102, 250, 574, 598–9; *VCH* Oxon X, p. 41. Kenilworth: SP.28/182, 185; SP.28/136/4, 6, 8; Dugdale, p. 249.

11. THE DISINTEGRATING CHURCH

1. For background, see G. Davies, *The Early Stuarts 1603–1660*, Oxford, 1959, Chs III, VIII; J.S. Morrill, 'The Church in England, 1642–1649', in Morrill; Hughes, pp. 62–87, 291ff. etc. Bishop of Worcs.: *HMC* Salisbury VI, pp. 265–7. E.245(32).

2. Howes: see Ch. 2, 'Rising Tensions', above; *LJ* IV, pp. 108, 230. Doughty; [Bloxam and Staunton] *Notices of the Churches in Warwickshire*, Warwick, 1847, p. 149, and BL Add 15670/437. Frankton etc: *VCH* II, p. 41. Quakers: J. Besse, *A Collection of the Sufferings of the People called Quakers*, 1753; W. White, *Friends in Warwickshire*, Birmingham, 1873; B. Reay, *The Quakers and the English Revolution*, London, 1985; N. Penney (ed.), *The Journal of George Fox*, Cambridge, 1911, II, p. 338. Saye: *VCH* Oxon IX, p. 101; *CPM* 1646 (BL Add 15670–71/177, 102, 214, 254, 222: résumés in Matthews).

3. Hawes: E.77(33, 34). T. Edwards, *Gangraena*, 1646, facs. edn. The Rota and Univ. of Exeter, 1977, III, pp. 19–20, 81, 107, 172–3, 238, 250–1. Cromwell: Carlyle's *Letters and Speeches of Oliver Cromwell*, ed. S.C. Lowes, Methuen, 1904, I, p. 493, Letter CX.

4. Wardington: *VCH* Oxon X, p. 221. Rowington etc.: QS VI, pp. 32, 56, 67–8. Stratford: *VCH* II, p. 41. Cirencester: J.H. Bettey, *Church and Parish*, Batsford, 1987, p. 96. Worcs: SP.28/235B/13, John Bridges' Depositions. Westbury: Corbet I, p. 93. Boarstall: Lipscomb, *Hist. of Bucks.*, 1847, I, p. 47, Cherington: *TBAS* 1887, p. 121. Adderbury: *VCH* Oxon IX, p. 32. Burton Dassett: church booklet notes by Eve Baker. Kineton: church booklet notes. P. Titchmarsh, 1983. Southam: *VCH* VI, p. 221. Whichford: QS II, p. 267, Shawell, Leics: SP.28/184, Rugby; *CSPD* 1638–9, p. 70; *DNB*. Edgbaston: *TBAS* 39, p. 10 (*Merc. Aul.*); SP.28/183, Edgbaston; Dugdale, p. 896; *CSPD* 1658–9, pp. 1–2. *VCH* VII, p. 362. Symonds, p. 190. Banbury: R.P.R. Carpenter, *The Story of St. Mary's Ch., Banbury*, Glos., n.d., p. 12; Beesley, pp. 148, 157–8; A. Wood, *Life*, op.cit. I, p. 276. Compton Wynyates: Dugdale, p. 550; N. Pevsner, *Buildings of England, Wks.*, p. 243. Firth & Rait, *Acts and Ordinances of the Interregnum*, 1911, I, pp. 265–6 (26 Aug 1643). Alcester: QS IV, p. 6 (Easter 1657).

5. E.75(37). Whitchurch: QS III, p. 4. Testimony: E.434(14) and Matthews, App; Hughes, 309ff. Monks Kirby: Hughes, pp. 318–9, 324; QS III, pp. 195–6. Leamington: Matthews; *CSPD* 1655, p. 175.

6. See Matthews, *passim*. and BL Add 35098, The Book of Sequests., 1646, and BL 15671. Whitby: I. Green, 'The Persecution of 'scandalous' and 'malignant' parish clergy', *Eng. Hist. Rev.* 1979, p. 513. Warmstry: E.199(23). Stratford: BL Add 35098/36r. Wootton: SP.28/182, Warmington; E.75(37); *CCC*, pp. 934–5; Hughes, p. 205. Darrell/Dayrell: BL Add 15671/18. Doughty: Bloxam & Staunton, op.cit., p. 149. H.B. Newman, 'The Sequestration of Royalists' Estates during the Civil War', Harvard Ph.D., 1940, pp. 103–4, 116–18. *Acts and Ords.*, op.cit., I, p. 256; I. Green, op.cit., pp. 520–1. G. B. Tatham, *The Puritans in Power*, Cambridge, 1913, pp. 67–8, Watkins: *CAM*, p. 1052. Oldys: J. Walker, *Sufferings of the Clergy*, 1714, II, p. 323 (reprod. in H.A. Evans, *Highways & Byways in Oxford and the Cotswolds*, Macmillan, 1908, pp. 60–1, and Beesley, pp. 397, 604, 621; résumé in *DNB*), Chipping Norton: *LJ* XI, p. 49.

12. ENDGAME: 1645

1. Loxley: E.270(33). Banbury district: Tibbutt, *passim* and extracts in Beesley, pp. 393–407, reproduced almost without comment. Whetham: *CSPD* 1644–5, p. 365. Halford: E.274(2). Northampton letter: E.260(12), 3 Apr 1645. Crawford: E.260(9,10,11).

2. Astrology: from George Wharton, 'An Astrological Judgement upon his Majesties present march begun from Oxford, March 7 1645', and William Lilly's response, in 'The Starry Messenger' of 14 June 1645, E.286(31) and E.288(17). Rumours: Luke, *passim*; E.260(10), *CSPD* 1644–5, *passim*, e.g. p. 398 (Massey-Stratford). Worcs: J.W. Bund (ed.), *Diary of Henry Townshend*, Worcester, 1920, II, pp. 225–9. Sherbourne: E.278(27): E.260 (20, 23, 24); E.281(3). Newport; Tibbutt, pp. 290, 514–15; Roundell, *Records of Bucks.*, op.cit., II, p. 307. Cromwell and Fairfax: Abbott, p. 348 and Luke; *CSPD* 1644–5, pp. 459, 476–7. Massey: *LJ* VII, p. 393; E.262(1): E.286(14); Clarendon IV, p. 38.

3. *CSPD* 1644–5, pp. 476, 482 etc.; Abbott, op.cit., I, p. 349; E.260(38). Brereton: Add 11331/163–4, 148, 306, reprod. in R. Dore, *Letter Books of Sir W. Brereton*, Rec. Soc. of Lancs. and Chesh., I, pp. 412, 425, etc. Digby, from Newport, Salop: *HMC* XIIIth Rpt., Portland I, p. 224 (19 May 1645). Bridges: *CJ* IV, p. 140, 12 May. Tibbutt, p. 535.

4. Tadmarton: Tibbutt, pp. 276–7, 532, 540; BL Add 11331/164 etc. *CCC* III, p. 1732. Cole: Matthew, p. 298. David and Jonathan repeated in Vicars, op.cit., IV, p. 151. Warwicks. quarters: SP.28/182–6; E.284(14, 17, 22, 23) (including 'The Wk. Scout', p. 14); E.285(4, 9). Tibbutt, pp. 537, 281, correspondence Luke–Bridges.

5. *CSPD* 1644–5, pp. 482–6, 492 etc. Cromwell and Brereton: BL Add 11331/306, 316–7, 221. Southam: SP.28/182–6. Tibbutt, pp. 281, 283, 537, 542, 617; *CSPD* 1644–5, p. 486. Warburton III, pp. 91, 97. E.260(39). Wroxall: SP.16/510/28, calendared *CSPD* 1645–7, p. 37). Kenilworth: SP.28/185. Stratford: SP.28/136/51. Pay: E.286(9).

6. *CSPD* 1644–5, *passim*, e.g. pp. 526, 535; Luke, pp. 292–4, 297, 305–6, 309. Coventry: E.262(2); E.260(41). Fairfax: R. Bell, *Memorials of the Civil War: The Fairfax Correspondence*, 1849, III, p. 228 (Marston, 4 June 1645). Plunder: SP.28/182–6 (Shawell in Rugby, SP.28/186; Flecknoe, SP.28/184). Clarendon IV, p. 42. King: E.292(27); W. Bray (ed.), *Diary of John Evelyn*, 1906, IV, p. 161. E.288(4, 21, 23, 24, 31).

7. Sprigge, op.cit., pp. 24, 30, etc. *CJ* May 1645. BL Harl 166/215. Vicars, op.cit., IV, p. 155. *CSPD* 1644–5, pp. 556, 578. Cromwell: E.288(28), Letter of a gentleman of Northampton to a friend in London. Digby: *CSPD* 1644–5, pp. 521–2, Digby to Nicholas, 25–6 May.

8   Naseby: contemporary accounts E.288(21–2, 31, 34, 37, etc.); best short account in (as often) Wedgwood, pp. 448–55; P. Young and R. Holmes, *The English Civil War, A Military History*, Eyre Methuen, 1974, pp. 236–50; M. Ashley, *Naseby*, Alan Sutton, 1992. Clarendon IV, p. 41. Southam: Tibbutt, pp. 574–5. Royalist feud: BL Add 29570/81–90; Warburton III, p. 100. SP.28/185, Upper Shuckburgh. Ghost: Baker's *Northamptonshire* I, p. 325, quoting a line of earlier sources through W.D. Rastall, *A History of the Antiquities of Southwell* (Notts), 1787, pp. 430–1. 'Suicide': Hutton, p. 178.

9. Prisoners: Rushworth, op.cit., VI, p. 45; E.288(22); E.293(3). Rugby: SP.28/186; Long Lawford, ib., p. 183; E. 292(16), repeated Sprigge, op.cit., p. 53. SP.28/182, Brinklow. Coventry: *CJ* IV, p. 202, 9 July, Quarters: SP.28/182–6. Radbrook, etc.: BL Landsdowne 578/23, reprod. in J.H. Bloom, *History of Preston-upon-Stour, Warwickshire*, Hemsworth, 1896, p. 35; *Trans. Bristol and Glos. Arch. Soc.*, vols. 12, 14, (1887–90), R.F. Tomes, 'Glos. Royalist Families'; J. Maclean, 'History of the Manor of Clifford Chambers'. Albright: *CCC*, p. 410; he later signed the Glos. ministers' Testimony. Stratford: SP.28/136/51; Buller E.284/22. Okey: H.G. Tibbutt, 'Colonel J. Okey, 1606–1662', *Bedfds. Hist. Rec. Soc.* 35 (1955).

10. Fairfax: *HMC* IXth Rpt. App. p. 437; Tibbutt, pp. 583–5, 622. Quarters: SP.28/185–6, Ilmington, Halford, Stretton. Worcester: Bund, *Townshend*, op.cit. II, pp. 236–9. Bridges: *LJ* VIII, p. 47, Bridges to CBK, 15 Dec 1645; and *HMC* VIth Rpt. App., p. 88. *CSPD* 1649–50, pp. 94, 111, 125; ib., 1645–7, pp. 1289–90; cf. *CAM*, p. 61, dated 8 Feb 1647.

CONCLUSION

J.F.C. Harrison, op.cit. (*see* Preface, note 2). D.F. Mosler, op.cit., p. 177. Baxter, op.cit., p. 44. Sprigge, p. 251. Numbers estimates: J.S. Morrill, 'The Stuarts', in K.O. Morgan (ed.), *The Oxford Illustrated History of Britain*, OUP, 1984, p. 317, and Morrill, p. 17. Finance: for detailed comment, cf. Hughes *passim* and 'Parliamentary Tyranny? Indemnity Proceedings and the Impact of the Civil War, A Case Study from Warwickshire', *Midland History* II (1986). Everitt: *see* Preface, note 1. Shakespeare: *Richard II* (III, iii). Wordsworth, 'The Solitary Reaper'.

SELECT BIBLIOGRAPHY

(Place of publication given only if outside London)

Abbott W.C., *The Writings and Speeches of Oliver Cromwell*, Cambridge, Mass., Harvard Univ. Press, 1937–41

Adair J., *Roundhead General: A Military Biography of Sir William Waller*, Macdonald, 1969

Ashton R., *The English Civil War: Conservatism and Revolution*, Weidenfeld & Nicholson, 1978

Baxter R., *Reliquiae Baxterianae*, ed. M. Sylvester, Parkhurst, Robinson, Lawrence & Dunton, 1696

Beesley A., *The History of Banbury*, Nichols & Son, 1841

Bloxam M.H., *Warwickshire during the Civil Wars of the 17th Century*, Warwick, Robert Spennell, 1880

Bulstrode R., *Memoirs and Reflections*, Charles Rivington, 1721

Bund J.W.W., *The Civil War in Worcestershire*, Birmingham, Cornish, 1905

Bund J.W.W. (ed.), *The Diary of Henry Townshend*, Worcestershire Historical Society, Mitchell Hughes & Clarke, 1920

Calendar of the Proceedings of the Committee for the Advancement of Money. 1642–1656, ed. M.A.E. Green, HMSO, 1888

Calendar of the Proceedings of the Committee for Compounding. 1643–1660, ed. M.A.E. Green, HMSO, 1890

Clarendon, Edward, Earl of, *The History of the Rebellion and Civil Wars in England*, ed. W.D. Macray, Oxford, Clarendon Press, 1888

Corbet J., 'An Historical Relation of the Military Government of Gloucester, 1645', in Washbourn, q.v.

Dore R.N., *The Letter Books of Sir William Brereton*, Record Society of Lancs. & Cheshire, 1984, 1990

Dore R.N., 'Sir William Brereton's Siege of Chester and the Campaign of Naseby' in *Transactions of the Lancs. & Cheshire Antiquarian Society*, vol. 67, 1957

Dugdale W. *The Antiquities of Warwickshire*, ed. W. Thomas, Osborn & Longman, Harding, Lepard & Co, 1730 (*see also* Hamper)

Eccles M., *Shakespeare in Warwickshire*, University of Wisconsin, 1963

Firth C.H. (ed.), 'The Journal of Prince Rupert's Marches' in *English Historical Review*, vol. 13, 1898

Fletcher A., *The Outbreak of the English Civil War*, Arnold, 1985

Gardiner S.C., *History of the Great Civil War, 1642–1649*, Harlow, Longman, 1901

Guttery D.R., *The Great Civil War in Midland Parishes*, Birmingham, 1951

Hamper W. (ed.), *The Life, Diary and Correspondence of Sir William Dugdale*, 1827

Hughes A.L., *Politics, Society and Civil War in Warwickshire*, Cambridge, 1987

Hutton R., *The Royalist War Effort, 1642–1646*, Harlow, Longman, 1982

James M., *Social Problems and Policy during the Puritan Revolution*, Routledge, 1930

Laurence A., *Parliamentary Army Chaplains, 1642–1651*, Woodbridge, Royal Historical Society/Boydell, 1990

Philip I.G. (ed.), *The Journal of Sir Samuel Luke*, Oxford Record Society, 1947–53

Matthews A.G., *Walker Revised*, Oxford, Clarendon Press, 1948

Morrill J.S. (ed.), *Reactions to the English Civil War, 1642–1649*, Macmillan, 1982

Mosler D.F., 'A Social and Religious History of the English Civil War in Warwickshire', Stanford University, 1975 (unpublished thesis)

Pennington D., 'The War and the People', in Morrill, q.v.

Ratcliff S.C. and Johnson H.C. (eds.), *Warwick County Records, Quarter Sessions Order Books*, Warwick, L. Edgar Stephens, Shire Hall, 1935–53

Roundell H., 'The Garrison of Newport Pagnell during the Civil Wars' in *Records of Buckinghamshire*, vol. 2, 1859

Roy I., *The Royalist Ordnance Papers*, Oxford Record Society, vol. 43, 1963–4

Rushworth J., *Historical Collections*, John Rushworth, 1721

Sherwood R.E., *Civil Strife in the Midlands, 1642–1651*, Chichester, Phillimore, 1974 (new edn., as *Civil War in the Midlands 1642–1651*, Stroud, Alan Sutton, 1992)

Snow V.F., *Essex the Rebel*, Nebraska, 1970

Somers, Lord John *A Collection of Scarce and Valuable Tracts*, ed. W. Scott, 1810

Spencer T., 'The Genealogie, Life and Death of the Right Hon. Robert, Lord Brooke', ed. P. Styles in *Dugdale Society Miscellany*, I, OUP, 1977

Sprigge J., *Anglia Rediviva*, 1647 (facsimile edn, ed. H.T. Moore, Florida, 1960)

Strider R.E.L., *Robert Greville, Lord Brooke*, Cambridge, Mass., Harvard Univ. Press, 1958

Symonds, R., 'Diary of the Marches of the Royal Army', ed. C.E. Long, Camden Society, vol. 74, 1859

Tibbutt H.G., *The Letter Books of Sir Samuel Luke, 1644–1645*, Bedfordshire Historical Society/HMC, 1963

Toynbee M. (ed.), 'The Papers of Captain Henry Stevens', *Oxford Record Society*, vol. 42, 1962

Toynbee M. and Young P., *Cropredy Bridge*, Roundwood Press, Kineton, 1970

Underdown D., *Revel, Riot and Rebellion: Popular Politics and Culture in England, 1603–1660*, Oxford, Oxford Univ. Press, 1987

Wallington N., *Historical Notices of the Reign of Charles I*, Bentley, 1869

Warburton E., *Memoirs of Prince Rupert and the Cavaliers*, Bentley, 1849

Washbourn J. (ed.), *Bibliotheca Gloucestrensis, A Collection of Scarce & Curious Tracts relating to the County & City of Gloucester*, 1825, Gloucester (privately printed)

Wedgwood C.V., *The King's War, 1641–1647*, Collins, 1978

Wharton N., 'Letters from a subaltern', ed. H. Ellis in *Archaelogia*, vol. 35, 1853

Whetham C.D. and W.C.D., *A History of the Life of Col. Nathaniel Whetham*, Harlow, Longman Green, 1907

Whitelock B., *Memorials of the English Affairs*, Oxford, Oxford Univ. Press, 1853

Wood A., *The Life & Times of Anthony Wood*, ed. A. Clark, Oxford, Clarendon Press, 1891–1900.

Woolrych A., 'The Civil Wars', in Worden (*see below*)

Worden B., *Stuart England*, Oxford, Phaidon, 1986

Vicars J., *Magnalia dei Anglicana*, Rothwell & Underhill, 1646

Young P., *Edgehill 1642*, Roundwood Press, Kineton, 1967

INDEX OF PERSONAL NAMES

Note: Not all minor or incidental references are listed

INDEX OF PLACE-NAMES

Subject Index